Routledge Revivals

A CRITICAL EDITION OF JOHN BEADLE'S

A CRITICAL EDITION OF JOHN BEADLE'S
A Journall or Diary of a Thankfull Christian

GERMAINE FRY MURRAY

First published in 1996 by Garland Publishing, Inc.

This edition first published in 2018 by Routledge
2 Park Square, Milton Park, Abingdon, Oxon, OX14 4RN
and by Routledge
52 Vanderbilt Avenue, New York, NY 10017, USA

Routledge is an imprint of the Taylor & Francis Group, an informa business

© 1996 by Germaine Fry Murray

All rights reserved. No part of this book may be reprinted or reproduced or utilised in any form or by any electronic, mechanical, or other means, now known or hereafter invented, including photocopying and recording, or in any information storage or retrieval system, without permission in writing from the publishers.

Publisher's Note
The publisher has gone to great lengths to ensure the quality of this reprint but points out that some imperfections in the original copies may be apparent.

Disclaimer
The publisher has made every effort to trace copyright holders and welcomes correspondence from those they have been unable to contact.
A Library of Congress record exists under ISBN:

ISBN 13: 978-0-367-18267-0 (hbk)
ISBN 13: 978-0-367-18268-7 (pbk)
ISBN 13: 978-0-429-06039-7 (ebk)

THE RENAISSANCE IMAGINATION

IMPORTANT LITERARY AND THEATRICAL TEXTS FROM THE LATE MIDDLE AGES THROUGH THE SEVENTEENTH CENTURY

edited by
STEPHEN ORGEL
STANFORD UNIVERSITY

A GARLAND SERIES

Deo plane, quod debet, retribuere nemo potest, quod tam copiose supra nos accumulaverit misericordiam; quod tam multa deliquerimus, quod tam fragiles & nihil sumus; quod tam plenus ille, & sufficiens sibi, nec bonorum nostrorum egens.
Bern. Serm. 3. De adventu Domini.

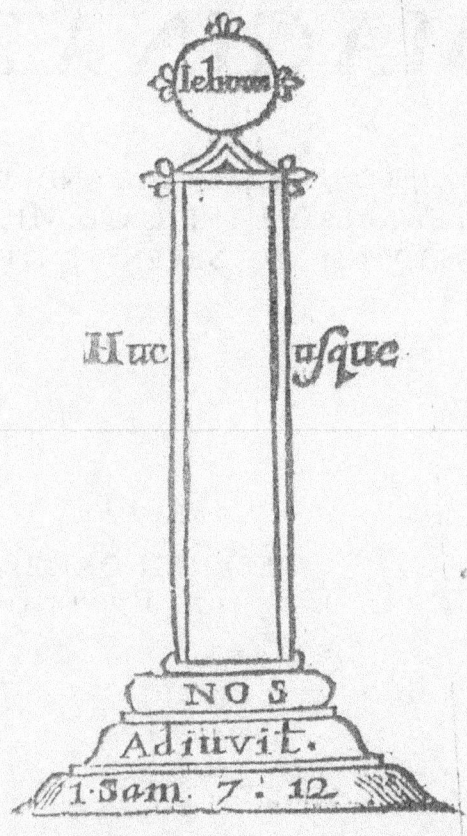

Curatorem mei rerumq; mearum ex pacto Deum habeo; illi bene notum est quid mihi sufficit, & quando conduceret; hactenus non fefellit, quando dubitare inciperem, & non simul ingratus esse inciperem. Foxius.

A CRITICAL EDITION OF JOHN BEADLE'S
A Journall or Diary of a Thankfull Christian

GERMAINE FRY MURRAY

GARLAND PUBLISHING, INC.
NEW YORK & LONDON / 1996

Copyright © 1996 Germaine Fry Murray
All rights reserved

Library of Congress Cataloging-in-Publication Data

Beadle, John, d. 1667.
   [Journal of a thankful Christian]
   A critical edition of John Beadle's A journall, or diary of a thankfull Christian / [edited by] Germaine Fry Murray.
       p.   cm. — (Renaissance imagination)
   Includes bibliographical references and index.
   ISBN 0-8153-1567-8 (alk. paper)
   1. Puritans—Doctrines—Early works to 1800. 2. Diaries—Authorship—Religious aspects—Christianity—Early works to 1800. 3. Spirituality—England—History—17th century—Sources. 4. Spirituality—Puritans—History—17th century—Sources. 5. Puritans—England—Religious life—Early works to 1800.
   I. Murray, Germaine Fry. II. Title. III. Series: Renaissance imagination (Unnumbered)
BX9318.B43 1996
248.4'6—dc20   96-2049

Printed on acid-free, 250-year-life paper
Manufactured in the United States of America

CONTENTS

Frontispiece of the Original Text	*ii*
Original Title Page	*vi*
Transcription of Title Page	*vii*

INTRODUCTION

Bibliographical Description	*ix*
Life of John Beadle	*xi*
Antecedents of *A Journall or Diary*	*xxx*
Traditional Influences on *A Journall*	*xxxvi*
The Text of *A Journall or Diary*	*lxv*
Bibliography for Critical Introduction	*lxix*

A JOURNALL OR DIARY OF A THANKFULL CHRISTIAN

Epistle Dedicatory	*1*
To the Reader	*9*
Chapter 1	*21*
Chapter 2	*31*
Chapter 3	*57*
Chapter 4	*71*
Chapter 5	*99*
Chapter 6	*119*
Chapter 7	*137*
Chapter 8	*147*
Contents	*163*

APPENDICES

Dedicatory Poem	*167*
Advertisement	*169*

SIDENOTES	*171*
CORRECTIONS TO THE TEXT	*193*
COMMENTARY TO THE TEXT	*197*
BIBLIOGRAPHY FOR THE COMMENTARY	*301*
GLOSSARY	*305*
INDEX	*313*

THE JOURNAL OR DIARY OF A THANKFUL CHRISTIAN.

Presented in some Meditations upon

Numb. 33. 2.

And Moses wrote their goings out, according to their Journeys, by the commandement of the Lord.

By *J. B.* Master of Arts, and Minister of the Gospel at *Barnstone* in *Essex*.

Whoso is wise, and will observe these things, even they shall understand the loving kindness of the Lord, Psal. 107. 43.
Who hath despised the day of small things? Zach. 4. 10.

Nihil tam conveniens Deo quam beneficentia, nihil autem tam alienum quam ut servet gratus homo. Lactan. de ira Dei ad Donat. cap. 16.

Αὐτὴ γὰρ ἡ εὐχαριστία ἡ ἀκριβής, ὅταν ταῦτα περιφέρωμεν δι' ὧν ὁ Θεὸς δοξάζεται ἰδεῖν μέλλει· ὅταν ἐκεῖνα φυλάσσωμεν ἀπαλλαγῶμεν.
Chrysost. Rom. Hom. 18.

London, Printed by *E. Cotes*, for *Tho. Parkhurst*, at the Three Crowns over against the great Conduit at the lower end of *Cheapside*, 1656.

The

Journal

or

Diary

of a

THANKFUL CHRISTIAN

Presented in some Meditations upon

NUMB. 33.2

And Moses wrote their goings out, according to their Journeys, by the commandement of the Lord.
By J.B. Master of Arts, and Minister of the Gospel at Barnstone in Essex.
Whoso is wise, and will observe these things, even they shall understand the loving kindness of the Lord, Psal. 107.43
Who hath despised the day of small things? Zach. 4.10.
Nihil tam conveniens Deo quam beneficentia, nihil autem alienum quam ut sit ingratus homo. Lactan. de ira Dei ad Donat. cap. 16.
For this is the genuine thanksgiving, when we do those things whereby God is sure to be glorified, and flee from those from which we have been set free. Chrysost. Rom. Hom. 18.
London, Printed by E. Cotes, for Tho. Parkhurst, at the Three Crowns over against the great Conduit at the lower end of Cheapside, 1656.

Introduction
BIBLIOGRAPHICAL DESCRIPTION

1656.

Title: THE | JOURNAL | OR | DIARY | OF A | *THANKFUL CHRISTIAN.* | Presented in some Meditations upon | NUMB. 33.2. | *And Moses wrote their goings out, accor-| ding to their Journeys, by the comman- | dement of the Lord.* | [rule, 83 mm wide] | By J. B. Master of Arts, and Minister of the | Gospel at Barnstone in Essex. | [rule, 83 mm wide] | *Whoso is wise, and will observe these things, even they shall | understand the loving kindness of the Lord,* Psal. 107. 43. | *Who hath despised the day of small things?* Zach. 4. 10. | *Nihil tam conveniens Deo quam beneficentia, nihil autem tam alienum | quam ut sit ingratus homo.* Lactan. de ira Dei ad Donat. cap. 16. |
Ἀυτη γάρ ἡ εὐχαριστία ἡ ἀκριβὴς, ὅταν
Ταῦτα πραττωμενδιών | ὁθεος δοξάξεσθαι
μέλλει ὅταν ἐκετνα φύγωμεν ὧν ἀπηλλάγωμτν |
Chrysost. Rom. Hom. 18. | [rule, 82 mm wide] *London*, Printed by *E. Cotes*, for *Tho. Parkhurst*, at the | *Three Crowns* over against the great Conduit at the lower | end of *Cheapside*, 1656.

Collation: Octavo. A^8, a-b^8, B-N^8. 120 leaves. Leaves of each gathering are signed except, A^1, A^2, and the last three leaves of all gatherings.

Pagination: A^{1r}- A^{8v}, a^{1r}-b^{8v} are not foliated or paginated. B^{1r}-N^{8v} are paginated. Errors in pagination: 128 for 125; 112 for 128.

Contents: A^{1r} [blank]. A^{1v} [single band of type ornaments, Imprimatur, *Edmund Calamy.* [single band of type ornaments]. A^{2r} [Title]. A^{2v} [woodcut 93 mm high of pillar on three-tiered pedestal containing the words "NOS Adiuvit 1 Sam. 7-12." The pillar is flanked by the words "Huc usque," and is crowned by a sphere containing the word "Iehova."] A^{3r}-A^{4r} [double band of type ornaments, 72 mm wide]. *The Epistle Dedicatory.* a^{4v} [blank]. a^{5r}-b^{6r} [double bands of type ornaments, 70 mm wide] TO

x   Beadle's A Journall or Diary of a Thankfull Christian

THE READER. b^{6v} [blank]. b^{7r} [double band of type ornaments, 70 mm wide, Latin dedicatory poem by C.G.]. b^{7v} [blank]. b^{8r} [single band of type ornaments, 70 mm wide, advertisment of T[homas P[arkhurst]. b^{8v} [single band of type ornaments, 70 mm wide] ERRATA. [single band of type ornaments, 70 mm wide]. B^{1r}-B^{7r} CHAP[TER]. I. B^{7v}-D^{8v} CHAP[TER]. II. D^{8v}-F^{1v} CHAP[TER]. III. F^{1v}-H^{3v} CHAP[TER]. IV. H^{3v}-I^{8r} CHAP[TER]. V. I^{8v}-L^{3v} CHAP[TER]. VI. L^{4r}-M^{2r} CHAP[TER]. VII. M^{2v}-N^{4v} CHAP[TER]. VIII. [woodcut tailpiece of shield containing two pomegranets and two bells, flanked by "Exod. 28.34."; underneath shield there is a scrolled band containing the proverb, "Thankfulnes A way to thriue"]. N^{5r} [band of type ornaments, 70 mm wide]. N^{5r}-N^{8r} The Contents:. N^{8r} [curved woodcut device, 28 mm wide]. N^{8v} blank].

Notes: The first word of chapter 1 begins with a decorative woodcut "S." The text of the Dedicatory Epistle, To the Reader, and each of the chapters is printed in roman type, except where italics is used to set off proverbial, classical, scriptural, or historical material. The Dedicatory poem and the Contents are printed in italics.

Running Titles: *The Epistle Dedicatory.* A^{3v}-A^{8v}. *TO THE READER.* a^{5v}-b^{6r}. *The Journall or Diary of a Thankfull Christian.* B^{1v}-N^{4v}. *The Contents.* N^{5v}-N^{8r}.

Copies used: B, the copy text, is a photostat of the copy in the British Library (Wing STC B1557). O is a microfilm of the copy in the Bodleian Library, Oxford. F is a microfilm of the copy in the Folger Library. P is a microfilm found in the Princeton Theological Seminary Library. U is a microfilm of a copy in Union Theological Seminary, New York. UB is a microfilm of the copy found in the University of Illinois Library at Urbana. UB2 is a microfilm copy of a second copy at the University of Illinois Library at Urbana.

Stop Press Corrections: Two stop press corrections were revealed by collating these seven copies of the book. The first is in the *sidenote* appearing on p. 1. line 13, sig. A^{3r}:

B	Rom. 4.20.
O	Rom. 4.20
F	Rom. 4.10
P	Rom. 4.10
U	Rom. 4.10
UB	Rom. 4.20
UB2	Rom. 4.20.

The second stop appears on p. 203, line 14, sig. L^{2r}:

B	heaven
O	heaven
F	beaven
P	beaven
U	heaven
UB	beaven
UB2	beaven

THE LIFE OF JOHN BEADLE

John Beadle was born to Samuel Beadle and Abigail Collins at Bramford, Suffolk in September, 1595, and was baptised on September 28, 1595.[1] John's father, Samuel, was born March 19, 1555, to John Bedle of St. Georges in Canterbury.[2] Samuel

---

[1] See Suffolk Record Office, Bramford Parish register, fiche #2, p. 70, for Beadle's baptismal record: "Baptized Anno 1595, John Bedle Sonne of Samuel 28 of September." Until now Beadle's date of birth was thought to be September 29, 1595, because it is recorded as such in James Strother, *Miscellanea Genealogica et Heraldica*, "Families of Catelyn and Beadle," ns 4 (1884): 418; and A.G. Matthews, *Calamy Revised, Being a Revision of Edmund Calamy's Account of the Minsters and Others Ejected and Silenced, 1660-2* (Oxford: Clarendon Press, 1934) 41. According to the Essex Record Office there was no statutory registration of births in England before the mid-nineteenth century.

[2] James B. Strother, *Miscellanea Genealogica et Heraldica*, "Families of Catelyn and Beadle," ns 4 (1884): 418.

Beadle was an Anglican who attended Corpus Christi College at Cambridge matriculating during the Easter term of 1577. Four years later he earned his B.A., and in 1584 took his M.A. He married Abigail Collins on August 16, 1586, at Bramford.[3] On March 30, 1594 he was ordained deacon and priest and was beneficed as vicar at Woolverstone, Suffolk in 1597.[4]

During their twenty-nine year marriage, Abigail and Samuel had seven children of whom John was the second oldest. According to a transcription of the family tree in the family Bible, their oldest son, William, was born on October 22, 1587; a daughter, Abigail was born not long after and soon died; Thomas Beadle was born on May 1, 1599, and buried in Kent on February 27, 1624; Nathaniel Beadle was baptized at Woolverstone on January 1, 1602; Arthur Beadle was baptized on January 26, 1603 and died July 22, 1625 in London after contracting the plague; and Dorothy Beadle, was born June 15, 1606 and baptized two days later.[5] On March 19, 1608, John's mother, Abigail, died and was buried in Woolverstone; Samuel died seven years later on Sunday January 18, 1615 "about 2 of the clocke in the afternoone."[6]

---

[3] Strother, 418.

[4] John Venn, comp., *The Book of Matriculations and Degrees: a Catalogue of those who have been Matriculated or been admitted to any Degree in the University of Cambridge from 1544 to 1659* (Cambridge: University Press, 1913) 52; John Venn, comp., *Alumni Cantabrigienses*, 10 vols. (Cambridge: University Press, 1922) 1: 115. See also, R. Freeman Bullen, "Catalogue of Beneficed Clergy of Suffolk, 1551-1631," *Proceedings of the Suffolk Institute of Archaeology* 22 (1936): 296.

[5] Strother, 418-419.

[6] Strother, 418. Samuel Beadle's will was proved in the Consistory Court of Norwich in 1616; a copy of the will can be gotten from the Norfolk Record Office, reference no. 47 Sayer. Very little is known about Samuel Beadle's siblings, parents, or relatives. It is probable, however, that Samuel was related as an uncle or a cousin to the well-known William Bedell (1571-1642), Bishop of Kilmore, the son of John Bedell, a small

Introduction xiii

Like his father, John Beadle attended Cambridge University matriculating sizar at Pembroke College during the Easter term on July 8, 1613.[7] He earned his B.A. in 1617, was ordained deacon in the Church of England on May 11, 1618, at the age of twenty-two, and received his M.A. in 1620.[8] Shortly after his graduation he married Rose who was born in Braintree, Essex on December 21, 1598.[9] After their marriage, they stayed in Braintree where their first two children were born: George was born on January 12, 1621, and baptised four days later; Agnes was born on October 11, 1623, and baptised eight days later.[10]

On December 13, 1623 at the age of twenty-seven, Beadle was made rector of Little Leighs by his patron Robert Rich, Earl of Warwick.[11] *Lees-parva*, as the parish was called, was the

---

farmer, descended from William le Bedell, who held Bedels Hall and other farms in Writtle, Essex in 1251. John Bedell held a small farm at Black Notley, Essex, since known as "Bedalls." William Bedell and his brother were educated at Braintree, Essex. William's father and grandfather were loyal Puritans and friends of Sir Walter Mildmay of Chelmsford, a prominent Puritan Essex businessman and aristocrat who founded Emmanuel College, Cambridge. Throughout his life, John Beadle maintained a friendship with Hervey Carew Mildmay, a relative of the Mildmay family, who was a church elder in Romford, Essex, and a member of the Braintree Classis (See Essex Record Office, document D/DMS C3, "To my much honoured [----] freinde Carew Harvy Myldmay Esquir . . . Romford).

[7]John Venn, comp., *The Book of Matriculations and Degrees*, 52; John Venn, comp., *Alumni Cantabrigienses*, 1: 115; see also, T.W. Davids, *Annals of Evangelical Nonconformity in the County of Essex* (London: Jackson, Walford, and Hodder, 1863) 41.
[8]*Alumni Cantabrigienses*, 1: 115; *The Book of Matriculations and Degrees*, 52; *Calamy Revised*, 41.
[9]Strother, 419.
[10]Strother, 419.
[11]See *Calamy Revised*, 41; Richard Newcourt, *Repertorium Ecclesiasticum Parochiale Londinense*, 2 vols. (London: Printed by Benjamen Motte, 1710) 2: 388; *DNB 1*, 1379; Barbara

small parish to which his friend John Fuller refers when he observes of Beadle in the "To the Reader" section of *A Journall or Diary of a Thankfull Christian*: "As for this author's painfulnesse, and faithfulnesse, it's well known to all that know him, how greatly they shined forth in him, whilst in a very small place, and how since advanced by the bounty of his truly Noble and Honorable Patron". During his nine years as rector he and his wife had five more children. Thomas was born February 1, 1624 and died in June 1631; Dyonisius was born between 1624 and 1626 and died in November of 1627; Abigail, their second daughter, was born October 28, 1627; Susanna was born September 2, 1629, and Samuel, the last to be born at Little Leighs, entered the world on January 26, 1630.[12]

While rector at Little Leighs, Beadle became associated with the renowned Thomas Hooker who settled in Essex in 1626 as a guest lecturer[13] at St. Mary's Chelmsford and served as curate to John Michaelson then rector of that parish.[14] Also during his stay in Little Leighs, Beadle and John Fuller[15]

Donagan, "The Clerical Patronage of Robert Rich, Second Earl of Warwick 1619-1642," *Proceedings of the American Philosophical Society* 120.5 (1976): 417.

[12] For birth dates and baptismal dates of most of Beadle's children see Strother, 419. Unfortunately, no parish registers for Little Leighs survive before 1680 and so it was not possible to verify the dates given in the transcription of the family tree in Beadle's family bible.

[13] In his *Ecclesiastical History of Essex Under the Long Parliament and the Commonwealth* (Colchester: Benham and Company Limited, 1932) 31, Harold Smith explains that the lectures at Chelmsford were held on Tuesdays and in former times had been delivered by neighboring beneficed clergy; however, because of Hooker's reputation any modern knowledge of the Lecture is in connection with Thomas Hooker, from 1626 to 1629 or 1630.

[14] Davids, *Annals of Evangelical Nonconformity in Essex*, 151.

[15] John Fuller wrote the commendatory preface for Beadle's book. According to T.W. Davids, Fuller originally settled in Great Waltham, Essex, but "later removed to London" in 1656

Introduction

became friends. According to Fuller "we oft breathed and powred out our souls together in Prayer, Fasting, conferences . . . Fuller suggests that Beadle's relationship with Hooker was more than acquaintance when he compares their relationship to that of Elisha and Elijah: "he had the happinesse of a younger *Elisha* . . . to be watered by the droppings of that great *Elijah*, that renowned man of God in his generation Reverend Mr. *Thomas Hooker*."

Hooker's ministry and his preaching in Essex against conformity to some liturgical rites of the Church of England became widely known throughout the county and adjacent counties. Moreover, his "great popularity and influence especially with young ministers, to whom he [was] a great oracle, and their principal library"[16] concerned not only the conservative clergy in the county, but the ecclesiastical authorities in London—especially Bishop Laud. Consequently, Hooker was asked by the Archbishop Laud to lay down his ministry and lectureship in 1629.[17] The somewhat heated controversy was briefly quelled by a kinsman of Beadle's, Samuel Collins, who was at that time a close friend of Bishop Laud's.[18] Nevertheless, Hooker continued to preach

---

(541). After the Act of Uniformity, he was ejected from his living at St. Martin's, Ironmonger Lane, in London (541).

[16] See the summary of Samuel Collins's letter to Dr. Arthur Duck, Bishop Laud's Chancellor, in *Calendar of State Papers, Domestic, Charles I, 1628-1629*, 554.

[17] *DNB* 9: 1189.

[18] Samuel Collins became vicar of Braintree in Essex on February 15, 1610, on the presentation of Robert Lord Rich who would later become Robert Rich, Earl of Warwick. He retained his living until he died in 1657 See *DNB* 4, 830-831, for brief details of his life. Also, see T.W. Davids, *Annals of Nonconformity in the County of Essex*, 150; Thompson Cooper, "Dr. Samuel Collins, Provost of King's College, Samuel Collins, Vicar of Braintree," *Notes and Queries*, 2nd series 10 (1860): 42; and Richard Newcourt, *Repertorium Ecclesiasticum Parochiale Londinense*, 2: 89. A summary of Collins's written mediation of the Hooker affair with Laud's Chancellor, Dr. Arthur Duck, is

nonconformity and opened a school in Little Baddow with the future missionary to the American Indians, John Eliot. Again, complaints about Hooker's extreme nonconformity were made to Bishop Laud on November 3, 1629,[19] triggering a petitionary written response sent to Laud by forty-nine beneficed, pro-Hooker clergymen on November 10, 1629. It was a response fashioned to prevent any type of disciplinary action, including imprisonment, against Hooker. Beadle was the ninth signer of this petition which urged Laud "to understand that we all esteeme and knowe the said Mr. Thomas Hooker to be, for doctryne, orthodox, and life and conversation honest, and for his disposition peaceable, no wayes turbulent or factious, and so not doubting but he will contynue that good course, commending him and his lawfull suite to your lordship's honourable favor, and entreating the continuance of his libertye and paines there, we humbly take our leave, and remaine your honour's humbly at command."[20] The entire controversy was rendered moot in 1630, when Hooker peacefully left England for Holland, briefly returned, and then traveled to the American colonies to become pastor in Hartford, Connecticut. It should be noted that as a

---

found in *Calendar of State Papers, Domestic Series, Charles I, 1628-1629*, 554, 567. According to Barbara Donagan, Collins's participation in the Hooker affair is notable because he represented "an older generation of Puritans which found the radicalism of younger men like Hooker and Beadle antipathetic not merely because it disturbed the settled tenor of their lives, stirring up conflict with the authorities and among the Puritans themselves, but because it cast into doubt their acceptance of the duty of obedience to the state church, which to their just post-Elizabethan minds was after all the true Protestant church, and to the king who embodied the Protestant state" ("The Clerical Patronage of Robert Rich," 412).

[19] See *Calendar of State Papers, Domestic, Charles I, 1628-1629*, 87.

[20] For a reprinted text of the petition see Davids, *Annals of Evangelical Nonconformity in Essex*, 153-158. Also, see *Calendar of State Papers, Domestic, 1629-1631*, 92, for a summary of the petition.

Introduction *xvii*

result of Beadle's relationship with Hooker and his written defense of his person and teachings, Archbishop Laud and the ecclesiastical powers in London seemed then to have deemed Beadle, along with 10 other ministers, one who was "not conformable in preaching or practice."[21]

Despite Beadle's very public agitation, on May 31, 1632, he became pastor at Barnston in Essex upon the resignation of the previous pastor William Wright.[22] Beadle attained the appointment because of the intercession of his kinsman Samuel Collins[23] with Bishop Laud. According to a letter from Samuel Collins to Bishop Laud, Collins himself had been offered the position at Barnston by Robert, Earl of Warwick, but turned it down because of his attachment to his parish and flock in Braintree. Nonetheless, he used his influence with Laud to help his relative in obtaining a respectable benefice, probably also hoping to mitigate the more nonconformist religious and political positions which John seemed to be enthusiastically embracing at the time. Collins believed that an appointment to a parish and "pastoral" visit with the Bishop himself would help foster an attitude of conformity in his younger more radical friend, who had been easily impressed by Hooker's nonconformist doctrines. He wrote to Laud:

> My good lord, I am come with a kinsman of mine to your lordship, whom I humbly desire may be admitted into the rectory of Barndston, which my lord [Robert, Earl of Warwick] offered me. But I desire your honour, when we come before you, to let him

---

[21] *The Calendar of State Papers, Domestic, Charles I, 1629-1631*, #104.

[22] See Richard Newcourt, *Repertorium Ecclesiasticum Parochiale Londinense*, 2: 39. Also, see Edmund Calamy, *The NonConformist's Memorial; Being An Account of the Lives, Sufferings, and Printed works of the Two Thousand Ministers Ejected from the church of England, chiefly by the Act of Uniformity Aug. 24, 1662*, 3 vols. (London: Printed by J. Cundee, Ivy-Lane, 1802) 2: 188.

[23] Collins was probably a brother or close relative of John Beadle's mother, Abigail (Collins) Beadle.

xviii   *Beadle's* A Journall or Diary of a Thankfull Christian

> know that you expect from men some account upon what terms I am settled at Brayntree. I also humbly pray your lordship to give me charge, in his presence, to prevent and suppress to the utmost of my power all conventicles of both sexes in my parish, and to be careful to keep all my people, or what quality soever, to conformity in receiving the sacrament. And withall, to intimate that your lordship hath so watchful an eye over us in Brayntree, as that few things can be spoken of or done but they come to your lordship's eare. These things spoken at this present, will both settle this young man in the conformable way wherein he now is, and may procure me much peace.[24]

For Beadle the move from Little Leighs proved to be a modest financial windfall, since at Barnston the Earl of Warwick supported the pastor at £90 a year as opposed to £50 a year at Little Leighs.[25] Indeed, by the time Beadle and his expectant wife moved to Barnston with their seven children in 1632, he was in need of a more substantial living so that he could properly care for his growing family. According to Fuller, despite the more generous benefice, Beadle's modest living at Barnston still never enabled him to enjoy financial security;". . . his outward estate is not overmuch, (he being rich especially in *Asher's* blessing, many children)." In the next thirteen years, John and Rose had seven more children: Hannah was born on September 30, 1632; Mary on June 29, 1634; John was baptized on September 8, 1636; Dorothy was baptized on December 27, 1638; Lucy on October 22, 1640; the second son to be named Thomas was

---

[24] T.W. Davids, *Annals*, 346-347. For a summary of the letter to Laud see *Calendar of State Papers, Domestic, Charles I, 1631-1633*, 341.

[25] Barbara Donagan, "The Clerical Patronage of Robert Rich," 403. Also, Fuller refers to Beadle's financial step upwards when he observes how he had since "advanced (by the bounty of his Truly Noble and Honorable Patron to a higher, and but necessary subsistence . . . " (14).

Introduction   xix

baptized on September 25, 1642; and Joseph, the youngest of the twelve surviving children, was born on April 4, 1644.[26]

Clearly, Beadle's family life was very eventful. This can also be said about his public life as an outspoken nonconformist minister. During his thirty-year tenure at Barnston, Beadle actively dissented from Church norms and openly supported the institution of presbyterial government throughout England. In addition, he was an avid and loyal apologist for Cromwell's government, even when it became clear that Cromwell would fall. As early as 1633, only a year after Beadle had come to Barnston, Archbishop Laud disciplined him for "omitting some parts of divine service, and refusing conformity. But upon his submission and promise of reformation, I dismissed him with a canonical admonition only."[27] Apparently, the influence of Thomas Hooker's doctrines was not easily exorcized from Beadle's thinking because in 1638, he was again in danger of being severely admonished by the Archbishop for preaching nonconformity. In the "Account of His Province To the King, for the Year 1638," Laud describes the incident:

> The[re] was one Bedle a minister of Essex, came into this diocese, and at Harbledown near Canterbury ... preached very disorderly, three hours together at a time, and got himself many ignorant followers. But so soon as ever he was enquired after by my

---

[26] Beadle himself entered into the parish register the baptismal dates of his children who were born at Barnston. However, he did not specify their dates of birth. In Strother, "The Families of Catelyn and Beadle," 419, the children's dates of birth and baptism are listed. Interestingly, the transcription of the family tree in Beadle's family bible does not mention four of Beadle's children; namely, John, Dorothy, Lucy, and the second Thomas. Moreover, another discrepancy between the bible and the parish register occurs in the date of Joseph Beadle's baptism. Beadle lists it as April 10, 1645, and the bible entry lists it as April 6, 1644.

[27] William Laud, *The Works of the Most Reverend Father in God, William Laud*, 7 vols. (Oxford: John Henry Parker, 1854) 5 part II: 318.

officers, he fled the country, and I purpose, God willing, to speak with the chancellor of London concerning him.[28]

Whether Beadle was "convented" as a result of his "disorderly" preaching in Canterbury we do not know; however, we do know that throughout his thirty years at Barnston, he continued to openly dissent from the authority of the Church of England by participating in nonconformist associations and by signing and helping to disseminate statements in favor of presbyterial government.

The first such statement Beadle lent his support to was the "Protestation of 1641," a petition drafted by a committee of the House of Commons asking Charles to refuse the help of Irish troops in suppressing his opponents in England. John Pym, a member of the House of Commons, stirred that assembly to action because he was personally persuaded that the Catholics wanted to subvert and overthrow reformed religion in England. As a result, he called for unity among the members of the House of Commons and the entire nation, while insisting that the "protestation" contain a promise to maintain "the true reformed Protestant religion" in England. This solemn declaration was adopted by a large majority of that house on Monday, May 3, 1641, and was accepted by the Protestants in the House of Lords on Tuesday, May 4. On May 5, the clergy, the citizens of London, and citizens of adjacent counties were called upon to sign the protestation. Copies were sent to all parishes, with instructions that the minister should read it and ask the parishoners to sign it on some Sunday in the afternoon, after the sermon.

In Barnston, on July 11, 1641, Beadle presided over the public reading of the document, the gathering of signatures, and the final signing of the protestation; his signature is the first of 63 signatures on Barnston's copy of the document.[29]

---

[28] William Laud, *The Works*, 5 part II: 355. The chancellor referred to here is Arthur Duck, a friend of Samuel Collins.
[29] See Andrew Clark, "Barnston Notes, 1641-1649," *Essex Review* 25 (1916): 59. This article contains the full text of the Barnston copy of the "Protestation of 1641" and the names of the men who signed it. Also Clark alludes, as he does

Introduction

Again, in 1643, Beadle helped in the promulgation of the "Solemn League and Covenant," another affirmation of presbyterian rejection of episcopacy which the Scottish leaders and divines expected the English parliament to accept if it wanted Scotland's aid in defeating the Royalists. The English Parliament at Edinburgh publicly assented to the "Solemn League" in September 1643; however, it was not until October that it was sent to any parishes in the country for signatures. The Barnston version of the "Solemn League" was read and signed on July 13, 1643. John Beadle's name appears as the first of 49 signatures.[30]

As a result of Parliament's full embracing of the "Solemn League," the establishment of "classical presbyteries" throughout England was initiated in 1645. Essex was one of the first counties to petition for permission to organize for the swift

---

elsewhere in the article, to Beadle's "business aptitudes" and his exactness in record keeping (59). For a written text of the Protestation see Harold Smith, *The Ecclesiastical History of Essex*, 94-95; *Wing STC* P3867; and Samuel Rawson Gardiner, ed., *The Constitutional Documents of the Puritan Revolution*, 3rd ed. (Oxford: Clarendon Press, 1906) 155-156. For a discussion of the reason for the Protestation see Samuel Rawson Gardiner, *The History of England*, 10 vols. (London: Longmans, Green, and Co., 1884) 9: 351-357.

[30] See Andrew Clark, "Barnston Notes, 1641-1649," *Essex Review* 25 (1916): 63-64. As with the "Protestation of 1641," this article contains the Barnston text of the "Solemn League," as well as the names of the men who signed it. Also, Clark points out that the text of this document was not written by "Bedel, but by another hand." One can also find the text of the "Solemn League and Covenant" in S.R. Gardiner, ed., *The Constitutional Documents of the Puritan Revolution*, 267-271; *Wing STC* S4441; Edinburgh, 1643; and Harold Smith, *The Ecclesiastical History of Essex*, 1932, 95-99. S.R. Gardiner's *History of the Great Civil War, 1642-1649*, 4 vols. (New York: AMS Press, 1965) 1: 226-236, provides the circumstances surrounding the adoption of the "Solemn League."

and effective implementation of presbyterial government.[31] And by 1648, Essex county was divided into fourteen "classes."[32] John Beadle belonged to the eighth Classis, the Dunmowe and Freshwell Classis, made up of approximately 62 elders and ministers.[33]

It was because of the organization of Essex, and the effective communication it facilitated that what was called "The Essex Testimony" was swiftly disseminated and became widely known throughout the country, especially in London. Once again Beadle unequivocally supported its aims, and his signature heads the list of signers.[34] The document appeared in May, 1648, and was signed by 129 ministers. The full title of the testimony is "A Testimony of the Ministers in the Province of Essex to the Truth of Jesus Christ and to the Solemn League and

---

[31] Harold Smith discusses particulars of the guidelines for county *classis* organization in *The Ecclesiastical History of Essex*, 191-193.

[32] According to Harold Smith, in his article "The Presbyterian Organisation of Essex," *Essex Review* 28 (1919): 15, the idea behind the classis system "was that at least one elder . . . should be chosen from each parish; these and the approved ministers of the district should constitute the 'classis,' which was supposed to meet monthly for purposes of discipline, while the ministers would have also the function of ordination."

[33] In William Shaw's classic, *The History of the English Church During the Civil Wars and Under the Commonwealth, 1640-1660*, 2 vols. (London: Longmans, Green, and Co., 1900) 2: 383-384, he lists alphabetically the elders and ministers who belonged to the Dunmowe Classis. His list is more complete than the official document and list printed in 1648, which was essentialy the blueprint for the presbyterial organization of the Essex county. The official name of the document was *The Division of the County of Essex into severall Classes Together With the names of the Ministers and others fit to be of each Classis* (Wing STC D1738; London, 1648) B3r. Beadle's name heads the Dunmowe list. A more incomplete list of Dunmowe Classis members appears in T.W. Davids, *Annals*, 281-282.

[34] See Harold Smith, *The Ecclesiastical History of Essex*, 103.

Covenant, as also against the Errors, Heresies and Blasphemies of these times and the Toleration of them."[35] Its audience was the London ministers; its function was to serve as a manifesto for orthodox Presbyterianism and to unswervingly promulgate the work of the Westminster Assembly of Divines. In effect, it was Essex county's unqualified support for the aims stated in the "Solemn League" five years earlier. In substance, it flatly repudiated Roman Catholicism and other "carnal doctrines," stringently demanded the suppression of such "doctrines", forcefully rejected certain conformist worship practices, and unbendingly defended nonconformity and the primacy of conscience.

Beadle's staunch belief in Puritanism undoubtedly aided him in acquiring his postions at Little Leighs and Barnston, since his patron, Robert Rich, Second Earl of Warwick, was "the most visible and consistent supporter of the Puritan cause among the English nobility in the first half of the seventeenth century."[36] To entrench the Puritan way of life more firmly in Essex, Rich deliberately assigned nonconformist ministers to his parish holdings.[37] In all probability, one of the reasons why Beadle was not more seriously disciplined by Archbishop Laud was because Rich's high degree of lay control in the county

---

[35] It is interesting to note that "The Testimony" is found in the Wing *Short Title Catalogue* under the name of John Biddle, London, 1648; Wing STC B2878. For a discussion of the impact of the "The Essex Testimony," see Harold Smith, *The Ecclesiastical History of Essex*, 102-103.

[36] Barbara Donagan, "The Clerical Patronage of Robert Rich," 388. Throughout this article Donagan emphasizes the role that the clerical patronage of the Rich family played in influencing the widespread dissent to Anglicanism which characterized the religious landscape of Essex county.

[37] In many cases Warwick even defended and in fact protected such "troublesome" Puritans as Thomas Hooker, Hugh Peter, and Edmund Calamy (see Donagan, "The Clerical Patronage of Robert Rich," 394).

made "Laudian efforts at reform even more difficult."[38] Nevertheless, Beadle's penchant for nonconformity was not the only qualification Warwick expected of his ministers. He also demanded that his appointees be religious, zealous men of "good report and godly conversation;" "they were not to be pluralists, but vigorously controversial men;"[39] they were to be university educated;[40] furthermore, he emphasized that his ministers be not only highly competent preachers but that they also aspire to be publishing preachers.[41] With regard to the preaching abilities of Beadle, he was "returned as an able preacher" in 1650[42] by the ecclesiastical authorities in London.

And as for his publishing ability, it was just six years later that he wrote his first and only book, *A Journall or Diary of a Thankfull Christian*. In Arthur Wilson's "Autobiography," in which he describes his experiences as friend and confidant of Robert Rich, he fondly recounts a sermon of Beadle's which he heard in Leez on the Sunday morning of July 21, 1644. He recalls the inspiration the sermon provided him to record more religiously the providential occurrences, either trivial or important, which characterized his daily life. On that occasion Beadle chose his text from Numbers 33.1., the same

---

[38] Barbara Donagan, "The Clerical Patronage of Robert Rich," 391.

[39] Barbara Donagan, "The Clerical Patronage of Robert Rich," 396.

[40] According to Barbara Donagan, Warwick gave special consideration to Cambridge men; "it seems that of sixty-five incumbents of Rich livings between 1619 and 1658, some forty-eight had been Cambridge undergraduates, of whom eighteen were appointed by Warwick before 1642" (Donagan, "The Clerical Patronage of Robert Rich," 396).

[41] As Donagan points out, Essex clergy were not as productive as London clergy; however, they still managed to leave behind a respectably large body of work. The Warwick appointee usually published one or two works and failure to do so was frowned upon (Donagan,"The Clerical Patronage of Robert Rich," 397).

[42] *DNB* 1: 1379.

Introduction   xxv

text on which he based his handbook on diary writing almost twelve years later. Wilson summarizes the sermon and attests to the persuasiveness of its rhetoric by acknowledging that hearing it urged him to "run backe to the beginning of my life, assisted by my memorie & some small notes; wherein I have given a true, though a meane deleniation, of eight & forty yeares progresse in the world."[43] According to Wilson's account Beadle proclaimed,

> that every Christian ought to keep a record of his owne actions & wayes, being full of dangers & hazards; that God might have the glorie. For this command was given to Moses, as in the second verse, by God himselfe; that there might be a remembrance to posteritie of the deliverances which God had & would worke for that people. And soe everie man, though of the meanest qualitie, may see the hand of the Divine Goodnes Workinge for him in the many occurrences of life. Which, as it may be a register to his owne memorie, so it may bee an example of gratitude to those who shall read or heare it, when they shall reflect upon themselves; & make a like collection of God's mercie towards them; some more, some lesse, according as it pleases God to distribute his blessings.[44]

This is an invaluable entry; first, because it clearly indicates that as early as 1644, Beadle had largely developed the idea of the diary which would later become *A Journall or Diary of a Thankfull Christian*; second, it is a contemporary reference to his persuasive style of preaching. But, most importantly, this testimony more than hints at the commitment Beadle maintained throughout his career to announcing the need for

---

[43] Arthur Wilson's "Autobiography" is found in *Desiderata Curiosa: or a Collection of Divers Scarce and Curious Pieces relating Chiefly to Matters of English History*, ed. Francis Peck, 2 vols. (London: Printed for Thomas Evans in the Strand, 1779) 2: 475.

[44] Arthur Wilson, "Autobiography," in *Desiderata Curiosa*, 2: 475.

keeping a diary. As his name implies, and as his good friend John Fuller observes, Beadle saw himself, both in giving the above sermon and in writing *A Journall or Diary*, as delivering a message, as "executing a mandate of an authority,"[45] with that authority being God; "Well and timely then ought his Stewards and Bailiffs to demand, and call for by new rentals, those old Quit-rents and arrears long agoe due; which if denyed, we may well fear his straining for his right, and taking forfeit of all". In a sense, he viewed himself as God's baillif and messenger of justice in urging his audience and congregation to record what troubles had befallen them, what blessings had been bestowed on them, and then what praise and thankfulness were owed to God in return.[46] Beadle, seeing himself as a sacred clerk, "demands" that people render just praise and thanksgiving due to God by "chalk[ing] up his loving kindnesses" (Beadle, 228), and by keeping honest spiritual accounts.[47]

Beadle's concern for precision in spiritual accounting carried over into the care of his parish. Beadle was a conscientious rector who conducted his parish duties with efficiency and charity. His parish account books or registers hold evidence of both a thorough knowledge of business principles and a well-formed accounting ability. For example, with regard to Fast-Day collections, a notable feature of the Puritan period during the seventeenth century, Beadle took special care in recording and distributing alms. On these days special sermons were preached, the content of which was usually highly ideological. Collections were then taken up for the poor and

---

[45] See *OED*, 2nd ed.

[46] See the sidenotes on page 21 of *A Journall or Diary*, which discuss the meaning of Beadle's name.

[47] His demand for diary keeping is early outlined in *A Journall or Diary's* "Dedicatory Epistle" he proclaims that, "There is a book of three leaves thou shouldest read dayly to make up this Diary; the black leaf of thy own and others sins with shame and sorrow; the white leaf of Gods goodnesse, mercies with joy and thankfulnesse; the red leaf of Gods judgments felt, feared, threatned, with fear and trembling".

Introduction xxvii

other "straingers" or foreigners. From his meticulously kept records, it is clear that immediately after receiving the collection he distributed the money to the poor among the parish.[48] "The business-like Rector," as Clarke calls Beadle, also kept careful records of all gifts made to refugees from Ireland who came through Barnston. It is obvious from these records that Beadle was trained in bookkeeping methodology; in fact, the title of "clerk"[49] was assigned to him when his will was registered and probated in 1667.[50]

In essence, Beadle's life as pastor and preacher spanned the most tumultuous decades in the seventeenth century. His public life was daily impinged upon by the revolutionary events of the day. Undoubtedly, his active commitment to nonconformist doctrine, his support for theological presbyterianism, his complete loyalty to Cromwell's government, and his daily exertions as rector of Barnston parish were not responsibilities he held lightly or without personal cost. According to Edmund Calamy, whose "imprimatur" is found in Beadle's book, his friend struggled daily with his health; "He was long exercised with great weakness, which he bore with much faith and patience."[51] In a March 4, 1655, letter to his friend Colonel

---

[48] In his article, "Barnston Notes," Andrew Clark transcribes several records taken from Beadle's parish account books. One particular record is a transcription of a balance sheet listing the fast days from 1641 to 1645 and their collections. In his discussion about the balance sheet, Clarke adds that Beadle's "notes as to the distributions are very minute" *Essex Review 25* (1916): 65.

[49] According to the *OED*, the designation of "clerk" not only refers to the scholar or student, but also to a "keeper of accounts," and one who kept track of the "transaction of all business involving writing."

[50] See Essex Record Office, *Wills at Chelmsford (Essex and East Hertfordshire)* (London: British Record Society, 1958) 29. According to the Suffolk County Council Archives, John's father, Samuel Beadle of Woolverstone, was also a clerk and trained in bookkeeping methodology.

[51] See Edmund Calamy, *The Nonconformist Memorial*, 2: 188.

Carew Hervey Mildmay, Beadle refers at length to his sickness and gently apologizes for not writing sooner; "it hath pleased my good God to [letter torn] a longe and a sharpe sickness."[52] He indicates throughout that his health is poor and recounts that "once I confess I [---] [---] to aske Dr. Wright [a] question or two about the shape of my body." Beadle, however, survived the illness and continued to work as pastor of Barnston until he was ejected for nonconformity in 1662, as a result of the Act of Uniformity of 1660.[53]

Five years later, in 1667, at the age of seventy-two, Beadle died and was "buried on May 11, 1667;"[54] and his body was interred "beginning at the east end and north side" of the church.[55] Before Beadle died he had made out a brief will in which "all his goods" were bequeathed to his wife Rose. The will was registered on May 5, 1666[56] and later probated in September, 1667. Rose survived John for nine more years and

---

[52] See Essex Record Office document D/DMS C3 or "To my much honoured... freinde Carew Harvy Myldmay Esquire, Romford." This is the only letter by Beadle which the Essex Record Office owns. Carew Hervey Mildmay was a member of the famous Essex Mildmay family, whose land holdings rivaled those of Robert Rich, Earl of Warwick. He was also a member of the Becontree Classis, and was an elder in Rumford parish, Essex (*The Division of the County of Essex into severall Classes Together With the names of the Ministers and others fit to be of each Classis* (London, 1648; Wing STC D1738) A2r.
[53] Beadle's successor at Barnston, John Smith, was installed on December 13, 1662 (Richard Newcourt, *Repertorium Ecclesiasticum Parochiale Londinense*, 2: 40. Also, see A.G. Matthews, *Calamy Revised*, 41.
[54] Beadle's burial record is listed in the parish register, Essex Record Office, document D/P 153/1/1. On that same page of the parish register of burials is indicated the death of Beadle's third daughter, Susanna Beadle, who was buried on April 10, 1668.
[55] *DNB* 1: 1379.
[56] See Essex Record Office, document D/ABR 8/97.

Introduction xxix

then died in 1676 and was buried July 14, 1676.[57] She, too, prepared a will which she registered on October 13, 1672.[58] The will is approximately 2 1/2 folio pages long and is quite detailed in its stipulations. Moreover, it indicates how many of the Beadle children survived their parents and how many grandchildren were alive in 1672. According to the will, only six children of fourteen survived: Samuel, the oldest living son; Abigail, the oldest daughter, who married Thomas Watson; Mary, who married George Perry; Lucy, wife of John Mead; Dorothy, the youngest girl; and Joseph Beadle, the youngest son who later took Anglican orders in 1666-1667 and distinguished himself by serving as chaplain (c. 1679) to Charles II.[59] Like his father, Joseph published once. In 1679 he published *A Sermon Preached in S. Lawrence-Jewry Church on the Fifth of November, Anno Dom. 1678*, commemorating the Gunpowder Plot.[60] As for the Beadle grandchildren, only six are mentioned in Rose's will: Abigail's two sons, Samuel and James; Mary Perry's two children, Frances and Mary; Lucy's son, John; and Joseph's son, John.

---

[57] Essex Record Office, document, D/P 153/1/1.
[58] Essex Record Office, document, D/ABR 9/S44. Also, see Essex Record Office, *Wills at Chelmsford*, 29.
[59] Joseph was educated at Felstead School in Essex. At the young age of sixteen, he matriculated sizar at Gonville and Caius College, June 26, 1661. Joseph was awarded his B.A. between 1664 and 1665, and was ordained deacon in 1666, after which he served as a curate in Dunmowe, Essex. In the year his father died, 1667, he was ordained an Anglican priest at Ely, and three years later became vicar of Great Burstead, Essex, until he was given a rectorship at Chipping Ongar, Essex in 1680. He died in 1692 (*Alumni Cantabrigiensis*, comp. John Venn, part I, 1, 115).
[60] See *Wing STC* B1675 (London: Printed by R. Everingham for W. Kettilby, 1679).

ANTECEDENTS

The book Beadle produced, *A Journall or Diary of a Thankfull Christian*, is essentially a manual, a how-to book about how to write a spiritual diary; moreover, it is the only one of its kind written in seventeenth-century England. No religious or spiritual writer before Beadle's publication had extensively or systematically documented any rubric or tradition for diary-keeping. However, several religious writers did recommend keeping a journal of sorts, as part of daily devotional practise for the purpose of facilitating a complete examination of conscience, and an awareness of the movements of the soul and heart.[61] For example, Richard Baxter, in *The Saints' Everlasting Rest* , (1650), suggests that when one begins to take stock "it would not be unuseful to write out some of the chief and those Scriptures withall which hold them forth, and so to bring this Paper with you when you come to the Examination."[62] Baxter further suggests that after one has studied these written observations and has arrived at a conclusion concerning his application to life, one should permanently document his truth to stave off future backsliding:

> "be sure to Record this Sentence, so passed, write it down: or at least write it in thy Memory: At such a time upon thorough Examination, I found my state to be thus or thus: This Record will be very useful to thee hereafter. If thou be ungodly: what a damp will it be to thy presumption and security, to go and read the Sentence of thy Misery under thy own hand? If thou be godly: what a help will it be again the next Temptation to

---

[61] In her thorough treatise on the history of diary writing in England, entitled *Les Journaux Privès en Angleterre de 1600 à 1660* (Paris: Imprimerie Nationale, 1976) 355-359, Elisabeth Bourcier briefly discusses the place of Beadle, his predecessors (with the exception of Richard Baxter), and his successors in puritan devotional practice.

[62] (London, 1650; *Wing STC* B1383) Kkk4v, p. 428.

doubting and fear, to go and read under thy hand this Record?"[63]

Another Protestant devotional tract which discussed the efficacy of journal keeping as a vehicle for confession was Isaac Ambrose's *Prima, the First Things in reference to the Middle & Last Things,* (1654).[64] In a section called "Of the time of our Self-tryal," Ambrose, like Baxter, recommends that the sinner examine himself; "After supper, when you lie down, and are ready to sleep, and have great quietnesse and silence, without presence or disturbance of any, then erect a Tribunal for your own Consciences."[65] He goes on to suggest that the conclusions or "accounting" of "tryals" be recorded in a diary in order that the penitent may refer back during the year to his dealings with God and God's dealings with him:

> To this purpose we read of many Ancients that were accustomed to keep Diaries or Day-books of their actions, and out of them to take an account of their lives: Such a Register (of Gods dealings towards him, and of his dealings toward God in main things) the Lord put into a poor creatures heart to keep in the year 1641. ever since which time he hath continued it, and once a year purposes (by Gods grace) to examine himself by it...[66]

A third contemporary of Beadle's who wrote and spoke about the necessity of journal keeping was Edmund Staunton, a Puritan divine. In *A Sermon preacht at Great Milton in the county of Oxford at the funerall of Mrs. Elizabeth Williamson, late wife of Dr. Henry Williamson principall of Magdalen College. Whereunto is added a narrative of her godly life and death,* December 9, 1654, Staunton spoke much in the same terms as Ambrose, Baxter and Beadle concerning the purpose of keeping

---

[63] *Ibid.*, sig. Lll2v, p. 432.
[64] London; *Wing STC* A2962.
[65] *Ibid.*, p. 86.
[66] *Ibid.*, p. 87. Ambrose then provides a 2 1/2 page example of a "daily Register of a weak unworthy servant of Christ" (pp. 88-90).

a diary; "She kept a Diary of Gods dealings with her soule, and of those various dispensations she met withall."[67] Again, Mrs. Williamson used her diary as an aid to self-examination and as a tool for better understanding God's intentions for her. It helped her to "account" for various vicissitudes of her spiritual progress and the "returns" of grace with which God had chosen to reward her.

It is quite probable that Beadle had read about both Baxter's and Ambrose's instructions for journal keeping and decided to expand on them more completely. However, as I have already noted, Beadle's ideas on journal keeping pre-date both Baxter's and Ambrose's recommendations by many years as is evidenced by the eyewitness account of Arthur Wilson, a contemporary of Beadle, who witnessed Beadle preaching on the subject of diary-keeping on July 21, 1644. During that sermon Beadle's proof text was Numbers 33.2: "And Moses wrote their goings out, according to their Journeys, by the commandement of the Lord." In this text Beadle sees God setting a precedent for every Christian concerning the keeping of a journal. According to Wilson's own journal account, Beadle insists that

> every Christian ought to keep a record of his owne actions & wayes, being full of dangers & hazards; that God might have the glorie. For this command was given to Moses ... by God himself; that there might be a remembrance to posteritie of the deliverances which God had & would worke for his people And soe everie man though of the meanest qualitie, may see the hand of the Divine Goodnes workinge for him in the many occurences of his life. Which, as it may be a register to his owne memorie, so it may bee an example of gratitude to those who shall read or heare it, when they shall reflect upon themselves ...[68]

---

[67] Oxford, 1659; *Wing STC* S5343, sig. E24, p. 24. The sermon was preached in 1654 and printed in 1659.

[68] Francis Peck, ed., *Desiderata Curiosa, or a Collection of Divers Scarce and Curious Pieces Relating chiefly to Matters of English History*, 2 vols. (London: For Thomas Evans in the Strand, 1779) 2: 475.

Hence, for Beadle, the keeping of a journal was not simply a matter of preference, but an issue of obedience to God typified in His command to Moses. Furthermore, in the "To the Reader" section of *The Journall or Diary of a Thankfull Christian*, Beadle's friend, John Fuller, is even more explicit about the precedent underlying this obligation when he observes that God himself has "kept a Diary in the Creation of the world, Gen. I. to president this practise to us. Yea he keeps a Book of Remembrance for us that think upon his name . . . Registers our names in heaven, and shall we write down his name, works, love in water . . . ". Coupled, then, with the obligation to obedience, was the obligation to imitate God's example as *the* Record Keeper, and Author of Scripture, the ultimate record; as Beadle says at the end of his book, "God himself seems to keep a Journall by him of all the care he hath of us, the cost he bestows upon us, and the good things he gives to us. He hath a book of remembrance of every passage of providence that concerns us. And indeed, the Scripture for a great part is little else but a history of his goodnesse to his people". Moreover, if the Puritan believed that God himself keeps a record of every gracious soul's journey, then on judgment day the soul's journal must somehow mirror or match God's record. In essence, the soul faces God with a written record of his life, containing both the evil committed and the charity bestowed, with the judgment depending somewhat on how closely the solitary soul's diary corresponds to God's. Hence, the compelling issue for the solitary soul is whether or not he has kept an accurate record and whether or not he has he has been an industrious and faithful steward over the blessings of "God's goodnesse, [and] mercies with joy and thankfulnesse" evident in his life.[69]

---

[69] This theme of stewardship runs throughout the book and is most evident in the way in which Beadle and Fuller discuss the contemporary duties of a steward. First, Fuller says with regard to the diarist: "A Christian that would be exact hath more need, and may reap much more good by such a Journall as this. We are all but Stewards, Factors here, and must give a strict account in the great to the high Lord of all our ways . . . .

xxxiv   Beadle's A Journall or Diary of a Thankfull Christian

Clearly, Beadle was not unique in his belief that Christians should keep a written record of both their offenses against God and the benefits received from him. Spiritual diaries of the kind Beadle prescribes were written before Beadle's time, and we possess many manuscripts and printed examples of them.[70] Yet, it was not until the early to middle seventeenth century that the practise became prevalent, especially within the nonconformist community.[71] Indeed, Beadle's detailed treatise

---

Again, only a page later, Fuller observes, "then ought his Stewards and Bailiffs to demand, and call for by new rentals, those old Quit-rents and arrears long agoe due; wich if denyed, we may well fear his straining for his right and taking forfeit of all." Both examples undoubtedly allude to the "stewards" in the parable of the talents, Matthew 25.15-30, where each is given a certain number of talents, which the "lord" entrusts to them, in hopes that each may reap a return on what he has been asked to invest. Likewise, Beadle sees the diarist as a "steward" whose "returns must be greater then his ventures or he cannot live." Also, in another place, Beadle observes of Solomon, "God gave him wisdome, and moreover riches and honour more then any King had before him, or sould have after him, so that his returne was far above his venture."

[70] See M.M. Knappen, ed., *Two Elizabethan Puritan Diaries by Richard Rogers and Samuel Ward* (Chicago: The American Society of Church History, 1933), for two representative examples of Tudor Puritan diaries. For many other examples of pre-1656 Puritan religious diaries see William Matthews, comp. *British Diaries: An Annotated Bibliography of British Diaries Written between 1442 and 1942* (Berkeley: University of California Press, 1984) 3-26; and Patricia Pate Havlice, *And So to Bed: A Bibliography of Diaries Published in English* (Metuchen, N.J.: The Scarecrow Press, Inc., 1987) 12-16.

[71] According to Elisabeth Bourcier, diary keeping bourgeoned during the seventeenth century, crossing generational and class lines: "On assiste en Angeleterre, au xviie siècle, à une étonnante floraison de journaux religieux. Des hommes et des femmes, de tous âges et de toutes classes, profondément convaincus de leur nature pécheresse, tentent de s'améliorer, en

Introduction

was possible because he lived at a time when he was able to take full advantage of a variety of societal influences and cultural circumstances which made the codification of rules governing Puritan spiritual diary-writing both possible and necessary within the context of Puritan life. In brief, Beadle's instructional manual helped to popularize the already well-known practise of diary-writing among every level of the faithful and also to emphasize it as an important component of Puritan spirituality and Christian devotion.[72] He himself asks, with regard to the number of faithful keeping diaries, "Where is the man that makes conscience of private fasting and prayers, that shuts himself up in his closet, and wrastles with God in secret, that his Father that seeth in secret may reward him openly? To conclude, how few are there that keep a Diary by them of all Gods gracious dealings with them?"

---

faisant un inventaire régulier de leurs fautes, de leurs manquements, mais aussi des bénédictions divines. Si le puritanisme, en mettant l'accent sur le combat spirituel que le chrétien doit livrer en liu-même, contibue dans une large measure au développment et à la poplarité de ce genre d'écrits, la nécessité de scruter sa conscience, d'en observer attentivement les fluctuations, n'est pas une idée nouvelle" (*Les Journaux Privés en Angleterre de 1600 à 1660*, 353).

[72] Robert A. Fothergill claims that the influence of Beadle's book is "widely attested to," and he further deduces that because it appeared "comparatively late in the day it must be regarded as summing up and re-iterating precepts which were already common and had been followed for at least a half a century (*Private Chronicles: A Study of English Diaries* (London: Oxford University Press, 1974) 17.

TRADITIONAL INFLUENCES

Essentially there were three specific circumstances which made possible Beadle's thorough discussion of the diary form. They were: 1) the Puritan's psychological need for a structured confessional experience where he specifically documented his shortcomings while also enumerating his blessings; 2) the increased knowledge of accounting theory and practise, the language of which was ingrained in the Puritans who made up a substanital portion of the new merchant middle class;[73] 3) and, finally, the Puritans' keen interest in recording and understanding the symbolic and cosmic significance of the public and environmental workings of Providence, a practice which complemented their interest in the private workings of Providence and which probably also derived from the already entrenched practise of keeping commonplace books, and from the medieval and Renaissance fascination with prodigies and the ordinary workings of natural events.

The Puritan Diary as Confessional

First, there is little doubt that the Puritan proclivity for diary-keeping stemmed from the Puritan's need for self-reflection, for a regimented examination of conscience, for the giving of public and private penance, for assurance of election and forgiveness, and for offering thanks for the benefits and blessings bestowed on him by God.[74] Indeed, the Puritan diary,

---

[73] Thus, financial and accounting vocabularies dominate the language of late sixteenth- and seventeenth-century diaries and diary literature.

[74] Many students of the spiritual diary conclude that Puritans used the journal or diary as a part of a strict method of religious self-development. For example, see Robert A. Fothergill, *Private Chronicles: A Study of English Diaries* (London: Oxford University Press, 1974) 17. Steven Kagle similarly maintains that an important "motive for many Puritan diarists was a journal's potential as a weapon against despair. For . . .

or a "Register-book for Conscience," as Beadle calls it, in order to fulfill these needs (especially the examination of conscience), was used as a confessional vehicle or more specifically as a replacement for the Catholic sacrament of auricular confession which had given pre-Reformation generations a spoken assurance of forgiveness.[75] Beadle's prefatory instructions also attest to the confessional nature of the spiritual diary, when he commands, "providences must be registred. Who can number the stars, or sands; Gods blessings, or our sins? the most eminent of the first magnitude are to be noted down; as all our sins are to be laid to heart, but especially the most hainous." Concomitantly, William Haller early observes that "The diary like the autobiography, of which it was the forerunner, was the Puritan's confessional. In its pages he could fling upon his God the fear and weakness he found in his heart but would not betray to the world."[76] Furthermore, the Puritan

---

Puritans, salvation was dependent on the arbitrary will of God to choose whom he would for salvation or damnation. The Puritan creed taught that the process by which sinful man became regenerate was rarely sudden or strikingly evident; rather, it was usually a long and difficult process the evidence of which would be difficult to perceive. Many Puritans hoped that by keeping a rigorously exact diary they would be able to find a pattern which would give them confidence in their own election" (*American Diary Literature*, Boston: Twayne Publishers, 1979) 30.

[75] Alan MacFarlane notes that after the Reformation, diary-writing rapidly proliferates, particularly during the second half of the seventeenth century (*The Family Life of Ralph Josselin: A Seventeenth-Century Clergyman*, Cambridge: University Press, 1970) 5. Probably, the need for a confessional replacement accounts for this upsurge.

[76] In *The Rise of Puritanism* (1938; New York: Harper & Row, Publishers, 1957) 30, William Haller was the first historian to recognize the confessional motivation behind the diary form. Several students of Puritan history and literature have echoed and have expanded somewhat on his observations. See Owen Watkins, *The Puritan Experience: Studies in Spiritual*

diary conflated the practise of confession with the examination of conscience which are two separate processes in the Catholic tradition. The examination which preceded confession and the tradition of the *septenary* interrogation of the confessional[77] between priest and penitent, which asked the penitent the circumstances of his sins, are both replaced with the self-interrogation of the diary.

In coalescing elements of the two, Beadle's rubric retains many elements of the Catholic examination of conscience.[78] For example, when a Catholic prepared for confession, he was asked to consider several personal circumstances such as "The

---

Autobiography (New York, 1972) 18; Baird Tipson, "The Routinized Piety of Thomas Sherpard's Diary," *Early American Literature* 13 (1978): 69; Elisabeth Bourcier, *Les Journaux Privés en Angleterre de 1600 à 1660* (Paris: Imprimerie Nationale, 1976) 357; and, finally, see Theodore DeWelles, "Sex and Sexual Attitudes in Seventeenth-Century England: The Evidence from Puritan Diaries," *Renaissance and Reformation* 12(1988): 48, who discusses the psychological need the Puritans possessed for a form a confession.

[77] The *septenary* is comprised of seven questions concerning the circumstances of each sin confessed: who, how much, why, in what place, at what time, by what means and instruments, how often.

[78] An excellent example of this combination in practice is the private seventeenth century *Diarie of Elizabeth Viscountess Mordaunt* (Duncairn, 1856). Toward the beginning of her diary, she lays down her rules for keeping her diary and they sound quite similar to instructions given to Catholic penitents: "when I come to account for my sins of cummition, and omision, which I must stricktely dow, and senserely repent of, that by God's assistance hauing dune that, I may Laye me doune and rest in pece, with a full ashuranc, that they shal neuer more be layde to my charge, so as to condemne me . . . That I may the beter kepe this resolution, Lorde geue me Grace constantly to examen my selfe, by these foloing rueles or the like . . . " (6-7). What follows in her diary, corresponds almost exactly to the scheme for the Catholic examination of conscience.

Introduction   xxxix

state of [his] degree, person, or calling;" "The offices and daily expercises, wherein [he] [has] beene occupyed;" "The places wherein [he] [has] liued or dwelt;" and "the persons with whom [he] [has] kept company, & byn most conuersant."[79] Similarly, Beadle recommends that the diarist record, "his effectual calling, and of his age in Christ"; "all the men and means that God hath in providence used for our good"; while also suggesting that "it will be of singular use to put into our Diary, what Times we have lived in, what Ministers we have lived under, what Callings we were of, what Wealth was bestowed on us, what places of Authority and Command were committed to us." Beadle also strongly reminds the "thankfull Christian" to "remember your sinfull estate, when you were in a naturall estate, and therefore in the gall of bitternesse, and in the bond of iniquity."

Another part of the Catholic examination of conscience which Beadle adjusts to the diary form is the penitent's self-interrogation concerning his obligation toward God, toward his neighbor, and toward himself. Traditionally, the penitent asked himself if he had sinned against God, his neighbor, or himself "by thoughts, by words or by deedes." Further, he would ask himself with regard to his relationship with God if he had "loued God, wyth all his harte, and with hys soule, as was bounde to doe: But hath setled his affection [on] . . . the vanitie of this worlde, forgettinge his creator altogether."[80] He would also check "in lyke maner for beinge ingratefull towards the benefites of god; and for not rendering unto him due thanks therefore, and for that he hath not endeuoured to serue and loue more earnestly the giuer of al goodnesse."[81] In chapter 6, Beadle's prescription for self-accusation bears a striking resemblance to these questions. He begins the chapter with this

---

[79] William Warford, *A Briefe Treatise of Pennance*, ed. D.M. Rogers, *English Recusant Literature, 1558-1640* (1624; Yorkshire, England: The Scolar Press, 1973) *155*: 21.

[80] Henry Suso, *A Short and an Absolute Order of Confession*, ed. D.M. Rogers and A.F. Allison, *English Recusant Literature* (1575-8); Yorkshire, England: Scolar Press, 1969) *5*: sig. A5r.

[81] *Ibid.*, sig. A6r.

instruction: "when you have read over your Journall, and made such use of it as hitherto I have shewed you; ask youre owne hearts these three questions: The first concerns God; the second, our neighbour; and the third, ourselves." He then lists a number of questions the diarist should ask himself: "What honor do I bring to God for all this?" "I have all from him, but do I anything for him?" "Can I say with St. *Paul, His I am, and him I serve?.* He is the *alpha* of all my happinesse, why should not he be the *omega* of all my thankfulness?"

The Catholic penitent was also obliged to examine his actions toward his neighbor; "First let him blame himselfe, for not bearing to his neighbour such affection as he ought: for not releuing his neede with such faueur and helpe as he coulde and shoulde: For not hauing due compassion of his miserie, and for not praying to god for hym as was his parte."[82] In addition, he was to "accuse himslef of the crymes apperteining to hys degree, calling and office, declaring that he hath don contrary to the rule and equitie of his vocation."[83] Likewise, Beadle encourages the following interrogatory: "What good do I to my neighbour? . . . What good do I in the Town where I dwell, to the family where I live? to my relations, wife, children, servants, with whom I converse; are any of these the better for me? . . . How do I promote the good of my neigbour, by my alms, prayers, counsels, labours?" Finally, the Catholic penitent was to account for his sins against himself:

> I accuse my selfe, that I haue not
> vsed such dilgence in the dayly examining of
> my conscience, and amendment of my life, as
> I ought to haue done: for which I aske God
> hartily pardon.
> I accuse my selfe, that I haue
> greatly offended Almighty God, in that haue
> not giuen him due thankes for all his bene-
> fits that I haue receiued continually at
> his handes: for which I aske him hartily
> pardon. . .
> I accuse my selfe, for that I haue

---

[82] Henry Suso, *A Short and an Absolute Order of Confession*, sig. A8v.

[83] *Ibid.*, sig. B2r.

Introduction

> been proud, and vaine-glorious in my inward thoughts & cogitations: for which I aske God hartily pardon.[84]

Again, Beadle's recommended questionare strikingly resembles its Catholic counterpart:

> Let every man therefore ask his owne heart upon a serious survey of his Journall, thus much: Am I bettered by all this health, and wealth, and good dayes? . . . Do I grow? At such a time, I had a great affliction, a long sicknesse; Am I more humble since? . . . Am I more holy, more humble, more heavenly, more meek, more mercifull, more faithfull, more fruitfull in my place? Or, am I not rather worse . . . Be sure that after all these questions be strictly asked and seriously answered, you make it . . . your very work to be thankfull for all Gods mercies; otherwise, why do you keep such a Journall.

The purpose behind Beadle's written adaptation of the Catholic examination of conscience and the oral *septenary* was to aid the diary keeper's memory in permanently recording the dialogue between his conscience and his sinful self so that he might then absolve himself. However, the adaptation possessed a not easily surmounted limitation: how was the writer to be sure that he had been forgiven in the eyes of God?

Whereas in confession the priest functions as a proxy for Christ and speaks with His voice, the puritan diary keeper serves as both examiner and penitent; therefore, he had to detach himself in such a way as to render "a scientific judgment on himself; his conscience examines his experience as would an eternal, objective observer, God."[85] In a pre-Beadle devotional tract entitled *The Saints' Everlasting Rest*, Richard Baxter demands that during self-examination one should "resolve to

---

[84] George Dowley, *A briefe Methode for frequent Confession* in *The Key of Paradise*, ed. D.M. Rogers, *English Recusant Literature* (1623; London: Scolar Press, 1979) *394*: sig. Y1r-Y2r.

[85] Baird Tipson, "The Routinized Piety of Thomas Shepard's Diary," *Early American Literature* 13 (1978): 69.

judg thy self impartially; neither better nor worse then thou art, but as the Evidence shall prove thee;"[86] and then after the judgment "when by all this pains and means thou hast discovered the truth of thy state, then pass the Sentence on thy self accordingly."[87] This kind of objectivity on the part of the diarist was virtually impossible, and thus, assurance of God's favor became more elusive and uncertain. The only way this limitation could be overcome was by rigorous and prolonged daily examination which would ultimately produce a written and therefore visual pattern of one's life, character, and circumstances which would, in turn, produce proof of forgiveness and election. Over a period of several months or years a pattern of assurance emerged and was augmented by the very act of keeping a diary which "proved" the diarist's commitment to penance, reform, and thanksgiving. According to Michael McGiffert, "the keeping of a journal, which seems to have been an important point of Puritan piety, was itself a means of assurance, or was so intended. Ability to sustain this methodical, painful discipline could be regarded as a mark of a gracious soul, and the regularity of the exercise may itself have contributed to the diarist's composure."[88]

---

[86] (London, 1650; *Wing STC* B1383) Lllr, p. 429.
[87] *Ibid.*, Lll2r, p. 431.
[88] *God's Plot: The Paradoxes of Puritan Piety, Being the Autobiography & Journal of Thomas Shepard*, ed. Michael McGiffert (Amherst: The University of Massachusetts Press, 1972) 18. In their edition of *The Diary of Samuel Pepys*, Robert Latham and William Matthews insightfully comment on the "duality" which cannot but develop in the Puritan diarist and which is evidenced in Pepys's self-examination: "Egocentric and charged with feeling as the diary is, it often reads as though it had been written by an *alter ego,* by another man in the same skin, one who watched understandingly but rather detachedly the behaviour and motives of his fellow-lodger. The diary-form lends itself to this kind of duality, since the diarist is at once performer, recorder and audience ... Through large areas of Pepys's diary, however, the diarist is both the observer and the observed, the penitent and the priest, the

Introduction *xliii*

As with the absolution of auricular confession, this written record was meant to give its writer assurance of forgiveness, and a greater awareness of personal sinfulness, while also validating and ordering both his personal and his communal existence.[89] In other words, the Puritan believed that because his life experiences, his successes, his failures, his faults, were written, or in a sense stored permanently on the page, that his narrative arrangement of all of these circumstances constituted both a true mirror of himself and of his favor in the eyes of God. Thus, constant review of this document and disciplined, honest expansion upon it would make more clear one's relationship to God, one's realization of salvation, and one's innate sinfulness. More than once Beadle instructs the diarist to review often what he has written: "The keeping of such a Journall, especially if we look often into it, and read it over, will be a notable means to encrease in us that self-abasement & abhorrency of spirit that is most acceptable in the sight of God."[90] In short, the keeping of a journal attempted to

---

patient on the couch and the psychiatrist too, the man in the street and the behavioural sociologist" (Berkeley: University of California Press, 1970) 1: cix. Also, see n. 73.

[89] In "Literary Reflections of the Puritan Character," *Journal of the History of Ideas* 29 (1968): 23, Cynthia G. Wolff, concludes that "a man's daily record is intended to mark God's blessings as well as his own sins. Some fortunate diarists were able to perceive God's workings within their souls, and this sign of blessedness permitted them to escape from lonely religious despair and move more confidently toward the society which they sought.
  Sometimes the sign of grace was the journalist's sense of inspiration in his praying; yet often, God's blessings were seen in more tangible terms."

[90] As for the usefullness of the diary as an aid to memory, Beadle observes "look often into this Journall, and read it over: of all imployments in the world, a studious is the most ingenuous; wherein the understanding, judgement, and memory . . . are principally employed." In this same vein, Beadle says,

externalize one's sinful actions and one's faults in the same way as auricular confession was meant to externalize the penitent's sins as they were spoken to the priest. Or, as Fuller says concerning the confessional nature of the diary, these "Records well kept, and diligently read, would not only procure rest . . . But might also stir us up to honour our deliverer."

It is worth noting here that keeping a written record of personal sins to guard against forgetting them was not an exclusively Puritan activity. In fact, Catholic confessional manuals often encouraged this practice. For example, in a small but popular seventeenth-century confessional treatise entitled, "Mirrour to Confesse Wel," the author advises "that before thou goe to the Sacrament of confession, thou must thinke vpon thy sinnes, and examen thy conscience wel, reading such thinges as be noted heere. Thou maist also write thy sinnes, and reade them before thy ghostlie father, yf thy memorie doe not serue thee."[91] This suggestion is also made in Vincenzo Bruno's *A Short Treatise of the Sacrament of Penaunce*, 1597; "Whereunto will be no small help for those which haue no great memorie, to note euerye day in the examination which they make at night, such faultes as they shall finde: to the ende, that when they are to goe to Confession, they may the better remember themselues, and by looking vpon them somewhat before, make their Confession with more peace."[92] In another much more lengthy manual on how to prepare for and offer a good confession, William Warford, a Jesuit, suggests that the

---

"To be able to read our Lives even from the wombe to this present moment; from the cradle, within some few dayes of he grave, would surely be a study as profitable as delightful." As for the diary aiding in the ordering of one's existence, Beadle observes, "When you have read over this Journall, and seen what you have, cast up also all your wants, and see what at present you stand in need of."

[91] D.M. Rogers, ed. *Six Spiritual Bookes* in *English Recusant Literature, 1558-1640* (Yorkshire, England: The Scolar Press, 1977) *343*: sig. A11v, p. 22.

[92] D.M. Rogers, ed. *English Recusant Literature, 1558-1640* (Yorkshire, England: The Scolar Press, 1972) *101*: sig. D4r, p. 77.

Introduction

Christian keep a double entry tally of his sins throughout the day so that he may compare the noon-time tally with the evening tally and "be sory for it [sin] from our hart."[93] In addition, Warford advises that a tally of two-weeks be taken and compared in order that "it may appeare what amendment hath beene made, or omitted."[94] For Catholics, however, this practice was merely a preferential convention and was not considered a substitute for confession; rather, it was considered a preparatory aid for making a complete confession.

The Diary and Spiritual Account Book

The second cultural circumstance which undoubtedly influenced the keeping of spiritual journals and, therefore, the development of Beadle's pattern for journal-writing, was the increased knowledge of bookkeeping methodology and accounting theory which became ingrained very early in the Christian sensibilty.[95] Puritans especially made up a large majority of the merchant class in England, in the seventeenth century, so it is not surprising that they heavily borrowed from the language and theory of commerce. In his book, *The Family Life of Ralph Josselin: A Seventeenth Century Clergyman*, Alan MacFarlane concludes that one reason for the "rapid growth of diary-keeping after the Reformation" had to do with the "increased interest in house-hold accounting."[96] Likewise, P.A. Spalding observes that the majority of early diaries in England and America "developed, almost unawares, as the

---

[93] *A Treatise of Pennance*, ed. D.M. Rogers, *English Recusant Literature* (Yorkshire, England: The Scolar Press, 1973) 155: sig. I3v, p. 198.
[94] *Ibid.*, sig. I4r, p. 199.
[95] Moreover, several of Christ's parables portray business situations and business practice whose ramifications his audience would have immediately grasped. See Matthew 18.24, Luke 16.1-13.
[96] Cambridge: At the University Press, 1970, 5.

amplification of account-books or other domestic records."⁹⁷ The language of accounting, already imbedded within his consciousness, furnished the Puritan with a vocabulary allowing him to objectively document his private life, while also adding to it a sense of mathematical precision which made it more presentable and seemingly ordered in his eyes and in the eyes of God. Beadle himself maintains that when keeping a diary "a methodicall way is a successfull way." Samuel Pepys's diary, one of the most famous diaries ever written in the seventeenth century, was directly influenced by the "methodical way" of accounting. Pepys "was by nature a man of system, and one to whom the keeping of records was necessary to the art of living. The diary was one of a series of records, which by the 1660's included petty-cash books, account books, letter-books, memorandum books . . . All were a means to a disciplined life, methods of canalising the stream of experience."⁹⁸ Indeed, the "keeping" of a diary, like the "keeping" of accounts, became the "practicall part of Religion," a practical aid in keeping the sacred account book, so that the Puritan with greater credibility could "well convert his spiritual

---

[97] *Self-Harvest: A Study of Diaries and the Diarist* (London: Independent Press Ltd., 1949) 64. Further, see Arthur Ponsonby's very early study of diary-writing in which he wonders at the mixing of business records and intimate information in the same diary (*English Diaries*, London: Methuen & Co. Ltd., 1923) 19-20.

[98] Robert Latham and William Matthews, eds. *The Diary of Samuel Pepys*, 10 vols. (Berkeley: University of California Press, 1970) 1: xxviii. Latham and Matthews further observe that "the diary is a concomitant of Pepys's delight in book-keeping. The rough notes from which the existing version may have been written were, as we have seen partly accounts, and the diary manuscript bears some of the marks of a book-keeper's hand, in its precise spacing and lining . . . but in the matter itself not a little reflects the mind of a man who believes there is a vital correspondence between values and dates" (cvi).

Introduction

examination into a kind of general audit, totalling up sins and graces and exulting in spiritual riches."[99]

An additional piece of information should be taken into account in considering the Puritan's borrowing of accounting nomenclature: and that is, the instructions of confessional manuals were also imbued, consciously or unconsciously, with the language of accounting and finance, which the Puritans in all probability borrowed and then adapted to the practice of spiritual journal-writing.[100] In fact, the *septenary* of questions asked by the priest during confession directly influenced the invention of double entry bookkeeping and the ethics of early accounting business practice.[101] The seven questions which asked the specifics of each sin: who, how much, why, in what

---

[99] Cynthia G. Wolff, "Literary Reflections of the Puritan Character," *Journal of the History of Ideas* 29 (1968): 24.

[100] In an early confessional manual, the writer declares that "he that wil wel & onely make his Confession must first of al cal himself to *accompte* certain houres of the daies;" in addition, he must enter into a "particular *accompt* with God, and with a man's own conscience in his secrete chamber I closest place, considering that there he goeth to give *accompt* of his life unto God, and unto the Priest in his name" [emphasis mine] (*A Brief Form of Confession*, Antwerp: Apud Iohannem Foulerum, 1576) 2-3, a seventeenth century confessional manual uses even more explicit financial language in describing man's imperfect nature and daily proclivity toward sin: "Euen so a sinner doth behaue himselfe very vnwisely and foolishly whiles he yet liueth, yf he do not runne to christ by the Sacrament of pennance, to obtaine by this means the *bill of his acquittance* . . And because we run euery day in new *debt*, we must also oftentymes aske a new *acquittance of paiment*, as long as our Lord remaineth with vs" [emphasis mine] (George Dowley, "A Briefe manner to Examine the Conscience, for a Generall Confession," in *The Key of Paradise*, ed. D.M. Rogers, *English Recusant Literature* (Yorkshire, England: The Scolar Press, 1979) 394: sig. Z1r-Z1v.

[101] See James A. Aho's article, "Rhetoric and the Invention of Double Entry Bookkeeping," *Rhetorica* 3.1 (1985): 21-43.

place, at what time, by what means and instruments, how often, are the same questions which shaped the method expounded by Luca Pacioli's late fifteenth- century treatise on double-entry bookkeeping called *De Computis et Scripturis* (1494).[102]

Pacioli advised that these seven questions should be answered with regard to every transaction and account. His purpose in writing such a work was to help "serve all the needs of the subjects regarding accounts and recording."[103] Secondly, Pacioli wished to inculcate in businessmen a love for truthful, moral, orderly, and systematic business practice; as Pacioli exhorts,

> Let him who wants to know how to keep an orderly Ledger and its Journal pay strict attention. So that the reader may fully understand the procedure, the case of one who is just starting in business wil be used. How to keep accounts and books will be illustrated in order that each thing can easily be found it its proper place. If each thing is not in its right place, great trouble and confusion would arise. As the saying goes, 'Where there is no order, there is chaos.'[104]

Thus, Pacioli hoped that order and the full documentation of the circumstances of each transaction, which his method imposed, would witness to the veracity and trustworthiness of the businessman. Further, Pacioli insists that "businessmen should commence their affairs with the name of God at the

---

[102] Pacioli was a fifteenth-century Franciscan conventual who was the first to record the principles of double-entry bookkeeping in *De Computis et Scripturis*, (1494). This treatise provided the basis for all subsequent discussions of what has been called the "Italian method." And for the last 350 years it has continued to serve as the basis for accounting technique world wide.
[103] *Pacioli on Accounting*, eds. R. Gene Brown and Kenneth S. Johnson (1963; New York: Garland Publishing, Inc., 1984) 25.
[104] *Ibid.*, 26.

Introduction   xlix

beginnings of every book, always bearing His holy name in mind."[105] By keeping books in God's name, the merchant further affirmed the truthfulness of his business dealings and accounts before men and before God. Pacioli's instructions carry with them a theological motive as well; for he believed that accounting would ultimately aid the merchant in becoming a more vigilant steward over the assets and liabilites bestowed on him by God. In turn this divinely willed stewardship would then give glory to God. As Pacioli urges,

> In the divine offices of the Holy Church, they sing that God promised a crown to the watchful ... Record everything that you require day by day, in the manner stated in the following chapters. But above all keep God before your eyes, never forgetting to attend to religious meditation every morning, as the following holy verse says: "Time is not wasted by religious meditation any more than wealth is lost by charity." And to this our Savior exhorts us in St. Matthew, when he says: '... seek ye first the kingdom of God, and his righteousness; and all these things shall be added unto you.'[106]

For the orderly keeping of business transactions, and for authentication of their accuracy, Pacioli originally advises that three separate books be kept: the first is called the Memorandum; the second, the Journal; and the third, the Ledger.[107] The Memorandum (later called a Memoriall or Waste Booke) is a chronological compendium of every transaction, large or small; the Journal is the private book, where the businessman fully relates his assets; the Ledger is the third book, where each of the entries from the Journal is posted twice.[108] Later, when accounting practice had developed, other books were created such as The Remembrance

---

[105] *Ibid.*, 27.
[106] *Ibid.*, 34.
[107] *Ibid.*, 35.
[108] *Ibid.*, 36-48.

Beadle's A Journall or Diary of a Thankfull Christian

Book, "a kind of small waste Booke, to put in some briefe notes to helpe the Memory what businesse you are to performe."[109]

Pacioli's methodology spread rapidly throughout Europe, where the Dutch and the English efficiently adapted its principles to their economic contexts. In England, one of the earliest accounting manuals to appear was James Peele's, *The Maner and Fourme How to Keep a Perfecte Accompte* (1553), which was clearly an almost word for word adaptation of Pacioli's treatise. Peele's argument for this new practice hinged on its ability to help the merchant achieve more true "reconyngs;"

> For emongest althynges nedefull in any nacion, touchyng worldy affaires, betwene mana and man, it is to be thought that true and perfect reconyng, is one of the chief, the lacke wherof, often tymes causeth, not onely greate discencion, but also is an occasion of greate losse of time ... For that his reconynges, through want of a perfect order haue been negligently kepte, fearyng that he hath been deceiued, when that he is not throughly hable to saie (with a cleare conscience) whether he haue been deceiued of any thyng at all, or not.[110]

In 1569, Peele wrote a treatise on accounting theory called *The Pathe Waye to Perfectnes* where he again stressed how accounting practice could create good will between businessmen— "surelye amonges all thinges in this world, that passeth betwene man and man: there is nothinge more nedefull then perfect & playne order in reconinge, for it encreaseth frendshippe and amitie, whereas the contrary: procureth great discorde, strife and debate."[111] And thus, if strict accounting

---

[109] John Carpenter, *The Most Excellent Instruction for Keeping Merchants Accounts* (London, 1632; STC 4661) sig. B2v, p. 4.

[110] James Peele, *The Maner and Fourme How to Keep a Perfecte Accompte* (London, 1553; STC 19547) sig. A3r.

[111] London, 1569; STC 19548, sig. *3r. Other accounting manuals which were extremely popular in the late sixteenth and early

Introduction   li

method could accomplish this among men it could surely accomplish this between God and man; "Even thus it is with a believer that can in a straight venture upon God in Christ according to a promise: his returns are often above his ventures. Faith is the greatest gathergood in the world."

Undoubtedly, Beadle was well aware of and, as his parish records show, fairly adept at the accounting methods growing ever more popular during his life-time. He himself was a clerk,[112] and the parish records from Barnston surviving him indicate a definite bookkeeping expertise.[113]. Likewise, the accounting terminology and business vocabulary Beadle and John Fuller consciously use throughout *A Journall or Diary of a Thankfull Christian* also betray a deliberate effort to adapt this language and theory of "reckoning" to personal diary writing. Beadle borrows Pacioli's and his English successors' ideas concerning the purpose of accounting and applies them to the keeping of a spiritual journal. For Beadle, and for many diarists of the late sixteenth- and seventeenth-centuries, the diary becomes a conflated spiritual version of the Memorandum, the Journal, the Ledger, and the Remembrance book of bookkeeping practice.[114] In the "To the Reader," section John

---

seventeenth centuries were Hugh Oldcastle, *A Briefe Instruction and maner How to Keepe Bookes of Accounts* (London, 1588; STC 18794); John Carpenter, *A Most Excellente Instruction for Keeping Merchants Accounts* (London, 1632; STC 4661); Gerard de Malynes, *Lex Mercatoria* (London, 1635; STC 17224); Richard Dafforne, *The Merchants Mirrour or, Directions for the Perfect Ordering and Keeping of His Accounts* (London, 1651; STC 17224); Richard Dafforne, *The Apprentices Time-Entertainer Accomptanty* (London, 1640; STC 6188).
[112] See n. 29.
[113] For examples of Beadle's parish accounts, see Andrew Clark, "Barnston Notes, 1641-1649," *The Essex Review* 25 (1916): 65-67.
[114] For example, in the diary of Captain Adam Eyre (1614?-1661), personal, religious, and family details are combined with business details: "Then I went to Sara's, where I dyned

Fuller draws a comparison between the earlier comparison treated by Pacioli for a full and exact recording of transactions and the Christian's sacred obligation when keeping his diary:

> We have our State Diurnals, relating the
> Nationall affaires. Tradesmen keep their
> shop books. Merchants their Accompt books.
> Lawyers have their books of presidents.
> Physitians their Experiments. Some wary
> husbands have kept a Diary of dayly disburse-
> mentsw ... A Christian that would be
> exact hath more need, and may reap much more
> good by such a Journall as this. We are all
> but Stewards, Factors here, and must give
> a strict account in that great day to the
> high Lord of all our ways, and of all his
> wayes towards us.

---

with Mr. Ellize, the lawyer, and spent 1s. 8d., and 4d. for threid, and so home... This day I received a fall from my horse, but God preserved mee from hurt therby, and praysed by His name therefore; but I can never sufficiently set forth his praises" (*Yorkshire Diaries and Autobiographies in the Seventeenth and Eighteenth Centuries* (Edinburgh: The Publications of the Surtees Society, 1877) 65: 78. Another diary combining the keeping of business accounts and the keeping of personal accounts in John Harington's diary of 1646-53, which is a record of business and governmental transactions, as well as religious and church matters (Margaret F. Steig, ed., *The Diary of John Harington, M.P.*, Somerset Record Society, 1977). Probably, the best examples of a account books and spiritual diaries are *The Diary of Ralph Josselin, 1616-1683*, also called *A Thankful Observacion of Divine Providence & Goodness towards Mee, & a Summary View of My Life*, ed. Alan MacFarlane (London: Oxford University Press for British Academy, 1976), and *The Day Book of Giles Moore of Horsted Keynes Sussex, 1655-1679*, ed. F. Stenton Eardley (London: MacMillan & Co. Ltd, 1939), 79-113. Finally, a late example of a diary in which the influence of accounting is evident is *A Journal and Account-Book of Timothy Burrell*, ed. Robert Willis Blencowe (Sussex Archaelogical Collections, 1850) 3: 117-172.

Introduction

Moreover, very early on in *A Journall or Diary*, Beadle compares the Christian's relationship to Christ with that of a merchant "venturing" capital for a higher return on his investment; he says, "every true believer is a Merchant adventurer, whose returns must be greater then his ventures or he cannot live." Concomitantly, just as the merchant needs books of account to document his "ventures" and "returns," so Christian diarists who "such as will be well stored with such a treasure of experiments, had need keep a constant Diary by them of all Gods gracious dealings with them."

In addition, Beadle reassures the "thankfull Christian" that the keeping of such a diary and the recording of "memorials by you of his goodnesse to you" will improve his relationship with God, "enlarge your love to him, and fortifie your hearts." This assurance is reminiscent of early accounting theory which held that the adoption of the double-entry method would build trust between merchant and customer:

> There is a great affinitie betweene
> Faith, Trust, and Confidence; in
> Diuinitie Trust and Confidence are two
> handmaides vnto Faith, euen as Faith is the
> hand whereby we apprehend Gods mercies, to
> repose our trust in him, and to be
> confident thereof. But in Humane actions
> the word Trust is more proper, which
> imploieth a credit or beliefe which we
> giue or repose vpon others or others doe
> attribute and giue vnto vs.[115]

Many early bookkeeping experts also believed that double-entry was a gift from God which should be used not only to benefit the merchant, but the rest of the community as well. To better ensure this fiduciary relationship between the Christian and Christ, Beadle, like Pacioli, exhorted the diarist "to set Jesus Christ above all, for he is the *summa totalis* of all our comforts. The *Grecians* set the *summa totalis* of their bills of accompt in the top of the page, as we do in the bottome. Christ and riches, Christ and honors, Christ and liberty is the totall

---

[115] Gerard de Malynes, *Lex Mercatoria* (London, 1635; STC 17224) sig. Kkr.

sum of all we enjoy . . . All in all, set him above all." The impetus for what Beadle urges here finds its origins in Pacioli's insistence that "businessmen should commence their affairs with the name of God at the beginnings of every book, always bearing His holy name in mind."[116] By beginning the diary in Christ's name, as is done with the account book, the Puritan witnesses to the veracity of his tally, listing "returns of prayer," "new mercies," "wants," and faults to be ultimately balanced by God at the last judgement. Or, as Beadle observes toward the end of his book, "At the last day it is said, the books shall be opened, and is not this one of those books? and the dead shall be judged out of those things which were written in those books."

But the most important benefit of applying accounting principles to personal diary writing was the creation of a sustained and conscious connection between the Puritan's private and public existence. Order in one's books could not help but bring divine satisfaction. For like the goal of business account keeping, which was "to give contentment unto the Bookowner, and to shew him (or them, whom they do concern) at all times, and in every degree, how his Estate standeth in the so written books,"[117] the goal of the thankful Christian was to be a diligent steward over both his soul and the benefits awarded to him by God so that he might give contentment to God—"A Christian that would be exact hath more need, and may reap much more good by such Journall as this. We are all but Stewards, Factors here, and must give a strict account in that great day to the high Lord of all our ways, and of all his wayes to us." If a Christian could be strict in keeping his business accounts, which were important for his success and livelihood on earth, surely he could keep strict spiritual accounts for his final "audit." As Fuller commends, in the "To the Reader" section, "If thou fearest to be overstrict in practicall godlinesse, sure without fear thou wilt be soon over loose and carelesse:

---

[116] Pacioli, *Pacioli on Accounting*, 27.
[117] Gerard de Malynes, *The Merchants Mirrour. or Directions for the Perfect Ordering and Keeping of His Accounts* (London, 1651; STC 17224), B2v.

thou fearest not be strict for thy estate and outward concernments, why art thou lesse carefull for thy soul? many not exact in casting up their books, they have cast them up; thy Audit will be strict, so should thy accounts be." In accounting for one's private concerns, one participated in the spiritual counterpart of his secular business, using a kind of sacred numeration, a "divine Arithmetick," in order to help one thrive "in this spirituall soul-trade." Beadle, all the while acting as a faithful and loyal steward, instructs his readers in this "divine Arthmetick" or sacred "accounting" when he counsels each Christian in keeping his private books to "mark what returns, what answers God gives to your prayers"; to "reckon how many ways those wants are supplyed with other comforts"; "to reckon often, not onely what you have, and what you want, but what you may want; cast up all hazzards . . . and reckon upon losses"; and to "make [a] collection of praises from friends, that the summe maybe made up the more full."

The Diary as Book of Providences

The final component of the Puritan spiritual diary which explains more fully its role as a confessional vehicle is its concern with documenting and interpreting the public and natural workings of Providence in the family, in the society and in the body politic. In brief, the Puritans, in both England and America, interpreted every natural phenomenon or worldly event as either a portent or a sign of God's will toward his people on earth.[118] This belief in the doctrine of providence crossed denominational lines; however, the Puritans were among the most zealous interpreters and recorders of God's

---

[118] For what is still the most definitive discussion of the American Puritans' understanding of providence see Perry Miller, *The New England Mind: The Seventeenth Century* (1939; Boston: Beacon Press, 1954) 227-235. Also, for a discussion of American diary writing and its reliance on the providential memorial convention see David Sanford Shields, "A History of Diary Writing in New England, 1620-1745," diss., University of Chicago, March 1982, 154-186.

providential manifestations in the world, and they created what can be described as a method of exegesis for interpreting God's handwriting in the book of nature. "They insisted that providence be acknowledged as the surest sign of God's sovereignty,"[119] and they "sincerely believed that there was a link between man's moral behaviour and his fortune in this world, whether in bodily health or professional success."[120] Again, this concern with passages of Providence was closely related to the Puritan's constant need for salvific assurance. Assurance was possible if the Puritan's private confessional record was in consonance with his assessment of the public mercies or trials bestowed on him by Providence. And if the two recordings did not balance, "the correct reaction on the part of a believer stricken by ill fortune was therefore to search himself in order to discover the moral defect wich had provoked God's wrath, or to eliminate the complacency which had led the Almighty to try him."[121] Apparently, the close observance of illustrious providences could then act as a catalyst to reform and conversion and an assurance of election. Moreover, the Puritan also believed that by both noticing and then documenting "special providences," either trivial or important, he would be able to glean a pattern of God's workings in the community or in his family; this knowledge would allow no harm to befall him unless God permitted it.

Alongside the Puritan's accounting of his "own and others sins with shame and sorrow," he detailed all blessings, notable judgments, and remarkable happenings in his life. He would also chronicle any conspicuously symbolic judgments which had befallen others. Very often, the puritan diarist would remark on an historical event, anecdote, or quotation which held a particular significance to a contemporary situation or which providentially taught a moral lesson concerning human nature

---

[119] Herschel Baker, *The Wars of Truth: Studies in the Decay of Christian Humanism in the Earlier Seventeenth Century* (Gloucester, Mass.: Peter Smith, 1969) 15.

[120] Keith Thomas, *Religion and the Decline of Magic* (New York: Charles Scribner's Sons, 1971) 87.

[121] Thomas, 83.

Introduction lvii

or God's will.[122] He undoubtedly borrowed this convention from the already ingrained practice of keeping a commonplace book, used during the Renaissance and throughout the seventeenth century "as a stimulus and guide to thought and expression."[123]

The "places" were also used as "sedes argumentorum unde depromuntur quae ad aliquid probandum conducunt; unde etiam vocantur loci communes, exempli gratia, ex nomine, ex genere, ex causa, et cetera."[124] Puritan diary practise borrows and subsequently applies the rhetorical motivation for the "places" by encouraging the diarist to record examples of both contemporary and historical *Divina Exempla*, which aid the diarist's memory, while also furnishing proof and thus making a case for his holiness and election. Consider, for example, the

---

[122] We should also remember that the Puritan viewed all of human history as an expression of God's inscrutable purpose, where the salvific events of the future were typified in the seemingly ordinary events and personages of the present, as Beadle assumes, "Of all imployments in the world, a studious is the most ingenuous; wherein the understanding, judgement, and memory, the most noble faculties of the [H3v] soul, are principally imployed: Of all studies the study of History seems to be most excellent: Hence even the Scripture it self is for a great part Historicall; that the hearts of people might be the better taken with it, and delight in it: Of all Histories, the History of mens Lives, is the most pleasant: Such History, amongst many commendations that may be given to it, this is not the least, that it can call back Times, and give life to those that are dead; & like a Landskip give a lively discovery of the actions of the Grandees in former ages. But of all Histories of Lives, I should think, the History of a mans owne Life (even out of common principles of self-love) must needs be most acceptable."

[123] Sr. Joan Marie Lechner, *Renaissance Concepts of the Commonplaces* (New York: Pageant Press, 1962) 69.

[124] John Micraelius, *Lexicon Philosophicum terinorum philosophis usitatorum ordine alphabetico sic digestorum ut inde facile liceat cognosse praesertim si tam Latinus quam Graecus* (Jena, 1653) 601.

way in which Walter Powell, a seventeenth century diarist, describes the purpose and function of his diary:

> a booke of ould remembrances
> collected by me Walter Powell
> of the agess of me & my ffrindes
> and children.
> and of the matters happening
> in my occasions, collected out of
> ould Almanacks, wch I have
> filed togeather from yeare to
> yeare, as in the blanks thereof
> they are written more at large.
> of all wch, this booke is a shorte
> breviat to be caried about me
> helpe my memorie concerning
> those things & vpon all occasions.[125]

Beadle himself alludes to the relationship between the commonplace book and the Puritan diary, when he urges the thankful christian to note in his diary the promises of Christ as they are evidenced to him in every day events: "The good word of the Lord should be your *Vade mecum*, your companion, you should have the promise alwayes with you." In addition, Beadle, as has already been noted, considers the journal or diary a "memorial" to God's goodness containing "*memorandums* of great mercies vouchsafed" to posterity.

The sacralizing of the commonplace impulse is especially evident in the number and size of the collections of "illustrious passages" published in the late sixteenth and seventeenth centuries.[126] Three such collections that Beadle seems to have used himself in writing *A Journal or Diary* are Edmund Rudierd's *The Thunderbolt of Gods Wrath, or an Abridgement*

---

[125] *The Diary of Walter Powell*, Joseph Alfred Bradney, ed. (Bristol: John Wright & Co., 1907) xi.
[126] In *Religion and the Decline of Magic*, Keith Thomas discusses at length the popularity of collections of providence, finding their Protestant source in John Foxe's *Acts and Monuments* (New York: Charles Scribner's Sons, 1971) 93-96. Beadle relates three anecdotes whose source probably was Fox. See commentary, 28/24, 41/1-2, 143/26-30.

Introduction   lix

of Gods Fearefull Judgements, (1618);[127] Thomas Beard's *The Theatre of Gods Judgements*, originally published in 1597 and much expanded in later editions;[128] and Samuel Clark's *A Mirrour or Looking-Glasse both for Saints and Sinners*, originally published in 1648, and later enlarged into a second edition.[129] These compendia furnished ministers and their

---

[127] (London, 1618; STC 21437). The rest of the book's title is *Wherein is represented the admirable Justice of God against all notorious sinners, great and small, specially against the most eminent Persons in the World whose exorbitant power had broke through the barres of Divine and Humane Law. Collected out of Sacred, Ecclesiasticall, and Pagan Histories . . .*
[128] Rudierd's *The Thunderbolt of Gods Wrath*, is an abridgement of Beard's work (London, 1648; Wing STC B1565, 4th ed.) The source for two anecdotes that Beadle relates is probably Beard's *Theatre of God's Judgements*. In a strikingly similar fashion, Beadle's description of Zoroaster's demise (38/6-8) is strikingly similar to Beard's relation of the story (sig. H3v). In addition, Beard's *Theatre* is most probably the source for Beadle's discussion of the Diaz case. See Beadle, 38/9-20 and Beard, sig. Q4r.
[129] The rest of the title is *Held forth in about two thousand Examples: Wherein is presented, as Gods wonderful Mercies to the one; so his severs Judgments against the other. Collected out of the most Classique Authors both Ancient and Modern with some late Examples observed by my self. Whereunto are added, the Wonders of God in Nature; and the Rare, Stupendious, and Costly Works made by the Art, and Industry of Man . . .* (London, 1654; Wing STC C4548, 2nd ed.) Beadle seems to have used *Mirrour or Looking-Glasse* as the source for eleven anecdotes given in *A Journall or Diary* since, in several cases his wording and Clark's is quite similar. The following chart delineates the anecdote Beadle records and its corresponding source in Clark.

     Lycurgus Beadle, 15/6 Clark, sig. Cc5v.
     Zoroaster Beadle, 38/6-8 Clark, sig. Gg5r.
     Serving man Beadle, 38/31-36 Clark, sig. O7v-O8r.

faithful with a body of lore which ostensibly demonstrated God's intimate connection with His creation and "like the mystery of the Incarnation it brought God and man into an intimate relation with no jeopardy to God's sovereignty but with the prodigious increase of man's dignity. If everything that happens--the traffickings of daily life no less than the great movements of history--can be referred to God for causality and therefore justification, then everything assumes a dimension in infinity."[130] In a sense, the Puritan saw in ordinary and extraordinary events of his communal and personal life, direct participation by God; and therefore, if the Puritan could record the trappings, the outward signs of this involvement he could discern the will of God toward him and toward his community. If God's will toward him was favorable, if there were no physical signs of trouble, he could interpret this as a sign of absolution and election. However, this theory also worked in reverse and carried with it a certain inevitable lack of certitude. As Keith Thomas observes concerning the loopholes in the theory,

> At the same time it can hardly escape notice that the doctrine of divine providence had about it a self-confirming quality. For there was no way in which the theory once accepted could be faulted. If the wicked man encountered adversity this was clearly a punishment from God; if a godly man

---

King Edgar Beadle, 40/22-29 Clark, sig. G6v.
Conrad III Beadle, 79/38-79/5 Clark, sig. V8r-V8v.
Alexander &
pauper Beadle, 95/2-6 Clark, sigs. I7r, K1v.
Mahomet Beadle, 108/39-109/5 Clark, sig. F5r.
Saladin Beadle, 109/10-20 Clark, sig. Bb7r.
Duke of Exeter Beadle, 109/20-22 Clark, sig. Cc1r.
Bern Beadle, 143/26-30 Clark, sig. Cc2v.
Tamerlane/
Baiajet Beadle, 153/2-8 Clark, sigs. Cc5r-5v.

---

[130] Herschel Baker, *The Wars of Truth*, 14.

Introduction

was smitten then he was being tested and tried. The pious Christian for whom events went well could thank God for his good fortune without in any way being worried by the equal prosperity of his reprobate neighbour, since he knew that the absence of worldly afflictions could sometimes be a dreadful signs of God's lost love.[131]

Furthermore, there were certain events that were viewed theologically, such as, sickness and disease, natural disasters, untimely deaths, deaths of children, and prosperity and misfortune. And the job of the diarist was to note them and assign providential meaning to them. In fact, many of the Puritan diaries which survive do document these occurrences in relation to their communities and families. For example, John Hull's (b. 1624) diary contains "Some Passages of God's Providence, About Myself and in Relation to Myself; Penned Down That I May Be the More Mindful of, And Thankful For, All God's Dispensations Towards Me."[132] Similarly, Alexander Jaffray (1614-1673), at the beginning of his spiritual diary, articulates the spiritual utility of recording God's actions in the world: "it might be useful for a believer to be very punctual in observing all the passages of Divine Providence [that concern] him, and those related to him, for whom he is making daily supplications and putting up petitions;...and that these, for the better remembering of them, be written down and often perused."[133] Henry Newcome (1627-1695), another famous diarist of the seventeenth century, remarks at length about the necessity of paying close attention to the working of the Almighty:

> what men have so writ of themselves
> hath made posterity a truer and more
> exact account of passages of divine
> providence towards them than could be

---

[131] Thomas, 82.
[132] *Transactions and Collections of the American Antiquarian Society* (Printed for the Society, 1857) 3: 141.
[133] *The Diary of Alexander Jaffray*, John Barclay, ed. (London: Harvey & Darton, 1833) 1-2.

> done by any other that hath come after
> them, that hath taken in hand the lives
> of men deceased and gone. That it is
> little question but those lives that have
> been so written by others, had been much
> fuller representations of goodness
> and admirable providence if some remem-
> brances had been made thereof...to record
> divine providences is not the least portion
> of God's praise, of our duty, and of
> posterity's patrimony.[134]

And finally, another representative journal which closely interprets the workings of Providence is that of Mary Boyle, Countess of Warwick (1624-1678), who recorded "the daily frame of her own heart towards God, his signal providences to herself and sometimes toward others, his gracious manifestations to her soul, returns of prayer, temptations resisted and prevailing; or whatever might be useful for caution or encouragement, and afford her matter of thankfulness or humiliation."[135]

Thus, along side the recording of their examination of conscience and the recognition of their sins, Puritan diarists, as Beadle notes, also kept track of "judgements, great changes, overturnings, and the sins of the age," while also noting "the works and operations of God, wherein God hath exceeded to them; but we must also consider, wherein they and others have exceeded against God in their transgressions . . . and the judgements both spirituall and temporall of our times, else we may be equally destroyed, and sure shall not keep a faithfull Journall." For the Puritan it was essential that the personal and private records be congruent and complementary, and that the blessings outnumber the punishments; any overabundance of

---

[134] *Autobiography of Henry Newcome* in *Remains Historical and Literary connected with the Palatine Counties of Lancaster and Chester* (Chetham Society, 1852) 26: 1-2.

[135] *The Memoir of Lady Warwick: Also Her Diary* (London: The Religious Tract Society, 1847) 28. It is likely that Lady Warwick had read Beadle's book because her husband, Charles Rich, was the brother and successor of Robert Rich, Earl of Warwick and Beadle's patron.

punishments and any imbalance between one's sins and one's interpretation of Providence could otherwise indicate the displeasure of the Almighty with the diarist. More specifcally, their diaries were made up of essentially three parts: one part accounted for private sins, the second recorded and interpreted providential blessings and the third kept track of what were deemed to be providential punishments. Beadle mandates this organization when he says, "There is a book of three leaves thou shouldest read dayly to make up this Diary; the black leaf of thy own and others sins with shame and sorrow; the white leaf of Gods goodnesse, mercies with joy and thankfulnesse; the red leaf of Gods judgments felt, feared, threatned, with fear and trembling." In effect, this is the fundamental blueprint for the Puritan spiritual diary.[136]

Yet even though the organization of the diary was relatively simple, there nevertheless existed necessary requirements for the proper delineation of one's life. While continuing to use financial nomenclature, Beadle specifically recommends that the diarist "keep an account of the various and changeable condition of the Times in the Countrey where we live, either in prosperity or adversity, with the fruits and effects of both"; "keep a Diary of the severall and most remarkable judgements that God hath in our time inflicted upon notrious offenders, whether perons in high places, or such as moved in the lower orbe"; "remember, and for that end put into your Journal all deliverances from dangers, vouchsafed to you or

---

[136] Steven Kagle, without any mention of Beadle's directives, likewise considers a similar impulse in the American Puritans: "The major but not exclusive reason for the popularity of diary keeping by the American Puritans was an appreciation of its confessional, revelatory, and directive functions. By keeping a spiritual journal a Puritan could privately consider the conviction of sinfulness which his society viewed as a necessary step toward salvation, record natural and human events in which he could find God's principles, and plan actions or reason judgments to allow the better adherence to God's commandments" (*American Diary Literature*, Twayne Publishers, 1979) 30.

yours;" "consider seriously, and observe very strictly, what the Nationall Epidemicall sin of the time and present generation may be." Finally, Beadle advises that the diarist should memorialize his personal conversion, the circumstances surrounding that conversion, his calling, and "all the men and means that God hath in providence at any time used for our good."[137]

Each of Beadle's recommendations is accompanied by several layers of the anecdotal proof originating from scripture, classical literature and patristic literature, and from contemporary life. In order to illustrate his method, let us look at his suggestion that "every man keep a strict account of his effectuall calling, and of his age in Christ . . . set down the time when, the place where, and the person by whom he was converted." Beadle illustrates the rationale behind this command by first giving the reader two scriptural and therefore typical examples of conversion: the first being that of St. Paul and the second that of Onesimus. Next, Beadle further proves that it is important to record one's calling and spiritual mentors when he refers to the fact that both St. Cyprian and St. Polycarp give thanks to their spiritual mentors. Finally, he rounds out his evidence in support of his command with a more contemporary anecdote when he refers to Theodore Beza's testimony concerning his conversion: "Amongst many things that *Beza* in his last Will and Testament, gave God thanks for, this was the first and chief, that he at the age of sixteen yeers, had called him to the knowledge of the Truth. Let every one that can know his age in Christ, set down this in his Journall." With every diaristic suggestion Beadle makes throughout *A Journall or Diary*, he consistently resorts to this "heaping up" of

---

[137] Beadle, 97. The recording of these observations was especially noticable in the diarists who wrote during or after Beadle's time. For example, see *Diary of Alexander Jaffray*, John Barclay, ed. (London: Harvey & Darton, 1833) 50-30; *The Diary of John Hull*, in *The Transactions and Collections of the American Antiquarian Society* (Printed for the Society1, 1857) 141-142; and *The Diary of Thomas Naish, 1685-1728*, Doreen Slatter, ed. (Wiltshire: The Museum, 1965) 22-23.

Introduction

material to amplify, exemplify and mostly to persuade his audience of the spiritual benefit of keeping a spiritual diary.

In the end, Beadle's book encourages the keeping of a "Gather-book," a "Mirrour of mans Estate,"[138] a proper reckoning of man's soul before God, and of a man's outward estate before God. Nevertheless, it is also a "Factor-book"[139] where there is entered every "return" of prayer or blessing, and every providential memorial proving the veracity of the diary keeper's life. Assuredly, Beadle's structure, method, and the coalescing of the form's influences which helped to spur its development, aided in standardizing the practice of journal keeping among the Puritan middle-class, while also influencing its further development as a confessional vehicle and a tool for self-discovery in years to come.[140]

THE TEXT

Establishing the text of *A Journal or Diary of a Thankful Christian* was relatively unproblematical. Since no manuscript of *A Journal* is known, I have compared seven photocopies of the text. Three unavailable copies for comparison are located at the Massachusetts Historical Society Library, Boston,

---

[138] "Gather-book" is an accounting term. See Gerard de Malynes, *Lex Mercatoria* (London, 1635; STC 17224) sig. B2v.

[139] Also, an accounting term wherein is recorded "each particular received, or parcell of wares alone, that commeth into his [merchant's] hands" (Gerard De Malynes, *Lex Mercatoria*) sig. B2v.

[140] See Ronald Klug's, *How to Keep a Spiritual Journal* (Nashville: Thomas Nelson Publishers, 1982), a Protestant treatise on journal keeping whose rubric follows Beadle's almost exactly. Klug believes that the journal is a means for attaining spiritual discipline and perspective; "journal is also a tool for self-discovery, an aid to concentration, a mirror for the soul, a place to generate and capture ideas, a safety valve for the emotions, a training ground for the writer, and a good friend and confidant" (9).

lxvi   Beadle's A Journall or Diary of a Thankfull Christian

Massachusetts; Trinity College Library, Cambridge, England; and Congregational Libary, London, England.

In preparing the text I have remained faithful to Beadle's punctuation except where the meaning of a passage is obscured by a misplacement of punctuation. Also, I have incorporated the errata found on sig. b6v into the text. It must be noted, however, that the third erratum directs the reader to "put out *all* after the word *Journies*," yet the correction was actually made before or during the printing. Thirdly, turned letters, repeated letters, repeated words and parts of words have been corrected. Lastly, where a letter has been mistakenly left out of a word or a word has been left out or misplaced in a sentence or the wrong letter has been used in a word, I have indicated the correction by bracketing the letter or the word. In every case the erroneous reading in the text has been given in the corrections.

In addition, there are twenty-three errors in Beadle's sidenote scriptural references which I have corrected. These corrections appear both in the commentary and in the corrections.

Finally, there are several instances in the text where Beadle quotes a scriptural or patristic Greek passage which sometimes contains abbreviations. Where this occurs, I have given the full Greek quotation or phrase without abbreviations.

John Beadle's only book or publication, *A Journal or Diary of a Thankful Christian*, 1656, was printed by Ellen Cotes, a printer of London and widow of Richard Cotes. Her printing establishment was at Barbican, Aldersgate Street from the years 1653-1680(?)[141] On October 1, 1655, Thomas Parkhurst, bookseller, "entred for his copie under the hand of Master Stephens warden a booke entituled *A Journall or Diary of a thankfull Christian*, by John Beadt,[142] ministr."[143] Parkhurst

---

[141] Henry R. Plomer, *A Dictionary of Printers and Booksellers who were at work in England Scotland and Ireland from 1641 to 1667* (London: The Bibliographical Society, 1968) 52.

[142] The transcription misspells Beadle's last name.

[143] *A Transcript of the Register of the Worshipful Company of Stationers from 1640-1708*, 3 vols. (London, 1913) 2: 13. The unusual spelling here is that of the Stationers record.

was a bookseller in London operating "at the Three Crowns at the lower end of Cheapside, near the Conduit." Throughout his career he was on friendly terms with chief presbyterian divines of his day and began to publish their works and other theological tracts in July 1654. John Dunton, a loyal friend and one-time apprentice of Parkhurst dubbed him "the most eminent Presbyterian Bookseller in the Three Kingdoms," who "printed more Practical Books than any other that can be named in London."[144] According to the manuscript entry on the copy of the British Library, the publication date for *A Journal or Diary of a Thankfull Christian*, was April 25, 1656.

---

[144] See the memoirs of Parkhurst's one time apprentice John Dunton, *The Life and Errors of John Dunton*, 2 vols. (New York: Burt Franklin, 1969) 1: 205; for more details of Parkhurst's life see Henry R. Plomer, *A Dictionary of the Booksellers and Printers Who Were at Work in England, Scotland and Ireland from 1641-1667*, 230; and *DNB*, 15: 311.

BIBLIOGRAPHY

This bibliography includes only works frequently cited or of special importance for Beadle's life and writings. Other works are full identified in the footnotes. I have used the following abbreviations:

DNB = *Dictionary of National Biography*
OED = *Oxford English Dictionary*, 2nd edition.
STC = Pollard and Redgrave's *Short Title Catalogue*
Wing STC = Wing's *Short Title Catalogue*

Calamy, Edmund. *The NonConformist's Memorial.* 3 vols. London: Printed by J. Cundee, 1802, Vol. 2.

Calendar of State Papers, Domestic Series, Charles I, 1628-1629. John Bruce, ed. London: Longman, Green, Longman, & Roberts, 1859.

Calendar of State Papers, Domestic Series, Charles I, 1629-1631. John Bruce, ed. London: Longman, Green, Longman, & Roberts, 1860.

Calendar of State Papers, Domestic Series, Charles I, 1631-1633. John Bruce, ed. London: Longman, Green, Longman, Roberts, 1862.

Clark, Andrew. "Barnston Notes, 1641-1659." *Essex Review* 25 (1916): 55-69.

Davids, T. W. *Annals of Evangelical NonConformity In the County of Essex.* London: Jackson, Walford, and Hodder, 1863.

Donagan, Barbara. "The Clerical Patronage of Robert Rich, Second Earl of Warwick, 1619-1642." *Proceedings of the American Philosophical Society* 120 (1976): 388-417.

Essex Record Office. *Wills at Chelmsford.* London:
British Record Society, 1958.

Laud, William. *The Works of the Most Reverand William
Laud, D.D.* 7 vols. Oxford: John Henry Parker,
1853, Vol. 5, part II.

Matthews, A.G. *Calamy Revised: Being a Revision of
Edmund Calamy's Account of the Ministers and
Others ejected and Silenced, 1660-2.* Oxford:
Clarendon Press, 1934.

Newcourt, Richard. *Repertorium Ecclesiasticum
Parochiale Londinense.* London: Printed by Benj.
Motte, 1710.

Peck, Francis. *Desiderata Curiosa: or, A Collection
of Diverse Scarce and Curious Pieces Relating
Chiefly to Matter of English History.* 2 vols.
London: Printed for Thomas Evans, 1729, Vol. 2.

Pollard and Redgrave. *A Short Title Catalogue of
Printed Books in England, Scotland, & Ireland,
1475-1640.* 2nd ed., 2 vols. London: Bibliographical Society, 1976-1986.

Smith, Harold. *The Ecclesiastical History of Essex:
Under the Long Parliament and Commonwealth.*
Colchester: Benham and Company Limited, 1932.

Thomas, Keith. *Religion and the Decline of Magic.*
New York: Charles Scribner's Sons, 1971.

Strother, James B. "Families of Catelyn and Beadle."
Miscellanea Genealogica et Heraldica n.s. 4
(1884): 418-419.

Wing, Donald. *A Short-title Catalogue and of Books Printed in England, Scotland, Ireland, Wales, and British America and of English Books printed in other Countries, 1641-1700.* 3 vols. New York: Clarendon University Press, 1945-1951.

A Critical Edition
of John Beadle's
*A Journall or Diary of a
Thankfull Christian*

To the Right Honorable,
truly Noble and Religious Lord
Robert Earl of *Warwick*,
Baron of Leez, etc.
And to the Right Honorable the Lady
Eleanor Countess of *Warwick*,
His most Pious and Vertuous Consort;
Such an encrease of Grace on Earth,
as may bring them to fulnesse of
Glory in Heaven.

RIGHT HONORABLE,

AS there is no Grace that giveth more glory to
God, so there is no Grace that hath [A3r] more
honour from God then Faith: Who though he doth all
our work for us, and therefore should have all the
glory from us; yet is pleased that Faith should go
away with the praise of that which himself only
doth. *Daughter thy Faith hath made thee whole*,
saith Christ to the woman, that by the touch of his
garment received virtue from him and was healed. *By
faith the Israelites passed through the Red-sea, as
on dry ground. By faith the wals of Jericho fell
down.* When we know that the Waters of the one, and
the Bulwarks of the other obeyed the soveraign
authority of the Word of Gods command. Yea further,
as there is no Grace that brings more glory to God,
so is no [A3v] Grace that yeelds more benefit
to us then Faith: It is a Grace as the most usefull,
so the most successefull, and of the largest capacity
for our good. *As thou hast believed, so be it done
unto thee*, saith our Saviour to the Centurion. He
that is inlarged in his faith cannot be straightned
in his comfort. Through Faith God the Father is our
portion, God the Son is our pledge, God the Holy

Ghost our earnest; Heaven our home, Holinesse our way, the Angels our gard, the Saints our company, the World our servant, and the Promise under seal our security. And what would we, what can we have more? yea such is the large capacity of this Grace of Faith, that could we be rich in [A4r] that grace, we might have our wils even with an overplus. *Oh woman,* saith our Saviour to the woman of Canaan, *great is thy faith, be it unto thee even as thou wilt. Luther* was so strong in faith, and therefore so powerfull in Prayer, that when *Frederick Myconius* his dear friend was sick, he prayed for his recovery, and used these words, *Hoc peto et volo, fiat voluntas mea,* This I aske, and this I will, and let my will be done; a while after *Myconius* recovered according as he had prayed. Whereupon *Justus Jonas* said of *Luther, Iste vir potuit quod voluit,* That man could have what he would.

Now the reasons why through faith we may have what we will, and more then we will, are these three. [A4v]

First, Because by Faith we live the best life in this world; From life to life, how vast a distance is there? from the life of the highest Angell to the life of the lowest Mushrome, how great a difference? 1 There is the life of the Vegetation, and that is the life of Plants. 2 There is the life Sense, and that is the life of Beasts. 3 There is the life of Reason, and that is the life of Men. 4 There is the life of Faith, and that is the life of Saints. Now according to the kinde of life, such is the capacity of the creature. The life of a Beast is more excellent then the life of a Plant, and therefore more capable of good. The life of a Man is better then the life of a *Beast*; and the life of [A5r] a Saint far above the life of a meer Man. *The righteous is more excellent then his neighbour,* saith *Solomon;* and therefore more capable of good, the good of the body and the soul, the good of this

life and of that which is to come. As we have
believed, so shall it be done unto us, much faith,
and much comfort, whilst we live: rich in Faith,
and rich in Glory, when we shall go hence and be no
more seen.

Secondly, Because other Graces make us like
unto God, as Wisdome, Holinesse, and Righteousnesse; but Faith makes us Sons of God: *As many as
received him, to them he gave power to become the
Sons of God, even to them that believe in his name.*
And if we be Sons, we are capable [A5v] of an inheri-
tance incorruptible and undefiled, and that fadeth
not away, reserved for us in the heavens; *For if
Sons, Heirs, Heirs of God, and co-heirs with Christ,
who is heir of all things.* Such a man is capable of
being heir to an Esquire of a vast estate; not
because he is like him, but because he is his
Son. Other graces make us like unto Christ, as
Humility, Zeal for Gods glory, and Love to the
Brethren: but Faith makes us members of Christ: and
it is our membership, our union to Christ, our communion with Christ, that makes us capable of all that
grace and glory that he hath for us, for he is only
the Saviour of his body. A painted arme and a wood-
den legge are like those [A6r] members, but they
draw no virtue from the head. It is, because we by
faith live in Christ, and grow up with Christ, *That
of his fulnesse we receive grace for grace.*

Thirdly, Because Faith is a grace by which we
venture upon the willingnesse and power of Christ
to save and succour us. Every true believer is a
Merchant adventurer, whose returns must be greater
then his ventures, or he cannot live; even so it is
with every believer, if God whose thoughts are
above our thoughts, should not send in to our Faith
more then we come for, we should live but barely.
The believing Palsie man and his friends, venture
upon Christ for health; but when [A6v] Christ saw
their faith, by which they brake through all diffi-

culties (for they would uncover the roof of the
house where he was, rather then not come to him) he
gave him health, and the pardon of his sins too,
which was more then they came for. The Prodigal son
ventures far upon his Fathers love, yet craves no
more but the place of an hired servant; but he is
entertained as a Son, he is clad with the best
robe, and fed with the fatted Calfe; he hath a Ring
for his hand, and Shooes for his feet, very rich
supplies not only for necessity, but sober delight,
which was more then he desired. *Jacobs* sons venture
into *Egypt* for Corn in a time of Famine, and they
return with Corn, and [A7r] Money in their sacks,
yea with very good news at last, *Joseph is alive
and Governour of all Egypt*. Even thus it is with a
believer that can in a straight venture upon
God in Christ according to a promise; his returns
are often above his ventures. Faith is the greatest
gathergood in the world; for it is not only according to our faith, but often above our faith. When
the prayers of faith are answered mercies are
multiplyed. When *Solomon* through faith beg'd of God
for a wise and understanding heart, by which he
might be able to judge his people; God gave him
wisdome, and moreover riches and honour more then
any King had before him, or should have after him,
so that [A7v] his returne was far above his venture.

Are these things so? what an happy condition
are they in then that believe in the name of the
Lord Jesus? and who would not upon these terms make
it good to their own souls, that they have obtained
this precious grace of Faith? And that they have
this grace, I know no better evidence then this,
Thath they have high thoughts of it, and set a great
price upon it. Now undoubtedly such as have a true
esteem of faith, will improve all times and
talents, will imploy all means for the service of
their faith, that they may abound therein. And what
better means can be used for the advancement of

faith in the growth and strength [A8r] of it, then a
rich treasure of experience; every experiment of Gods
favour to us, being a good prop for our faith for
the future. *Thou breakast the heads of Leviathan in*
pieces (saith the Psalmist) *and gavest him to be*
meat to the people inhabiting the wildernesse: that
is, Thou (O Lord) didst ovethrow *Pharaoh* and his
Host in the Red-sea; which experiment of thy power
and goodnesse, was as meat to the people in the
Wildernesse, which might uphold their hearts in the
midst of those many evils that were either feared
by them, or infli[c]ted on them in that vast, and
howling desert. God hath, and doth, and will, is
the language, and should be the constant tone [A8v]
of faith amongst all the Saints of God. So did
Jacob plead with God when he was ready to meet
with his brother *Esau*; *With my staffe I passed over*
this Jordan, and now I am become two bands. Deliver
me I pray thee from the hand of my brother, from
the hand of Esau. So did *David* argue before *Saul*,
I slew the Lion and Bear, and this uncircum-
cised Philistine shall be as one of them. So did
aged *Paul* reason, *I was delivered out of the mouth*
of the Lion, and the Lod shall deliver me from
every evill work, and will preserve me unto his
heavenly Kingdome, to whom be glory forever and
ever, Amen. Now doubtless such as will be well
stored wil such a treasure of experiments, had
need keep a [a1r] constant Diary by them of all
Gods gracious dealings with them.

    To commend which duty to such as desire to grow
in this grace of Faith, and abound therein with
thanksgiving, is (Right Honorale) the main scope
of this present Subject, which I have taken the
boldness to dedicate to your Honors; and do humbly
pray that it may passe abroad under your Name and
Patronage. If any aske why I trouble the Presse,
that in these dayes is so opprest with a glut of
Books. I answer, that it was not out of any vain

humor of mine to appear in Publick, who am so far
privy to mine own want and weaknesses, that I may
truly say, not onely as [a1v] St. *Paul, I am lesse
then the least of all Saints;* but as *Ignatius* once
said of himself, *Non sum dignus dici minimus,* I
am not worthy to be called the least: So that I
could never judge my self able to write any thing
that might endure the test of your judicious eyes,
or the censure of this criticall age. But indeed,
that which principally hinted to this service, was
partly a desire I had to promote a common good;
being very confident that such Christians who walk
much with God, and observe him in the wayes of his
Providence, may be provoked to this duty, and reap
much good thereby. For without doubt, this work
here commended, is very usefull, though the duty be
seldome [a2r] practised, because the subject is
rarely handled. It is as untroden a path, as ever I
have gone; who have had scarce a little day hole of
light to direct me, much lesse a Cloud of witnesses, or a Pillar of fire, or a Star to guide me.
Partly, and indeed, that which chiefly incouraged
me hereunto, was the memory of those great favours
which I have received from both your Honors; the
one my most Noble Patron, *Qui curat oves oviumque
Magistros,* A true friend to the Church of God, and
the Ministers of it. The other, my most bountifull
Benefactor. Nor would I give your Honors thanks *in
aurem vel in angulo,* but so publickly that I may
have as many eye-witnesses of my hearty [a2v]
acknowledgment of your goodness, as there may be
courteous Readers of the Book. And do presume that
if your Honors will be pleased to throw away an
hour or two in the perusall of these lines, you may
be hence encouraged more and more to observe God in
the wayes of his providence, and keep some
memorials by you of his goodnesse to you and yours;
which may much encrease your faith in him, enlarge
your love to him, and fortifie your hearts against

the evils of these times. *Considius* a Senator of
Rome, one day boldly told *Caesar, That the Senators
durst not come to Councell for fear of his Souldiers.*
He replyed, *Why then doest thou goe to the Senate?* He
answered, *Because* [a3r] *my age takes away
my fear.* Antient Christians should be very bold and
couragious in evill days, because they are or
should be stored with much experience, which will
much encrease their faith, and abate their fears.
God in rich mercy to you and many others, hath
added to your lives many daies, and your hoary
heads are a crown of glory to you, being found in
the way of righteousness; and therefore you are by
this time I hope above the fears and flatteries
of all the world. Now that the God and Father of
our Lord Jesus Christ, who hath abounded toward you
both, not only in the outward comforts of Honor and
Wealth in the eyes of men, but that which is far
better, in the knowledge of God [a3v] and practise
of holinesse before his Saints, would make you perfect to do his will, and work in you an encrease of
all those graces of his Spirit, that do undoubtedly
accompany salvation; that you may live in his fear,
die in his favour, rest in his peace, and rise to
his glory; is, and shall be the prayer of

YOUR HONORS
Much obliged, And
Most humble Servant,
John Beadle. [a4r]

To The Reader

Christian Reader,
    OUR blessed Saviours caveat about what, and how
we hear of the things written by God, as how to
hear and read also Books written by men, is now
most seasonably needfull; when many soul-sick
stomachs are so childishly weak, they know not how
to refuse the evill, and choose the sound and good
food for souls.
    To quicken then thy appetite to this savory meat,
held forth in this Pious Tract (that thy soul may
eat, walk in its [a5r] strength, blesse God, and
the dresser of it) let me walk with thee a while in
the withdrawing room of a Preface, about some few
things concerning the Author and work it self.
    I presume not my single testimony to add to the
credit or value of either (the Surety should be of
more note and worth then the Principall) yet my
duty of honour and love to him, my zeal and desire
to advance such a designe, emboldens me beyond my
ability, with a learned pious Ancient, in a subject
not unlike this, Of the ungratefull enemies of
Grace, in his time, the Pelagians.
    Concerning the Author of this *Journall of a
Thankfull Christian*, my knowledge hath been above
twenty years standing; we were of an intimate
society and vicinity for many years, we took sweet
counsell together, and walked unto the house of God
in company. He was my guide, and my acquaintance,
as *David* hath it. We oft breathed and powred out
our souls together in Prayer, Fasting, and conferences. When walking after the Lord in a
wildernesse, we had lesse allowed [a5v] liberty, but
more inward enlargednesse of Spirit. At which time
he had the happinesse of a younger *Elisha* (not to
powre water on the hands, but) to be watered by the

droppings of that great *Elijah*, that renowned man
of God in his generation, Reverend Mr. *Thomas
Hooker*, and hath had ever since the blessing and
favour of much of his spirit resting on him, as was
said of *Elisha*. And having mentioned that Name of
pretious memory, Worthy Mr. *Hooker*, now at rest
with the Lord (Saint *Hooker*, I may call him as
Latimer, Saint *Bilney*) it is a reall practise of
this Christian Diurnall, to acknowledge with all
hearty thankfulnesse to God in Christ, before the
world, that great mercy, and unspeakable blessing,
which *Essex Chelmsford*, this Author, my self, and
many others enjoyed, in the labours of that
Powerfull, Soul-saving, Heart-searching Minister of
Jesus Christ: for which rich grace and compassion
towards us, we hope some of us shall blesse and
praise his glorious Name, in a better world, to all
eternity. [a6r]

As for this Authors painfulnesse, and faithfulnesse, it's well known to all that know him, how
greatly they shrined forth in him, whilst in a very
small place, and how since advanced (by the bounty
of his truly Noble and Honorable Patron, to a
higher, and but necessary subsistence) they have
continued and increased; In Catechizing, Preaching
on the Lords dayes, and working dayes, holding up
the use of those soul-feasting Sacraments, even
unto these our dayes; wherein these Wels have been
either stopt up, or lesse drawn at; these choice
dishes, either set off the table quite, or seldome
fed on, to the leannesse of many souls.

Neither is he only a Practicall, but in life
and practise a Preacher as in other particulars, so
in the subject of this Treatise, Thankfulnesse;
which as he hath put forth a monument and memoriall
of herein to God and Man; so I hope, his name shall
live in it, and I heartily desire, thy soul and
mine might live more thankfully by it. As *David*
towards the end of his Book of *Psalms*, so this

singer of *Israel* towards the end [a6v] of his dayes,
summons a consort of all, to blesse the Lord; for
which thankfulnesse in so many gratulatory Psalms,
some have thought the former, and we may in charity
hope the latter, a man after Gods own heart.

Which sacrifice of Thanksgiving and Praise,
exciting others also, and calling them to it, is
now the more signally exemplary in him, as his outward estate is not overmuch, (he being rich especially in *Ashers* blessing, many children) and
whilest he with many other burning and shining
lights, once rejoyced in, yet now are become Lamps
despised, by many at ease, and troden out as
snuffes, before God put on the extinguisher of
death.

I say now, to set himself over the Thanksgiving, and set out such a Psalm of praise, is
thankfulnesse in deed, and worthy of an *Higgaion
Selah*. Psal. 9.16.

For the work it self, as *Solomon* of vir-
tuous woman, Let it praise it self in the gates;
its subject being Praise and Thankfulnesse, it will
carry its commendation in its Name and Title, [a7r]
as some Emperours, *Commodus, Pius*, did; a work worthy of thanks and praise.

Besides the ground (or plain song, as I may
phrase it) and matter of it, the forme and descanting about it, set off with many Historicall appli-
cations and Scripture allusions, yea minding us of
some duties obsolete and quite out of fashion; all
these graces, may render this a new song; and so
not only profitable, but more pleasurable and
acceptable to the Reader.

In a word, the whole is Pillar of Praise, an
Eben-ezer set up to the name of the most high God;
an *Ed*; a Stone of witnesse, both of Gods goodnesse
to us, and of our evill and unthankfulnesse against
him.

Praise and thanksgiving is a service becoming

the upright, proper to the Saints, a work of pure
grace when purely offered; Confessions, petitions,
nature, outward wants may excite to; but as they
say of vain swearing, cursing, it's all Devill, no
profit, pleasure tempts to it; and as one of
murmuring, called it the Devils mouth: so cont-
rarily blessing, praising is all God, such a mouth
is the [a7v] mouth of God; it's the service of triumphing Saints, and spirits of men made perfect;
Angelicall, Heavenly, most spirituall, and of highest divine extract. The fire must come from above
that kindles this Sacrifice. Christ alone is the
Master and teacher of this musick, who only can
teach it, and tune our hearts for it, *Psal.* 51.17.
& 119.7.
   2. Yea tis a better blessing (a thankfull
praising heart) then the blessings for which we
commonly blesse God; these are earthly, temporall,
mostly; this is a gift of especiall grace, an
unspeakable gift.
   Praise compared with petitionary Prayer, that
excellent piece of Divine worship, excels it as
far, as it is better to give then to receive.
   3. It is the most proper homage and service to
God; therefore by God styled, *Glorifying him*,
Psal. 50.23. Who though he be in his name exalted
above all blessing and praise; yet it suits him
best to receive, and is the highest we can give,
and therefore is called, *A blessing of God on our*
part; so much as man a worme, so far the lesse, [a8r]
can blesse him that is so infinitely the greater.
   Some Divines make the third part of Divinity,
Gratitude, Thankfulnesse.
   It's not only to continue in eternity, the only
service, when believing, confessing, and mourning
for sin shall be no more; but here in this world,
it's ever needfull, as salt to every sacrifice, for
all things, at all times, *Ephes.* 6.
   I will praise the Lord at all times, whilest I

have any being, saith *David*.
   Thou art my praise, said weeping *Jeremy*.
   Paul in sufferings above many, in Doxologies above all.
   The Church consuming, saw mercy to blesse God for.
   Job blessed God taking away, as giving.
   Jesus Christ who lived under the Crosse, and died under the Curse, yet had oft, *Father I thank thee*, in his blessed lippes. [a8v]
   4. It's most profitable to our selves: as a sinfull oath is fitly called a word compassed about with death, so this blessing with life, and many blessings; the showres of heavenly blessings descend upon the ascending of these vapors; we give for our selves in thanksgiving, as the Italian forme of begging is, *Do good for your selves*; we are the greatest receivers. We manifest Gods goodnesse herein, but procure our own, yea blesse our selves, in blessing him.
   Now this Treatise is a help to this heavenly exercise. A sacred Ephemerides, The Annales, Chronicles of the glorious Acts of the King of glory, The Court-Rolles and Register-book for Conscience to keep Courts by.
   Which Records well kept, and diligently read, would not only procure rest (as his Chronicles did to him in *Esther*) to our souls, in this restlesse night of our life; and as by past bounty did cause *David* to return to rests in the plurall, *Psal.* 116.7. But might also stir us up to honour our deliverer, [b1r] the God of our mercies and salvations, as *Ahasuerus* advanced *Mordecai*.
   This Book affords wood, call thou to God for the Lamb and fire; for this sacrifice, the matter and heads in it are fuell for our Faith and Thankfulnesse.
   We have our State Diurnals, relating the Nationall affaires. Tradesmen keep their shop

books. Merchants their Accompt books. Lawyers have their books of presidents. Physitians their Experiments. Some wary husbands have kept a Diary of dayly disbursements. Travellers a Journall of all they have seen, and hath befallen them in their way. A Christian that would be exact hath more need, and may reap much more good by such a Journall as this. We are all but Stewards, Factors here, and must give a strict account in that great day to the high Lord of all our wayes, and of all his wayes towards us.

This Journall is now (in our generation so ungratefull, and unmindfull of Gods judgements and mercies) a word in season running on its wheels. We must be holy Antipodes to sinfull times. [b1v] We like froward children, either cast away what we have, if not all we desire; or dote on what we have received, and neglect to return acknowledgement and observance; our owne glory we seek, not the glory of God that gives all.

Many earthly Lords in these dayes of overturning, losing their Rentals, have lost their Quit-rents. The most high heavenly Lord Jesus Christ, is the greatest sufferer and loser in our dayes, he hath lost his quit-rents of Praise and Thanksgiving from men; yea he hath lost and suffered in his name, glory, day, worship, law, government, offices, officers; well and timely then ought his Stewards and Bailiffs to demand, and call for by new rentals, those old Quit-rents and arrears long agoe due; which if denyed, we may well fear his straining for his right, and taking forfeit of all.

Satan that cunning wrastler hath twitched us, or rather bewitched us in our present age, from one side and extream to another; the whole fabrick of Religion (which we expected to be [b2r] repaired and reformed) is almost quite cast down; many are fallen from Formality to Prophanenesse, from Superstition to Atheisme: which was the Prophesie of

Worthy Mr. *Greenham* of these dayes, long since
expressed in his works, when he instanceth of a
Papist that fell to Familisme, and thence to
Atheisme in his dayes.
      Many by idolizing some prescribed formes, now
cast off all formes of prayer; and too many from
Cathedrall chanting, are come to reject that sweet
heavenly Gospel service of singing of Psalms: yea
so far from keeping a Diary of bypast mercies, that
they slight and omit dayly blessing of God in
their families, and at their meals, for their dayly
bread and present mercies, though contrary to
Scripture precepts and presidents; as if their food
suited not their stomachs unlesse it were profane,
(like themselves) that is, not sanctified by the
Word and Prayer.
      The sacrifice of Thanksgiving was to be eaten
on the same day, as one well notes; and in well
ordered families singing Psalms, as Prayers, hath
been a dayly exercise. [b2v]
      Twas a grave and just reproof of a right
Reverend Father in this City, present with his
Brethren on their days of Humiliation and Prayer,
he commended their large Confessions and Petitions,
but discommended their failing in Thanksgiving.
      And 'twas well answered by another, to one complaining of many wants and weaknesses, Be
thankfull, be thankfull.
      We look more after our priviledges by Christ,
then our duty we are to practise towards him; like
Tenants, not so ready with their Rents, as to see their
Covenants from the Landlord be made good to
them.
      But Ingratitude is a sin condemned by the light
of nature; the Heathen had their Hymns to their
Gods. *Lycurgus* made no law against it: man in
requiting kindnesses being a law to himselfe.
      In *Athens* a servant ungratefull after manumission, his Master had an action against him, and

might reduce him to bondage. [b3r]
   The unthankfull and unholy goe together in the
Word, and are parallel with the evill.
   Unthankfulnesse is the grave, the hell of benefits, the curse of blessings, a wind that dries up
mercies. *Let nothing be lost,* saith our Saviour;
Bernard applies it to favour from God.
   Nor only mercies and signall works of gracious
providence, but judgements, great changes, overturnings, and the sins of the age are to be registred in this Christian Journall, as this Author
well mixes the ingredients of this Diary.
   As we have two ears, to hear the rod threatning, as the Word promising; so two eyes, to see
sins and sufferings, blessings and mercies. Some
would have us note the works and operations of God,
wherein God hath exceeded to them; but we must also
consider, wherein they and others have exceeded
against God in their transgressions, as *Job* hath
it; and the judgements both spirituall and
temporall of our times, else we may be equally
destroyed, [b3v] and sure shall not keep a faithfull Journall.
   There is a book of three leaves thou shouldest
read dayly to make up this Diary; the black leaf
of thy own and others sins with shame and sorrow;
the white leaf of Gods goodnesse, mercies with joy
and thankfulnesse; the red leaf of Gods judgments
felt, feared, threatned, with fear and trembling.
   But what needs this waste, may some say, *of*
      time and paines? it's too strict and
      precise a practice, a hard saying, at
      least a duty too legall for Gospel liberty.
   Answ. 1. Gods law is a law of liberty to a
gracious heart. None of his commands grievous; yea
and each command requires not only the duty it
self, but the help and means to that duty to be
observed, as Divines generally hold. Now this Diary
is a Directory and help to praise and thank-

fulnesse; yea indeed to the practicall part of
Religion. The Pharisee was thankfull for spirituall
mercy, and our righteousnesse by Christ must exceed
Scribes and Pharisees, upon the [b4r] penalty of the
losse of heaven, *Luk.* 18. *Mat.* 5.20.

2. Nor is this imposed on all upon pain of damnation, or so exacted as the totall of all mercies, providences must be registred. Who can number the stars, or sands; Gods blessings, or our sins? the most eminent of the first magnitude are to be noted down; as all our sins are to be laid to heart, but especially the most hainous.

3. If thou fearest to be overstrict in practicall godlinesse, sure without fear thou wilt be soon over loose and carelesse: thou fearest not to be strict for thy estate and outward concernments, why art thou lesse carefull for thy soul? many not exact in casting up their books, they have cast them up; thy Audit will be strict, so should thy accounts be.

4. Lastly, the ingenuity of grace in the soul, cals for thus much, not only to endevour what may safely carry thee to heaven, but that which may most advance Gods glory, and thy souls prosperity and happinesse. [b4v]

God kept a Diary in the Creation of the world, *Gen.* I. to president this practise to us.

Yea he keeps a Book of Remembrance for us that think upon his name, he numbers our hairs, bottles our tears, writes us upon the palms of his hands, forgets not any of our works of love to his name; Registers our names in heaven, and shall we write down his name, works, love, in water, in the dust on earth? Shall he lay up our drosse, and not we his gold? Shall he remembring us, blesse curses to us; and shall we by ingratitude and forgetfulnesse of him, curse his blessings to us? He hath called us to inherit a blessing, and to blesse them that curse us; and shall not we blesse our blessed God

that blesses us? So much the more now as we expect
and desire some settlement of truth and peace.
    Bring in your tallies of old, if you look for
new mercies to be put upon your account.
    But why do I detain thee so long without in the
portall of a Preface? go in, set thee close to this
divine Arithmetick; [b5r] sums are best cast up in
solitarinesse; retire into thy self, set thy heart
on Gods wayes to thee, and on thine own wayes to
him. I heartily desire thy thriving in this
spirituall soul-trade.
    Study, not only the notional Numeration, Addition and Multiplication of particulars recited and
set down in this Christian Journall; but above all
look to the rule of Practise, which in this is the
true Golden rule indeed.
    I may say (to conclude) of this Book as one of
the Scripture, *They are words to be lived and practised, not read only.* And as another of the 119
*Psalm, They are good and true Catholicks indeed who
follow both sound faith and good manners.* This
musicall lesson of Praise and Thankfulnesse must be
well practised.
    Which that thou mayest do, both make thy Journall, and thy life and journey to heaven, answerable to such a Journall, go to him, and set out
in his strength, *Who is the wonderfull numberer,* as
Daniell styles him; who can teach thee to number
thy dayes, sins, Gods dispensations to thee
and others; [b5v] yea and how to profit by all,
even the Lord Jesus Christ, who is the Way, Truth
and Life, without whom we can do nothing, and by
whom we can do all things; In whom craving thy
prayers and praises for him that is lesse then the
least of all his servants and mercies; yet is, and
rests thy soul-friend and servant in him our common
Savior.

Ironmonger-lane
London. Octob.
12. 1655.

John Fuller. [b6r]

Chap. I

THE JOURNALL OR DIARY

Of a Thankfull Christian

NUMB. 33.2

And Moses wrote their goings out according to their journeys, by the commandement of the Lord.

CHAP. 1.

The Preface, wherein an entrance is made to the words, and the duty of a Journall or Diary is propounded.

SUch is the corruption of all, even the best men by nature, that though in their adversity they seek God early, yet in their prosperity they forget him commonly. They that in a dark [B1r] evening are glad of a little star-light, in the day are scarce thankfull for the Sun, *when he goeth forth in his strength.* It is observable, that the Psalmist taking notice of Gods good hand of Providence over Travellers, Captives, Sick men, Sea-men, and divers others; repeats this passage foure times in Psal. 107. *Then they cry unto the Lord in their trouble.* And he doth as often add, *Oh that men would prayse the Lord for his goodnesse!* Which is as much as if he had said, I know they will perform the first duty, I wish they may not forget the latter: How many are there that on their sick dayes make new

promises, but being recovered, forget God, and
follow their old lusts? It is a most provoking sin
to forget God, and the great mercies he hath bestowed on them. *How often did the provoke God in
the wildernesse,* (saith the Psalmist of the
Israelites) and grieve him in the desert? But how
did they provoke him? As by many other sins there
mentioned, so by this especially, *They remembred
not his hand, nor the day in which he delivered
them.*
  It so far provokes God, that,
    1. There is scarce any other sin that God
gives his people so great a charge to take heed of,
as this sin of forgetfulnesse: So he charged the
people of *Israel*, by the hand of *Moses*, divers
times, as Deut. 4.9. Where having declared what God
had done for them, he adds this charge, *Onely take
heed to thy self, and keep thy soul diligently,
lest thou forget* [B1v] *the things which thine eyes
have seen, and lest they depart from thy heart all
the dayes of thy life.* The like charge is given
them, Deut. 6.12. Where having told them what they
were like to enjoy in the Land of *Canaan,* according
to Gods promises and oath; that which they never
took care of, nor bestowed cost for; he chargeth
them to beware, lest they forget the Lord.
    2. So far is God provoked by the sin of
forgetfulnesse, that as he takes special notice of
it, so he reproves it very sharply. In Psal. 78.
where you have an history of Gods goodnesse to his
people, this sin of forgetfulnesse, is two severall
times noted; *They forgat Gods works, and the
wonders he had shewed them,* vers. 11. *They
remembred not his hand, nor the day in which he
delivered them from the enemy,* vers. 42. In Psal.
106. this sin is thrice laid to the peoples
charge; as, *They remembred not the multitude of thy
mercies,* vers. 7. *They soon forgat his works,* vers.
13. *They forgat God their Saviour, which had done*

great things in AEgypt, vers. 21. How sharply
doth our Saviour Christ reprove his Disciples
for this sin? Who, when he bad them *take heed and
beware of the leaven of the Pharisees*; thought he
had said that, because they had taken no bread with
them: whereupon, Christ takes notice of this
sin, and reproves them for it. *What,* (saith our
Saviour) *do ye not remember the five loaves, and
the seven loaves, and how many baskets ye took up?*
This forgetfulnesse [B2r] proceeds from your grosse
ignorance, and your great unbelief. *Were
there not ten cleansed?* saith our Saviour of the
Lepers, *but where are the nine? There are not found
that returned to give glory to God, save this
stranger.*

3. So far is God provoked by this sin, that
he often plagues it most severely. So saith the
Lord by the Prophet *Isaiah* to the people of *Israel*,
*Because thou hast forgotten the God of thy salva-
tion, and hast not been mindfull of the rock of thy
strength; therefore shalt thou plant pleasant
plants, and shalt set it with strange slips. In the
day shalt thou make thy plant to grow, and in the
morning shalt thou make thy seed to flourish: but
the harvest shall be an heap in the day of grief
and of desperate sorrow. Summa est, omnia mala
illis provenire ex impio Dei contemptu,* saith judicious *Calvin* on the words. The summe of all that
the Prophet had said is this: That all manner of
evills were like to befall them because of their
wicked contempt of God. And who contemns God so
much as he that forgets God, in whom is all our
strength and salvation? Let them sow, and plant,
and fetch their seeds and slips from a far
Countrey, and therefore the most choyce and precious; yea let them have great successe, let them
flourish betimes; that is, *Initio omnia tibi suc-
cedant pro voto, erunqt; priora foelicia ac
prospera, at postea incides in summas aerumnas et*

calamitates; saith *Vatablus* on the place: In the beginning let all succeed according to their desire; let the first undertakings [B2v] be happy and prosperous; yet afterwards thou shalt fall into extreme miseries and calamities. Or as *Junius, Regionem tuam colueris, et studiosissimé confirmaveris, ut certum ex ea fructum percipias, etc.* Take all care of thy Countrey, and strengthen it what thou canst, yet in one moment the *Assyrian* shall destroy all.

Luther had wont to say that three things would destroy Religion, (and if Religion be blasted, what good can be expected?) carnall security, worldly policy, and forgetfulnesse of Gods benefits. But more of this afterwards.

Are these things so? How great is Gods goodnesse to us? How singular his loving kindnesse towards us? who knowing our mold best, and how ready we are to forget him and his benefits, hath in all ages and times afforded many speciall means for the helping of our dull memories; that divine favours being remembred, Gods glory might be advanced, his judgements prevented, and our comforts enlarged. Hence a pot of *Manna* must be kept in the Ark, that after ages might know and remember how God had fed his people with Angels food. For the like use twelve stones must be set up neer the banks of *Jordan*, & other twelve stones in the midst of that River, that they and after generations might remember that God had miraculously made way for the twelve Tribes of *Israel*, through that flood, to the [B3r] Land of *Canaan*. The same people were appointed to make fringes upon their garments, with a ribband of blew, that they might look upon it and remember God and his commandements. For this purpose God set apart solemne dayes, and appointed publick feasts; as, the feast of Tabernacles, and Pentecost; which as they were typicall resemblances of better things promised, so were they *memorandums*

of great mercies vouchsafed. For this end God hath
ordained Sacraments, as that of the Passover under
the Law, and this of the Lords Supper under the
Gospel; that as at the celebration of the one,
Israel might remember their deliverance out of
AEgypt; so we at the administration of the other,
might remember Christ, by whom we are *saved from
our enemies, and from the hands of all that hate
us*. This Supper is not onely a representing, a
sealing, and a conveying signe, but a commemorative
signe. *Do this in remembrance of me*, saith Christ.
There is no Gospell-ordinance, whether prayer,
reading, or hearing of the Word, but there is such
mention made of Christ as we ought to remember him.
But this ordinance of the Supper hath this signall
note of excellency stamped upon it above all, a
speciall charge from Christ to remember him when
that is administred; *Do this in remembrance of me;
for, as often as ye eat this bread, and drink this
cup, ye shew*, that is, *ye make a commemoration of
the Lords death till he come.* [B3v]

    Sometimes (that we may come to the subject matter intended) God appointed Records and Registers
of his mercies, Histories and Journalls of the
noble acts and loving kindnesses of the Lord to his
people, to be kept and conveyed to posterity, that
the generations to come might know them, even the
children that should be born, *who should arise and
declare them to their children*. Thus the Lord
commanded that the History of *Amalek* should be written in a Book, their malice and Gods mercy, their
war and overthrow; and it must be rehearsed to
posterity, that it might never be forgotten. What
this Book was, we shall not much enquire. Some say
it was the Book of *Jasher*, mentioned Josh. chap.
10. which was a Chronicle of the acts of the people
of the Lord, which is lost. Some say it was the
Book of the *Judges*. Some say it was a Book of the
Battails of the Lord, mentioned Numb. 21. 14.

Others, and that most probably, that it was no
other but this Book of Exodus; *Junius* and *Calvin*.
But why this History must be written in a Book is
more worthy of our inquiry, and more sutable to
to our purpose. And the reasons may be these two:
    1. That a thankfull remembrance of so great a
deliverance from so malicious an enemy, might be
continued in the generations following.
    2. That the people of God knowing what sentence
was denounced against *Amalek*, [B4r] which should be
executed in due time, (as it was in th Reign of
Saul) might be the better encouraged to fight
against them, and through faith expect the victory
over them: And thus in this Chapter God would have
the Journals of the people of *Israel* from *AEgypt* to
the Land of *Canaan* recorded, that the great things
God had done for them by the way, might not be
forgotten; for so it said in the Text. *Moses
wrote their goings out according to their journey,
by the commandement of the Lord.*
    In this Chapter two parts are observable,
    1. An *Israelitish* Journall is recorded, from
vers. 1, to *v*. 50.
    2. A direction is given them, concerning
their proceedings in and with the Land of *Canaan*.
Which is threefold:
    1. That they should cast out the inhabitants,
v. 52, 53.
    2. That they should destroy their idols, *v*. 52.
    3. That they should divide the Land amongst
them by lot, *v*. 54.
    The two former whereof are seconded with a most
sharp threatning, that if they did not punctually
observe Gods command therein:
    1. For the present, that people should prove
a continuall snare unto them.
    2. For the future, what God had intended to
these their enemies, should fall upon their own
heads: all this to the end of the *ch*. [B4v]

Chapter One

In the *Israelitish* Journall two things are to be considered,
  1. The duty is in generall propounded, *v.* 1, 2.
  2. You have an Historicall enumeration of their several Journeys, in *v.* 2.
In which three things are to be noted in the second verse.
  1. the matter that stands upon record, and that is *their journeys, according to their goings out.*
  2. The Scribe that recorded them, and that was *Moses, Moses wrote, etc.*
  3. The authority by which he did it; and that was the *commandement of the Lord,* he had very good warrant for what he did. The first of these, namely, the matter that stands upon record, *their journeys,* is that which I shall principally take notice of.
In which Journall this is observable,
That there is not onely a particular relation of the place from which, and the place to which they journeyed, as from *Rameses* to *Succoth,* etc. but also a singular mention is made of all the great passages of Gods good hand of providence over them, together with their murmurings and rebellions, by wch they provoked him. All which are in this *ch.* implyed, and some particulars are expressed, as you may find, *v.* 9, 14, 38, 40. This *ch.* being but a short Epitome or abridgement of the whole History. So that in the *Israelitish* Journall you shall finde how here God gave them bread from heaven, there water out of [B5r] the rock, in one place he delivered them from the violence of the mighty waters; in another, from the fury of their potent enemies: Now he saved them from the cruelty of the *AEgyptians,* at another time from the malice of the *Amalekites;* and soon after, from the sting of the fiery Serpents. To day he gives them Manna and Quails, good food for their hungry bodies; to morrow he delivers them his Law, with many divine

ordinances and statues, for the good of their souls: In all their goings out he afforded them plentifull pledges of his care of them, bounty to them, and patience towards them. Who, notwithstanding the many grievous sins by which they provoked him, being full of compassion, forgave their iniquities, and destroyed them not; *yea, many a time he turned away his anger, and did not stir up all his wrath, for he remembred that they were but flesh,* etc.

By this time we are come to the Observation that is intended, and may hence be collected, and that is this,

To keep a Journall or Diary by us, especially of all Gods gracious dealings with us, is a work for a Christian of singular use.

I say, of Gods gracious dealings with us, in a more especiall manner; because it is good also to observe and keep a good account of the severall occurrences of the [B5v] Times we meet with, as they have reference to the Countrey and Nation we live in. It is good to keep an History, a Register, a Diary, an Annales, not onely of the places in which we have lived, but of the mercies that have been bestowed on us, continued to us all our dayes. This was the practice of *David* the Servant of the Lord, who made a Psalm and Song in the day that the Lord delivered him from the hand of all his enemies, and from the hand of *Saul. Moses* writes his Book called *Deuteronomy*, which is nothing else but a repetition of the Journeys of the people of *Israel*, and the great things God had done for them, in their goings out to that day. There was scarce any thing in *Israel*, but was typicall; their Meats, their Drinks, their Manna, their water out of the rock their Prince, Priest, Prophet; their sacrifices, their whole service; yea, the very Land of *Canaan* was a type of heaven, and was not their voyage a type of our pilgrimage? their journey from *AEgypt*

Chapter One

to *Canaan*, a signe of our passage from bondage to
liberty, from darknesse to light, from a vale of
tears to thee joyes of heaven? See this parallel in
six passages.

1. They were brought out of *AEgypt* with mighty
hand, and we are delivered from the slavery of sin
& Satan, by the arm of the Lord. The Creation of
the world, Sun, Moon, and Stars are the work of
Gods fingers; and all the great things he doth for
us in the world, [B6r] are but finger-work in comparison of our Redemption by Christ, that is indeed
the work of his arm.

2. They had many and mighty enemies that stood
in their way, and opposed them. The *AEgyptians*, and
the *Amalekites, Sihon,* the King, and *Og* the Giant;
and *we in this way fight not with flesh and blood
alone, but against principalities and powers
against the rulers of the darkness of this world,
against spiritual wickednesses in high places.*

3. They had a red Sea to passe thorough, and we
our temptations and tryals to passe over; for, *all
that will live godly in Christ Jesus shall suffer
persecution.*

4. They had a bunch of grapes in the wildernesse, and we a taste of Gods goodnesse in this present evill world. It is sometimes fair weather
over head, though foul under feet; we have peace
with God, though trouble in the world. When *Joseph*
dealt roughly with his Brethren, yet even then they
carryed home corn and money in their Sacks: As it
is never so well with us, but we have cause to
be humble; so it is never so ill with us, but we
have cause to be thankfull.

5. They had a mixed multitude went up with
them; and we have sheep and goats in the same fold,
wheat and tares in the same field, corn and chaffe
on the same floor, good fish and bad in the same
stream, Saints and Hypocrites in the same visible
Church. In the Ark amongst eight, there was a *Cham*;

[B6v] in Christs family amongst twelve, there was a *Judas*; in the primitive times, amongst the seven Deacons, there was a *Nicholas*. Our best Congregations are mixt companies, in heaven only the Assembly shall consist of holy ones, *the spirits of just men made perfect*.

6. Lastly, they had a Journall of all Gods mercies, and why not we a Diary of all Gods gracious dealings with us? If this last hath nothing of type in it, I am sure it hath of president; for, *whatever was written before, was written for our learning*. [B7r]

Chap. II

The matter whereof a Journall or Diary is compounded, and first Nationall and publick.

IN the prosecution of this Subject in hand, I would do these two things:
1. Discover the materials whereof this Journall doth consist.
2. Shew the manner how it is to be used. For the materials, they are twofold:
   1. Either Nationall, and more publick.
   2. Personall, and more private.

For those that are Nationall, and of publick concernment, they may be reduced to these five heads.

1. Take notice what Kings and Princes, what Magistrates and Governors have ruled over us; for commonly, Such Prince, such people. They that come of the yeelding Willow, and not of the sturdy Oak (as a Marquesse of *Winchester* had wont to say) will yeeld with the Time, and ever be of the Religion of the King their Master: They can be Pagans under *Diocletian* the Heathen [B7v] Emperor, and Christians under *Constantine* the Reformer: Such again will turn *Arians* under *Constantius* the Heretick, Back-sliders under *Iulian* the Apostate, and with *Jovinianus* for preferment turn Orthodox. Hence the Ancients were wont to place the statues of their Princes and Patriots neer their fountains; intimating thereby, that if their Magistrates were good, they were the springheads of much happinesse to the people; but if wicked, the originall of misery and

mischief. If wicked *Jeroboam* set up idols, *Regis ad exemplum*, all *Israel* are made to sin through his example. If *Hezekiah* be forward in reforming Religion, so are the People. When certain Embassadors praised the *Lacedemonian* Souldiers for their good order, in being well regulated by Martial dissipline who were before mutinous and injurious; one of them answered, *Nos iidem sumus qui ut nuper, sed alius nunc nobis est Dux*: We are the same we had wont to be, but now we have another Generall. The Nation is happy, that can say of their chief Governor, as one of *Saul's* Courtiers spake of *David*, when he commended him to his Master, *He is a cunning player on the Harp, a mighty valiant man, and a man of war, and prudent in matters; a comely person, and* (that which made all excellent) *the Lord is with him*. He is a great Souldier, and a good Scholar, like another *Caesar*, that did as much by Arts as by Arms; he is a wise States-man, and as religious as noble; [B8r] so ruling over men that he is just, ruling in the fear of God. Goodnesse and Greatnesse, when they meet together in the Grandees of the World, huge swelling titles in their Coyns and Charters are accompanyed with grace and godlinesse, if like a ring with a rich Diamond, that raiseth the price of it very high. Oh! how winning and prevalent are such mens examples? He that carries a light in a dark evening in *London*, seldome goes alone; and that ship in the Navy that hath the Lanthorn, and sets out the light, shall not want followers. It is so in a good example, though given by a mean person; but if the light of Magistrates so shine before men that they may see their good works, how do they glorifie God, and indevour by all means to walk in those wayes? And the reason is, because Subjects study the lives of their Princes more then their laws, and esteem their examples as currant as their coyn: Hence it is, that as their personall virtues are publick ornaments, so their proper vices are a Kingdomes injuries.

2. Observe what that Religion is, that by those Magistrates is imbraced, and how the truth is countenanced or opposed by them.

Charls the Great was wont to set his Crown upon the Bible, as *Canutus* sometimes put his Diadem upon the Rood, both thereby intimating, that as all honor was due to [B8v] God, so true Religion was the best basis for Government, and that Piety was the best Policy. The Lions that upheld *Solomon's* throne were of pure gold. A Princes Religion should be pure, not polisht; it should be undefiled before God, as well as pretended in the sight of men. And indeed the best way to facilitate the affairs of State, for the best advantage of a Common-wealth, is to carry on Religion, and seek the glory of God in the first place. It is obervable, that the *Israelites* in their journey to *Canaan*, went no faster, nor no farther then the Ark. And when they returned from *Babylon* to their owne Land, they first set up the Altar, and offered Burnt-offerings, they kept the feast of Tabernacles, and built the Temple before they set up the Wall. And had we in our generation been as wise, and observed Gods and his peoples method; that is, first sought the Kingdome of heaven, and the righteousnesse thereof, then all outward good things had been added to us. Had we sought Gods glory before our owne grandure, we had better provided for our owne and the Kingdomes safety. It is observed, that the Disciples at sea, in the absence of Christ, by reason of a storm, rowed slowly and dangerously; but as soon as they willingly received Christ into the ship immediately, they came to the land whither they intended. The most politick Pilots that ever sate at the stern of any Common-Wealth, were never able through the depths [C1r] of State to drive on their designes with successe, unlesse they took Christ along with them.

They that trust much to their owne pates and
policies, without an eye to God, are like Boys that
stand on their heads, and fling up their heels
against heaven; as this standing is dangerous to
the state of the Body, so that trusting to carnall
policies, with a neglect of Religion by some, and a
contempt and a reall opposition against the truth by
others, are as destructive to the body of any State
in the world. The Bishop of *Monte Pulciano* told
Charls the Emperor in the Councell of *Trent*, that it
was one of the chief instructions Pope *Paul* the
third gave to his Legat, to commend to that
Assembly, That *Principalities cannot be preserved
where Religion is lost*: And it was a good Law that a
Danish King of this Land made, *That at the generall
Court of every Shire, the Bishop of the Diocesse
should accompany the Sheriffe; that the one might
countenance Gods law, the other mans.* Much like the
practice of good *Jehosaphet*, whose heart was lifted
up in the ways of the Lord. He sent with his
Princes the Levites, to teach in the Cities of *Judah*.
The Princes are said to teach; that is, either by the
Levites, whom they did company, countenance, and
encourage in the work; or rather the Princes
taught the Law of the Land, the Levites the Law of
God, and both did mutually help each other. [C1v]

3. Keep an account of the various and changeable condition of the Times in the Countrey where
we live, either for prosperity or adversity, with
the fruits and effects of both. *Omnium rerum est
vicissitudo*. There are no sublunary comforts but
are subject to change. We have sometimes sun-shine,
and sometimes rain; we have sometime day, and sometime it is night with us. The Church of the
Jews under the Old Testament had sometimes War, and
sometimes Peace. *Jabin* King of *Canaan* mightily
oppressed *Israel* twenty years; but the Lord discomfited *Sisera* his Commander in chief with all his
host before *Baruch*, and the Land had rest forty

yeers. How punctuall is the holy Ghost in observing
the very circumstances, not onely of person and
place, but of the very time, how long they had War,
and how much longer time they injoyed Peace? Under
the reign of *Solomon*, that people enjoyed much
peace. *Judah and Israel were many, as the sand
which is by the Sea shore in multitude, eating, and
drinking, and making merry.* But in the dayes of
Abijah his Grandchilde, *Israel* and *Judah* fought one
against another, *so that there fell down slain of
Israel five hundred thousand chosen men at that
battle.* I challenge any man that is most verst in
History, to give me a parellel.

The Church of the *Jews* under the Gospel, about
the time that *Stephen* was stoned, through the heat
of persecution was [C2r] scattered abroad,
throughout the Regions of Judea and Samaria: But
when *Saul* became *Paul*, and of a Persecuter turn'd a
Preacher, *Then had the Churches rest throughout
Judea and Galilee, and Samaria, etc.*

This one thing amongst other is recorded in the
sacred Journall of the *Israelites*; sometimes they
had plenty, and sometimes they wanted bread and
water; sometimes they had peace, and sometimes
their enemies made war against them; sometimes they
enjoyed health, and sometimes the plague brake out
amongst them: And thus it hath been in all the generations and ages of the world. *England*, that some
have called *Terra Florida*, or *the fortunate Island*,
that, with *Capernaum*, hath been lifted up to
heaven, in the enjoyment of peace and plenty, the
Gospel of peace, and the peace of the Gospel
together, for many years; so that enough cannot be
spoken upon this subject, to the praise of God, the
envy of our enemies, and the blot of our
ingratitude. But we have had our changes. We have
sinned away all our comforts. Our peace brought
plenty, our plenty nourisht pride, our pride begat
contention, our contention drew the sword, and the

sword a civill sword, the sharpest and sorest of
all Gods judgements, hath turned our peace into
war, our plenty into penury, our friends into
enemies; so that our blood hath been spilt, and
our treasure spent, and our glory stained, [C2v]
almost beyond all example. Where every day,
Marte cadunt subito per mutua vulnera fratres.
In a battle betwixt *Sylla* and *Marius*, both
Romane Commanders, a Souldier having slain one, and
afterward understanding that it was his Brother, in
anguish of spirit thrust his sword into his own
bowels. *Titus Vespasian* Emperor of *Rome*, wept when
he saw the destruction of *Jerusalem*, and the great
slaughter of the *Jews*, chiefly occasioned through
their owne civill dissensions; but that which hath
heightned our misery, and I fear aggravated our sin
very much, we grew to that height of heat and bit-
terness, that we rejoyced over our brethren when we
obtained any victory against them. *Pliny* reports
this of the Dragon, that fighting with the
Elephant, he got under the belly of that mighty
beast, where he suckt out the blood so far, that at
last the Elephant fell, but with his fall crusht
the Dragon to death. He that wins most by a civill
war, will be a great loser at the last. *Philip* Duke
of *Burgundy* his embleme of a flint-stone and a
steel striking one against another so long till
both are consumed, doth lively set out the miseries
of that fire that is made by domesticall arms. A
forain enemy cannot wish us a greater mischief, nor
themselves a greater advantage, then our intestine
wars. Hence [C3r] the *Turks* use to pray unto
God, to keep the Christians at variance; which
caused one of their Emperors to say to his Councell, disswading him from making war with the
Germanes, because of their multitude and fortitude;
that he feared them not, because (saith he) sooner
would his fingers be all of a length, then their
Princes be all of one minde.

4. Keep a Diary of the severall and most remarkable judgements that God hath in our time inflicted upon notorious offenders, whether persons in high places, or such as moved in a lower orbe. The holy Ghost takes speciall notice of such in the Scriptures. Few men went to the grave in peace, that by their monstrous impieties made war against heaven and his Church. As, what became of *Pharaoh* the bloody, and *Achitopel* the crafty? of *Balaam* the covetous, and *Corah* the rebell? of *Haman* the proud, and *Herod* the fox? As their lives were wicked, so their ends were fearful. In like manner, what became of *Absalom* the disobedient, and *Ela* the drunkard? of *Zimri* and *Cosbi* the unclean? of *Ananias* and *Saphira* those lyars? Were not all these taken away with a stroke in their sin? What became of those *Romane* Nimrods, as *Maxentius* the Tyrant, and *Julian* the Apostate, with others, who hunted the Saints of God to death in those ten persecutions mentioned in Ecclesiasticall Histories? How few of [C3v] their hoary heads went to the grave in peace?

To come neerer to our owne times. What became of wily *Winchester*, and bloody *Bonner*, with many others that ruled the roste in those Dog-dayes of Q *Mary's* reign? Few of those bloody and deceitfull men lived out half their dayes: But when the scumme was at the highest, it fell into the fire; for though God did bear them up for some time in their essence, yet he would not bear them out at all in their malice. God hath leaden feet, but iron hands; though he comes slowly, yet he strikes surely. It is good to mark the ends of men. *Mark the perfect man* (saith the *Psalmist*) *and behold the upright, for the end of that man is peace.* Balaam did so as wicked as he was, which made him wish that he might dye the death of the righteous, and that his latter end might be like his. In like manner mark the end of the transgressors, for they shall be destroyed together, *the end of the wicked shall be cut off;* that is, they shall not dye the the common death of all men, but shall be cut off in the midst of their dayes. If their lives be tragical, their deaths are seldome comicall. *Zoroastes* the inventor of Magick (as some Historians affirm of him) laught at his birth, but dyed a wofull, and lamentable death, being banished from his Countrey. *Alphonsus Dyazius* a Spaniard, a rigid Papist, procured a notorious cut-throat to murther his Brother *John* [C4r] *Dyazius,* a sincere Protestant, because he could by no means turn him from the truth; but the righteous Lord would not suffer such an unnaturall villany to go unpunished; for not long after he was haunted by the terrors of his owne conscience, that being at *Trent* when the Councel sate there, (for he was one of the Popes Lawyers) he hanged himself about the neck of his owne Mule. How have some godly Divines taken good pains in writing the stories of Gods judgements upon notorious malefactors, as Drunkards, Swearers, Sabbath-breakers, and such like? Would others be perswaded in their generation, to take speciall notice, and keep some account of such memorable accidents, the benefit would be singular. *The righteous shall see and fear* (saith the Psalmist). What shal they see? That God destroyes the mighty man, that boasts himself in mischief, that God takes him away, and plucks him out of his dwelling place, and roots him out of the land of the living.

A Serving-man, being at a Tavern in *Essex,* and threatning to swear the Constable out of the Town, if he came there; in a drunken fit running after one to make him pledge him a pinte of sack at a draught, fell down the stairs, and dyed instantly, *Novemb.* 1. 1626.

A Fisher-man (that I knew) bringing Mackerell to a Port-town in Suffolk, where the people (because they were new, and the [C4v] first that

came that yeer to Town) pressing eagerly to buy
them, and some against his will being entred
into his boat, he took up a stone, and sware by the
name of God he would make them stand further off,
instantly sunk down, and soon after dyed.

How many in my time have I noted! Would others
do the like, how would men consider such things,
and understand the righteous judgements of the
Lord?

5. Finally, consider seriously, and observe
very strictly, what the Nationall Epidemicall sin
of the time and present generation may be. Where
iniquity abounds, it is hard to determine, but
questionlesse every age hath a peculiar distemper.
In times of commotion, when the bands of love are
broken into severall parties and factions, as they
have been lately amongst us, it is more easily discerned.

A noble Gentleman of singular abilities, and
one much employed in affairs of State in his time
(whom I knew well) advised his friends at such a
time to buy up all the Pamphlets that were printed,
if of any considerable worth; for when people fall
out, they commonly speak out; and if they be once
drunk with passion, and their distempers boyl to
any height, the most secret venome will swim on the
top: By which means you may easily feel the pulse
of the present time, and discover what is the
Nationall and most predominant sinne: [C5r] and it
will be worth our paines to know it.

Which that we may the better doe, let us look
back a little to the generations behinde us.

1. Some times have been more notorious for
drunkennesse. *Scaliger* in his Book *de Lingua
Latina*, observes this of the *Germans* in his time,
that their *vivere* was *bibere*, not only in their
pronunciation, as he noted; but in their practice,
as other well observed, who lived that they might
drink.

Seneca foretold so much of some times, that men should be so drowned with this sin of drunkennesse, that *plurimum meri sumpsisse virtus esset*, it should be esteemed a virtue to strive with the Brewers horse who should carry more liquor; and with some it hath been of that esteem, that not *as drunk as a Begger, but as drunk as a Prince*, hath been a kind of proverbial commendation of some.

When *Aeschines* commended *Philip* King of *Macedon*, for a Joviall man, who would drink freely; *Demosthenes* being by, told him, that this was a good quality in a Spunge, but not in a Prince.

Drunkennesse is a sin that layes men open to all iniquity more then any sin. *Ebrietas in se culpas complectitur omnes*. What sin is not a Drunkard subject to? *Their eyes shall behold strange women*, (saith *Solomon*) *and their hearts shall utter perverse things*. And a sin it is that God hath more frequently and suddenly plagued [C5v] with death in the very act then any other sin.

Edgar a King of *England*, observing in his time that excessive drinking abounded in the Land, through the example of the *Danes* that dwelt in divers parts of the Kingdome; to prevent that evill, ordained that their cups they drank in should have certain pins or nails put in them, beyond which if any drank at one draught, he should pay so much money.

2. Some generation hath been more infamous for that sin of Swearing, and that by the name of God, even at every word here in England. Insomuch that a family in this Land, and that no mean one, was so notorious for this sin, that they had the name of the *Bygods* given them, and were so usually called.

I remember, Mr. *Fox* in his History of the *Acts and Monuments of the Church*, reciting many evidences whereby he proved the antiquity of Priests Marriage, sets down the copy of a Release made by

Chapter Two
41

William Bygod, Lord of *Little Bradley*, to *Henry Denardestone* Clerk, and *Alice* his Wife; and questionlesse that name of *Pigot* was originally the same, though in succession of time, and very wisely
5 it was changed: *Omne peccatum suam habet excellentiam:* Every sin hath some peculiar vilenesse, wherein it may be said to excel other. There's not any sin that doth more plainly discover the great profanenesse of [C6r] the heart, as common swearing,
10 especially by the name of God, *for out of the abundance of the heart the mouth speaketh.*

    3. Some times that are gone over our heads, and therefore far behinde us, have been infected with an itching humour after Superiority, wherein persons not
15 content to abide in the calling that God set them in, have indevoured to go beyond their proper line, and so broke their ranks. Thus *Absalom* was not content with the place of a Son, nor *Hazael* with the rank of a Subject, nor *Jezebel* with the condition of a Wife,
20 whose desires should be subject to her Husband, whose right it was to rule over her. Thus the lowest of the people under the countenance of *Jereboam* would be Priests, and it was a small thing in the eyes of *Corah* and his company, that God had brought them
25 nigh unto himself to do sevice, but they must seek the Priesthood also. Thus *Jeroboam* the Servant of *Solomon* is not contented, unlesse he may lift up his hand against his Master. How sad was that time amongst the *Scythians*, who whilest they
30 made their third Expedition into *Asia*, and tarryed seven yeers (as *Justin* in his History reports) were turned out of their beds and possessions by their servants that were left behinde to keep their cattle, and at their return were kept out by force
35 of Arms by those slaves who had taken their Wives, and possessed their goods. Not much unlike that of the [C6v] people of *Israel*, servants ruled over them, and there was none to deliver them.

    Caesar riding one day through a Towne, was

asked by one, whether there were any striving for
offices and places of honour in that place, answered that he had rather be the chief man in that
little Village, then the second person in *Rome;* an
itching humour it is after greatnesse, that hath
run in a blood from *Adam* and *Eve* to this day, who
were not content with their standing, but would be
as Gods, knowing good and evill: Now as the root of
this humour is extreme pride, so the fruit is confusion; first I say pride is the cause, there are
none that are so low in their deserts, but are very
high in their thoughts; even the bramble hath great
thoughts and high words too of his shadow, and it
was but a shadow. *Absalom,* and *Hazael,* and *Iezebel,*
and *Ieroboam* thought they could manage the affairs
of a Kingdome better then *David,* or *Benhadad,* or
Ahab, or *Solomon.* Every simple cobler thinks he can
go beyond his Last, and preach far better then his
Priest: *Ye Sons of Levi* (saith he) *take too much
upon you*: But the fruit of such ambition is mischief and confusion.

    Some Countrey Pesants that behold the stars to
glister in the horizon on the top of a mountain,
think if they were there they could reach the
heaven, & order the stars, but being exalted on
that mountain, they are as far to seek as before.
What became of [C7r] *Absalom* the Rebel, and *Hazael*
the Traitor, and *Iezebel* the Proud? of *Ieroboam* the
Servant, and *Corah* and his company? As none did so
ill, so none sped worse, their mischief lighted on
their own heads, and (like to *Phaeton*) their
violent dealing on their owne pates. Those *Scythian*
slaves, though their Masters could not beat them
with their weapons, yet at the sight of their
Masters rods and whips ran all away, and at last
perished.

    But you will ask me, What may be the sin of
this time? Some wood is more apt to breed worms,
and some cloth more ready to breed moths, and some

times have their peculiar sins. But, what is the
sin of this age? which is more considerable for us,
then the looking back to the times that are past.
    1. Some say our great divisions, our most bit-
ter contentions, and that amongst Brethren, is the
sin. And indeed this evill is grown to that height,
that they that should dye one for another, can
hardly live one by another. Surely such divisions
amongst those that professe godlinesse, cause great
thoughts of heart, for the neerer the union is, the
more dangerous is the breach; broken bones are not
so soon healed, nor sinews that are cut so soon
knit, as great gashes in the flesh may be cured; if
a cable rope be broken, it is very hardly tyed
together. If the Father and the Son, if the Husband
and the Wife fall out, they are hardly reconciled;
[C7v] and, as *Solomon* saith, *A brother offended is
harder to be won then a strong City.* We do not finde
that *Paul* and *Barnabas* ever met together again after
they parted asunder, through their sharp contention. Which made *Cosmus* a Duke of *Florence* say, We
are commanded to forgive our enemies, but we never
read that we are bid to forgive our friends. And
that which makes our contention so much the more
grievous, is, that one speciall means that God hath
appointed for the uniting of Brethren, is become a
ground of the greatest quarrell. The Lords Supper
is a feast of Loves, a communion ordained to
nourish union, and yet at this feast we have found
a bone of contention, and an apple of strife. And
it is observable, that when any listen to seducing
spirits, and separate from this ordinance, they
grow sowre and sullen to their dearest friends.
Our Saviour Christ foretelling the evills of the
latter dayes, gives this as a badge of the last and
worst, the old and cold age of the world: *Iniquity
shall abound, and the love of many shall grow cold.*
But what is the cause of both? *Many false Prophets
shall arise, and shall seduce many;* and surely the

difference of judgement will ever cause a distance
in affections. Firebrands though they doe not smoak
more when they are out of the chimney, yet I am
sure they offend more, and may prove dangerous.
The novel opinions of these times kept within dores
do too much harm; but [C8r] spread abroad by the
boutefewes of these times through their burning
charity are ready to set all on fire. And most
people either out of ignorance or easinesse, are
like foot travellers, who when they come to a stile
that stands neer a gap, leave the stile and go in
at the breach; take up any error that causeth division, rather then take the pains to try the
spirits, to prove all things, and keep that which
is good. Unity is the highest mystery in heaven,
and would be the greatest happinesse on earth,
could we enjoy it. Union is from God, division from
the Devil, who where he comes with his cloven feet,
separates chief friends; and surely such are factors for hell that cause divisions, that observe
Machiavel's rule, they divide that they may rule;
but surely the end of such wayes will be their owne
confusion. The champion Milo when he thrust his
hands into the clefts of an Oak, thinking thereby
to make the breach the wider, was caught, and there
held till he was devoured by wilde beasts. God
grant that such envyous persons, that do sow the
tares of division, may reap the fruit of such
labours, even confusion. He graciously fulfill his
promise, and give us one heart and one way; He hear
the prayers of his dear Son, and grant that we may
be one; He turn our heart-burnings into heart-
breakings, and unite us fast together in the *unity
of the spirit, with the bond of peace.* This I confesse is one of the sicknesses of these [C8v]
times, which alone is enough to make a gracious
heart weary of his life, and long to be at home in
heaven, out of the reach of so mischievous an evil.
Melanchthon, when he lay on his death-bed, discov-

ered not only much willingnesse to dye, but much
joy at the thoughts of his approaching end; and
being asked by one the reason of it, answered, that
it was because he should then see Christ and his
Church above, where he was sure there was no such
contentions amongst brethren, as was here, which he
often lamented with tears. This I say is our sicknesse, but yet my finger is not upon the plague-
sore.

2. Some peradventure will think Hypocrisie to
be that sin; and indeed much profession of Religion
without the power of godlinesse is common in these
dayes, wherein men have learned the art of looking
one way, and rowing another; pretending one thing,
and doing quite contrary. These are not like onely
Apothecaries boxes, that have golden titles, and
nothing in them, but like painted sepulchres, full
of rottennesse and noysome filthinesse. There are
seven abominations in such mens hearts. These men
are like curious pictures of men and women, drawn
to life; but if you look behinde them, you may see
store of dust and cobwebs. Or, they are like to
some of our Innes in Market-towns, where you may
see a Crown for the Signe, and a [D1r] Begger for
the Host; an Angel at the dore, and a Devil for the
Hostess: who under the glorious profession of
sanctity, dare act the greatest villany. *Jehu* his
pretence is zeal for the Lord of Hosts, but his
plot is the Kingdome. *Ahab* and *Jezebel* proclaim a
Fast, pretending the punishment of blasphemy, but
they intend thereby to take away *Naboth's* both life
and vineyard. And though all hypocrites have not
attained to this height of hellish iniquity, yet
they are like some children that are sick of a disease they call the Rickets, who have great heads,
and big bellies, but shrimpled hands, and weak
knees. They are men of great parts, but no gifts,
not one of many are given to good works whilest
they live; and when they dye, something is given to

the poor by their Testament, but not by their Will.

It is said that *Isaac* digged more Wells, and found more water then *Abraham*; and questionlesse the knowledge of most men in this latter age of the world, exceeds that of former times; *The earth is full of the knowledge of the Lord, as the waters that cover the earth*: Nay, mens knowledge is profound, like waters that came out of the Sanctuary; it is grown deeper, from the ankles to the loyns; but it is to be feared, the waters of the Sanctuary have put out the fire that should burn in the Sanctuary, and that our great knowledge hath quite drowned our zeal, so that all those mens religion is run [D1v] out of the heart into the head. The world is full of such, who are like the heads that *Jehu* caused to be laid at the gate of *Jezreel*, a great many heads, but never an heart amongst them all. The *Toad* some say hath a pearl in the head, I am sure it hath poyson in the belly. These speak like *Cato*, but live like *Lucullus*. *Leah* had bad eyes, but she was fruitfull; *Rachel* had a better sight, but she was barren. Our Fathers saw lesse, but did more; these men professe *they know God, but in works deny him, being abominable, and unto every good work reprobate*; such knowledge will end in utter darknesse, and this tree of knowledge rob them of the tree of life. *Quis non irascatur* (saith St. *Aug.*) *videns homines ore Deum confitentes, negantes moribus? Quis non irascatur videns homines seculo verbis et non factis renunciantes?* Who can choose but be angry, that shall see men that confesse God with their lips, and deny him in their lives; that shal see men renounce the world, and the lusts thereof, in words, but not in deeds? Such men are like rogues that use to lye in the Church porch, whilest others make it but the way to their attendance upon divine ordinances, and religious duties. These men rest in an outward profession of religion, and a very form of godlinesse, and go no

further. I wish some men were called as these be
Hypocrites; or be as they are called, solid and
judicious Christians: But questionlesse many such
are miscalled, they have a name to live, but are
dead [D2r]. Like many of the Popes of *Rome*, if the
man were a Coward, they called him *Leo*; if a Clown,
Urbanus; if a Tyrant, *Clemens*. Such hypocrisie is
hated of all.

    The Cardinal of *Lorreign* a bitter enemy to
Geneva, and the reformed Churches, when Bernardinus
Ochinus offered him his service in writing against
the Protestants, slighted him with the greatest
scorn, because he knew he had dissembled and played
the hypocrite. And *Trajan* that wise and worthy
Emperor, professed, that he had reason to hold himself discharged of all debts to those, that
offended more by prevarication, then they ever
deserved by industry: But yet this is not the sin.

    3. There are others that will say, that
Apostasie is the sin of this age; and certainly
there may be some reason for it, for we are a
people given to backsliding; and how hath the
secret hypocrisie of many broken out into open
apostasie in these times? These are like gallant
ships with glorious titles, as the *Bonaventure*, the
Triumph, etc. but in a storm are *ventorum
ludibrium*; if the temptation come from the fears or
flatteries of the Times, they are taken with many
foolish lusts, which drown men in destruction and
perdition, and so they make shipwrack of faith and
a good conscience.

    There are three sorts of persons that are most
dangerous, I wish all to take great heed of them. [D2v]

    First, such as might have been good, but are
not; as, the *children* of *religious parents*,
servants that have lived much in *religious
families*, and *people* that have lived long under a
powerfull fruitfull Ministery, but are not bettered.

Secondly, such as seem to be good, but are not;
that can transform themselves into the shape of
Saints, who have the voyce of *Jacob*, and the hands
of *Esau*; that speak like the Lamb, but are ravening
Wolves. Oh! how hath Religion suffered under the
pretence of Religion in later times?

Thirdly, such as have been good (at least in
the hopes of many) but are not. These are trees
whose fruit withereth, *without fruit, twice dead,*
and plucked up by the roots.

The first are civill persons that have no
faith, too good for the Devill, but not good enough
for God. The Lord deliver us from such, for they
may prove unreasonable, because they have no faith.

The second sort are Hypocrites, and the third
Apostates, the most bitter enemies to holinesse,
and the power of godlinesse. Such was *Iulian* the
Apostate.

It is said, that tame Foxes, if they break
loose, and turn wilde, will do more mischief then
any. *Iulian* was once a Christian, and a forward
professor, but turning back to Heathenisme, drew
more from the Faith by fraud, then any of his
predecessors did by force. Baldwine and Bolsack
turned Apostates, and were hired by the Papists
to write [D3r] the Life of *Calvin*, and proved
desperate adversaries to the truth. *Parsons* and
Harding had sometimes a taste of the truth, but
falling away, proved most bitter enemies to the
Church of God. The greatest enemies that any man
can have, are those of his own house. He was of the
society of Jesus that betrayed him. Such Apostates
are not onely injurious to others, but in conclusion are the greatest enemies to their owne souls.

To fall backward is more dangerous to the body,
and to apostatize is most dangerous to the soul.
What became of *Iulian* the Apostate his *Vicisti*
Galilaee? which taking a handfull of blood and
slinging it up into the air against Christ, told

Chapter Two 49

all the world that his end was miserable. *If any man draw back* (saith the Apostle) *my soul shall have no pleasure in such.*

Henry the fourth, King of *France*, after his revolt to Popery, was perswaded by the great Duke about him, not to readmit the Jesuites into the Land, who had been justly banished by the State. He answered, Give me then security for my life: and thereupon admitted them, and gave them one of his owne houses for a Colledge; but did that secure him? certainly it did not; the Jesuites would never trust him, for first one by their procurement stab'd him in the mouth, and after that another to the heart, and that was the end of so great an Apostate. And surely he that draws back from [D3v] the God of truth must needs embrace error; if from the God of wisdome, will be a fool; if from the God of happinesse, cannot but be miserable.

This is a great sin, but not that sin.

4. So that if I may take liberty to expresse my thoughts, with humble submission to better judgements, I am of opinion, that not onely an unwillingnesse to submit unto, but a most violent opposition against the Kingly government of Jesus Christ in his Church, by his owne officers and ordinances, is the sin of this present generation. It is very observable, that the offices of Christ have met with strong opposition, some in one age, and some in another, more apparently.

Some times have been more notorious for the opposition that was made against his Propheticall office, as when the *Circumcellians* defaced and burbt the Scriptures: So did the *Papists*, who made it death for any Protestant to have and read any part of the Old or New Testament. The same grand Hereticks have made their Injunctions, Precepts, Traditions, of equall authority with the Word of God: So did the Councel of *Trent* at their fourth Session.

Some *times* have been more infamous for the opposition that was made against the Priesthood of Christ, who made peace for us by his Death, and still maintains our peace by his Intercession. Thus the *Papists* have mightily [D4r] opposed Christs Priesthood, by their doctrine of Justification by Works, their figments of Purgatory, works of Supererogation, prayers to Saints. Every man (say they) must suffer for his owne particular; yea, the works of one may suffice for another: So say the *Rhemists* in their Annotations, Rom. 8. 17. Col. 1. 24.

But these times are such as do more cleerly fight against the Kingdome of Christ; and herein cunningly they strike at the root, and undermine all his offices, the end whereof, *viz.* his Kingly office, being to support the Priesthood and Prophesie of Christ in their vigour and efficacy, that as a Prince and Captain of salvation to the Elect, he might bring them to God. A practicall, vigorous, open opposition of Christs Kingly office exercised in his ordinances, was never more eminent then in these dayes. Wherein there are so many *Gallioes*, or *Gadarens*; *Gallioes*, that care not for tose things, as either too far below their greatnesse, or too heavy a yoke to put their necks under; or *Gadarens*, who say plainly, We will not have this man reign over us, but desire him to depart out of the Countrey; who are not only an unwilling, but a rebellious people in the day of his power.

The reverend and learned Ministers of *London* met together in their Provinciall Assembly, in their Vindication of this government, to use their owne words, say as [D4v] much: *We are not ignorant that this government hath many adversaries.* The ignorant person hates it, because it will not suffer him to go blindfold to hell; the profane person hates it because it will not suffer him to eat and drink his owne damnation, by unworthy coming to the Lords

Chapter Two

Supper; the Heretick hates it, because after two or three admonitions it rejects him; the Jesuite hates it; because it is an invincible bulwark to keep out Popery; the Schismatick hates it, because the main designe of it is to make all the Saints of God to be of one lip, one heart, and one way. And above all, the Devill hates it, because if rightly managed, it will in a short time blow up his Kingdome.

And indeed, hence are all our miseries and mischiefs. Church-discipline is like the hem to the garment, rend off that, and how soon will all Religion ravell out to nothing? It is like the hedge to the Vineyard, if that be pluckt up, how soon will the Boar out of the Wood, and the wilde beasts of the field devour it? What a company of Hereticks and Schismaticks break in upon it? all that passe by the way pluck it: *Antitrinitarians, Antinomians, Antiscripturists, Socinians, Familists, Quakers,* etc. would dig up this Vineyard by the very roots. How are Christs ordinances despised, the authority of the Scriptures questioned, Gods faithfull Ministers misused? They were never [D5r] more learned, more pious, or more painfull; and yet never more scorned and undervalued then at this day. All Sectaries and Schismaticks, though they difer much amongst themselves, yet agree all in this, an irreconcileable hatred of, and bitter opposition against a godly faithfull Ministery.

But it is no wonder, for if the Cartwheel turn round, it is impossible that the spokes should stand still; if the Church and her discipline suffer under so many turnings and changes, surely her officers can have no rest.

Now, if any ask what the reason is that this government, formerly so much commended, so much desired, is now so mightily opposed, as the most tyrannicall.

I answer: It is not because we have attained to

more light then our Forefathers had, as is
pretended; but,
    1. Partly, because the instruments are changed,
the actors upon the stage that oppose it are new
men. It was notable advice that *Benhadad's* Councel
of War gave him after that *Ahab* had beaten him in
that first battle. *Take the Kings away every one
out of his place, and put Captains in their roomes.*
It is an old and most politick device, If a designe
receive a check, it may easily be driven on by
changing the instruments, and hath often prevailed,
where God hath not stept in and prevented it, as he
did here. [D5v] That which is unsufferable in a
Prince, may be commendable in a Captain. The same
errors that were formerly taught, and as generally
loathed, because the broachers of them were
Prelaticall, are now embraced gladly, and swallowed
downe greedily, because taught by such as have a
name of Sanctity. Take away the Bishops every one
out of his place, that so mightily opposed this
discipline; and set up some rare gifted men in
their room, that shall as much persecute and oppose
it; and then the same people that earnestly
laboured for this government, will now as violently
resist it.
    2. Because of the wickednesse and perversnesse
of mens spirits, this being the last and worst age
of the world, and we are faln upon the very dregs
of time. This government is very strict, and mens
secure lives will not easily submit to Christs
severe laws: We are become their enemies, because
we tell them the truth.
    3. But chiefly, because of the crosse and
froward disposition of most men: If they be commanded any duty, they peremptorily reply, *There is
no hope, we will walk after our owne devices, and
we will every one do the imaginations of his evill
heart.* If they be forbidden any thing, *nititur in
vetitum,* they eagerly pursue what before they stub-

Chapter Two

bornly refused: Let people be denied what is petitioned, they grow the more boldly importunate, even to a kinde of violence; let their [D6r] desires be granted, they not onely loath what before they liked, but grow higher in their demands.

Whence *Franciscus Sodorinus* Cardinall of *Preneste* was heard to say to Pope *Adrian* the sixth, that to grant to some people their petitions was but the way to slight the grant, and prepare for more. How many instances may we give of this?

When God commanded Circumcision, though under the sharpest penalties, how unwillingly did people submit to it? The neglect whereof had wel-nigh cost even *Moses* his life. And now the Lord hath taken it away, both *Jews* and *Gentiles* will be circumcised.

Time was when Christians met in Lanes and Woods to hear the Word, even with the perill of their lives, being wholly restrained from all places of publick meetings. Oh! how much did they desire that Temples might be granted to them! And what cost were they at, when they had liberty given them to enjoy them! But in our dayes, when we assemble freely in such publick places, every thing is too much that is bestowed on them; with *Judas* and Jeroboam we cry out, *What needs this waste?* and, *It is too much.* And with what scorn and contempt do many turn their backs against those places, and creep into corners?

The same people, when they were restrained from hearing Sermons, especially the [D6v] Sermons of some men; How did they then flock to our Congregations, as Doves to the windows? they went from strength to strength, notwithstanding the many penalties they endured: But now they have liberty to attend the same persons and places, they say, *Depart from us, we desire not the knowledge of those wayes.*

Time was when Baptisme was willingly and generally embraced by most, provided that their children might not be baptized with the signe of

the Crosse, which was then enjoyned; but now when
that offensive ceremony is removed, many of these
care not whether ever their infants be admitted
into the Church by that Sacrament or no.
    Heretofore people came most willingly and fre-
quently to the Lords Supper, provided they might
not be brought up to the Rail, at which most
stumbled, and be dispensed with as touching their
gesture; but now, when what was desired is granted,
and that burthen (that neither we nor our Fathers
were able to bear) is removed, they loath that
spirituall Manna, and ordinarily turn their backs
upon that royal feast and company.
    These people, when they were forbidden to meet
together in private, where they used to afflict
their souls before the Lord, for their owns sins,
and the evils of the times, by prayer and fasting;
and that notwithstanding the severest censures of
those in power, who [D7r] condemned such meetings as
unlawfull Conventicles; yet did meet, and that frequently, and (it is hoped) fruitfully: Now having
free liberty granted, so to assemble temselves,
seldome come together for such a purpose. Martyrs
have formerly gone more willingly to the stake to
be burned, then these to this excellent ordinance,
where their hearts may be warmed and refreshed.
    Even so, when this goverment was strongly
opposed by the State, and all hopes of enjoying it,
altogether frustrate, how did our Fore-fathers pray
for it, preach for it, dispute for it, print for
it; yea, suffer even to bonds and imprisonment for
it? Insomuch that divers lost their liberties, and
some hazarded their lives. Amongst the rest, Mr.
Udall a learned and godly Minister, was at a
generall Assizes condemned to dye for writing in
defence of it: the Story of whose Imprisonment,
Examinations, and Arraignment, I have seen: Yea, of
so high account it was with some in those days,
that the King of *Denmark* and the King of *Scots*

Chapter Two

wrote their Letters in his behalf to Queen Elizabeth, requesting that he might not suffer for that Cause: Yea, King *James* then King of *Scotland*, in a Speech of his to the Generall Assembly, told them that he blessed God the he was born in *Scotland*, and was a member of such a Church; his reason was, because the Church of *Scotland* excell'd other Churches in discipline; [D7v] *England* had true doctrine, but wanted true discipline. And now that we may enjoy it, the State in a full Parliament declaring for it, men loath and abhor it as the most tyrannical and Antichristian, and cry out, *Not him but Barabbas*, and choose rather to put their necks under any heavy yoke, then submit to this gracious discipline, formerly so much desired.

Now the God and Father of our Lord Jesus Christ advance the Kingdome of his dear Son, that he may be Governor amongst us, that he may rule in us, and reign over us; even he that is the Prince of peace, that came into the world with a *song* of peace, that going out of the world left us a legacy of peace, whose government is a government of peace, whose Ministers are Embassadors of peace; whose wayes are wayes of pleasantnesse, and all whose paths are peace. He unite our hearts together in the unity of the Spirit, with the bond of peace. That God that could find out a way to make peace betwixt himself and mankind, He that can never come too late in any danger, that can never be to seek in any straight; heal our wounds that grow so deep, repair our breaches that grow so wide: He in his good time give us one heart, and one way, that we may fear him for ever; for the good of us, and our children after us. *Amen*. [D8r]

Chap. III

What personall and private passages of Providence those are which ought to be recorded in our Journall or Diary.

THus far of our National and more publick concernments, that are to be remembred: I come now to shew what Personall and private occurences are to be recorded; And they are these five that are most observable.

1. Let every man keep a strict account of his effectual calling, and of his age in Christ; and (if it may be) set down the time when, the place where, and the person by whom he was converted.

I know every one cannot relate it, as Paul could, in all the circumstances: *It came to passe as I made my journey, and was nigh unto Damascus, about noon, suddenly there did shine from heaven a great light round about me, and I fell to the ground, and heard a voyce,* etc. But yet some can with the same Apostle say, *I was a persecuter, a blasphemer, and injurious, but I obtained mercy*: Or, with the blinde man whom Jesus cured; *One thing I know, that whereas I was blind, now* [D8v] *I see.* I was an ignorant, proud, profane person, and without God in the world, but by his grace I am that I am.

There are some questionlesse that can most punctually set down the severall circumstances of their conversion. It was a prophesie of the times under the Gospel. It shall be said of some in *Babylon* that they knew God, and this and that man was born there; and of *Zion*, this man was born in her: Yea,

the Lord himself shall count when he writeth up the
people, that this man was born there. Onesimus
could tell that *Paul* was his Father, he could tell
the time when, and the place where he was converted, for he begat him in his bonds.
    Cyprian had wont to call *Caecellius, novae
vitae parentem*, his spirituall Father. St. *Paul*
could say that *Andronicus* and *Junia* were in Christ
before him. There is a seniority amongst the
Saints. God hath his elder and his younger children. It is good to know our age In Christ.
    Polycarpus could say, Thus many yeers have I
served my Master Christ, and hitherto hath he dealt
well with me. *Remember this day*, saith *Moses* to the
Israelites. What day was that? The day that they
came out of *AEgypt*, from the House of bondage. So I
say, Remember the day wherein God took you, not
from toyling in brick and clay, but from the
slavery of sin and Satan; not from following the
sheep, as he did *David*, [E1r] whom he made a King;
but from following the world and your own unruly
lusts. You keep an account of the day wherein you
were born, and why not of the day wherein you were
born again? You remember your Marriage-dayes, and
why not much more the day on which you were married
to Christ? You have your Register-books for the
one, and why not Diurnalls for the other? Would you
be perswaded to do thus, it might provoke you to
say as sometimes *Sarah* said when *Isaac* was born,
Who would have said (that knew my age) *that Sarah
should have given children suck*? Who that knew me
in the dayes of my vanity and vilenesse, that knew
me in the School, or at the University, or when I
was an Apprentice, when my life was as full of disorder, as a toad was of poyson; who would have said
that Christ should ever have been formed in me? But
by his grace I am that I am, and God hath made me
laugh.
    Some acts of God, are acts of common pro-

vidence, and so he feeds us, and cloaths us, he
doth as much for the creatures; for he feeds the
Ravens, and cloaths the Grasse. Some acts of God,
are acts of speciall priviledge; and thus he gave
Abraham a childe in his old age, and made *David* of a
Shepherd a King. Some acts of God, are acts of
pattern; and thus he shewed mercy to *Manasseh*, and
Mary Magdalen, & *Paul*. For this cause (saith that
Apostle) *I obtained mercy, that in me first* [E1v]
*Jesus Christ might shew forth all long-suffering,
for a pattern to them that should hereafter believe
in him to life everlasting.*

    Some acts of God are acts of wonder: It is a
wonder that any soul is saved; I am sure it is a
wonder that ever God should think of me, look after
me, strive with me, wait upon me, that he might be
gracious to me; nay, it is not onely matter of
wonder now, but will be cause of admiration unto
all eternity; Who am I, and what am I, that God
hath brought me hitherto! It is the Lords doing,
and it is wonderfull in mine eyes.

    Amongst many things that *Beza* in his last Will
and Testament, gave God thanks for, this was the
first and chief, that he at the age of sixteen
yeers, had called him to the knowledge of the
Truth. Let every one that can know his age in
Christ, set down this in his Journall.

    2. Take speciall notice of all divine
assistance, and that either in the performance of
the duties that are required of us, or in bearing those
evills that are inflicted upon us.

    For the first, we know that all our sufficiency
is from God, all our fresh springs are in him, and
therefore all our full streams of prayse should run
to him. It is our sin, and should be our shame,
that though *the Oxe knows his owner, and the Asse
his Masters crib* (as the Prophet saith) that is, by
a common [E2r] instinct of Nature, they acknowledge
that as all their provision is from him, so all

their strength to draw or bear is due to him: *Yet we do not consider;* that is, we doe not so know God, as to acknowledge, that as we have all from God, so all is due to God. *He* it is that *giveth power to the faint, and to them that have no might, he encreaseth strength. But the youths shall faint and be weary, and the young men shall utterly fall.* If *David* will go out in the Name of the Lord, in the strength and by the assistance of God, he shall return a victor over the mighty Giant: But if *Goliah* will go out against *David* with a sword and a spear, trusting onely to his own strength, he shall fall. *Moses* had a great charge to go to *Pharaoh*, and to bring the people of *Israel* out of the Land of *AEgypt*; and how oft doth he through unbelief cavil at the call, as unfit for that service? seven or eight times he replyes upon God as unwilling, because unfit to go: But through Gods most gracious assistance, he finished that work to the glory of God, the confort of his people, and the shame of that proud enemy; and this is recorded. *I have fought the fight,* (saith St. *Paul*) *I have finished my course, I have kept the faith;* and this is written down in a book.

Secondly, assistance in withstanding violent temptations, in undergoing heavy burthens, and conflicting with sundry evils, should not be forgotten. There is a time [E2v] when Kings go not forth to War, but no time wherein Christians have not some combate with temptations, but God either prevents them, or assists us in them, and makes us victors over them, and gainers by them. It is written of St. *Augustine*, that after his conversion to the Faith, he was much vexed with inward conflicts; and after long struggling with them in the use of means, and not prevailing as he desired, he heard a voyce saying to him, *In te stas et non stas;* whereby apprehending, that the way to fall was to stand in his owne strength; by faith in prayer he did fly

unto God in Christ, and his free grace, and so
obtained victory.
   At my first answer (saith St. *Paul*) *no man
stood by me, all forsook me; I pray God it be not
laid to their charge. But God stood by me, and
strengthned me, and I was delivered out of the mouth of
the lion.* And indeed at such a time a gracious heart can better bear Gods stroke, then
endure his absence. St. *Paul* makes speciall mention
of this: *Faith is the gift of God*; and amongst many
singular benefits that we have by that grace, this
is not the least, It hath a singular dexterity in
helping the heart at a sudden pinch; in mustering
up spirituall, and those present forces against an
unexpected temptation. A lively faith is the best
leaver at a dead lift. See it in the case of
Joseph, fiercely and unexpectedly assaulted by his
beastly Mistris. Many arguments are brought in of a
sudden, by which [E3r] he is fenced so impregnably
against her solicitations, that he comes off more
then a conqueror.
   1. It is a sin (saith he) against the great
trust my Master hath in me, *He hath committed all
into my hand*, etc.
   2. It is a sin against my place and dignity,
There is none greater in the house then I.
   3. It is a sin against my Masters interest, *You
are his wife.*
   4. It is a wickednesse, *a great wickednesse
against God.*
   The like you shall read of *David*, who when he
was reviled by *Shimei*, with those words, *Come out
thou bloody man, thou man of Belial,* etc. which so
far provoked *Abisha*, and edged his spirit against
him, that he could hardly hold his hands; yet bare
all patiently, being armed against such an assault.
   Three arguments are suddenly mustred up by
Faith, by which he comes off with victory.
   1. My Son rebels, and he is more violent

against me. My Servant takes away my good name; my
Son would not only take the crown from my head, but
my head from my shoulders.
    2. *The Lord hath bidden him curse me*, and
therefore let him alone.
    3. The Lord will look on me, and not onely do
me good by this, but for this affliction. [E3v]
    It is good to set down every affliction we have
met with in our time, and to observe Gods carriage
towards us in them, with the benefit we receive
from them.
    4. Remember, and for that end put into your
Journal all deliverances from dangers, vouchsafed
to you or yours. And indeed, what is our whole
life, but a continued deliverance? We are daily
delivered, either from the violence of the creature, or the rage of men, or the treachery of our
own hearts; either our houses are freed from
firing, or [our] goods from plundering, or our
bodies from danger, or our names from reproaches,
or our souls from snares. This being the difference
betwixt a gracious and a gracelesse heart; a godly
man is delivered, a wicked man is but reserved. God
knows how to deliver the godly out of temptations,
and to reserve the unjust unto the day of judgement, to be punished.
    Jacob is delivered from the treachery of his
Uncle *Laban* at one time, and from the fury of his
Brother at another; both are remembred.
    David is delivered from the paw of the Bear, and
the mouth of a Lion; both of them are mentioned
before *Saul*.
    Jeremiah cannot forget the dungeon out of which
he was saved; nor *Daniel* the Lions den, out of
which he escaped; nor *Jonah* the Whales belly, out
of which he was delivered. Read their Prophesies,
and you shal [E4r] finde the stories. Mr. *Beza* in
his last Will bequeaths thanks unto God, that being
infected with the plague at *Lusanna*, and aspersed

Chapter Three

by his enemies with grievous calumnies, God
delivered him from both.

2. That being tossed up and down in the first
Civill wars of *France*, for many moneths, God had
preserved him from six hundred dangers.

Our deliverances are more then we can number,
greater then we can value. Who so is wise, and will
observe them, even they shall understand the loving
kindnesse of the Lord. Every night God setteth his
watch about us, and every day he commands his Angels
to pitch their tents for our safeguard. And alas,
what is all our care and prudence, without his
watchful eye of providence over us! *Except the Lord
keep the City, the watchman waketh but in vain.*

When *Noah* and all his train went into the Ark,
it is said the Lord shut him in. It is good to open
the dore in the morning, and to shut the dore in
the evening by prayer: pray when we open them, that
God would dwel with us; and when we lock up our
dores, that God would shut us in, otherwise we cannot be safe.

Take but a little notice of the preservation of
our children; nay, but of one childe, and you will
say that all our care is nothing without his
watchfull eye. I will give you a memorable instance
of a Childes [E4v] deliverance; who, whilest divers
in the family, with many other friends were met
together to fast and pray, went out to a pond very
much frozen, (for it was in an hard cold Winter)
either to slide, or to whip his top, I remember not
which; where two holes were made in the ice for the
safety of the fish, and the taking up of water,
into one of these he fell up to the arm-holes; the
childe was soon mist, and search being made, he was
found there: Had the hole been wider, or he not
  spread out his arms, or he not seasonably found out
(for it was about the time the company brake up) he
had perished. I was then at the house, an eye-
witnesse of that deliverance.

Another example I shall give you of a Man.
A certain *English* Captain in the Wars of
France, under *Henry* the fourth, whom Queen
Elizabeth assisted against his own subjects; being
quartered in a Town lately taken from the enemy,
carryed himself with that civility toward his Landlord, as became an ingenuous Gentleman; and yet
with that fidelity too, as suited with the honor of
his command in chief; that he won very much respect
from the Master of the family: Insomuch, that some
time after, the enemy having taken the Towne again,
beaten the Kings party, slain many, and wounded
more even unto death; at the end of the day, when
the Armyes were retired, the Townsmen [E5r] came out
to cut throats, and to take the pillage: By providence
this Landlord before mentioned, came to this Gentleman, sorely wounded, and ready to dye; whom he
bestrides, and drawing his sword protests he would
there dye, rather then his friend should suffer any
further harm: And so by the help of others, he
brought him home to his own house, where by
chirurgery and good diet, with all carefull
attendance, he recovered. This story I heard the
Gentleman relate to me and others.

Thus God creates deliverances; and indeed,
preservation from danger, is nothing else but a
continued creation. There is scarce any thing in
the wayes of God more remarkable then Deliverances.
And indeed, it is necessary that God should take
the charge of us at all times; for our dangers are
so many and great, that none are wise enough, or strong
enough to deliver us, but the Lord.

4. All the instruments, all the men and means
that God hath in providence at any time used for
our good, must not be forgotten: As,

1. What Parents we have had, how godly they
were, and how religiously tender they were of our
eternal welfare; what care they took of us, what

cost they bestowed upon us, what prayers they made
for us, what pains they took with us, in correct-
ing, in instructing us for our temporall and [E5v]
eternal good. It is a very rich priviledge to
come of godly and religious parents, to be heirs of
so many promises which they daily laid up for us,
and so many prayers that they continually made
in our behalf, is a very rich portion. The *Jews*
would often boast that *Abraham* was their Father,
and *Moses* chose rather to owne him, yea though he
suffered with his posterity, then to be called the
Son in law to *Pharaoh's* daughter, and enjoy the
pleasures of sin for a season, *Solomon* keeps an
account of this mercy: *I was my Fathers Son*; that
is, I was his darling, his beloved Son; and, *I was
tender and dear in the sight of my Mother: And thus
he taught me, and said unto me, Let thine heart
retain my words*, etc, The like honorable mention he
makes of hs Mother: *The words of King Lemuel, the
prophesie that is Mother gave him. Lemuel* is a
name given to *Solomon*, as *Mercer* observes upon the
place. He is called also *Jedidiah*, because the Lord
loved him; and here *Lemuel* by his Mother, because
she had dedicated him to the Lord.

    2. Remember what Schoolmasters we have had.
Dr. *Andrews* Bishop of *Winchester* was so thankfully affected with the care that Mr. *Mulcaster* had
of him whilest he was his Scholar, that when he
came to great preferment in the Church, he placed
his picture over his study dore.

    Mr. *Calvin* did so far acknoledge the love [E6r]
and care of *Maturinus Corderius* his Schoolmaster,
that he dedicated his Commentary upon the first
Epistle to the *Thessalonians* to him. And *Persius*
had so honorable an esteem of his Master *Cornutus*,
that he writes his fifth Satyr to him, and expres-
seth his thankfulnesse to him in very high language.

Hinc ego centenas ausim deposcere voces,

> *Ut quantum mihi te sinuoso in pectore fixi*
> *Voce traham pura, etc.*

3. What noble *Mecaenas*, what bountiful Benefactor we have had, by whose cost and kindnesse our good education hath been furthered, and our comfortable maintenance enlarged.

St. *Augustine* thankfully acknowledged that by the liberall contribution of *Romenian* a noble Gentleman, his studies in the Liberall Arts were much cherished and advanced.

4. To conclude: It will be of singular use to put into our Diary, what Times we have lived in, what Ministers we have lived under, what Callings we were of, what Wealth was bestowed on us, what places of Authority and Command were committed to us.

Plato when he was ready to dye, gave God thanks for three things:
1. That he was made a Man.
2. That he was born in *Greece*. [E6v]
3. That he lived in the time of *Socrates*.

Blesse we God, that such a Kinsman brought us up in our younger yeers, that such a Scholar was our Tutor in the University, such an one relieved us, such a friend preferr'd us.

The Lord give mercy to Onesiphorus, saith *Paul* to *Timothy, for he oft refreshed me, and was not ashamed of my chain. When he was at Rome, he sought me out diligently. The Lord grant unto him that he may finde mercy from the Lord in that day; and in how many things he ministred unto me at Ephesus, thou knowest very well.* Yea, let not the meanest or lowest instrument of our good under God be forgotten. *Who hath despised the day of small things?* Even a Raven may sometimes bring bread and meat to a poor Prophet, and a poor Widow sustain a Messenger of God. A wicked Physitian, or a drunken Chirurgeon, may instrumentally under God save our

lives. Even a cypher, as very a nothing as it is,
if joyned to 10, make it 100; if added to 100,
makes it 1000. Poor despised *David*, that stood but
as a cypher in Kings *Saul's* account, & his Brothers
judgement, in the name of the Lord slays
Goliah, and wrought a great salvation for *Israel*.
The Lord *Cromwell*, K *Henry* the Eights favourite,
did not onely remember *Friscobald* the rich
Florentine, that was so bountiful to him in his
travel; but he considered a very poor man, and gave
him maintenance to his *dying* day, whose Father had
given him many a meals meat. [E7r]

    5. And finally, mark what returns, what answers God gives to your prayers, and set them down with a *Selah*, as most remarkable pledges of his love. *Moses* did so; who having fasted and prayed for the people, who had made them a Molten-calfe, and he recieved a gracious answer; writes that down—the *Lord heard me at that time also*. It seems *Moses* took speciall notice of such answers to prayer, for he records a like passage, when God separated the Tribe of *Levi* for his service, he prayed, *and the Lord* (saith he) *heard me at that time also*.

    Hannah did so; she told *Eli* that she had received a man-childe from the Lord by prayer; *for this childe I prayed* (saith she) *and the Lord hath given me the petition I asked of him*.

    All a Christians happinesse is laid up in promises, and all those promises hang upon the pin of prayer. The prayer of faith is the great engine of the people of God, by which promises are made out into evidences; and such returns of prayer should be recorded.

    What grace Jesus Christ had either to do or suffer the will of God, he had by promise, as you may see, Isa. 11. 2,3,4. & 42. 1,2,3,4. & 61. 1,2,3,4. and the good of all those promises he fetcht out by prayer. He had a word of command as well as we, *Ask of me*; and he had a word of [E7v] promise, *and I will give thee, etc.* And he prayed very much, he spent whole nights in prayer, and was heard in what he prayed; and he takes speciall notice of it, *I knew that thou hearest me alwayes* (saith he to his Father, when he raised *Lazarus*.) *In the dayes of his flesh* (saith the Apostle) *when he had offered up prayers and supplications, with strong crying and tears to him, that was able to save him from death, and he was heard in the thing he feared*; and this is recorded. Now this God is our God, he will hear us and deliver us as he hath said. Undoubtedly if he give us an heart to pray, he will encline an ear to hear; who delights as much to grant his peoples petitions, as they can to receive his grants. As King *James* said once to a great Courtier, to whom he gave a great summe of money, I am better pleased that I can give, then you are satisfied that you may receive.

Tiberius was so in love with *Sejanus* his favourite, that he never denyed him any thing that he asked; he often prevented his asking by his bounty: But our God is so willing to grant our desires, that he doth not onely give us what we ask, but more then we ask, nay more then we should ask, more then we can ask or think, and that exceeding abundantly.

Give us this day our daily bread, is the rule by which we are directed to ask for necessary and convenient comforts; and certainly, [E8r] what we may not labour for, we may not pray for; but we must not labour to be *rich*.

Now though Nature is content with little, Grace with lesse, yet God is so bountifull as to afford us exceedings; *he will fill our hearts with food and gladnesse:* He will give us not onely a house to dwell in, but a stately one; not onely a coat to cover us, but a costly one; not onely a table to

Chapter Three 69

sit at, but a table well spread, and a cup running
over, and that in the sight of our enemies; which
is more then we should ask for.
   So high was *Roger* Bishop of *Salisbury* in favour
5   with King *Stephen*, that he would say of him, Let
that man beg of me what he will, I will grant him,
though it be half of the Kingdome; and sooner shal
he be weary of asking, then I shall be of giving.
   God will give in mercy, as long as we ask in faith.
10   When Sir *Walter Raleigh* asked a favour of Q
Elizabeth, she said to him, *Raleigh, when will you
leave your begging?* he answered, *When your Majesty
leaves giving.* God is much more bountifull; who did
not give over granting *Abraham* his requests for
15   *Sodome*, till he left asking; and who can tell, but
that if he had gone on, and prayed that if five
persons that were righteous had been found in
Sodome, the City might have been spared for their
sakes, according to his request? Can we think that
20   God will hear [E8v] the young Ravens when they cry,
and neglect the Doves that mourn in the valleys?
That he will hear the young Lions when they roar,
and forget the Lambs that bleat after Sheep?
That he will hear *Hagar* and her *Ismael*, varlets and
25   vile ones, that cry unto him in their extremities;
and will he turn his back upon the tears, or stop
his ear to the prayers of his owne children that
cry unto him daily, in the name of Jesus Christ?
Undoubtedly he cannot. St. *Ambrose* was wont to say,
30   the better to comfort *Monica* St. *Austin's* Mother,
who prayed often for him, even with tears, *Impos-
sibile est ut filius istarum lachrymarum periret,*
It is impossible that a Son of so many tears should
perish. As long therefore as God gives us an heart
35   to pray for any mercy, let us not be out of heart.
And why so? Because then we beg no more but what
God hath commanded us to ask, and we ask no more
then what he hath promised to give, and he hath
promised no more but what he is able to perform,

and he shall perform no more but what he shall have glory for, and we know his glory is dear to him.

Let me therefore advise every believing soul to be much in prayer, and with the *Psalmist* to hearken what the Lord will speak, for *he will speak peace unto his people*. And what returns of those prayers they meet with. If they can say, for this Wife I prayed, for this Childe, this deliverance, [F1r] this successe I prayed, and the Lord has granted me the request I put up unto him. Let such experiments be put upon this account, with a *Selah*.

Chap. IV

*The manner how a Journall or Diary is to be used, and
first what is to be done by way of observation.*

THus far of the materials whereof a Journall may be
compounded: Now in the next place I shall speak of the
manner how such a Journall is to be used. And here in
two things would be commended to the Christian Reader.
    1. Rules of Observation: And,
    2. Rules of Practice.
For observation take notice of these three Rules:
    1. Labour by faith to see and observe God in all
things that are bestowed on you, continued to you;
say as *Elisha, Here is the mantle, but where is the
God of Elisha*? Here is health, and peace, and
liberty; but where is the God of these comforts?
The Name of God; that is, the wisdome of God, the
power and faithfulnesse of God, is written
[F1v] upon every spire of grasse, upon every drop
of rain, in such great letters, that he that runs
may read. Let the same minde be in us that was in
Jacob, the Israel of God, who when he told his
Wives his resolution to leave his Uncle *Laban*,
useth this language, *God hath taken away your
Fathers cattle, and given them to me.* And when he
met with his brother *Esau*, who asked him of the
children whose they were; he answered, *they are the
children which God of his grace hath given me.* At
the same time urging his Brother to accept the
blessing that he had sent him, he useth this argument,
*I have seen thy face, as though I had seen
the face of God.* And again, *Take what is brought
thee, because God hath dealt graciously with me.*
He that cannot see God in a judgement, will never
be truely humble; and he that cannot see God in a

mercy, can never be truely thankfull. Check your
selves therefore often for this neglect, as this
Jacob did, who when in his journey to *Laban* he had
in a vision a sight of a Ladder, whose foot stood
on the earth, and whose top did reach to heaven,
and the Angels of God were ascending & descending
upon it, and the Lord stood above it: All which was
a lively discovery of Gods provident care of him;
said, *God was in this place, and I knew it not.* So
say you, God was in this friend that relieved me,
in this ordinance that refreshed me, in this creature that comforted me, and I observed him not.
There are none of the [F2r] wayes of God, wherein
he useth either the ministery of Angels, or the
wisdome of men, or the strength of any creature;
but God is at the top of the Ladder, and orders
all, though we observe him not.

    We may by an eye of reason see a man in his
works, though his person be not present: As, when
we see a piece of ground well ploughed, the fences
well made, the cattle well ordered, we say, Here is
a good Husband, though we do not see the Farmer:
When we see a house built very well, and every room
well contrived, we say, Here is a good Work-man,
though we do not see the Carpenter. And may we not
as well by an eye of faith behold the wisdome,
goodnesse, and power of God in his works, though he
be invisible. Say you therefore, Here is so much of
the prudence of a Prince, so much of the policy of
a State, so much of the valour and faithfulnesse of
a Governour; but how much do you observe of God,
who rules the hearts and wayes of all men? Here is
so much of the cost of a Father, so much of the
affection of a Mother, so much of the faithfulnesse
of a Friend, but how much of the mercy and wisdome
of God?

    A great Cardinall (that I have read of) writing
down in his Diary what such a Lord did for him, how
far such a Prince favoured him, what incouragement

Chapter Four

he had from such a King, and how such a Pope [F2v]
preferr'd him, but not a word of God; one reading
of it, said, This man remembred his friends, but
forgat God. Like another *Haman*, who when he told
his friends, and *Zeresh* his Wife, of the glory of
his riches, and the multitude of his children, and
all the things wherein the King had promoted him,
who had advanced him above all the Princes and Servants at the Court, and what honor Queen *Esther* did
him, who invited him onely with the King to the
banquet, never made any mention of God. Do you
rather as *David*, who when he had told King Saul how
he had slain the Lion and the Bear, said moreover,
The Lord that delivered me, etc. He comes over with
it again, rather then not mention the Name of the
Lord, and let *Saul* know he observed Gods great
power in that victory.

All the letters in the Alphabet, without a vowel,
will not make one word; nor all the stars in
the firmament, without the Sun, will make a day;
nor all the world, the profits of it, or pleasures
in it, can make a man happy without God.

The *Jews* (some say) when they read the Book
Esther, let the book fall on the ground, and they
give this reason for that ceremony, though they
esteem it a Canonicall piece of Scripture, yet
they somewhat undervalue it, because the word of
God is not found in all the Story. Though a man
have as much health, strength and beauty [F3r] as
Nature can afford him; and to that as much wealth,
honor, and friends, as the world can bring him; and
to all these as much learning as Tutors can put
into him; yet if he be a man without God, he falls in
the thoughts and estimation of such as are
spirituall, and can discern him, though they may
acknowledge him a very discerning man.

2. Labour by faith to see and observe all these
good things in God. For as *omnia mala* may be seen
in summo malo: All evils in the world may be seen

in sin, the chief evil; as blindnesse, nakednesse,
poverty, death, hell; for he that is ignorant, is
blind indeed; he that is without God, is naked
indeed; he that hath no grace, is very poor; he
that is dead in sins and trespasses, is truely
dead; he that is under the power of sin, and given
up wholly to his hearts lusts, is in an hell above
ground. So *omnia bona* are *in summo bono,* all good
things are in God the chiefest good. All creatures
may be seen in the Creator, as all the stars may be
seen in the sun. So the Apostle thought, who called
God the God of all comfort. Honor is not the God of
comfort, nor liberty, nor health, or wealth; nor
hath honor the comfort of liberty, nor liberty the
comfort of health, nor health the comfort of children or wealth, etc. But the comfort of all these
may be found in God. Hence he is called *our Son. He
will be a Sun and a shield to those* [F3v] *that walk
uprightly.* The light and comfort of all these
things may be found in God, as the light of all the
stars may be seen in the Sun: As a Sun he gives
all the light, so as a shield he gives all the protection to all men, and means of our good: The
shield in ancient times (to which the holy Ghost
seems, as some think, to allude) was made so big,
as it covered the whole man, and all his armour; as
appears by that speech of *Ajax,* to or of *Ulysses,*
when he contended him about the armour of *Achilles*:
    Opposui molem clypei, texique jacentem.
In his flight he came to me, and I covered him with
my shield, and so saved his life. So I say, as a
Sun and shield all comfort is from him. Hence he
that can call the Lord his God, may call God any
thing that at any time he stands in need of. As
David sometimes did, whilest compassed about with
many enemies. *The Lord is my rock, and my
fortresse, my deliverer, my high tower, my buckler;*
and why so? He *is my God,* and in that all. If he be
my God (saith a believer) he is my Father, and no

Chapter Four 75

father like him for affection; if my God, my
Friend, and no friend like him for faithfulnesse;
my Physician, and none like him for skill; nay, my
Bed-maker, and none can make my bed so easie as he.
5   So that if we lose the comfort of any creature; as
the comfort of a wife by death, of health by
sicknesse, of liberty by a prison, of wealth [F4r]
by poverty; they may all be found in a God; who is
health in sicknesse, liberty in prison; yea, all
10   things in the want of all. He that is the *Alpha* and
Omega hath said it, *He that overcometh shall
inherit all things*: But how shall that be? *I will
be* (saith the Lord) *his God, and he shall be my
Son*. All comfort is divided amongst the creatures,
15   as by severall channels, but united in God as the
fountain.

    The King of *Bohemia* (as some have reported) when
he was beaten out of *Prague*, and therefore almost
out of all in that Kingdome, was encouraged by some
20   great Commanders about him, that he had many
Princes his friends and Allies, that were potent,
and would readily assist him; to which he made no
answer, but wrote the word *DEUS* in great letters;
implying thereby, that all these must be found in
25   God, or they could do him no good; whence some
pickt out his meaning, and found *Denmark* in *D*,
England in *E*, *Hungary* in *U*, and the *Swedes* in *S*.

    But I have read that *Herod* in a speech that he
made in the head of his Army that was ready to joyn
30   battle with the enemy, the better to encourage his
Souldiers, had this passage: *Where justice is, God
is; and where God is, there is no want of men or
fortitude*. God is a perfect good, as well as a
solid good. *Id bonum perfectum dicitur* (saith *Lac-*
35   *tantius*) *cui nil accedere, solidum cui nil decedere
potest*: [F4v] That is a perfect good, to which
nothing can be added; that a solid, from which
nothing can be spared. Hence it is, that God in
wisdom and mercy plucks these stools from under us,

that we sit so securely upon, that we may look up
to him, and finde that comfort in him that we lost
in them. When *David's* Captains and Commanders,
that so long had stuck so close to him, spake of stoning
him, he comforted himselfe in his God. When *Habbakuk*
could finde no blossome in the fig-tree, nor fruit
in the vines; when he could finde nothing in the
fold, nor in the field, nor in the stall; yet he
would *rejoyce in the Lord and joy in the God of his
salvation*; because all might be found in a God.
When *Micah* looked upon the miserable face of the
Time in which he lived, wherein there was scarce a
good man to be found, nor a friend to be had, the
best was but as a bryar, and a mans enemies were
those of his owne house; so that neither the childe
of a mans loyns, nor the wife that lay in his
bosome were to be trusted; he resolves to look up
to God. *Therefore I will look unto the Lord, I will
wait for the God of my salvation, there I shall
finde all comfort.* How happy is he then that hath
the Lord for his God! He is one of St. *Paul's* rich
men, *as having nothing, yet possessing all things*.
So that I shall conclude this passage with that of
the Prophet, *Let not the wise man glory in his wisdome, neither let the mighty man glory in his
strength, nor the rich man in his [F5r] riches, but
let him that gloryeth, glory in this, that he
knoweth me*, etc. Not the wise man in his wisdome,
Satan is wiser then he, and yet a Devill; nor the
strong man in his strength, for the Horse is
stronger then he, and yet a Beast; nor the rich man
in his wealth, the Earth is richer then he, and yet
he treads upon it every day; *but let him that
gloryeth, glory in this, that he knoweth the Lord
to be his God. Happy is the people that is in such
a case* (saith the Psalmist) *yea, happy is that
people that hath the Lord for their God*. That any of
us have the cap and the knee from our
inferiours, is our priviledge, but not our happi-

Chapter Four

ness; that any of us have the uppermost seat in the
Church, or chiefest room at a feast, is our honor,
but not our happinesse; that any of us eat the fat,
and drink the sweet, when others eat ashes as
bread, and mingle their drink with their tears, is
our comfort, but not our happinesse; *but happy is
that people that is in such a case; yea, happy is
that soul that can say, The Lord is my God.*

Thirdly, observe well the *mediums*, the choyce
wayes and means by which all good things are conveyed to us. It is good to know how we come by what
we have.

These three wayes take speciall notice of as
most observable. All good things come to us:
1. By Christ, savingly.
2. By the promise, certainly.
3. By the creatures, sensibly. [F5v]

1. Observe how all good things come in by Jesus
Christ savingly. God gives all good things to his
through Jesus Christ. *If God spared not his owne
Son, but delivered him up for us all, how shall he
not with him also freely give us all things?* Peace
with him, and liberty, and riches, and honor with
him, are a good portion indeed. *All things are
yours*, saith the Apostle to the *Corinthians, Paul
and Apollos, things present and things to come,
etc.* But how come they in? *Ye are Christs* (saith
the Apostle) *and Christ is Gods.* All comes to us by
Jesus Christ, as all the corn in *AEgypt* came
through *Joseph's* fingers, so all comforts come to
us by Jesus Christ, who is our Mediatour; who hath
not onely by his blood purchased all things for us,
but sanctified all to us; he turns our waters into
wine, and makes our bitter waters sweet. Hence as
all our duties are presented from us to God by
Jesus Christ, and therefore are accepted; so all
things are conveyed to us from God by Jesus Christ,
and so are sanctified. Christ is not onely our
Mediator, but our Husband also, and so we enjoy all

good things with him and by him; we have conjugal
communion with him; so that we may say as *Hamor* and
Sechem said to their people (the better to perswade
them to be circumcised, and to marry into *Jacob's*
family) *Shall not all their cattle, and substance,
and every beast of the field be ours*? So, if we be
married to Jesus [F6r] Christ, and become one with
him, shall not all be ours through him who is heir
of all? Not onely his wisdome to inlighten us, and
his power to uphold us, but the world to supply us;
so that if this Husband of ours be honorable, we
cannot be mean; if he be rich, we cannot be poor;
and so a little with him is a great portion, when
the whole world without him is nothing. Hence
the Saints of God, out of their love to Jesus
Christ, do use to set Jesus Christ above all; *his
name* also *shall be above every name*. Princes in
their Proclamations, Charters, and Grants, set
their names in the beginning, on the top, as *James
by the grace of God King of England, etc*. Subjects
do always use to subscribe their names to their
Wills, Letters, Leases in the bottome: Both the Old
Testament and the New, wherein the Will of God is
contained, have the name of God set down in the
beginning, as *In the beginning God created*, etc.
Gen. 1.1. *In the beginning was the Word, and the
Word was with God, and the Word was God*, Joh, 1.1.
It is good to set Jesus Christ above all, for he is
the *summa totalis* of all our comforts. The *Grecians*
set the *summa totalis* of their bills of accompt in
the top of the page, as we do in the bottome.
Christ and riches, Christ and honors, Christ and
liberty is the totall sum of all we enjoy. Let us
make Jesus Christ our *Generalissimo*, Commander in
chief, Primate, Supreme, All in all, set him above
all. [F6v]

    1. Above all comforts and outward contents.
Like those brave *Germane* Ladies in a siege; who
when the Emperor at the surrender of the Town gave

them liberty to carry with them what they could, but excepted the men, who were to stand to his mercy; left all their gold and silver, with their rich jewels, and took up their Husbands, and carryed them out with them. Let us leave all, so we may enjoy Christ. *Let Ziba have all* (saith *Mephibosheth* to *David*) *so that the King return.* Let the men of the world have all the wealth, though we be impoverished; let them have all the honour and friends, though we be disgraced and forsaken, so Jesus Christ may rule in us, and rejoyce over us, and be all in all to us.

2. Set Jesus Christ above all the men and means of any good. Men are apt to make idols of such as have been instruments of their outward peace and happinesse: Christ will admit of no corrivals, he will be all or none. When *Tiberius* the Emperour of *Rome* sent to the Senate, and required that the Image of Christ might be set up in the Capitoll, they returned this answer from their Priests, that if he were set up, all the other Images of their gods must down; if Jesus Christ be set up, all our Idols must fall, our Dagons will fall before the Ark.

3. Set Jesus Christ above all your duties, parts, gifts, and abilities. Your selfishnesse [F7r] proves often your greatest prejudice. Like the viper in *Paul's* bundle of sticks, which he brought in to make a fire and warm his fingers with, would sting you to death, did not God in mercy prevent the mischief. If you compose your selves with such sparks, you shall lie down in sorrow, if God be not more gracious to you. In all your duties therefore it is best to do as *Joab* did, when he had won *Rabbah*, he sent to *David* to take the Crown; and good reason, for all the men and means, the money and ammunition were *David's*. So here, all your sufficiency is from Christ, *you can do all things through Christ that strengthens you.* Let

him therefore go away with the Crown. Be not like
proud *Haman*, whom nothing could content, but the
royall apparell, the royall horse and crown. Christ
will part with any thing to you but his crown, but
his glory; take heed of usurping that. What part or
member of the body soever is used in getting the victory,
by the consent of all the head is crowned:
However you speed, let Christ have the crown.
    When *Caesar* and *Bibulus* were Consuls, *Caesar* did
all, *Bibulus* did nothing, being overawed by *Caesar*:
whereupon the Wits of *Rome* would in jest subscribe
their Letters, *Julio & Caesare consulibus*: Do you so, if
through the grace of Christ you can bear
afflictions patiently, perform duties fruitfully,
pray with heart, confesse with sorrow, [F7v] beg
with life, hear with fruit, say, we can do all
things by Jesus Christ assisting us.
    2. Observe how all good things are bestowed
upon you, continued to you, by the Promise
certainly. All providences to a gracious heart, are
but as so many fulfillings of promises. Carnall men
have nothing but by common providence; but whatever
this man hath, he enjoys by speciall promise; so
that his peace is the peace of promise, his liberty
the liberty of promise, his deliverance the
deliverance of promise. Labor therefore to see
every comfort you have noted in your Journal, conveyed to you in and by a promise. Thus did *Joshua*,
who when the people were setled in the Land of
Canaan told them, that they knew in their hearts
and souls, that not one thing had failed of all the
good things which the Lord their God had spake concerning them, all was come to passe. It is good to
observe how Gods judgements are executed upon
transgressors, according to his Word, and to say as
Jehu did, when the fiercenesse of Gods wrath was
poured out upon *Ahab* and *Jezebel*, *This is the bur-*
then that the Lord laid upon him, and this is the
word of the Lord that he spake by Elijah the Tish-

Chapter Four

bite. When we see Adulterers brought to shame, and
a morsel of bread, say, This is according to the
Word of the Lord, who hath said, *Whoremongers and
adulterers God will judge*. When ye see swearers,
and blasphemers, and perjured [F8r] persons,
punished with a stroke from heaven, say, This day
is this Scripture fulfilled in our eyes, *God will
not hold them guiltlesse that take his name in
vain*. But it is far more comfortable to see all
good things bestowed according to a promise, and to
be able to say as *David, Thou hast dealt well with
thy servant, O Lord, according to thy Word*. So did
Solomon, when he sate upon the throne of his Father
David, *Blessed be the Lord God of Israel who hath
fulfilled with his hand that which he spake with
his mouth*. And again in the same prayer, *The Lord
hath performed his word that he hath spoken, for I
am risen up in the room of my Father David, and am
set on the throne of Israel, as the Lord hath
promised*. We talk much of Providences, and indeed
we are apt to make Providences, to serve our turns;
as *Jonah*, though a Prophet, and a good man, when he
was sent to *Nineveh*, and not willing to go upon
that Embassage, but to *Joppa*, and finding a ship
going to *Tarshish*, Oh surely (thought he) here's a
providence, God would have me now go rather to
Tarshish, so providence leads me; and indeed this
is a great part of the Religion of our time, here
was a providence, and there was a providence; yea,
a continued *series* of providentiall actings: but no
man asks, Where is the Precept requiring, or
the Promise encouraging? He that walks by common
providence, without a speciall Precept to guide
him, or singular Promise to comfort him, walks by a
dark [F8v] Lanthorn, and will finde that his successes will prove but pitfalls in the conclusion,
and will fall short of an happy issue; according to
that saying:
      ------*Careat successibus opto*

Quisquis ab eventu facta notando putat.
But let every wise man observe how his successefull proceedings are fruits of a Promise. So did the Virgin *Mary; God hath holpen his servant Israel in remembrance of his mercy, as he spake to our Forefathers, Abraham and his seed forever.* So did Zachariah; *God hath raised up for us a horn of salvation in the house of his servant David, as he spake by the mouth of his holy Prophets, that we should be saved from our enemies, and from the hands of all that hate us; to perform the mercy promised to our Fathers, and to remember his holy convenant.* Go you, and do likewise; see how Promises run out into Providences. As, when we see a sincere course of life blessed; say, This is according to Gods Word, who hath said, *No good thing shall be wanting to them that walk uprightly.* When you see the children of honest godly parents prosper, you may see the promise that day fulfilled, which saith, *The righteous walks in his integrity, and his children are blessed after him.*

    Now that we may do this, that we may the better discern in what channel, by what promise such a comfort flowes in to us, [G1r] foure things would be skilfully attended:

    1. Endevour to sort the promises, and to know their several kinds. Some are absolute, some conditionall; some are generall, some are particular, made to some persons; some for this life, some for the life to come. *Godlinesse* (saith the Apostle) *hath the promises of this life, and of that which is to come.* Some promises are encouragements, as 1 Cor.5.20. Some are comforts, as 1 Cor.10.13. Some bring rewards, as Psal.84.11. Some contain priviledges, as Joh.1.12. Tradesmen sort their commodities, by which they live; so should believers promises to which they trust, and from which they have all.

    2. Be sure you understand the language of the

Chapter Four

Promise. Take heed that the Promise give not an
uncertain sound, nor let the promise be a *Barbarian*
to you. Let the promise be cleered to you. Christ
was very near to *Mary Magdalen*, when he appeared to
her after his resurrection, but she thought he had
been the Gardener.
   As for example:
   Touch no unclean thing, and I will receive you.
This promise is neer to us, but few understand what
it saith. *Touch not;* that is, be not married to
your lusts, be not wedded to your wills, but be
divorced from every evill way: Scripture is the
best interpreter of Scripture, another text will
open it: *It is not good* (saith the Apostle) *as the
case* [G1v] *standeth, for a man to touch a woman;*
that is, to be married.
Take another instance:
   *He that confesseth and forsaketh his sins shall
   have mercy;* that is, he that forsaketh his sins, as
the young married woman leaves her Father and
Mother, and is joyned to her Husband; that is, she
leaves them in regard of communion with him, for
she must now live with her Husband, in regard of
subjection to them; for *her desires must be subject
to her Husband, and he must rule over her*: So the
soul leaves his sin in regard of communion with it,
subjection to it, as formerly; and now saith to
Christ, as Paul did when converted, *What wilt thou
have me do*? How few understand the language of that
promise, Heb.13.5. *I will never leave thee nor forsake thee*? Where there are five negatives in the
Originall, ὀν μὴ σε ἀνῶ οὐδ οὐ μήοε ἐγκαταλίπω.
I will never never never never never leave thee.
With the *Latines* two negatives do more strongly
affirm, with the *Grecians* they do more firmly deny.
That you may thus understand the language of the
promise; *Let the word of Christ dwell plentifully
with you;* nay, *in you, in all wisdome.* The good
word of the Lord should be your *Vade mecum,* your

companion, you should have the promise alwayes
with you, as *Saul* his spear and his cruse of water
at his beds head. Let it lead you walking, watch
with [G2r] you sleeping, talk with you waking. By
this means it will be cleared to you.

3. Endevour to understand well the extent of
Promises, their latitude, and what their boundaries
are; that is, know how much they dish out unto
you, how far they will go with you: If the promise
will go but a mile, do not compel it to go twain:
Some promises are made to particular persons, and
will not reach you, as the promise to *Abraham* of a
childe in his old age. Sometimes a particular promise will go farther, as that to *Joshua*, *I will
never leave thee nor forsake thee.* Which St. *Paul*
makes use of as a good motive to young married persons to take heed of covetousnesse, and be content;
*For he hath said, I will never leave thee, nor forsake thee. No good thing shall be wanting to those
that walk uprightly,* is a promise that must be considered with boundaries and limits. This shall be
fulfilled in Gods time, in Gods measure, after his
manner, and by his means, and according to your
capacity, *secundum modum recipientis*; the head is
more capable of blood and spirits then the little
finger, a Pottle-pot will hold more then a Pinte:
Some man can use abundance of honor and wealth,
better then you can (it may be) a low and mean condition.

4. Be skilfull in the method of applying
promises. A methodicall way is a successfull way.
Therefore, be sure you make good [G2v] the main
promise, and then the rest will follow: *I will be
thy God,* is the main promise, the summe of a all
promises. Can you say as *David, Thou art my God?*
You may say then, *The Lord is my rock, my
fortresse, my deliverer.* Can you say as the Psalmist, *I am thine?* You may then say, *Save me,
sanctifie me, deliver me, provide for me according*

Chapter Four

to thy Word. God that by promise hath given us his
Son, cannot but fulfill every promise to us
according to our necessity. There can be no limit
in that love, no bound nor bottome in that bounty.
If *Pharoah* will give *Jacob* and his family *Goshen*,
the best of all the Land of *AEgypt*, to dwell in, he
will provide for them wagons and victuals for the
way. If you be justified by the death of Christ,
you shall certainly be saved by his life. So the
Apostle argues. Primitive acts of Gods grace, are
engaging acts; there was no reason that a sinner
should be justified, but there is a great deal of
reason that a justified person should be saved; if
God will take you as his owne, he is bound to make
you as his own for ever.

3. Observe how all those good things mentioned
in your Journall, are dispensed to you by the creatures sensibly. There is a vast and and infinite distance betwixt God and man, majesty and meannesse,
and therefore we enjoy him, and receive good from
him by men and means. All things both in heaven and
earth are at his command. All [G3r] creatures are
his, and for our service; not onely the cattle of a
thousand hills are his, but the strength of those
hills are his also. In all which observe Gods wisdome and goodnesse in this threefold choyce.

1. His wisdome and goodnesse in the choyce of
the instruments. Why this man, and that means,
rather then any other? God often chooseth where man
leaves, and leaves where man chooseth. He is wiser
then the wisest, and better then the best. Of all
the Sons of *Jacob*, who would have thought of
Joseph, the youngest, and sold by his Brethen;
that he should have proved the instrument of pre-
serving his Father and his family from perishing in
the famine, and providing for them a dwelling place
in the Land of *AEgypt*? And yet God made choyce of
him. Amongst all the Sons of *Jesse*, even *Samuel* the
Seer would not have chosen *David*, the youngest, and

the least regarded, and therefore set to keep the
sheep, to be the man whom God would anoint amongst
his Brethren, to be King of *Israel*: And yet God
made choyce of him, and leaves *Eliab*, and *Shammah*,
and *Abinadab*, though proper persons, great
Souldiers, and prime Courtiers. When this *David* was
sent by his Father into the Camp to visit his
Brethren, none would have judged him a fit man to
encounter with *Goliah*, yea even *Saul* himself could
not believe it; *Thou art not able* (saith he) *to go
out against this* [G3v] *Philistine, to fight with
him; for thou art but a youth, and he is a man of
war from his youth.* And yet God chose him as the
man that should slay that Giant, and save *Israel*
that day. *Jethro* a *Midianite* shall give good
counsel to *Moses*, and *Gideon* shall be fetcht from
the threshing floor, and made Captain Generall over
all the forces of *Israel*; he shall save them from
the hands of the *Midianites*, and that with three
hundred men alone. This God doth, not onely to magnifie his power and wisdome, whose wayes and
thoughts are above ours, past finding out; often
secret, but allwayes just; but to check the haughty
thoughts of proud man, who is ready to limit the
holy one of *Israel*, and to conclude, that if God go
not his way to work, that cannot be effected, which
is promised and expected.

 It was the fault of good *Melancthon*, though a
man of excellent parts, and very serviceable for
Christs cause, who was extreme pensive, for fear of
some sad issues of the great meeting at *Auspurge*;
who though very humble, yet had this pride; his
projects must like the counsels of God unerringly
and unchangeably stand, or the cause was lost;
whereupon *Luther* wished *Spalatinus* his friend to
exhort him, yea charge him in his name, *Ne fiat
Deus*, that he make not himself a god.

 It was (as some have observed) the proud humour
of *Ferdinand Alvares* Duke *de Alva*, to neglect the

advice of others, if beneath him, though never so
good; and would [G4r] rather stumble then beware of
that block that another had warned him of, because
he scorned the instrument. Such an one was
Cardinall *Matheo Langi* Archbishop of *Saltzburg*, who
at the Diet of *Ausburg* confessed that the reformation of the Masse was needful, that liberty of
meats was convenient, but that *Luther* a poor Monk
should reform all, and tell them what was to be
done, must not be endured. But he that walks much
with God, and observes him in the wayes of his providence, shall in his owne experience finde that he
receiveth least from those from whom in reason he
might expect most, and most oftentimes from those
from whom he could expect nothing. Even the
AEgyptians shall favour the *Israelites*, and lend
them jewels of silver and gold for their better
accommodation in their journey. It was the Lord
indeed that gave them favour in the eyes even of
their enemies. The very Ravens in a famin shall
bring *Elijah* food morning and evening; and when
that means fails, a poor Widow shall provide for him,
when never a Prince nor noble Lord in *Israel*
did bear so much love to the Prophet, as to sustain
him in that extremity. *Ebedmelech* the *AEthiopian* is
very kinde to *Jeremiah*, and through his interest
with the King, works out his inlargement: When his
own Countrey-men cast him into the dungeon,
Nebuzaradan by the commandment of *Nebuchadnezzar*,
[G4v] King of *Babylon*, delivers *Jeremy* out of
prison, & gives him liberty to go whither he
please, when *Zedekiah* his own King shuts him up in
prison. It is an excellent rule, therefore I wish
all that fear God to observe it. Use means, love
prayer, and trust God; which was well implyed in
that embleme of some Heathens: A man with his hand
on the plow, but his eye in heaven. *There is no
restraint with God*, saith *Jonathan* to his Armour-
bearer. If there be many means, God must blesse

them; if but few means, he can multiply them; if
they be contrary means, he can use them; if there
be no means, he can create then, or work
without them: He it is that appoints all means of
our good: He gives virtue to those means that he
appoints, he draws out of that virtue that he gives,
he blesseth that virtue that he draws out, and by
the finger of his providence points us to the use
of those means that he will blesse; and in the want
of all will work wonderfully for our good. In the
Creation, God had light without Sun, Moon, or
Stars. He made the earth fruitful, and caused
every plant to flourish when there was no rain, nor
any man to till the ground, and could finde out an
help for *Adam* that was most meet, though he could
not.

    2. Observe Gods goodnesse in the choyce of the
time. As God doth all things well, so he doth all
at the best time. The greatest things that God hath
done in the [G5r] world, he hath done fo r his Church;
and the greatest things that God hath done for his
Church, he hath done as by the most unlikely instruments, so at the most unlikely time; yet those
instruments were the best instruments, and that time
the best time. The *AEgyptians* had wont to picture Time
with three heads. *Time past* with the head of a greedy
wolfe, as one that had devoured much time. *Time
present* with the head of a crowned Lion, triumphing
in the enjoyment of the present time. *Time to come*
with the head of a dog, fawninng on that which is to
come. But all our times are in Gods hands (and in better hands they cannot be) our time to come into
trouble, our time to continue in trouble, and our
time to come out of trouble, is at his dispose. God
seldome comes at our time, always at his owne. And
if deliverance from dangers, successe in our
endevours, supply of our wants had come sooner or
later, it had not been so good for us. Christ is
said to be sent at the fulnesse of time, or at the

Chapter Four

full time; so called, because it was just at that time
that God had designed. *Moses* was sent to deliver
Israel out of *AEgypt*, at the full time, though the
tale of bricks were doubled, and their burthens
encreased; and at the end of 430 years, even the
self-same day as it was promised, it came to passe
that all the hosts of the Lord went out for the
Land of *AEgypt*. Christ came to his [G5v] Disciples
when they were distressed by a storm at Sea, in the
best time, though it were at the fourth Watch in
the night, and they most in danger. Our extremity
is Gods opportunity to magnifie his wisdome and
goodnesse to us; when we are worst, God is ever
best; when we are at our wits end, then he makes
the storm a calm, and brings us to our desired
haven. When we know not what to do, he knows how to
deliver.

   Three persons Christ is said in the Gospel to have
raised from the dead; one was dead, but not carryed
out, and that was *Jairus* his daughter. A second was
dead, and carried out, and that was the widows Son of
Naim. A third was dead, and carried out, and
buried in the grave, where he had lyen foure days,
so that he began to stink, and that was *Lazarus*.
All these he raised at his owne time, and that the
best time. He works as wonderfully in raising con-
verts from the grave of sin. Some are dead, but not
carried out; these are civill persons, who are dead
in sin, but more modest and moderate, whose disor-
ders are not so notorious, and in the publick view
of the world; if they are drunk, they are drunk in
the night. Some are dead and carried out; these
with *Absalom* will play their pranks on the house
top, that are almost in all evill in the midst of
the congregation and assembly. Some are dead,
carried out, and [G6r] buried; whose filthy lives
stink in the nostrils of God and men. And yet when
Gods time is come, if he speak but the word only,
Lazarus come forth, they shall live in his sight.

Even *Manasseh* the bloody, and *Mary Magdalen* the
filthy, and *Paul* the persecuter, shall be converted.
    In all our tribulations, both Nationall and Per-
sonall, it is good to wait on God; who can and will
at his owne time deliver our persons from trouble,
and our Nation from the grave of sorrow; yea, even
when our bones are dead and dry, and scattered;
he can then prophesie over us, and cause a gracious
resurrection, but *we must wait till his time come,*
as the eyes of servants upon their Masters, until he
have mercy upon us. We are all for the time present,
we would all be Masters, no servants. *Wilt thou now*
(say the Disciples to our Saviour after his resurrection) *restore the Kingdome to Israel?* Who answered them, *It is not for you to know the times and*
seasons that the Father hath put in his owne power.
And it is good to wait:
    1. It is *bonum honorandum,* an honorable good.
Happy are these thy servants (saith *Sheba's* Queen)
that stand continually before thee, O King Solomon.
But a greater then *Solomon* is here.
    2. It is *bonum utile,* a profitable good. The
longer we wait, the better we speed. *Abraham* waited
long for a Son, *Hanna* waited long for a childe; so
did *Zachary* and *Elizabeth,* [G6v] and had they not
all a most gracious issue?
    When two Monkes came to King *Will. Rufus,* to buy
an Abbots place, and endevoured to out-bid each
other; a third Monk that came to wait on them, was
asked what he would give, and answered, Not a
penny, I came to wait on him that shal have the
place: upon which he gave the waiter the place.
    3. It is *bonum jucundum,* a pleasant thing to
wait: For all Gods wayes are wayes of pleasantnesse, and all his paths are peace.
    4. It is *bonum aequum*: It is most just that we
should wait upon that God that would wait upon us,
that he might be gracious unto us.
    Some Historians have made this difference

betwixt *Charls* King of *Sicily*, and *Fabius* the *Romane* Generall; the first staid till the opportunity was past, and so lost all; the second waited till the time came, & *cunctando restiuit rem*, by waiting the fittest season, he restored the Common-wealth to her former beauty. *I had fainted* (saith the Psalmist) *unlesse I had believed to see the goodnesse of the Lord in the land of the living.* But he adds by way of advice to others, *Wait on the Lord, be of good courage, and he shall strengthen thy heart. Wait I say on the Lord.* Waiting is nothing else but faith and patience and hope lengthened out to Gods time.

3. Observe Gods wisdome and goodnesse to you in the choyce of the [G7r] measure; just so much comfort in the creature, and no more. He it is that gives us our daily bread, that feeds us with convenient food, that is, an allowance fitted to our size and stature, a proportion suitable to our condition. A crust of Gods carving is better then a banquet of our owne providing. I am sure that is true that the Psalmist hath taught us, *A little that a righteous man hath is better then the riches of many wicked ones.* Because that little is Gods allowance. Plentifull provisions have oftentimes large bills of accompt. How hard a matter is it to enjoy much, with an *Omnia bene*! Many rich owners are like weary Sumpter-horses, who having travelled all day under the burthen of some great treasure, at night lie down in a foul stable with gall'd backs: so these at last are laid down in their graves, with galled & distressed consciences. And if it so fall out that their spirits are quiet, that the tears of the oppressed do not cry out against them, yet high places are slippery, and great estates lie open to the blasts of envy and malice. It is as great a mercy to be able to want that patiently, that God denies justly, as to use that wisely that God bestowes bountifully. Gods

measure is ever best; so much health, and no more; so much liberty, and no more; so much riches, and no more; so much content in a wife, so much comfort in a childe, so much love from a friend, and no more. It may be our neighbor hath ten talents, [G7v] and we but two, Gods allowance is ever best; beg we for our daily bread, but let God be our carver. *Joseph* thought that his good old Father had been mistaken when he laid his right hand on *Ephraim's* head, who was the younger; and his left on *Manasseh*, who was the elder. And we are ready to entertain hard thoughts of God, who oftentimes layes an heavy hand upon his Saints, that are his first-born, and is very open-handed to others. *I was envyous at the foolish* (saith the Palmist) *when I saw the prosperity of the wicked, when all the day long I have been plagued, and chastened every morning.* But God is wise, and knows what is best. Some live upon their lands, and some by their labours, and some by both; some live upon their trades, and some by alms, and some upon their friends. God often teacheth his by the want of some mercies how to value others, and to be thankfull for them, and fruitfull under them. Fulnesse is the bane of thankfulnesse, and want a good antidote against wantonnesse. I am sure surfet kills more then famine; more birds are taken with a net, then slain with a gun. The roaring of the Canon is good Rhetorick to commend peace, and that Spring is usually most pleasant that is ushered in by a sharp Winter. Yea further, the meanest condition is sometimes the safest. *Iob* on the dunghill speeds better then *Adam* in Paradise. *David* with his sling and his stone hath better [G8r] successe against *Goliah*, then he could have expected in *Saul's* brave armour which he had not proved. And I am sure a poor man on foot may get to heaven as soon as the rich on horseback. God grant I may go to heaven on foot (saith good Mr. *Welsh*) when he saw the Bishop of

Chapter Four

London ride in all state to the Court. I have seen
a great Lord in his Coach drawn with six horses,
stayed at the turning of the street either by a
Carman or a Colliar, when many a poor man on foot
hath slipt by, and got safe home. We are apt to
think those men that have most wealth are of best
worth, and we usually call them the best men of the
Parish, and our betters. Like ignorant people that
judge those Luminaries of heaven, as the Sun and
Moon, to be the greatest, because the lowest; when
stellae primae magnitudinis seem lesse, but are
not, because higher. The things of this world are
such as commonly the best want them, and the worst
have them, and they are often reserved for their
owners, to their hurt. *Dantur bonis ne videantur
mala, dantur malis ne videantur summa bona*: They
are sometimes given to good men, lest they should
seem evil; sometimes to wicked men, lest they should
seem the chiefest good things. Some have lost their
fingers for gold rings, some their lives for their
purses, others their souls for their mammon. Many
Papists in the *Parisian* massacre were butchered with
the Protestants for their wealth, which made them
[G8v] *Hugenots*. *Naboth*'s vineyard was his greatest
fault, not blasphemy against God and the King. It was
his land that cost him his life. *Sir Iohn Cornwall*
Lord *Fanhope* at his death durst say, that not himselfe, but his brave house at *Amphtel* was guilty of
treason. *Solon* told *Croesus*, when he shewed him his
great treasure of gold, If your enemies Iron be
better then yours, he will carry away all your
gold; and so it fell out afterward. *Silver and gold
I have none*, saith *Peter* to the lame man. *All these
things will I give thee*, saith the Devil to Christ.
If these things were so very good, as the world
judgeth them to be, *Peter* should not have wanted
them, nor would the Devil ever have offered them.
In sublimitate metus, in mediocritate quies: A mean
condition hath safety, when high places are full of

fears. The poor of the Land of Judea are spared by
Nebuchadnezzar, and left behinde to till the land;
when *Zedekiah* the King had his eyes put out, his
Princes slain with the sword, and the wealthy
carried into captivity. *Mediocria firma*; a middle
estate betwixt poverty and riches, *food convenient
for us*, which the Wise man prayed for, is the more
secure, when excesse hath danger. Which made *Scipio
Africanus* say, when he was required to joyn with the
Priest, who prayed for more encrease to the *Romane*
State; No, our State is rich enough, I will rather
pray the gods to keep and continue what we have.
[H1r]. How many when they have found their blood
too rank, have been at the charge with a Chirurgeon
to let some out?

 However God deal with you, whether he give you
more or lesse, it will be your wisdome to hold
these three conclusions fast:

 1. Conclude, that if God did see you fit to use
more, he could and would afford more. Are you
straightned in outward comforts? It is not because
there is any want in God, the want is rather in
your selves. So much God told David by Nathan the
Prophet; *I anointed thee to be King over Israel,
and delivered thee from the hand of Saul; and I
gave thee thy Masters house, and thy Masters wives
into thy bosome; and gave thee the house of Israel
and Judah; and if that had been too little, I would
moreover have given thee such and such things.* He
saith to every childe of his, as *Ephron* the *Hittite*
said to *Abraham*, when he came to buy the field and
the cave in *Machpelah*, to bury his dead in; *The
land is worth* 400 *shekels, but what is that betwixt
thee and me?* What are riches, and honour, and
peace, and liberty? They are indeed of great value,
but they are little betwixt you and me, who am a
great God, and have given you my Son; and can there
be any limits in that love? any bounds or bottome
in that bounty? I am a great God, and can do more

for you then you can ask or think, and that exceeding abundantly. When one, [H1v] and he a poor man, asked *Alexander* a penny, he told him, it was too little for him to give; whereupon he asked a talent, he then told him, it was too much for him to beg. But of God we may say, he loves to give above our petitions, yea, our thoughts, and that very bountifully. *Jacob* confessed so much to *Joseph*, *I had not thought to have seen thy face; and loe, God hath shewed me also thy seed.*

2. Conclude, that it is a rich mercy when your mindes are conformable to your means; and should your means come up to your mindes, it might be a misery. In every estate to be content, requires not an ordinary measure of grace; *St. Paul* attained to it, but he had learned so to do. It is an hard lesson, we had need to take out that lesson betimes. Yea, it is hard to learn to be contented, to be full, and to abound; for commonly they that have most are the most discontented persons; and the more they have, the more they would have. *He that loveth silver* (saith *Solomon*) *shall not be satisfied with silver; and he that loveth abundance, with encrease.* Whence one told *Alexander*, that had he the Eastern Empire in on hand, and the Western in another, he would not be contented. Whereas on the other side, *Diogenes* the *Cynicke* housed in his tub, and making even with his victuals and the day together; being invited to a great feast, could say, I had rather lick salt at [H2r] *Athens*, then feast with *Craterus*. It is reported of one of the old Philosophers, that when he saw a Prince going by, with the greatest pomp and state that might be, he said to some about him, See how many things I have no need of. He that hath food and rayment, and is therewith content, may say with *Cato*, (as *Aulus Gellius* reports of him) *Si quid est quo utar utor; si non scio quis sum, mihi vitio vertunt, quia multis egeo; et ego illis, quia*

nequeunt egere. I have neither house, nor plate,
nor garments of price in my hands; what I have, I
can use; if not, I can want it: Some blame me,
because I want many things; and I blame them,
because they cannot want. And it is not strange
that herein a Heathen should go beyond a Christian.

3. Conclude that God hath many wayes to throw
these things in upon you, if he see them good for
you; and as many wayes to take them from you, if he
perceive they prove hurtfull to you. He that can
blesse a little, can blast a great deal. He can
raise you up on high, and bring you downe again.
Job one while was the greatest man in all the East,
and in a short time stript of all; and again, the
Lord blessed the latter end of *Job* more then his
beginning; who gave him twice as much as he had
before. You are but Tenants at will to the great
Landlord of all the earth, and all you have are but
moveables. To be [H2v] able to bear extremities of
heat and cold discovers a strong constitution;
such were our *Henry* the fifth, King of *England*, and
Gustavus Adolphus King of *Sweden*; of whom it is
reported in the History of their Lives and Wars,
that no weather, of heat, or cold, or wind, or
storms, came amisse to them. I am sure it is an
argument of a very gracious heart, that is strong
in the Lord, and in the power of his might, to be
able to bear comfortably severall conditions, even
in their extremes. This may be seen in *Joseph*, who
of all the twelve Patriarchs is only mentioned with
honour amongst those famous believers in Heb.11.
Today he is his Fathers darling, the Son of his
love, and none greater in that family then he, to
morrow he is sold for a slave by his owne Brethren,
and carried into *AEgypt*. Now he is advanced by
Potiphar, one of the prime peers of that Kingdome,
and none greater in that house then he: By and
by a jealous Husband at the complaint of his
beastly Mistris, casts him into prison, where the

Chapter Four

irons entred into his soul: Not long after that he
is advanced by King *Pharaoh* to great honour, even
as high as Subjection could permit, or Soveraignty
endure; for onely in the throne the King would be
above him. And in all these turns and changes
Joseph kept his integrity. In the Countrey, and in
the Court; in the Prison, and at the Palace, *Joseph*
was sincere [H3r] and faithful; neither did his low
estate deject him, nor the high sail of honor and
greatnesse overwhelme him, but he kept upright in
both. Now as affliction cometh not forth of the
dust, neither doth trouble spring out of the
ground, as *Eliphas* told Job; but from on high: So
promotions come neither from the East, nor from the
West, nor from the South, but God is the Judge; he
putteth down one, and setteth up another.

Chap. V

The manner how a Journall or Diary is to be used, according to the rules of Practise.

AND thus far of the rules of Observation. We come now to the rules of Practice, which are to be followed, for the better improvement of such a Journall or Diary; and they are these twelve.

1. Look often into this Journall, and read it over: Of all imployments in the world, a studious is the most ingenuous; wherein the understanding, judgement, and memory, the most noble faculties of the [H3v] soul, are principally imployed: Of all studies the study of History seems to be most excellent: Hence even the Scripture it self is for a great part Historicall; that the hearts of people might be the better taken with it, and delight in it: Of all Histories, the History of mens Lives, is the most pleasant: Such History, amongst many commendations that may be given to it, this is not the least, that it can call back Times, and give life to those that are dead; & like a Landskip give a lively discovery of the actions of the Grandees in former ages. But of all Histories of Lives, I should think, the History of a mans owne Life (even out of common principles of self-love) must needs be most acceptable. To be able to read our Lives even from the wombe to this present moment; from the cradle, within some few dayes of the grave, would surely be a study as profitable as delightfull. It seems that *Jacob* had some skil in the art of memory, though he wrote not such a story; who when he prayed unto

God that he might be delivered from the hands of
his Brother *Esau*, that he might the better prevail
with God, he argues from the experience he had of
his former goodnesse, and gives him a brief narrative of his life, in some particular passages of
providence; *With my staffe I came over this flood
Jordan, and now I am become two bands.* And
questionlesse this duty was taught every *Israelite*,
who when they came yeerly to offer [H4r] their basket of first-fruits to the Lord, did use to run
over a short history of their Fathers lives
(wherein their condition had been wrapped up) in
these words: *A Syrian ready to perish was my
Father, and he went downe into AEgypt, and sojourned
there with a few, and became there a Nation great,
mighty, and populous: And the AEgyptians evill
intreated us, and laid upon us hard bondage; and
when we cryed unto the Lord God of our Fathers, the
Lord heard our voyce, and brought us out of AEgypt
into this Land*, etc. It is reported of *Ahashuerosh*,
that one night when he could not sleep, he sent for
the Book of the Chronicles of his owne Kingdome,
and they were read before him: Now of all the parts
of that History, that which concerns things done in
the time of his Reign was principally chosen;
wherein was written what good service *Mordecai* did
him in discovering the treason of *Bigthan* and
Teresh against him, which probably was most acceptable to him, as may appear in the sequel in that
History.

Tamerlane the most victorious Emperour of the
Tartars, the night before he fought that fatall
battle with *Bajazet* the *Turkish* king, having cast
himself upon a rich carpet in his pavillion, called
for a Book, wherein was contained a history of the
lives of his Ancestors; which he used often to read
for this end, that he might the better imitate that
which was worthily done by them, and learn also to
decline such dangers as they [H4v] by their oversight

Chapter Five

had faln into. And surely such Histories of our Fathers
are but next dore to our owne, and may provoke us
to look into our owne lives with more care and caution. And I am assured, to read a story of our owne
lives, would be a study (next that of the holy
Scripture) as pleasant and profitable as any.
   2. When you have read over this Journall, and
seen what you have, cast up also all your wants,
and see what at present you stand in need of. When
Israel and his family went down into *AEgypt*, it was
fair weather all the way, they had rich provision
for their journey. *Joseph* his Son came out too meet
him in great state, and they were received into
Goshen, the best of all the land of *AEgypt*: But
when *Israel* went out of *AEgypt* towards *Canaan*, they
met with many storms, their wants were great, their
enemies mighty, their dangers grievous; a red Sea,
a howling Wildernesse, bloody *Amalekites*, and fiery
Serpents were in their way. So falls it out with
any Christian; who, though whilest he walked in the
broad way, that leads to more then an *AEgyptian*
darknesse and bondage, he had no cause of complaint, but all went well with him; yet when he set
his face to heaven, and walkt in that narrow way
that leads to life, then found that his wants were
many, and his temptations great. The best, even in
the midst of their abundance, have their just [H5r]
complaints; and he that hath most, hath not all.
One man hath wealth, but no honour, he is under a
cloud; another hath wealth and honour, but not a
dayes health scarce in a moneth; a third hath all
these, but not a childe. The life of the best is
like a shuttle-cock kept up a while betwixt two
battle-dores, and at the last falls to the ground:
Betwixt prosperity and adversity, good dayes and
evill, light and darknesse, our lives run on, and
at the last we are laid in the grave.
   The *Germanes* have a proverbiall saying of the
three Princes Electors, that the *Paltsgrave* hath

the honour, *Brandenburg* the land, but the Duke of *Saxony* the money. No man hath all. Even *Adam* in Paradise was taught to want something, he must not eat of the tree of the knowledge of good and evill. *Moses*, one of the five grand favourites of heaven, called in one chap. five times *the servant of the Lord*. And to be a servant of God is a great honor; *Deo servire regnare est*, To serve God is to reign. And yet *Moses* must not go into the Land of *Canaan*, though he begg'd hard for it: *Let it suffice thee*, (saith God to him) *speak no more to me of that matter*. I know no man that enjoys that abundance of all good things, but I may say to him as our Saviour to the young man in the Gospel, *One thing thou lackest*. If the possession of many things make us proud, God knows how by the [H5v] want of one thing to keep us humble. Oh be sure that one thing be not that *one thing necessary*; namely, *faith*, by which we may see God in all, enjoy God with all, and love God above all.

3. In the midst of all our wants, reckon how many wayes those wants are supplyed with other comforts. God usually makes us a good amends, as *David* said to *Abisha*, when *Shimei* railed on him; *It may be God will requite me for this cursing this day*. If *Adam* may not eat of the fruit of the tree in the midst of the Garden, yet of the fruit of every tree in the Garden besides he might freely eat. If *Moses* may not goe into the Land of *Canaan*, yet his body shall have the most honorable buriall that ever man had; the Lord buried him, and no man knows of his sepulchre unto this day, and his soul went to heaven, which was far better. If we be straightned in outward comforts, and enlarged with spirituall graces; if we be weak in body, and strong in the Lord; if poor in the world, and rich in faith; if forsaken of friends, and God stands by us, we have no great cause to complain.

Travellers into forain parts will tell you, that those Countreys that are most Paganish, are most

stored with gold and silver, and that those lands
that are without those rich mines, have more of the
knowledge of Christ and his wayes. One man [H6r]
hath little to live upon but his labours, but he
hath a very strong and healthy body. Many times the
poorest men have most children, which some esteem a
great blessing, though others look upon it as a
burthen, and put it into the bill of charges. Even
Haman, when he boasted before his wife and friends
of his great wealth and honors, reckons the multitude of his children amongst his great preferments.
If one childe be a blessing, then ten children are
ten blessings. *Children of youth* (saith the Psalmist) *are like arrows in the hand of a mighty man;
happy is the man that hath his quiver full of them.*
And certainly many a man would willingly part with
half his estate for the fruit of the loyns and
wombe. If God send mouths, he will provide meat.
Ashur's blessing was children, but God will provide for him and them. *Ashur shall be blessed with
children,* (saith *Moses*) *but let him be acceptable to
his Brethren, and let him dip his foot in oyl; his
shoes shall be iron and brasse; and as his dayes
be, so shall his strength be: His bread shall be
fat,* (saith *Jacob*) *and he shall yeeld royall
dainties.* Every childe that cometh into the world,
commonly hath two breasts.

    The like may be said of any other wants, and the
several wayes by which God is pleased to supply
them very graciously to his; yea, sometimes to
those that are without. It is said of *Galba* the
Emperor of *Rome,* that he had a crooked body, but a
good head; [H6v] insomuch that one said of him,
Ingenium Galbe male habitat: Galbo's great wit had
but an homely habitation. *AEsop* was much deformed,
but very wise; and *Erasmus,* a plain man, but a
great Scholar. Such a man (and blessed be God there
are many such) is but one story high in the world;
but a very godly man, and high in Gods favour, and

esteem of all his people.

To conclude, could any man live the dayes of *Methuselah*, and should all his way lie by Weepingcrosse; God reconciled in Christ, with the enjoyment of heaven at the last, would make amends for all.

4. Take great notice of the singular peculiar excellency of all Gods dispensations towards you above the world. Your waters are become wine, your gleanings are better then the vintage of the world. God dealeth with you as with Sons; the Servant shall have his wages, and it may be a livery, but the Son shall have better: He is the Saviour of all, but especially of them that believe. Every passage of providence towards you, if you be the Lords, hath something more speciall in it. God hath choyce mercies for a chosen generation, peculiar favours for a peculiar people, hidden comforts for his hidden ones; that which eye hath not seen, nor ear heard, nor can enter into a carnall heart to conceive. [H7r]

See this made good in three passages.

1. Such have ever what the world hath, and something more, an overplus; the meanest Christian way vie comforts with the greatest men of the world, as *Paul* sometimes with the false Apostles. *Are they Hebrews? So am I. Are they Israelites? So am I. Are they the seed of Abraham? So am I. Are they Ministers of Christ? I am more; in labours more abundant*, etc. So a gracious heart: Are the men of the world honorable? So am I that am a Son of God, and a partaker of the divine Nature. Have they friends? So have I, that have union to, and communion with Jesus Christ and his members. Are they rich? So am I, that am rich in faith, and an heir of heaven; as poor, yet making many rich; as having nothing yet possessing all things; as sorrowing, yet always rejoycing. I can take more content in my tears, then they in their dayes of jollity. Have they health, peace, liberty, money? I

am more; in comforts more singular, in promises
more abundant. God deals with his and the world,
as *Joseph* dealt with his Brethren; their sacks were
all fill'd, and their money put into their sacks.
But *Benjamin* shall have the silver cup, which
proved a pledge of love at the last. All are
bountifully feasted, but *Benjamin's* messe is best.
God is good to all, but his owne shal [H7v] have
something over and above; riches, and the God of
riches; honour, liberty, health, and a good right
to them, with a gracious use of them; which the
world never had. And not onely so, but in that
salvation wrought for mankinde, by the death of
Jesus Christ, Gods owne people have something more
then others; according to that of the Apostle, *He
is the Saviour of all men, especially of them that
believe.* He saves all; that is, from that inevitable
ruine the sin of *Adam* had involved them in, and
making them salvable upon conditions of another
covenant; so that now salvation is not impossible, as
it was before Christ, but may be offered to any
man, even the Jailor, a boysterous bloody fellow,
upon condition of believing; according to the tenor
of that commission, *He that believeth shall be
saved.* So that a speciall salvation is afforded to
believers. *Christ was a ransome for all,* 1 Tim. 2.6.
but the Saviour onely of his body, Eph. 5.23. He
redeemed all from present ruine, but called, and
justified, and glorified onely whom he knew before,
and had predestinated to be conformed to his Image.
He saves none thus, but those for whom he prayed,
and he prayed not for the world.

   2. Such, even in those outward enjoyments,
have something more singular then the world; that
little that a righteous man hath, is better then
the great revenues of [H8r] the wicked; their wealth
is better, their liberty better, their honor better, their peace better then other mens. For they
have these things & mercy with them, and a blessing

upon them. They have these things, as by the same
convenant, so with the same love that they enjoy
Jesus Christ, and a little blessed is better then a
world enjoyed. It is said of *Isaac*, that he sowed
his ground, and received an hundred fold, and the
Lord blessed him. He waxed great, and grew on till
he became very great; but the Lord was with him,
and blessed him. Others have a bit and a whip, a
crust and knock; rich and reprobate, honorable and
damned. Abundance, and go ye[t] cursed at the last.
A little in mercy is abundance, and abundance with
blessing is Gods plenty. And indeed, he that can
blesse a little, can blast a great deal. If *Cain*
till the ground, and and sow his seed, the earth is
cursed to him, it shall not bring forth, or yeeld
to him her strength. Hence the word in the Greek,
ἐυλοία, signifies both *bounty* and *blessing*; and
indeed that is truely bounty that is thus blessed,
Rom.15.29. 1 Cor.10.16. 2 Cor.9.5.

3. God ever gives to his owne, satisfying
mercies, contenting goodnesse. No man but a childe
of God could ever truely say as *Jacob* did, *I have
enough, Joseph is alive. My redeemer liveth.* There
is much difference between the men of Gods hand, that
are the men of this world, and the men of his
heart; [H8v] and there is as great a difference
betwixt the filling of the belly, and the satisfying of the soul. *Thou fillest their bellies* (saith
David, speaking of the men that are his hand) *with
thy hid treasures; but as for me, I will behold thy
face in righteousnesse, I shall be satisfied when I
awake with thy likenesse.* These outward things to
the world is but a belly-full, and how soon is the
belly emptyed? but *they that hunger and thirst
after righteousnesse, shall be satisfied.* God gives
the world the worlds goods, but not the Saints
goodnesse. He gives the world, as sometimes he did
to *Israel*, their request, but sends leannesse into
the soul; a fat purse, and a fat heart; a whole

Chapter Five

estate, and a whole heart; a fat body and a lean
soul; but he deals better with his own, he fulfils
the desires of them that fear him. If he afflict
them, he sanctifies their afflictions, or they are
not satisfied. If he give to them, he gives them
all things that concern life and godlinesse, or
they are not satisfied. If he forgive them, he for-
gives all their iniquities, and remembers their sin
no more, or they are not satisfied. Hence it is
observable, that the Saints of God in the Old
Testament, are ever mentioned in the Gospel with
honor, but their faults and failings never
remembred. *Ye have heard of the patience of Job*
(saith *James*) so we have read something of his
impatience, but that is quite forgotten. Ye have
read of the Faith of *Abraham*, of the Grief of *Lot*
for the [I1r] conversation of the wicked, of the
Zeal of *David*, the Wisdome of *Solomon*, etc. But
their sins are not remembred in the Gospel. On the
contrary, those wicked ones whose names are
recorded in the Old Testament, are never mentioned
in the New Testament but with some blot; as, *Cain,
who was of that wicked one; Ismael, the persecuter;
Esau, the profane; Balaam, the convetous; Corah,
the Gainsayer,* etc. But what saith
the Lord of these? *In those dayes, and at that time, the
iniquity of Israel shall be sought for, and there shall
be none; and the sins of Judah, and they shall not
be found; for I will pardon them whom I reserve.*
    5. Take great heed that the want of some one
thing, do not rob you of the comfort of all the
mercies that you enjoy besides. For such is the
perversnesse and waywardnesse of mans nature, that
though some have had more, have more, and look to
enjoy more then they can either want or wish for;
yet they are more troubled with the sense of one
want, then they are comforted in, or thankful for
all they have. This was not onely the fault of
Ahab, whom not the royalties of the Kingdome, nor

the Cities he had built, nor the Ivory house that
he had made, would content and comfort, unlesse he
might have *Naboth's* vineyard also, which was denyed
him. Nor was this the fault of *Haman* alone, who
though he did what he listed, and had what he
pleased, under the favour of his royall [I1v]
Master; yet lost the comfort of all, because *Mordecai* would not bow. What avails all (saith he) *so
long as I see Mordecai sitting in the Kings gate?*
but it was the fault of good *Rachel*, that was able
to wrestle with God; who, though she had what a
loving Husband could afford her, yet would die of
the sullens, because she had no Son. Yea, even
Abraham (as some think) failed in this, who brake
out into this discontented speech before God, *What
wilt thou give me, seeing I go childlesse?* As if
all had been nothing, no not Gods being his shield,
and exceeding great reward, unlesse God gave him a
Son: Though some have thought that his complaint
reached higher, (to whom I encline) *What wilt thou
give me?* all hitherto is nothing, if I goe
childelesse, if Christlesse, if Saviourlesse; for
it is such a Son that I have waited for, in whose
seed the Nations of the earth shall be blessed; and
it is such a Son that thou hast promised me; and if
not such a Son, all is nothing.

6. Reckon often, not onely what you have, and
what you want, but what you may want; cast up all
hazzards. Who knows what lies in the wombe of the
next morning? All the pomp of the world is but a
fancy and may soon vanish.

It is said of *Agrippa* and *Berenice*, that when
they came to *Jersulem* to hear *Paul*, they entred
with great pomp; the word in the orig. is μΣΤὰ
πολλῆς φαντασίας, *with great fancy*, [I2r] *with great
pomp*. And how soon are affairs changed in a Kingdom, or in a family? *Haman* the great Minion in the
Court of *Ahashuerosh* is hanged on that tree that he
prepared for *Mordecai*. It hath been observed by

Chapter Five

Historians, of *Tiberius*, Emperor of *Rome*; of *Mahomet* the Great, Emperor of the *Turks*; and of *Henry* the Eight, King of *England*; that there was no security in their love, but that such as were highest in their favour, were neerest to ruine. Who ever hath read the stories of *Bajazet* and *Bellizarius*, who fell from the highest pinnacle of greatnesse, to the lowest extreme of all scorn and misery, but will acknowledge the uncertainty of all sublunary comforts? *Saladine* the great Sultan of *AEgypt*, and Conqueror of the East, to shew the frailty and vanity of all wordly felicity, commanded on his death-bed, that no Princely solemnity should be used at his Funerall, more then his shirt fastned to the point of a Launce, and carried before his dead body, a Priest going before, and crying aloud to the people in this sort: *Saladine, of all the great riches and honor that he had in his life, carries no more with him at his death then his shirt.* A Duke of *Exeter*, that marryed K. *Edw.* the fourth his Sister, was seen barefoot, begging in the Camp of the Duke of *Burgundy*. Hence a wiseman will cast up his hazards, and reckon upon losses, thus. Here is a fine house, & a most pleasant habitation; but a fire may suddenly levell it even with [I2v] the ground. Here is a competent estate of *land*, but riotous children may spend it; here is a great summe of *money*, but as that fire that came down from heaven, that consumed the sacrifice, and the wood; and lickt up all the water in the trench about the Altar that *Elijah* caused to be made: so sicknesse, or surityship, or long Suites in Law, or a Civil war, may consume all. I have those comforts in wife, children, relations, friends, that few have; but how soon death may deprive me of all, I know not: *And he died, and he dyed* is the end of every mans story; and the winding sheet of the strongest man, and the choycest friend. I have health, strength, and such personall endowments that many want; but I may suddenly by some noysome disease, or violent distemper, be stript of all. Yea, which is more then all this, I have peace with God and mine owne conscience; it is fair weather over head, though foul under foot; though I meet with some trouble in the world, yet the lamp of God shines upon my tabernacle, and the Almighty is with me, as *Job* sometimes said of himself; yet I may be forsaken, and left to my self, and the most dreadfull terrors get hold of me for a time; yea, God may write bitter things against me, and make me possesse the sins of my youth; for there is no evill of sin, but that against the holy Ghost; nor evil of sorrow, but that of the bottomlesse pit, but may befall me. When *Joseph* dreamt of [I3r] his great preferment, he never dreamt of his imprisonment. We often look upon that we have, but seldome consider what we doe or may want.

When a great City was burnt to ashes, *Seneca* had this saying, *Una dies interest inter magnam civitatem et nullam:* One day makes a great difference betwixt a great City and none. *Is not this great Babylon* (saith *Nebuchadnezzar*) *which I have built for the house of my Kingdome, and the honor of my Majesty, by the might of my power? Whilest the word was in the Kings mouth, there fell a voyce from heaven, saying, Oh Nebuchadnezzar! to thee be it spoken, The Kingdome is departed from thee,* etc. The same hour was the thing fulfilled. Christs prophesie of the ruine of the Temple, and those stately buildings that the *disciples* shew'd him, was dreadfull; *Verily, I say unto you, there shall not be left here one stone upon another, that shall not be thrown down.*

7. In the next place, from hence study seriously the vanity of all creature-comforts, honors, pleasures, riches, friends; *O quantum est in rebus inane!* Oh how much vanity is in these things! was the saying of *Perseus* long agoe. By

this time we are faln upon the dregs of time, the
last and worst age of the world; and now these
things run a tilt, and therefore have the lesse in
them. *Vanity of vanities, saith the Preacher, all
is vanity.* *Vanitas est debitae entitatis vacuitas:*
Vanity is nothing else but the want of a just
entity or being. [I3v]
  Now, 1. A just being is a present being, but
these things are often furthest off when we have
most need of them. God onely is a present help in
trouble, and can be with us in all places, according to that promise to *Jacob.*
  2. A just being is a constant being, but
these things last not, our pleasures end in pain,
our plenty in penury, our honor in contempt; *The
fashion of this world passeth away*; the, Τὸ σχῆμα,
the *species,* the *figure,* the *image;* like a brave
picture drawn upon the ice, that under the heat of
the Sun is soon gone. God onely is from everlasting
to everlasting.
  3. A just being is a perfect being, that hath
all excellencies in it; but these things want something still: *Nihil est ab omni parte beatum*:
Nothing here is in every part compleatly happy;
onely God is a perfect good, and he that enjoys
him, needs no more.
  4. A just being is a solid being, that hath
no evill in it at all; but these things are not
onely vanity, but vexation of spirit. *Augendi cura,
et amittendi metus*: A care to get, and a fear to
lose, like burs, stick close to our choycest comforts. These things at the first sight seem very
good, but better considered, are not so. *Quae cito
aspecta placent ea melius inspecta displicent*; as
Seneca could say, They are seemingly good, but not
certainly so. Like *Calipolis,* a City, that at a
great distance seems beatifull; but if you [14r]
come nigh to it, answers not expectation; but God
onely is a solid good; *he is light, and in him*

there is no darknesse at all. He is altogether excellent.

See the vanity of these things yet further in foure passages.

1. They are so vain, that all the world, the profits of it, the pleasures in it, were it ten times better then it is, are not enough to make up one childes portion, though a servant behinde the Mill, or a drudge in a Kitchin, if godly, the eternal, almighty, alsufficient God, is but enough to be his portion: *Thou art my portion, O Lord,* saith *David.* This one promise, *I will be thy God,* will outweigh them all.

2. They are so vain that a fancy, a conceit, a jealousie, a humour, an ungrounded fear, will rob a man of the comfort of them all (and what are these things without their comfort?) and make him run quite away from them, as the *Syrians* once did from their camp, and all their treasure. One man will not live, because his minion will not love. Another man will hasten to the grave, because his commodities are dead, and lie on his hand.

3. They are so vain, that had one man as much wealth and honor, as much pleasure and outward concontent as his heart could desire, or the world afford him, yet within 24 hours he would be weary of all, and must go sleep; God draws the curtain [14v] of the night, and hides them all from the world under that dark canopy. Here *omnium rerum est satietas,* all things have their fulsomnesse, and therefore we have day and night. In heaven no night, there we shall never be weary of our enjoyments, but delight in them unto all eternity.

4. They are so vain, that suddenly when we least think of it, they are gone. Good news from them is like the sound of bels in a storm; sometimes that pleasant ring is very neer, and suddenly it cannot be heard. I have seen a man compassed about with plenty, and variety of all earthly com-

Chapter Five

forts that can be imagined, in a short time come to
nothing; his honor, wealth, friends, peace
liberty, health, beauty, posterity, attendants;
like a great flock of birds, with one shout scared
quite away, and return no more; pluckt all from
him, and never any more recovered. Oh! study much
the vanity of all sublunary contents. You can never
have high thoughts of Jesus Christ, his
promises, ordinances, union to him, communion with
him, till you have low thoughts of the things of
the world. *Solomon* first wrote his *Ecclesiastes*,
before his *Song of Songs*; he could first say by
experience, *All is vanity*, before he could set it
downe under his owne hand that *Christ* was *the chiefest among ten thousand*, and *altogether lovely*. [15r]

Therefore, in the next place, be very moderate
in the use of these things. Take heed you lash not
out too much of your love upon them, and delight in
them. Take heed you make them not idols, lest God
pluck them away from you. As it is an high point of
wisdom to seek these things remisly, so it is an
argument of a great measure of grace, to use them
soberly, and part with them willingly. *Quantum
canis Appula tantum*. Like the dog that runs by the
river *Nilus*, where the Crocodiles lie, and wait for
their prey; but a sip, a taste, and be gone, lest
they be surprised and devoured by them. For *Jonah*
to be glad of his gourd was safe, but to be exceeding glad, was sinful. And his vexation was greater
in the losse, then his content was in the enjoyment
of it; his very life is now a burthen to him,
because his gourd is pluckt away from him. And
indeed, strong affections to these things are good
for nothing, unlesse to breed strange afflictions:
How many have lost their dispositions amongst their
advancements; because when riches and promotion
come, they set their hearts too much upon them.
Magistratus virum indicat; give a man place and
power, and you may soon see what he is; those

snakes of corruption that lay hid in the cold
winter of want and meannesse, will stir abroad in
the sunshine of honour and greatnesse. [I5v]
    It is reported of Pope *Sixtus quintus*, that
before he attained the Papall dignity, he was the
most humble crouching Fryer that (as my Author
saith) was ever lodged in an oven; but once seated
in that chair, the stoutest and proudest Prelate
that ever ware a triple crown. Some have observed,
that even *Judas*, before he had the Bag-office,
carried himself honestly and soberly; but afterward, he grew so covetous, that rather then he
would want money, he would sell his Master.
    Oh therefore take heed that your affections run
not out in so full a stream to these things. Height
of affection, as well as height of estate is
dangerous. *Set not your affections* (saith the
Apostle) *upon things on earth*. God would not take
away our affections, he would onely tune them. If
they be set upon these things, and not set upon
God, they are out of tune. Riches are like briars
and thorns, good to stop a gap with; but if you lay
them in your beds, and set your hearts on them,
this you shall have of my hand, you shall lye down
in sorrow. They are good servants, but bad Masters.
Let the world follow you as a servant, and be
thankfull; but do not you follow the world as a
Master, lest you prove the greatest slaves. If
riches have been thy god, make them thy slave.
Serve it as *Diagorus* did *Hercules* his image made of
wood; being in an Inne, and having nothing to
seethe his broth with, [I6r] made a fire with it.
All these things will I give thee, was the Devils
strongest temptation, and therefore reserved to the
last place. Hopes of preferment have overcome those
whom imprisonment and the fear of the losse of all
could not move. Take heed therefore, and beware of
covetousnesse. It is true, that temptation
prevailed not against our Saviour, but it may over-

Chapter Five

come us, because we have three enemies to contend
and fight with, Sin, World, and Devill; he had but
two, the World and the Devil, whose temptations
though fierce and frequent, could never prevail;
because, though like to us in all things, yet sin
was excepted.

9. But above all sublunary things, take great
heed you trust not too far, depend not too much
upon men; no, not those men that may have been
instrumental for your good. *Cease ye from man*
(saith the Prophet) *for wherein is he to be
trusted? Put not your trust in Princes,* (saith the
Psalmist) *nor in the Son of man.* Neither in this
generation, nor the next, for they are all but Sons of
men, and *every man at his best estate is
altogether vanity.* We are apt to think that the
next man may be better, but seldome comes a better,
because all are men. *Beware of dogs,* saith the
Apostle; but our Saviour Christ saith, *Beware of
men;* though more modest and moderate, yet if but
men, they will deceive, and peradventure persecute
you. The most intimate bosome friend may prove an
[I6v] *Achitophel,* if but a man. As you should not
fear them too much, so do not trust them too far;
not fear them, though they be made rich, and the
glory of their houses be made great; for *men of low
degree are vanity, and men of high degree are a
lye; if laid in the balance, they are altogether
vanity.* All *the Nations* (saith the Prophet) *are as
the drop of a bucket, and are counted as small as
the dust in the ballance.* All nations before God
are as nothing, and are counted to him lesse then
nothing and vanity. What then is one mighty man?
Ten hundred thousand times lesse then a drop. A
drop may wet, but it cannot drown; be not afraid of
him then, will you be afraid of nothing, of a
vanity, of a drop? Neither do you trust them too
far. *Trust ye not in a friend,* (saith *Micah*) *put no
confidence in a guide, keep the dores of thy mouth*

from her that lyeth in thy bosome. And why so? *ch.7. v.4. The best of them is a briar, the most upright is sharper then a thorny hedge.* And in *v.6. The Son dishonoureth the Father, the Daughter riseth up against her Mother, the Daughter in law against her Mother in law, and mans enemies are the men of his owne house.* Thou sayest (saith *Rabshakeh* to *Hezekiah*) *I have counsell and strength for the war, but they are but vain words.* Thou sayst, such a Prince is my friend, and such a great man is my kinsman, but they are but vain words. For he heapeth up riches, and cannot tell who shall enjoy them; not himself knows, much lesse thou. What was *Canaan* [17r] the better for the Sons of *Anak*, or *Bashan* for their *Og*, or the *Philistines* for their *Goliah*? So, what art thou the better for thy mighty friends? It is true, where goes the bucket there goes the rope, (as the *Spaniard* hath it in the proverb) the rope depends on the bucket: But if thy friend fail, where are all thy hopes? But above all, trust no mans judgement solely in matters of Religion; because a man of note, for great learning and piety. I will not pin my faith upon any mans sleeve, (saith Sir *Tho. More*) because I know not whither he will carry it: What if a very godly man? I never saw that Christian yet, but I might see something of a man in him; enough of the old man in the new man to trouble the best man. Grosse errors have been maintained by good men, to the prejudice of publick peace: Even *Peter* a good man, advised Christ not to go up to *Jerusalem*, but to favour himself; and when he was at *Antioch*, he dissembled, and many of the *Iews* dissembled likewise with him; yea, *Barnabas* was brought into the dissimulation also. When mens parts are great, their graces eminent, their names high, and their power large, we are in danger to be biassed by their counsels.

To conclude this passage, remember this advice

Chapter Five

one gave to his friend; it may do you good that
have much to do with men. [I7v]
    1. Have communion with few.
    2. Be intimate with one.
    3. Deal justly with all.
    4. Speak evill of none.
It is somewhat singular, but I am sure very
safe, to have one as our intimate and bosome
friend. *Alexander* had his *Ephestion*, and *David*
in the Wildernesse a *Jonathan*, and in the Court his
Hushai, called the Kings friend. Yea, even Christ
himself had *John*, if I may not say his Favourite,
yet certainly the Disciple whom Jesus loved above
the rest. And he is a wise man that will not put
all into his *Creed*, that puts up in his *Pater
noster*; nor will shew every man his minde or his
money, he may converse with. *Give unto Caesar the
things that are Caesars; unto God, the things that
are Gods.* Give faithfulnesse to men, but trust in
God. And I am sure, to speak evil of none, unlesse
we have a calling; to deal justly will all, with
whom we have any dealing, will bring us much comfort living, great peace dying, and and a good report
when we are gone hence, and shall be seen no more.
[I8r]

Chap. VI

More rules of the same kinde, that concern our practice.

 10. IN the tenth place, when you have read over your Journall, and made such use of it as hitherto I have shewed you; ask your owne hearts these three questions: The first concerns God; the second, our neighbour; and the third, our selves.
 1. Ask your own hearts this question, What honor do I bring to God for all this? Do herein as *Ahashuerosh* did, when he had read what good service *Mordecai* had done him, in discovering a treason; he asked those about him, *What honor and dignity hath been done to Mordecai for all this?* So do you, upon a survey of all the good things God hath vouchsafed to you and yours: Hitherto the Lord hath holpen me; he hath preserved me from many dangers, supplied me with many comforts, assisted me in many straights, afforded me many friends: But what honor hath God from me for all this? I live upon him, but do I live to him? I have all from him, but do I anything for him? [I8v] My times are in his hands, but are his praises in my mouth? He is never weary I see of doing me good, but am not I weary of doing him service? Can I say with St. *Paul, His I am, and him I serve*? He is the *alpha* of all my happinesse, why should not he be the *omega* of all my thankfulnesse? But may not my conscience answer as those Servants about *Ahashuerosh* did concerning *Mordecai, There hath been nothing done for him?* Nay, have I not

requited him evill for the good he hath done me? If
any spirit be grieved, it shall be his; if any day
be neglected, it shall be his; if any commandements
be broken, they shall be his; if my honor be called
for, and I be reproached; if my liberty be
threatned, and I be imprisoned; if my wealth or
ease be required, and I be endamaged or troubled:
How hardly comes any thing from me for God, that
hath done all for me? So that God may say to me, as
David sometimes complained of *Nabal*, the unthankful
churle, *In vain have I kept all that this fellow
hath in the wildernesse, so that nothing was missed
of all that pertained to him; and he hath requited
me evill for good.* In vain have I kept your house
from firing at such a time, your family from infection at another time; your person from danger, in
such a journey; your eyes from tears, and your feet
from falling, many a time; and you have requited me
evill for good. Say rather to God, as *Elisha* to the
good *Shunamite*, who had provided a chamber, [K1r]
and all things convenient for him; *Thou hast been
carefull for us with all this care, what is to be
done for thee?* Thou Lord hast been carefull of my
health, that it might not be impaired; of mine
estate, that it might not be wasted; of my name,
that it might not be reproached; of my soul, that
it might not be damned: Lord, what is now to be
done for thee? Is there any thing too great, too
good to part with to such a God?

    It was a brave speech of *Lewis* the 13. a late
King of *France*, in a journey neer *Paw*, in his owne
Kingdome. The inhabitants understanding that he was
coming, sent to know how he would be received into
the Towne, and what honor they should do to him. He
asked the messengers, whether there were ever a
Church in the Towne; if there were, he would enter as their
King, in state; if not, he would receive no honour in that
place, where Almighty God had no house, and
therefore no honor given him. A gracious heart would

Chapter Six

think all ill bestowed on him, if he had no spirit at all to glorifie God.

Boleslaus, a King of *Poland*, when he was to speak or do any thing out of concernment, would take out a little picture of his Fathers, that he carried about him; and kissing it, would say, I wish I may do nothing at this time unworthy [of] thy name. Say you as much, that can see God in every mercy, and [K1v] enjoy him with every favour; I wish that I who every day have tasted so much of Gods goodnesse, may do nothing this day to the dishonor of his name; but may blesse him, not onely with my lips, but honor him also with my life.

To give the same thing we receive from a friend, back again, is rudenesse amongst men; but with God, is true Religion. *Hannah*, after many prayers and tears, received a Son from the Lord, and she returned him back again to the Lord, as long as he lived. What health, strength, peace, liberty, parts, gifts, we receive from God, are best used, when they are bestowed on God in his service. And there is nothing lost this way; For he that offereth God praise, glorifieth him; and to him that ordereth his conversation aright, he will shew the salvation of God; that is, mighty and wonderfull salvation. Which made Cardinall *Wolsey*, once King *Henry* the Eight his Favourite, to say at his death, Had I been as carefull to serve the God of heaven, as I was to please the King of *England*, he would not have left me in my old age, as this man hath done.

2. Put this interrogatory to your owne hearts, What good do I to my neighbour? It is true, God hath done all this for me, and he hath dealt bountifully with me; but what good do others reap by me; either my Prince or Countrey, the Church or State? What good do I in the Town where [K2r] I dwell, to the family where I live? to my relations, wife, children, servants, with whom I converse; are

any of these the better for me? Even *Seneca* could
say, *Mallem mihi malèesse quàm mollitèr:* I had
rather be sick then idle, and do no good. But it is
the greatest affliction to a gracious heart, to be
wholly unusefull; he had rather not bee, then be
idle and unprofitable. If *Moses* the Servant of the
Lord, can do no good in *AEgypt*, he will go to
Midian. Every man therefore shall do well to put
this Querie often to his owne heart. Of what use
are my parts and gifts of body, minde, or estate?
Yea, is my very life and example sufficient to
others? How do I promote the good of my neighbour,
by my alms, prayers, counsels, labours? It is not
sufficient to say, *I do no body harm*. With which
plea, some are well enough satisfied: But remember
what question Christ askt his auditors; not *What
are you;* or *What know you more then others?* but,
What do you? *Hezekiah* could make a good answer to
such a question, *Lord remember how I have walked
before thee in truth, and have done that which is
good in thy sight*. So could *Nehemiah*, *Remember me,
O Lord, for good; and wipe not out the good deeds
that I have done for the house of God and the
offices thereof*. Our charity should be as a running
spring at our owne dores, that will not onely
supply our own wants, but run through our neigh-
bours pastures, [K2v] and water the field of a
stranger; yea, sometimes crosse the high-way, and
run into a common ditch. Whilest we have
opportunity, we should do good to all, but *especially to the houshold of faith*. Yea, *if our enemy
hunger, give him food; if he thirst, give him
drink; for in so doing we shall heap coals of fire
upon his head*.

    This indeed is to have the Spirit of Christ;
and, *if ye have not the Spirit of Christ, ye are
none of his*. Christ was a friend to his enemies,
and kinde to the unkinde. *Jonathan* was so friendly
to *David*, that he stript himself of his robe that

Chapter Six

was upon him, and gave it him; and his garments,
even to his sword and his bow. But Christ was a better
friend, who did not only lay aside his robe
of majesty, but laid down his life for us. *Greater
love hath no man then this, that he lay down his
life for his friends.* Christ did more, for he laid
down his life for his enemies. *Ebedmeleck* was very
mercifull to *Jeremiah*, that would let down cords,
and old clouts and rags into the dungeon where he
was, and so lift him out. Christ did more, who
would himself go down into the grave, that he might
deliver us who were dead in sins and trespasses,
and thereby free us from the bottomlesse pit.

It is reported of *Trajan* the Emperour, that he
rent off a piece of his robe to binde up the wound
of a common Souldier. Christ did more, who shed his
blood to [K3r] heal our wounds. *Pompey* the Great,
that noble *Romane* Generall, being ready to
undertake a piece of Service for the State, and
advised by one to desist, because the designe was
full of danger, answered; *Necesse est ut eam, non
ut vivam*: It is necessary that I go, not that I
live. Christ did more, for being perswaded by *Peter*
not to go up to *Jerusalem*, where he was to suffer,
but to favour himself, he was angry him, and said,
*Get thee behinde me Satan, thou art an offence unto
me, thou savourest not the things that are of God,
but of men.* *Judah* was a dutiful Son to his Father,
and a loving friend to his Brother *Benjamin*, who
was content to stay behinde in *AEgypt*, and be a
bondman to *Joseph*, upon condition his Brother might
be sent home to his Father. Christ did more, who
would not onely be a Servant, but he would die,
that we might live, and be reconciled unto his
Father.

Charls the fifth, in a great storm neer *Algiers*,
caused many brave Horses to be thrown over-board,
that the lives of a few Slaves might be saved.
Jonah the Prophet was a better friend to the

Mariners, who was content to be thrown into the
Sea, that the waves might be stilled, and their
lives might be secured. But Christ was the best
friend of all, who was willing to be cast into the
Ocean of his Fathers fury, that we might be set on
shore, and so passe from death to life. Now
certainly, he that is joyned unto [K3v] the Lord,
is one spirit. Ask your owne hearts therefore often
this question, What good do I for others, for whom
God hath done so much?

It is reported of Mr. *Fox*, who wrote the Book of
Martyrs, that he never denyed any man that asked an
alms for Jesus sake, and that he never refused anything that was given him; not that he might enrich
himself, but might relieve others, for he gave it
all away to the poor. A Student that was in want,
asking *Luther* some money, he bad his Wife give
him some; she pleading her owne necessities, he
took up a silver bowle, and gave it him. When you
have an opportunity of doing good, never plead you
have many children. *Cyprian* had wont to say, The
more children, the more charity. And our Saviours
counsell was to sell what we have, rather then
neglect this duty of doing good. *Let him that
stole, steal no more* (saith the Apostle) *but rather
let him labour with his hands, the thing that is
good.* But for what end? That he may have to supply
his own wants only? No, but rather that he may have
to give to him that needeth: So that there is no
man under heaven, from the highest Prince to the
lowest Pesant, that may plead an immunity from this
duty of giving. The omission whereof hath been as
prejudiciall to some, as the performance of it hath
been profitable to others. [K4r]

Mauritius the Emperor refusing to redeem a few
captive slaves from *Saladine* the *AEgyptian* Sultan,
which he might have done for a small matter, upon
which they were all slain; was afterward punished
by *Phocas*, who in a sedition being proclaimed

Chapter Six

Emperor by the Souldiers, caused his wife and children to be put to death before his face, himself all the while crying out, *Justus es Domine, et recta judicia tua.* But on the other side, memorable is the story of *Pyrhias*, a Merchant of *Ithaca*, who at Sea espying an aged man a captive in a Pirates ship, took compassion of him, and redeemed him, and with his person bought his commodities which the Pirate had taken from him, which were certain barrels of pitch. The old man perceiving, that not for any good service he could do him, nor for the gain of that commodity, but meerly out of charity he had done this, discovered a great masse of treasure hidden in the pitch. Whereby the Merchant in a very short time became very rich. At which time that Scripture was fulfilled, *He that giveth to the poor, shall not lack.* And that other Scripture, *He that soweth liberally, shall reap liberally.* Such giving is like the pouring of a pale of water into a dry pump, that will fetch abundance. Let us give that which we cannot keep, that we may have that in a time of need that we cannot lose. [K4v]

3. Ask your own hearts often what good you your selves get by all that God hath done for you. *If thou be wise* (saith *Solomon*) *thou shalt be wise for thy self.* As a wicked fool hath no foe like himself, so a wise Christian hath no friend like himselfe; who will be a gainer by every losse, and a saver by every comfort. Physitians and Chirurgions make much of their *probatum*'s, and so should every Christian of his experiments. Let every man therefore ask his owne heart upon a serious survey of his Journall, thus much: Am I bettered by all this health, and wealth, and good dayes; this Gospel of peace, and this peace of the Gospel that I have enjoyed so long? It is with these things as with the physick or dyet of the body, they will leave you better or worse then they finde you. But by all these good dayes, rich mercies, or sharp afflictions, do I

grow into more acquaintance with God, the world, and mine own heart; with God, and his holinesse; with the world, and its vanity; with mine owne heart, and its deceitfulnesse; that I may trust him more, and the world and my heart lesse? All grace in truth hath growth. *Ulterius* was *Charls* the fifth his Motto; by which he signified, the greater projections, more noble enterprises, were yet daily to be endevoured after by Princes. Christians must not stand at a stay, but with the Apostle, forgetting those things that are behind, reach forth unto [K5r] those things that are before. This being a cleer difference betwixt the first *Adam* and the second; The old creature in the beginning, and the new under the Gospel. The first *Adam* was made a man, and a holy man, all at once; but the Lord Christ was conceived in the wombe, and at the fulnesse of time was born of the Virgin *Mary*, and increased in wisdome, and in stature, and in favour both with God and man. In the beginning all the creatures were made in their full growth and strength, which made some to be of opinion, that *Mundus conditus fuit in Autumno*: That the creation of the world was in Harvest, when all things are in their full beauty. But now we must have an egge before a bird, a seed before a plant; a birth, and then a growth: So now every Christian must in time grow in grace, and the knowledge of the Jesus Christ, and proceed by degrees from faith to faith, from babes to grown men in Christ; and therefore where there is no growth, we may fear there is no grace. Ask your hearts then, Do I grow? At such a time, I had a great affliction, a long sicknesse; Am I more humble since? Where there is a rod of correction, there should be a word of correction. God teacheth by his rods; as *Gideon* taught the men of *Succoth*, with briars and thorns; and *blessed is that man whom God correcteth, and teacheth out of his law.* Oh that I could hear the rod, as well as

Chapter Six 127

feel it! A man of [K5v] wisdome shall see Gods
Name; hear the rod, and who hath appointed it. At
such a time God vouchsafed me great prosperity,
much successe in my calling; a long time of health,
with comfort in my relations: Am I more holy, more
humble, more heavenly, more meek, more mercifull,
more faithfull, more fruitfull in my place? Or, am
I not rather worse; more rich, and more covetous;
more honorable, and more proud; more healthfull,
and more wanton? But if you finde that the house of
David growes stronger and stronger, and the house
of *Saul* weaker and weaker; that your corruptions
are abated, and your graces encreased, happy are
you. And indeed the higher the Sun riseth, the
shorter are the shadows; as in a Pyramide, the
higher you go, the lesse compasse you finde; like a
flame of fire, the higher it ascends, the purer and
thinner is the flame; so the elder you grow, the
better you should be. If so, it is well. *These
things* (saith St. *John*) *I have written to you that
beleeve, that you may beleeve*; that is, that you
grow more and more in that grace of faith. Faith is
not like *Jonah's* gourd, up in one night, and down
in another; but like the sound of the trumpet on
the Mount, lowder and lowder; or like a great
bell that is long in raising, and strikes but a
while on one side; but at last is up, and makes a
great sound, and is heard afar off. Such was the
faith of the *Romanes*, small at the first, but [K6r]
afterwards it grew to that height, that it was
spoken of throughout the world.

When *Grave William* the Prince of *Orange* died,
his Son *Maurice* was but young; whereupon the States
were doubtfull whether they should choose him their
Generall or no. *Maurice* perceiving it by his
friends, wrote a Letter to them, and in it onely
these foure words, *Tandem fit surculus arbor*; A
young plant at last becomes a tree. Upon which they
made choyce of him; and he made his Motto good, for

he grew a brave Souldier, and proved not onely a happy instrument of their good, but a great ornament to himself and family.

I shall conclude this passage with a saying of St. *Augustine. Si vis pervenire ad id quid non es, semper displiceat tibi quid es: Si dixeris, sufficit, periisti.* If you would attain to what you are not, let it grieve you that you are as you are; that is, no better: You are undone if you think that what you are is sufficient.

11. In the eleventh place, Be sure that after all these questions be strictly asked and seriously answered, you make it your Tὸ ἔργον, your very work to be thankfull for all Gods mercies; otherwise, why do you keep such a Journall? *In every thing give thanks* (saith the Apostle) *for this is the will of God in Christ Jesus concerning you.* It is ordained by the *Rabbins,* (as some observe, who write the History of the *Jews*) that they should say a [K6v] benediction, and render particular praise and thanks to God for every benefit they receive; not only for every extraordinary mercy that befalls them, but in every action that they do; for their meat, drink, and every action that they do; for their meat, drink, and every good smell; for all the precepts of the Law, and of the Rabbins; for every new thing, and every strange thing that befalls them. And certainly, where God is never weary of giving, his people should never be weary of thanksgiving. God delights much in the praise of his servants. He loves a cheerfull giver, but much more a cheerful thanksgiver.

Give God thanks for all things, but especially for these foure:

1. For Jesus Christ, and the unsearchable riches of Gods grace in him; which is the fountain of all the good we enjoy, or hope to enjoy; *who was by God made sin for us, who knew no sin, that we might be made he righteousnesse of God in him.* He

that knew no sin in the act, knew all sin in the
weight. He that knew no sin by commission, knew all
by imputation. *The chastisement of our peace was
upon him, and by his stripes we are healed.* Who
made peace for his people by his death, and maintains this peace for them by his intercession; he
died once, but he prays ever; his passion is over,
but not his compassion; for he stands between us,
and all our harms, and will at last reward every
one according to his works. [K7r]
    Cyrus in a great expedition against his enemies,
the better to encourage his Souldiers to fight, in
an oration that he made at the head of his Army,
promised upon the victory to make every Foot-
souldier an Horseman, and every Horseman a Commander; and that no Officer that did valiantly
should go unrewarded. But Christ our Generall doth
promise more: *He that overcometh shall sit with me
in my throne; as I overcame, and am set with my
Father in his throne.* He will make us all Kings.
Oh therefore be thankful for Jesus Christ. It is
our sorrow, or should be our shame, that we cannot
be thankful for Christ as we ought: It is our comfort, and shall be our happinesse, that one day we
shal be. Eternity of time I confesse is little
enough to be thankful in for Christ, & all the rich
incomes we have with him; but endevour whilest you
are here to be thankfull for him; and certainly, he
that cannot be thankful for Jesus Christ, can never
be thankfull for any mercy.
    2. Be thankfull for afflictions. Blesse God
for every twig of his rod, every drop in his cup.
He holds the rod and the cup in the same hand by
which he gives you Jesus Christ: yea, he afflicts
you with the same love with which he gives you any
good. Afflictions are evill, *many and evill* (saith
Father *Jacob* to *Pharaoh*) *have the dayes of my life
been.* But being sanctified, they are necessary. So
St. *Peter*, to those he wrote his Epistle; *now for a*

season *(if need be) you are in* [K7v] *heavynesse, through many tribulations.* Even the best of us are sometimes like a top, that will go on longer then it is whipt; we will not mend our pace, and run the wayes of Gods commandements, without the rod.
  Some stories say, that there was a King of *Scotland*, that whilest he was a prisoner in *Mortimer's* hole, he scraped the History of Christs passion in the stone wall; which was more then ever he did in his palace. Afflictions wil make us run to God. *In their affliction* (saith God of his people) *they wil seek me early,* that is, speedily and instantly. *Out of the depths* (saith *David*) *I cryed unto thee, O Lord.* Deep afflictions should raise up strong affections. The Ark was neerest heaven when the waters of the flood were highest. Afflictions meeting with a gracious temper, will melt the heart, and make it tender and humble; and the lowest humility is neerest the highest majesty. *Aristippus* the *Cynicke,* fell on the ground before *Dionysius,* and kissed his feet, when he presented a Petition to him; and being askt the reason, answers, *Aures habet in pedibus*: He hath his ears in his feet. Never doth a poor prostrate soul, brought down to extremity, seek Gods face with prayers and tears in vain, but meets with a gracious answer. Now if afflictions sanctfied be so good, then surely you should be thankfull for them; this being one eminent excellency that praise hath above prayer, that we may praise God for that for which [K8r] we may not pray; though we may not pray for afflictions, yet we must blesse God for them. *Job* did so, *The Lord hath taken away, Blessed be the name of the Lord.*
  When one came to Mr. *Bradford,* and told him, that if he would recant, he should have the Queens pardon; he answered, If the Queen will let me live, I will thank her; if she will banish me, I will thank her; if she will burn me, I will thank her. So a gracious heart will say, If the Lord give me

Chapter Six

health or sicknesse, I will thank him; if I have
much or little, I will thank him; if I live or dye,
I will thank him. Ecclesiastical Histories report
this of one *Servulus*, who for a long time was
grievously afflicted with the Palsie, his life was
a lingring death, whose daily and ordinary speech
was, *God be thanked.*

3. Blesse God every day wherein he hath kept
you from scandall. It is our misery that our hearts
are so vile, but it is Gods mercy that they break
not out continually to his dishonor, and the
offence of brethren; that he sets bounds to those
waves of our unruly lusts, and saith, Hitherto and
no further. Esteem any condition better then a sinfull, and choose rather to suffer the worst, then
sin in the least. *Moses chose rather to suffer
affliction with the people of God,* (and who meet
with more sorrows then they?) *then enjoy the
pleasures of sin for a season.* And where might he
satisfie his lust more to the [K8v] full, then in
the Court of a King? *Socrates* had so vile an esteem
of sin, that he thought it would be one of the
greatest torments in hell, to be given up to those
sins that men most delighted in. *Major sum, et ad
majora natus,* (saith *Seneca*) *quàm ut sim mancipium
corporis mei:* I am greater, and born to greater
things then to be a slave or drudge to my body. Say
to the Tempter, as *Joseph* to his Mistris, *There is
none greater in the house then I; and shall I then
commit this great wickednesse?* Or as *Nehemiah;
Shall such a man as I flee? Shall such a man as I
be drunk,* or deal unjustly, or break my oath? These
sons of *Zerviah* are sometimes too hard for us.
These unruly corruptions sometimes prevail over us.
Our darling sin like *Jeptha's* daughter, comes out
with timbrels and dances, with many pretty smiles
and subtle reasons, and sometimes overcomes us, and
brings us low, and troubles us. We all run in a
race, how few get to the goal without a fall by the

way?
   There are two things that I desire daily to make the matter, not only of my praise, but admiration. And the first is, that God hath preserved from the beginning to this day, a little flock of sheep amongst a world of Wolves, and Lions, and Bears, that are set on mischief. And the second is, that God maintains a little grace in life, in the midst of so much corruption that the heart is poysoned with; a little faith, and a little [L1r] humility, in the midst of so much unbelief and pride. The reason why the Church is not wasted, is because the Lord is their God; why this grace is not overwhelmed, and that our corruption breaks not out every moment into most notorious scandalls, is, because the corruption is ours, but the grace is the Lords. Hath God kept you therefore any day, that your heels have not been tript up? Forget not to blesse him for such a mercy. A notable example of such a thankful spirit we have in *David*, who by the humble and prudent counsel of *Abigail*, being stayed from imbruing his hands in the blood of *Nabal* and his family, blessed God and her that he was prevented. *Blessed be the Lord God of Israel* (saith he to her) *which sent thee this day to meet me, and blessed be thy advice; and blessed be thou that hast kept me this day from coming to shed blood, and from avenging my self with mine own hand,* etc. In every affliction forget not to blesse God for this. It is mine affliction, not my sin. What ever the crosse be, it might have been worse, for it might have been my sin. Blesse God that either prevented the temptation, as he did for *David*; or assisted in the temptation, as he did *Joseph*, who left his garment, but kept his chastity, and chose rather to suffer then to sin.
   4. Blesse God not onely for what you have, and for what you want; but for what you hope to have. All is not come that is [L1v] promised by the Father, all is not come that is merited by the Son,

nor is all come that is assured to you by the Holy
Ghost; the best is yet to come. Here joy enters
into us, there we shall enter into joy. Here are
promises, there performances. Here is faith, there
is fruition. Here we enjoy God mediately, there
immediately. In heaven there is a Kingdome without
cares, a throne without a thorn, greatnesse of
state without corruption of manners, a treasure
without moths, honour without envy, joy without
tears, love without jealousie, and dayes without
end.
 A devout Pilgrim travelling to *Jerusalem*, and by
the way visiting many brave Cities, with their rare
monuments; and meeting with many friendly
entertainments; would often say, I must not stay
here, this is not *Jerusalem*. So do you, in the
midst of all the delicates that the world can
afford you, not onely with variety, but plenty; say
still of every one of them, This is not *Jerusalem*,
This is not heaven; these are but tents and
tabernacles, all no better then moveables; our mansions are in heaven, where we shall abide for ever.
But would you be thankfull for heaven, and do you
long to be there? Be truly thankfull then for Jesus
Christ. It is Christ that makes heaven to be
heaven. He that cannot be thankfull for Jesus
Christ, cannot be thankfull for heaven; nay, would
not go to heaven at the last. A wicked man [L2r] at
the day of Judgement, might he have his choyce,
would not go to heaven. *Dives* in hell torments,
when he discoursed with *Abraham* afar off, did not
desire to go to *Abraham*, but prayed that *Lazarus*
might come to him, he cared more for ease then
heaven; nor did he desire that his five Brethren
should go to heaven, but that one might be sent to
them, to testifie to them, that they might not come
into the place of torment. For certainly, they that
could not endure the presence of Christ with his
servants in his ordinances, will have no desire to

be with him in all his glory.

In the last place, because you may your selves come very far short of what you should do in this great duty of thankfulness; declare to others, as occasion is offered, what the Lord hath done for you, that they may blesse God with you. It is an argument of an ingenuous spirit, to acknowledge the courtesies of a friend; *non amotis arbitris, sed clarè et ut audiat hospes*; not in private, but in the presence of others: Much more is it an argument of a gracious heart to speak of the loving kindnesse of the Lord before many witnesses, that they may be provoked also to blesse God. *David* was of this mind; *I have not hid thy righteousnesse, O Lord, within my heart; I have declared thy faithfulnesse, and thy salvation; I have not concealed thy loving kindnesse and thy truth from the great congregation.* The Psalmist exhorteth to this duty very [L2v] much: *Sing unto the Lord, sing Psalms unto him, talk ye of all his wondrous works.* It was the Psalmist his practice: *Come and hear all ye that fear God, and I will declare unto you what God hath done for my soul.* Moses the servant of the Lord did so: *He told Jethro his Father in law, all that the Lord had done unto Pharaoh, and to the AEgyptians for Israels sake; and all the travell that had come upon them by the way, and how the Lord delivered them:* Which occasioned much prayse unto God from a *Midianite*; who said, *Blessed be the Lord, who hath delivered you out of the hand of the AEgyptians, and out of the hand of Pharaoh*, etc. Christ himself commanded the man whom he delivered from the legion of Devils, that he should goe home to his friends, and tell them how great things the Lord had done for him, and had compassion on him. And indeed, to return thanks unto God for all his mercies, is so great a debt, that we alone cannot pay, unlesse God give us time; (and no lesse then eternity is enough.) And therefore we had need make

collection of praises from friends, that the summe
may be made up the more full. The Psalmist goes to
all creatures both in heaven and earth, and makes a
collection. *Heavens, Angels,* (saith he) *Sun, Moon,*
and Stars; Kings and all people, young men and
maids, old men and babes, praise the name of the
Lord. Comemmoration Sermons which are in use in
Colledges, and some other places, are excellent:
And as there may be good [L3r] use made of them
divers wayes, so this way especially, that all may
be provoked to blesse God for their Benefactors.

    It is observable, that to beg prayers is the
common complement of friends at their parting, and
Ora pro nobis is the conclusion of all our Letters;
but we seldome beg praises. When do we say, I beseech you blesse God for me and with me, for such a
late deliverance, for such successe in mine
endevours, for such comfort in my relations? etc.
As if we served an hard Master, as if God had been
a barren heath or a wildernesse to our souls, as if
his service had no profit. Whereas, there is no
Master like the Lord, no service like his; whose
very work is wages. [L3v]

Chap. VII

An use of Exhortation, wherein Christians are perswaded to keep such a Journall or Diary.

AND thus far shall suffice to have been spoken of the manner how such a Journall should be used.
5 For the application of all, I shall onely exhort such as have not been acquainted with this duty, to set upon this work. Indeed there is latitude in Christianity, and the wayes of God, that all do not reach. *I have seen an end of all perfection* (saith
10 the Psalmist) *but thy commandement is exceeding large.* When things are come to their perfection, to their flower, they quickly fade; like a Lute string, if wound up to the highest, it breaks; but the course of holinesse, and way of righteousnesse,
15 have large limits and boundaries, that many come not at. There are sins that some seldome confesse, as Sacramentall sins, Sacramentall ignorance, Sacramentall unbelief, impenitency, uncharitable-nesse, etc. There are some things they seldome pray
20 for; Where [L4r] is the man who with *Agur* prayes, *Lord give me no riches?* We often in prayer presse the promise, but how few at any time presse the seal? wherein God is come under the power of law, under the power of his own law; wherein all his
25 wisdome, power, faithfulnesse, goodnesse, and mercy is under the power of his owne law; yea, so far engaged that he cannot go back: And yet how few urge the seal, and enter a suit with the Lord? There are some duties we seldome or never perform.

Where is the man that makes conscience of private fasting and prayers, that shuts himself up in his closet, and wrastles with God in secret, that his Father that seeth in secret may reward him openly? To conclude, how few are there that keep a Diary by them of all Gods gracious dealings with them?

Now that I may perswade such Christians, at least, as have any abilities and opportunites to enter upon this duty, I shall doe these two things:

1. Give some directions that may be as advantages to further this service.

2. Give some arguments that may encourage and provoke thereunto, and so conclude.

1. Therefore often remember your sinfull estate, when you were in a naturall estate, and therefore in the gall of bitternesse, and [L4v] in the bond of iniquity. God commanded his people so to do. *Remember and forget not how thou provokedst the Lord thy God in the wildernesse,* etc.

This charge the Apostle lays upon the *Ephesians, Remember that you being in times past Gentiles in the flesh, that at that time ye were without Christ, aliens from the Common-wealth of Israel, and strangers from the covenants of promise, having no hope, and without God in the world.* God promised that his people should do so. *You shal remember your wayes and your doings wherewith you have been defiled, and you shall loath your selves.* Paul did so: he oftentimes makes mention of his sinfull condition before his conversion, he is not ashamed to declare it before King *Agrippa; I thought verily with my self that I ought to do many things contrary to the name of Jesus of Nazareth; which thing I also did in Jerusalem, for many of the Saints I shut up in prison, and when they were put to death, I gave my voyce against them, and I punished them oft in every Synagogue,* etc. So much he telleth the Corinthians, *I am not worthy to be called an Apostle, because I persecuted the Church of God.*

The like he declares to *Timothy; Iwas a
blasphemer, a persecuter, and injurious.* Yea, he
was more then an ordinary sinner in his owne eyes.
Jesus Christ (saith he) *came into the world to save
sinners,* ὡνέγω ἐιμτ πρῶτος, *whereof I am chief;*
or *primus,* the first, as it is in the originall. He
was *primus,* the first, *non ordine, sed excellentia;*
not in order of time, [L5r] but in the excesse of
wickednesse, for *Omne peccatum suam habet excellentiam,* every sin hath his eminency. So did
Joseph's Brethren, when he dealt roughly with them,
and God lookt so mercifully on them as to afflict them
for their sin, *They said one to another, we are
very guilty concerning our Brother, in that we saw
the anguish of his soul, when he besought us, and we
would not hear.* And how have those old bruises,
and sins of youth, being sadly and seriously
remembred, caused much brokennesse and tendernesse,
much care and watchfulnesse in some all their days?
Themistocles told his friends, when being
banished out of his Countrey, and most honorably
entertained by the King of *Persia, Perieram nisi
periissem,* I had been undone, if I had not been
thus distressed. So may many a gracious soul say, I
had faln into hell if I had not faln into sin.
Onesimus therefore departed, (saith St. *Paul* to
Philemon) *that thou mightest receive him an*
αἰώνιον, *an eternall.* So it is in the Originall.
And thus if our sins were heavy, Gods mercies would
be weighty, and worth the recounting. Were
our sins often in our eyes, Gods praises would not
be long out of our mouths: We that see we have
deserved nothing, would be thankfull for every
thing; and rather then his mercies should be
forgotten, would keep some remembrances by us of
Gods goodnesse to us, who is every day mindfull of
us. [L5v]

2. Remember often your low and poor condition.
It is little peradventure that you have, but was it

not lesse? God commands his people this duty, *Remember that thou wast a servant in the land of AEgypt.* This they were enjoyned to do, when they came yearly to offer up their basket of first-fruits to the Lord. Thus they must say, *A Syrian ready to perish was my Father, and he went down into AEgypt, and sojourned there with a few,* etc.

Agathocles King of *Sicily,* who was by birth but a Potters Son, would alwayes be served at his Table with earthen vessels, that he might ever be mindful of his low & mean condition at first. *Jacob* did so, *With my staff I came over this Jordan:* His condition was low when the earth was his bed, a stone his pillow, and the heaven his canopie over his head; he is thankfull for this, because he forgat not his low estate. He that well remembers what he once wanted will not forget to be thankful for what at present he enjoys. Humility is a good spur to thankfulness. I have read of two garments in Scripture of excellent use: First, the garment of humility, *Be clothed with humility,* (saith *Peter*) *and the garment of praise.* Christ is said to appoint to them that mourn in *Zion,* the garment of praise for the spirit of heavynesse. The under garment is commonly plain, and of lesse worth, but the upper is very costly. Let humility be like the first: It is no matter how vile we be in our [L6r] own eyes; but let praise be the upper garment. *Be ye rooted and built up in Christ,* (saith the Apostle) *and established in the faith, abounding therein with thanksgiving.* He that is rich in faith, and low in humility, will make his upper garment costly; will be abundant in praises.

3. Labour to understand a mercy aright. Endevour to discern the height and breadth of a providence, weigh every benefit bestowed skilfully. The reason why the *Israelites* remembred not the multitude of Gods mercies, was (saith the Psalmist) *because they understood not his wonders*

Chapter Seven

in *AEgypt*. *Moses* told them that they had seen all
that the Lord had done before their eyes in the
Land of *AEgypt*, unto *Pharaoh*, and unto all his servants, and unto all the land. *The great temptations*
which thine eyes have seen, the signes and those
great miracles: And yet the Lord hath not given you
an heart to perceive, and eyes to see, and ears to
hear, unto this day. It is true, they had eyes and
ears, but they wanted an understanding heart to
perceive and discern God in all. Hence it comes to
passe, that as a proud man will not be mindfull, so
an ignorant man cannot remember God, and be
thankfull. It is good therefore not onely to remember our low and sinfull estate, that we may be humble, but to understand the loving kindnesse of the
Lord, that we may record his favours. The reason
why the Disciples forgat what Christ had done,
[L6v] and therefore mistook him, when he bad them
take heed of the leaven of the Pharisees and Sad-
duces, was, they did not understand the miracles of
the five loaves amongst the five thousand; nor the
seven loaves amongst the five thousand; nor the
seven loaves amongst the foure thousand, nor how
many baskets they took up. They did not well understand, nor seriously consider the mighty power of
his divine nature, by which he did all that. You
shall do well therefore to understand a mercy
fully, in all the causes, circumstances, manner and
means of working. Sometimes he works without means,
and then his works are miraculous; sometimes by
weak means, and then his works are wonderfull;
sometimes by contrary means, so that losses enrich
us, divisions unites us, and our routing in battle
makes us conquerors; and then his works are
glorious. Hence the Lord commanded his people to
understand why he gave them that good Land, to possesse it; not for their righteousnesse, for they
were a stiffe-necked people, but for his Name sake,
and for the wickednesse of those Nations which were

driven out before them. It is not an easie matter
for men to hit right on the true reason of Gods
despensations of mercy or judgement. Hence *Samuel*
advised the people of *Israel* to consider, that is,
to weigh & ponder wel in their hearts what great
things God had done for them. Now we all know,
things that are not known, and therefore lightly
valued, are [L7r] soon forgotten; when matters that
are looked at as things of price and worth, are
laid up very carefully. It is good therefore when
our thoughts dwell upon mercies. *Omnis festinatio
caeca*, swift passengers cannot be serious observ-
ers, a transient thought is too mean for a standing
mercy; one mercy enjoyed deserves more serious
thoughts then a million of miseries do one hearty
tear; our mercies are from God, our calamities from
our selves. Understand this well, and consider this
seriously, & you cannot be unmindful of the loving
kindnesse of the Lord.

  4. Would you write down the great things of
God in a book, that you might never forget them?
Take speciall notice of the actings of God in the
wayes of his gracious providence, whilest they are
new and fresh in memory, together with the workings
of your hearts, whilest they are so considered. Oh!
what vows, covenants, purposes, resolutions are
made and entertained then? *Omne novum valde mutat*,
saith *Scaliger*: New things, fresh mercies make a
wonderful change upon mens spirits for the present.
Omnia subita videntur majora, saith *Cicero*: All
sudden and unexpected passages seem very great at
first sight, and work very much upon the heart.
Observe then what joy, what thankfulnesse, what
meltings, what resolutions: And what you doe, doe
quickly, strike while the iron is hot. *Qui tardè
fecit, diu noluit*, saith *Seneca*: He that [L7v] is
slack in his performances, was but unwilling in his
resolutions. Oh! remember your first love, when you
were newly converted, and brought home to God; how

Chapter Seven

zealous, lively, active, forward, and savoury were
you in the wayes of God. So much the Lord tells his
people by the Prophet *Hosea*, that at their restitu-
tion, and Gods reconciliation with them, they
should sing as in the dayes of their youth, as they
did when they came out of *AEgypt*. *Then sang Moses
and Aaron*. A converted condition is a singing condition. God takes special notice of this. *I remember thee*, (saith the Lord of *Israel*) *the kindnesse
of thy youth, the love of thine espousals, when
thou wentest after me in the wildernesse, in a land
that was not sown*. Our first works and our last
works, are commonly our best works; when we begin
first to live the life of grace, and when we are
ready to die, and are entring upon the life of
glory, how excellent is our carriage, how savoury
our words, how heavenly our conversation? Even so it is
when we are delivered from any great danger;
when enlarged with any singular comforts, how
lively, how zealous, and how active are we? Call to
minde the fifth of *November*, 1605. when we were
delivered from that barbarous Gunpowder-treason;
how forward were we in making laws against Papists?
how severe in suppressing Jesuites? how zealous in
setling true Religion? [L8r]

It is reported of the City of *Berne*, when first
delivered from Antichrist, when that State cast off
that *Romane* bondage, and reformed Religion, that
they wrote the day of their Redemption upon pil-
lars, in letters of gold. And it is observable,
that in all the ages of the Church, God hath set
out himself to his people by such names and titles
as were most suitable to his present dispensations,
or such as were of the last edition. And why so?
But that his late mercies might be the better considered and remembred. Hence in the beginning he
was called the most high God, the possessour of
heaven and earth, who had made all by the word of
his power. Under those times *Melchisedech* blessed

Abraham, Blessed be Abraham (saith he) *of the most high God, possessor of heaven and earth.* And *Abraham* covenanted to take nothing from the King of *Sodome,* and that under these terms. *I have lift up my hand unto the Lord, the most high God, possessor of heaven and earth, that I will not take from a thread to a shoe-latchet; and that I will not take any thing that is thine.* Afterwards, when God entred into a covenant with *Abraham* and his seed, he was called the God of *Abraham,* and *Isaac,* and *Jacob.* And under those titles God gave his charge to *Moses,* when he sent him to bring his people out of the Land of *AEgypt; I am the God of thy Father, the God of Abraham, the God of Isaac, and the God of Jacob.* After that he was called, the God that [L8v] brought them out of the Land of *AEgypt,* out of the house of bondage. Such was the preface to his law, *I am the Lord thy God, which have brought thee out of the Land of AEgypt, out of the house of bondage.* And so it continued for many generations, even until he brought them out of *Babylon.* And then (saith the Lord) *It shall be no more said, The Lord liveth, that brought them out of the land of AEgypt*: but, *The Lord liveth, that brought the children of Israel out of the land of the North.* And now under the gospel, he is known by this most excellent name, *The God and Father of our Lord Jesus Christ.* And why so? But because our redemption by Christ is the last, and the great work he hath done for his Church, and most fresh in our memories. Whilest therefore mercies are fresh, and work most upon the heart, doe something in remembrance of Gods goodness; and why not then write them downe in a Journall? A small matter (I should think) whilest the heart is warm, and well affected with the present sense of some singular pledge of Gods loving kindnesse, may easily perswade to this duty.

    5. And finally, love the Lord for his good-

Chapter Seven 145

nesse. If any thing under heaven will constrain us
and help forward this duty, love will. *Oh! love the
Lord all ye his Saints*, saith the Psalmist. And indeed,
none but Saints can love him. He knocks at every
dore, and (as it were) pulls every man by the sleeve,
[M1r] and saith, *Oh!* love you the Lord; Let the
drunkard love his cups, and the adulterer his harlots,
and the covetous person his bags; but do you that are
Saints love the Lord. For, *the Lord preserveth the
faithfull, and plentifully rewardeth the proud doer.*
When one bucket goes downe, the other will come up.
When *Pharaoh* is drowned, *Israel* is saved. When *Haman*
is hanged, *Mordecai* is advanced. When proud doers are
plagued, the faithful are delivered. Oh! love the Lord
therefore. And indeed, love is all that God looks at
in us, and expects from us; and where there is love,
there is no lack. After so large a repetition of
the great things God hath done for *Israel, What* (saith
Moses to them) *doth God now require for all this, but
that you would love him?* And indeed love is *complementum legis*, the fulfilling of the Law. *Neither
circumcision, nor uncircumcision availeth any
thing*, (saith the Apostle) *but faith that worketh
by love.* Faith and Love are like a pair of Compasses; Faith like one point, fastens upon Christ
as the center; and Love like the other, goes the
round in all the works of holinesse and righteousnesse. Now certainly Love hath a good memory, or
would have a good memory: What we slight, we soon
forget; but what we love, we endevour to lay up
sure in our memories. *Ubi amor, ibi animus*: Where
our love is, our minde is. Where our treasure is,
there will our heart be. It was the eye that made
the match. That which [M1v] the eye sees not, the
heart desires not: And as love came in by the eye,
so it delights by the same dore to look after that
beloved object. Such a soul that hath seen God in
all things, and therefore loves God above all
things, delights still to look after God in all his

wayes, that he may love him more and more. Such a
soul loves God as *Jonathan* loved *David*:
   1. *Amore unionis*, with a love of union; the
soul of *Jonathan* was knit to *David*; for he loved
him as his own soul.
   2. He loved him *amore complacentiae*, with a
love of delight; for it is said that *Jonathan*
delighted much in *David*.
   3. He loved him *amore benevolentiae*, with a love
of good will; for *Jonathan* said to *David*,
*Whatsoever thy soul desireth, I will even do it for
thee.*
   Even so doth a gracious heart love God; not
onely with a love of union, and a love of delight,
but with a love of good will too; who saith to God,
as *Paul* at his conversion, *Lord, what wilt thou
have me to do?* Such an one is ready to suffer what
ever may be inflicted on him; and to do what ever
may be required of him; especially, whatsoever may
testifie how well he remembers God, and his loving
kindnesse to him. [H2r]

Chap. VIII

Severall arguments propounded, by which Christians may be provoked to keep such a Journall or Diary as hath been commended.

THat such Christians as have any abilities for the keeping of such a Journal or Diary as hath been commended to them, may be encouraged thereunto, I shal in the second place propound these foure arguments.

First, it is a most excellent duty, and practised by many, whose example we may follow: As,

1. It hath been the practice even of the very Heathens, even from a principle of common reason, who made use of white and black stones for these two ends: One was, They gave them to persons at their arraignment before the Judges: If any were condemned to death, they gave him a black stone; but if absolved and set free, a white stone. To which custome the holy Ghost seems to allude, in the Epistle to the Angel of the Church of *Pergamus*, in these words, *To him that overcometh, wil I give a white stone*, etc. [M2v] A second use of those was, That by them they might keep an account of all the good dayes or evill they had met withall in their lives. Hence *Persius* advised his friend *Macrinus* to remember a good day so.

Hunc Macrine diem numera meliore lapillo.
Count this day *Macrine* with a better stone.

2. Persons of good quality have a long time

practised this duty. How many noble *Theophilus's*
and *Elect Ladies* have such Diaries by them? But if
any men of worth be imployed in the service of the
State, either by Sea or Land, it is their common practise.
They that go to Sea, will tell you of their Journall book,
that on such a day they met aboard the Boneventure
they weighed anchor, and fell downe to *Gravesend;* on
such a day they met with the whole Fleet, on
another day they had stormy weather, or fought with
the enemy, etc. How exactly doth S. *Luke* set down
S. *Paul's* shipping towards *Rome,* how perfect a
Journall of that dangerous voyage, even day by day.
If they be employed by Land, and do either besiege
a Town, or are besieged; not a sally undertaken,
not a mine sprung, not a breach made, not a man of
note slain, not a tyre of Ordnance discharged, but
is every day recorded; as you may see in that
famous siege of *Ostende.* [M3r]

But in the 3. place, God himself seems to keep
a Journall by him of all the care he hath of us,
the cost he bestows upon us, and the good things he
gives to us. He hath a book of remembrance of every
passage of providence that concerns us. And indeed,
the Scripture for a great part is little else but a
history of his goodnesse to his people. And that
you may see that God is very punctuall in keeping
accompt of his mercies bestowed on us, you shall
find that in the Gospel of St. *John,* when Christ
turned the water into wine; it is said, *This is the*
beginning of miracles that Jesus did in Cana of
Galilee, and manifested forth his glory. And when
he healed the noble mans Son; *This is again the*
second miracle that Jesus did, when he came out of
Judea into Galilee. Thus God doth keep an account
of his mercies bestowed on us. This is the first
Magistrate, and this is the second Minister, and
this is the third affliction, and that is the
fourth deliverance you have had. And if we remember
them not to Gods glory, he will remember them to

Chapter Eight

our shame; as he did to *Eli, I did plainly appear unot the house of thy Father, when they were in AEgypt, in Pharaohs house; and I did choose him out of all the Tribes of Israel, to be my Priest, to offer upon mine Altar, and to burn incense, etc.*
The like he said to *Saul* by *Samuel, When thou wast little in thine owne sight, wast thou not made head of the Tribes of Israel, and the Lord anoited thee King over Israel?* And how doth God reckon up the many [M3v] [g]reat favors vouchsafed to *David*, especially in that great advancement of him to the throne, and delivering him from the hand of *Saul*? All these things are repeated to *Eli, Saul, David*, for the greater aggravation of their sins; nay, Gods very judgements executed are particularly recorded by him, as you may see in divers places, especially that of *Amos*, ch.4. v.6. to the end of that ch. his several judgements, and their incorrigiblenesse. Doth God keep a book of Remembrance, and shall we be without our Journall? God forbid.

Secondly, it is very just and equall, that we should thus remember God, who remembers us daily; and that not only for the supplying our wants, or delivering us in our extremity, but also in the accepting of our persons, and our sincere performances.

1. For the first: God remembred *Noah* when he was in the Ark, and sent him forth. God remembred *Abraham* in that great overthrow of the Cities in the Plain, and sent *Lot* to him, to warn him, to comfort him. God remembred *Rachel*, and gave her a *Joseph*. God remembred *Hannah*, and made her fruitfull. God remembers our wants, and supplyes them; our friends, and requites them; our enemies, and plagues them; nay, our very cattle, and preserves them. God did not only remember *Noah* in the Ark, but he remembred every living thing, and all the cattle. God chides *Jonah* for being angry for the losse of his gourd, upon this account; *Thou hadst*

pity [M4r] *on the gourd,* etc. *and should not I spare Nineveh, that great City, wherein there are so many children, and also much cattle?* Doth God remember and take care for oxen, and will he not much more remember his people? *No,* (saith the Lord) *I cannot. Can a woman forget her sucking childe, that she should not have compassion on the Son of her wombe? Yea, they may forget; Yet wil not I forget thee,* saith the Lord of his people. A Mother may break the bonds of Nature, but I cannot break the bonds of my Covenant. Why so? Because *I have graven thee upon the palms of my hands.* I may as soon forget my self, as forget thee; *thy walls are ever before me.* Now that which is continually before us, we well remember. Will not God forget us? And shall not we use all means that we may remember him? Rather then fail, chalk up his loving kindnesses.

    2. We never shewed any love to God in our lives, but he remembers it. *I remember* (saith God to *Israel*) *the kindnesse of thy youth, the love of thine espousals. Sarah* spake but one good word in that foolish fit of her unbelief, when she laught, and slighted the promise of a Son; she call'd her Husband *Lord; After I am waxen old, shall I have pleasure, my Lord being old also?* This one good word is not forgotten, but set down in a book by the hand of *Peter, Sarah obeyed Abraham, and called him Lord.* Not a prayer made, nor a tear shed, but he hath a book for the one, and a bottle for the other, rather then they should be lost. [M4v] *Put thou my tears into thy bottle, O Lord,* (saith the Psalmist) *are they not in thy book?* If Gods people meet together, and pray and speak often one to another, he hearkens and hears; that is, he doth most diligently attend to all they say; *and a book of remembrance shal be written of it before the Lord. Cornelius* was a most devout benefactor, and the Angel tell him that his prayers and alms were come up in remembrance before God. It is a mercy

Chapter Eight

that God will remember us, though it be with a rod
to correct us; but it is a rich favour indeed, if
he remember us with a staffe to support and comfort
us. As our remembrace of God or men is the summe
of all we do for them. *Remember me* (saith *Joseph* to
Pharaoh's Butler) that is, speak a good word for
me, do me the favour as work out my deliverance.
But the chief Butler did not remember *Joseph*, but
forgat him; that is, he did nothing for him; Even
so Gods remembrance is the *summa totalis* of his
goodnesse to us: He remembers us indeed, for he
pities us, and spares us, and pardons us, supplyes us
in all our necessities, and supports us in all our
extremities; he will not leave us in our straights,
nor leave us in our sins; and if we do or suffer any
thing for him, he hath a book of remembrance, and it
shall be written down. At the last day it is said,
the books shall be opened, and is not this one of
those books? and the dead shall be judged out of
those things which were written in those [M5r] books,
according to their works. Jesus Christ will read to
all the world the good works of his people out of
that book. *I was an hungry, and ye gave me meat; I
was thirsty, and ye gave me drink; I was a stranger,
and ye took me in; naked, and ye clothed me.* You
never did anything for God, but he hath put it down in
his book; it is very just and equall then, that what he
hath done for you should be written down in your book.

Thirdly, it is very necessary you should keep
such a Journall, and that in three regards:

1. In regard of the badnesse of your memory.
Memoria primùm senescit, (say Physicians) The
memory decayes first; old men and dying men will
tell you so; but the memory of a benefit sooner,
the memory of divine favours soonest of all. Some
things we can hardly forget, as our sorrows and our
pleasures. It was about 20 yeers ere *Esau* could forget
the sorrow he conceived for the losse of the
blessing, and the injury *Jacob* did him, in getting

it away from him. And he was so mindfull of his
pleasures that he forgat his bread. And there be
some things we can hardly remember, as our faults
and our friends. It was two full years (saith the
story) ere *Pharaoh's* Butler could remember *Joseph*,
or call his faults to minde, for which he suffered
imprisonment. *Many O Lord my God* (saith *David*) *are
thy wonderfull works which thou hast done, and thy
thoughts which are* [M5v] *toward us, they cannot be
reckoned up in order to thee; if I should declare
and speak of them, they are more then can be
numbred.* Then certainly, many of these mercies that
God hath vouchsafed to us, would quite be forgotten, did we not keep such a Diary by us.

    2. It is necessary, that thereby we prevent
the great sin of forgetfulnesse. To forget God is a
mother-sin, a root-sin. What will not that man be,
what will not he doe that forgets God? He is a very
wicked man. *The wicked shall be turned into hell*
(saith the Psalmist) *and all the nations that
forget God.* He is a proud man, and I am sure a
proud man is a wicked man. Through the pride of his
countenance he wil not seek after God; God is not
in all his thoughts, his thoughts are not of him;
or his thoughts are, that there is no God. He that
forgets God, forgets that God is. He that forgets
God is an hypocrite, and an hypocrite is a very
wicked man. *Consider this ye that forget God.* But
who were they? Such as took Gods name into their
mouths, and yet hated instruction, and cast Gods
words behind them. He that forgets God is a most
unthankfull person, and an unthankfull man is a
most wicked man. *Dixeris ingratum, dixeris omnia.*
Call a man an unthankfull man, and call him any
thing.

    There was a little City (saith *Solomon*) *besieged
by a great King, and a poor wise man delivered that
City by his wisdome, yet no mn remembred that poor
wise man.* It was a wicked part to forget that [M6r]

man, but most wicked it is to forget God. When *Tamerlane* (that victorious Emperor) had beaten *Bajazet* in battle, and taken him prisoner, he sent for him, and amongst other questions, asked him, Whether ever he were thankfull to God for making him so great a King? he answered, that he never so much as thought of him; which was a most wicked speech of a wicked man.

3. It is necessary to prevent the great danger of forgetting God. To forget God is a provoking sin. He that forgets God, sins not at an ordinary rate, and therefore shal be punished not after an ordinary manner. *Consider this ye that forget God* (saith the Lord) *lest I tear you in pieces, and there be none to deliver you.* Eli forgat God, and so did *Saul* and *Jereboam*, they forgat the great things God had done for them, and did not God plague them and their posterity? Forgetfulnesse of God makes him rage, not onely against the work of his hands, but the sheep of his pasture. *David* forgat God, and so did *Solomon*; and how severely were they punished? The one by his Son, who rebelled against him; the other by his Servant, that pluckt the greatest part of Kingdome from his posterity.

A Souldier of *Philip* of *Macedonia*, having begg'd the lands of one that had entertained him kindly, was branded with *Ingratus hospes* on the forehead, to his perpetual shame. It is reported of *Caesar* and *Alexander*; two of the most valiant Souldiers that ever [M6v] the world had, that the one would never give to, and the other forgive a unthankful man. *Because* (saith the Lord) *Pharaoh King of AEgypt saith the river* (that is *Nilus*) *is mine owne, I have made it for my self, therefore will I dry up the river, and cause the fish to stink.* What became of *Herod* the proud? who, after his oration, and the peoples acclamation, The voyce of a god, and not of a man, gave not the glory to God; the

Angel of the Lord smote him, and he was eaten of
worms, and gave up the Ghost. He that forgets God,
is unthankful to God; and he that is unthankful
forfeits all mercies; as the not paying of Custome
forfeits all a Merchants goods.

 It is written of one *Timotheus* the Son of *Conon*
a noble Citizen of *Athens*, that after he had
proudly said in a great assembly, *Haec ego feci,
non fortuna*: These things I have done, and not Fortune, (which that people adored as God) he never
prospered, but lost all the glory he had gotten.

 A poor honest man meeting with a very rich
neighbour in his Corn-fields, upon harvest, very
plentifully stored, consisting of many acres, said
to him, You have Sir a very rich crop; answered,
Yea, I wil have a good crop; and gave not God the
praise: Within a few dayes after, by a mighty storm
of wind the greatest part of his corn was blown out
of the ear, and with other wet weather it was so
wasted that it came to little. If we forget God, he
will forget us: He will remember [M7r] our sins, and
punish us for them; but he will forget our persons in
time of trouble. To wh^{ch} purpose I shall relate a
sad story, which I had from a good hand, in the
hearing of very many; and I believe it to be very
true. A man that on his sick bed, that proved his
death-bed, had one time an extraordinary appetite,
and desired something that he might eat; which
being brought to him, he did as much loath as
before he longed for; and therefore without touching any part of it, was carried away; suddenly, he
called for it again, his stomach to such provision
being as strong and quick as ever; which was done
accordingly, and set before him; but his stomach
rose against it, with as great abhorrency as
before. This was done a third time, upon the former
ground, & carried away again for the same reason.
At last he confessed that it was just with God so
to deal with him, that never craved a blessing from

Chapter Eight

God upon his meat when he sat down at his table, nor gave God thanks when he rose up, but forgat God the giver of all. And indeed it is just with God to forget us in our straights, that never remember him in our enlargements. The keeping of such a Journall would conduce much to the preventing of such an evil.

Fourthly, it is a very profitable course to have such a Journal or Diary by us; and you know, Who wil shew us any good? Who will bring us any profit? is the great question of the world, and prevails very far. Now it is profitable these 7 ways. [M7v]

1. As it would be an excellent way to advance the name and honorable memoriall of some, so it would thereby much promote the good of others: For would such as are of singular worth, and speciall note for their learning, piety, and usefulnesse in Church or Common-wealth, be perswaded to this duty of keeping a Journall, how easie were it for their posterity, or speciall friends, to write a history of their Lives, especially so far as concerned their parents, their birth and breeding, either in the University or Innes of Court; their great preservations from dangers, their great preferments to places of trust, with their employments and successe in those places, and such like? Other things might be added, as occasion is offered, from the relation of others; which as it would much conduce to the honor of the dead, so it would very far advance the good of those that survive them. Most people believe their eyes rather then their ears, and walk more by patterns then they do by any rules. *Mahomet* the Great, the first Emperor of *Constantinople*, did ever set before him the examples of *Alexander* and *Caesar* in all his Wars, whom he laboured to imitate. And it is reported of *Themistocles*, that he had always in his thoughts the victories of *Miltiades*, which made him unsatisfied, till he had imitated him. Christians

that have such a cloud of witnesses (not unlike the
pillar of a *cloud* to *Israel* in the *wilderness*) may
the better be guided through the dark labyrinths
[M8r] of this evil world, till they come to that
Canaan of unutterable joy and happinesse, of which
those worthies are now made partakers. And indeed,
who can behold their love to Gods truth, their
zeal for his glory, their patience in tribulation,
their courage in a good cause, their perseverance
in well-doing, their holinesse of life, their
prayers, fasting, tears, alms, temperance, modesty,
heavenly-mindednesse, with their triumph at their
death; but must needs ἀναζ ωπυρεατὸ χάριεματον θεοῦ,
stir up the grace that is in them; stir the coals
of their fervent desires, till they break out into
a flame, in being followers of those worthies as
they followed Christ. The *Lacedemonians* for the
better stirring up of young men to noble enterprises, used to have the statues of their most
famous Worthies, either Gown-men or Sword-men, set
up in their Senate-house, with this sentence in
golden letters, *Si fueritis sicut hi, eritis sicut
hi*: If you will be like these for their service,
you shall be like these for their honour. Some have
taken good pains in writing the Lives and Deaths of
such as have deserved well in their generations, a
Work in this regard very commendable. How many such
examples would be preserved, and left to posterity,
(which otherwise were like to be lost) were this
course of keeping Diaries observed?

2. This practice would bring Christians into
great acquaintance with God, and his most gracious
nature. So the Psalmist, [M8v] who having fully
discoursed of his providence over divers sorts of
persons, in answering their prayers, and relieving
them in their necessities; concludes, *Whoso is
wise, and will observe these things, even such
shall understand the loving kindnesse of the Lord.*
Now what better way to observe such things, then by

a constant keeping of such a Journal? Thence we may
discern his loving kindesse.
   1. How full it is; who giveth us richly all
things to enjoy.
   2. How free it is; who doth all for us for his
name sake.
   3. How firm it is; with whom there is no
variablenesse, nor shadow of turning; whose gifts
and calling are without repentance.
   And who would not endevour by all means to be
wel acquainted with God, whom to know, is wisdome
indeed; to fear, is godlinesse indeed; to enjoy, is
happinesse indeed?
   3. It will from hence much inlarge our love to
God; for we must needs love him that hath loved us
first, especially that hath loved us thus. Certainly
the more we know God, the better we shall love him.
I will deliver him (saith the Lord by the Psalmist)
*because he hath set his love upon me; And he hath
set his love upon me, because he hath known my
name.* Even Publicans (saith our Saviour) *will love
those of whom they are beloved, by whom they are
rewarded*: And shall not Christians [N1r] be in love
with such a God, whose mercies are more then we can
number, greater then we can value? And will not
this our love to God be beneficial to us? If we
love him, he will love us again, and in his love
there can be no lack, for they that seek him early
shall finde him. *He that loveth me* (saith Christ)
*shall be loved of my Father, and I will love him,
and manifest my self unto him*. And again, *If any
man love me, he will keep my commandements, and my
Father will love him; and we will come unto him,
and make our abode with him*. Now this God hath not
onely enough in himself to enable him unto all
this, (for he is the only wise and almighty God)
but he hath also enough to encline him thereunto,
for he is the Father of mercies, and the God of all
comfort. Yea, he hath enough to engage him; for he

is in covenant with us, and that convenant is under
seal, that by two immutable things, in which it was
impossible for God to lye, we might have strong
consolation.

    4. It will much enlarge our hearts in kind-
nesse and compassion to our brethren; for *because*
(as the Psalmist saith) *our goodnesse cannot extend
to God, it shall to the Saints that are in the
earth.* And surely he that loveth God, loveth him
also that is begotten of God. And such love to the
Saints is very profitable,

    1. For the present; for it is a good evidence
*that we are past from death to life, because we
love the brethren. He that loveth not his brother
abideth in death.* [N1v]

    2. For the future; it shall be remembred and
rewarded at the last day: For Christ will say to such,
*In as much as ye did all this to one of these my
Brethren, ye did it unto me. Come ye therefore ye
blessed of my Father, inherit the Kingdome prepared
for you from the foundation of the world.*

    5. The keeping of such a Journall, especially
if we look often into it, and read it over, will be
a notable means to encrease in us that self-
abasement & abhorrency of spirit that is most
acceptable in the sight of God. The more we look
upon the loving kindness of the Lord, the more vile
shall we be in our owne eyes. *When I consider*
(saith *David*) *the heavens, the work of thy fingers,
the moon and the stars which thou hast ordained;
What is man that thou art mindfull of him, or the
Son of man that thou visitest him?* Alas, man is not
onely frail, as a creature, but filthy also as a
sinner, yet the riches of Gods grace overlooks all;
so that God will bestow his thoughts upon him, and
visit him. We may be very mindful of such as we do
not, we cannot visit; but God will do both. *David*
in another place goes a step higher, *What is man
that thou takest knowledge of him, or the Son of*

Chapter Eight

man that thou makest account of him? Man is like to
vanity, his days are like a shadow that passeth
away. Man is not worthy that God should cast an eye
upon him, and make any account of him; and yet the
highest Lord will take knowledge of the lowest
worm; Majesty will make some [N2r] reckoning of
meanness. Oh! how will the serious survey of such a
Journal abase the soul before the Lord! When *David*
did but tell *Mephibosheth*, what he would do for
him, and he cryes out from the sense of his owne
vilenesse, *What is thy servant, that thou should
look upon such a dead dog as I am?* A dog; yea, a
dead dog; What more vile in the world? But when God
told *David* how he would build him an house, and set
up his seed after him; he replyes, *Who am I*, and
*What am I, that thou hast brought me hitherto? And
this was yet but a small thing in thy sight, O
Lord; but thou hast spoken of thy servants house
for a great while to come.* If God be great and good
in our eyes, we shall be little and vile in our
owne sight. If God be high in our hearts, we shall
be as low in our thoughts, as we are in our
deserts. And this will be for our profit; for if we
be mean in our owne account, God will set his heart
upon us, and magnifie us; for as *he resisteth the
proud*, so *he giveth grace to the humble.*

   6. This Journal, with a survey of all the
good things God hath bestowed on us, and continued
to us, will much provoke us to thankfulnesse. They
that have but heard much of Gods goodnesse, cannot
be unthankfull. Indeed, they that were born deaf
remain dumb; they that could never hear, can never
speak. They that could never hear the voyce of the
Son of God, and live, are tongue-tyed in his
praises: But they that have heard of him by the
ear, seen him [N2v] by the eye, and every day taste
of his bounty, their mouths will ever run over with
thanksgiving. Now certainly the more thankfull any
man is, the more successefull. As faith is the way

to thankfulnesse, so thankfulnesse is the way to
thrive. It is said that *Aaron* had on his robe round
about a bell and a pomegranate; the Bell signified
thankfulnesse; and the Pomegranate fruitfulnesse.
He that offereth me prayse (saith God) *glorifieth
me; and to him that ordereth his conversation
aright, I will shew the salvation of God.* I will
not be in his debt, but work some great extraordinary deliverance for him. *Let the people praise
thee, O God; yea, let all the people praise thee;*
(saith the Psalmist) *Then shall the earth bring
forth her increase, and God even our own God l shall
blesse us.* Prayers get mercies, but praises keep
them and enlarge them, with a blessing; and a little
blessed is better then the whole world enjoyed.

7. Such a course would very much help our
faith. Every experiment of Gods former goodnesse is
a strong prop for our faith for the future. When
Moses went up to the Mount to pray for *Israel*, and
against *Amalek*, he took the rod of God in his hand.
And the reason certainly was, because by that rod
God had done wonderful things for his people and
against their enemies; as by that he turned the
waters into blood, by that he brought frogs and
lice upon the land of *AEgypt*, by that he divided
the waters of the Red [N3r] Sea. And the very sight
of that rod did encourage *Moses* to trust in God for
the deliverance of his people, and the overthrow of
their enemies; and that from the experience of his
former goodnesse. Now questionlesse the best way to
be stored with such experiments, is to keep such a
Journal or Diary by us: And who can read such an
history, but must needs say, Why should not I trust
to, and depend upon such a God at all times, and
for all things?

First, I say, *at all times*; for there is not
prius et posterius in Deo; first and last in God,
as in man: He can do what he hath done, *I am* is his
name. *I have been young, and now am old*, was the

Chapter Eight

language of *David*, but not of *David's* God.
  Secondly, as *at all times*, so *for all things*;
for there is not *majus et minus in Deo*, not more
and lesse in God, he can do what he will do; he can
pardon all sins as well as one, supply all wants as
well as one, subdue all our enemies as easily as
one. *I cannot do as I have done*, is the voyce of
the creature, not the Creator. See how *Jacob*
reasons from experience, when he blessed *Joseph's*
Son. *The God which fed me all my life long unto
this day; The Angell which redeemed me from all
evill, blesse the lads.*
  Now is not faith a profitable grace? Faith is
the greatest gather-good in the world: What need he
care, why should he fear, what can he want, that is
rich in faith? For rich in faith, and rich in God,
and he that enjoyes [N3v] God, shall inherit all
things. By this faith strengthened, and by so many
experiments thus enlarged, he may erect a monument,
and say, *Hitherto the Lord hath holpen me*. And
thereupon look up into heaven, and thus admire at
the large allownace that is provided for him there,
with the Psalmist; *How great is thy goodnesse, O
Lord, which thou hast laid up for those that fear
thee!* If my friend will give me such entertainment
at an Inne by the way, how welcome will he make me
when I come to his house? If earth be such, what is
heaven? If my comfort in a cottage be so great,
what are the joys of those everlasting habitations,
not made with hands, but eternall in the heavens,
where I shall have glory with a double *hyperbole*,
καθ ὑπερβολὴν εἰς ὑπερβολὴν αἰώνιον βάρος δόξης,
an exceeding weight of glory. Oh! that our treasure
were laid up in heaven, that our conversation were
in heaven, from whence we look for the Saviour, the
Lord Jesus Christ; *who shall change our vile
bodies, that they may be fashioned like unto his
glorious body, according to the working whereby he
is able to subdue all things unto himself.* Heaven

wil make us amends for all, but Jesus Christ is
better then heaven. *Jacob's* Sons met with hard
measure whilest they travelled into *AEgypt* for
food; but *I am Joseph your Brother*, and Governour
of all *AEgypt*, did abundantly recompense them for
all their trouble. After all our sorrows and sufferings in this vale of tears; *Fear not, it is I.*
[N4r} All power is given unto me; your Captain,
your Brother, your Head will satisfie abundantly.
Paul had a desire to depart, and to be with Christ;
which is far better. Riches are good, but Learning
is better; Learning is good, but Grace is better;
Grace is good, but Glory in heaven is better;
Heaven is good, but Christ is far better. A picture
of the globe of the whole earth, set out with all
the brave things that Sea and Land can afford, with
this sentence encircling it round, *To be with Christ
is far better*, is a Christians embleme. Indeed Jesus
Christ is a Christians heaven; *in whose presence
there is fulness of joy, and at whose right hand
there are pleasures for evermore.* Whither he bring
us, who hath so dearly bought us; to whom with the
Father, and the Holy Ghost, be given by us and all
his Saints, all honor and glory, now and for
evermore, *Amen.* [N5v]

ΠάνΤοΤε δόεα θεω
Christianus gratulabandus
Exod. [device with bells and
pomegranates] 28.34
Thankfulnes Away to thriue
FINIS [N4v]

The Contents:

CHAP. I.
The Preface, wherein an entrance is made to the words, and the duty of a Journall or Diary is propounded.   pag. 1
To forget Gods mercies a provoking sin. 2 God is very gracious in affording means for the helping of our memories.   5

CHAP. II.
The matter whereof a Journall or Diary is compounded, and first Nationall and publick.   14
1. Take notice what Governours have ruled over us.   Ibid.
2. What Religion was by such countenanced.   16
3. How variable the conditions of the Times have been.   19 [N5r]
4. What remarkable judgemints God hath inflicted upon notorious offenders.   22
5. What the Nationall sin for the present generation may be: It's good to know that.   25
Some times have been more notorious for Drunkennesse.   26
Some for Swearing.   27
Some for Pride and Ambition.   28
Our generation (as some think) most guilty of Contention.   30
Some think, Hypocrisie.   33
Some think, Apostasie.   Ibid.
Enmity against the Kingly government of Christ in his Church is the sin of this age.   39

CHAP. III.

What personall and private passages of Providence those are which ought to be recorded in our Journall or Diary. 48

1. *Keep an account of our conversion.* Ib.
2. *Of all divine assistance, either for the doing of that which is required, or the bearing of such evils as are inflicted.* 51
3. *All deliverances from dangers.* 55 [N5v]
4. *All the men and means God hath used for our good.* 58
5. *All the returns of our prayers.* 62

CHAP. IV.

The manner how a Journall or Diary is to be used, and first what is to be done by way of observation. 66

1. *Labour to see and observe God in all things.* 66
2. *Labour to see and observe all things in God.* 70
3. *Observe the wayes and means by which all good things are conveyed to us.* 74
   1. *By Christ savingly.* 75
   2. *By the promise certainly.* 79
   3. *By the creatures sensibly.* 85

Wherein observe Gods wisdome in the choyce:
   1. *Of the instruments that are used.* 86
   2. *Of the time.* 89
   3. *Of the measure.* 93

In all which hold fast these three conclusions:
   1. *Where God sees any fit to use more, he can afford more.* 98 [N6r]
   2. *That it is a mercy when our mindes are conformable to our means.* 99
   3. *That God hath many wayes to throw these things in to us, and as many to take them from us.* 100

CHAP. V.

The manner how a Journall or Diary is to be used, according to the rules of Practise. 102

1. *Look often upon the Journal, and read it over.* Ibid.

2. *Cast up all your wants.* 105
3. *Reckon how many ways those wants are supplyed with other comforts.* 107
4. *Take great notice of the peculiar excellency of all Gods despensations towards you, above the world.* 109
5. *Take heed that the want of some comfort do not rob you of all other.* 114
6. *Reckon much upon what you may want.* 115
7. *Study much the vanity of all Creature-comforts.* 118
8. *Be very moderate in the use of these things.* 122
[N6v]
9. *Trust not too far, depend not too much upon men* 124

CHAP. VI
More rules of the same kinde, that concern our practice. 128
10. *Ask your own hearts 3 Questions.* Ib.
   1. *What honor do I bring to God for all this.* Ibid.
   2. *What good do I to my neighbor.* 131
   3. *What good do I reap by all for my self.* 137
II. *Labour to be thankfull for all.* 140
   1. *Especially for Jesus Christ.* 141
   2. *For afflictions* 142
   3. *For preservation from scandals.* 144
   4. *For heaven.* 146
12. *Declare to others what God hath done for you, to provoke them to blesse God with you and for you.*

CHAP. VII.
An use of Exhortation, wherein Christians are perswaded to keep such a Journall or Diary. 150
[N7r]
Directions to further this work. 151

1. *Often remember your sinful estate.* 152
2. *Remember your low & poor estate.* 155
3. *Labour to understand every mercy aright.* 156

4. Take notice of the actings of God, whilest they
are new.   158
5. Love the Lord for his goodness.   161
C H A P. VIII.
Arguments propounded that may provoke Christians to
keep such a Journall.   164
1. Ab excellenti, *It is an excellent duty.*
                                                        Ibid.
2. Ab aequo, *It is very just and equal.*   167
3. A necessario, *It is very necessary.*   170
   1. In regard of the badnesse of our memories.
                                                        Ibid.
   2. To prevent the great sin of unthankfulnesse.   171
   3. To prevent the great danger of forgetfulnesse.   172
4. Ab utili, *It is a profitable course, and that in
7 regards.*
   1. It would be an excellent way to perpetuate
the memoriall of some, and promote the good of
others.   175 [N7v]
   2. It would bring us into great acquaintance
with God.   176
   3. It would much enlarge our hearts with love to
our God.   177
   4. It would enlarge our hearts with kindnesse
and compassion to our Brethren.   178
   5. It would much encrease in us self-abasement
of heart.   179
   6. It would provoke us to thankfulnesse.   180
   7. It would very much help our faith.   181 [N8r]

Appendices

DEDICATORY POEM

Reverendi viri Mr. Jo-
hannis Bedle *Tractatum
pium, et eruditum, viz.
Grati erga Deum animi.*
5 *AStronomi populo collecta Diaria vulgant:
Theiologi haec reliquas vincit Ephemeridas.
Dat chartis loca visa suis spontaneus exul,
Alter ut incertos dirigat inde pedes:
Ad superas Coeli (namq; hic via lactea) sedes*
10 *Hinc pia mens foelix carpere discat iter.
Scribitur heu nimiùm, vitiatur casta papyrus,
Nugarum levium pondere praela gemunt,
Quas bis tinctorum, vel quas lymphata Tremen-
Secta parit, libros jurgia dura replent. (tûm*
15 *At pietas, candorq; nitent hoc Codice, pectus
Exhibet authoris pagina quaeq; sui.
Quicunq; inspicies, è nato nosce parentem,
Ore refert patrem. Quod docet, ipse facit.*
          C.G. [b7r]

ADVERTISEMENT

Books lately Printed for
Tho. Parkhurst, at the signe of
the Three Crowns, over against
the great Conduit at the
lower end of *Cheapside*.
 DR. *Richard Sibbs* his Commentary upon the Second Epistle to the *Corinthians*, published for publick good by *Tho. Manton*. in *Folio*.
 Mr. *John Cotton* his Exposition on the First Epistle of *John*, with Doctrines, Reasons and Uses. in *Folio*.
 There will be shortly extant, a Book Entituled, Cathechizing Gods Ordinance, or A short Treatise concerning that Ancient, approved and soul-edifying Ordinance of Catechisme, by Mr. *Zach. Crofton* Minister of the word at *Buttolphs* without *Algate*, *London*; in *Octavo*.

Curteous Reader

THou mayest expect within a short time to see published some new Pieces of Mr. William Fenners, who was so famous when living, and his works (though he is dead) hath such a sweet (though silent) voice.
         T. P. [b8r]

Sidenotes

p. 1
13 Rom[ans]. 4.20.
18 Mark 5.34.
20-21 Heb[rews]. 11.29,30.

p. 1
30 Mat[thew]. 8.13.
8 Mat[thew]. 5.28.

p. 2
37 Prov[erbs]. 12.26

p. 3
8 Joh[n]. 1.12.
13 Rom[ans]. 8.17.
27 Joh[n]. 1.16.
37 Mark 2.5.

p. 4
4 Luk[e]. 15.22.
15 Gen[esis]. 45.25,26.

p. 5
4 Psal[ms]. 74.14.
17 Gen[esis]. 32.10,11.
21 1 Sam[uel]. 17.36.
23 2 Tim[othy]. 4.7,18

p. 6
3 Ephes[ians]. 3.8.

p. 9
3 Mark 4.24.
3 Luk[e]. 8.18.
6-7 1 Tim[othy]. 6.4. ἀλλὰ νοεῶν. vid[e]. marg[in].
7 Isa[iah]. 7.16
19 *Prosp[er]. de ingratis--*

p. 9 (cont.)
21-26 *Congenitae in Christo gentis mihi castus ab alto. Insinuatus amor proprias excedere vires Me jubet.*
29-30 Psal[ms]. 55.13,14.
34 2 King[s]. 3.11.

p. 10
5 [2 Kings] Chap[ter]. 2.15.

p. 11
10 Deut[eronomy]. 33.24.
12 Job 12.5.
18 Neh[emiah]. 11.17. & 12.8.
23 φερώνυμοτ
35 1 Sam[uel]. 7.12.
36 Josh[ua]. 22.34.

p. 12
5 *Os Diaboli,* Irenaeus
26 Neh[emiah]. 9.5.
32 *Ursin.[us] Catech.[ism]*

p. 13
12 Ecclus[iasticus]. 23.11,12.
14 Job 36.27.
14-16 *Ascensus gratiarum descensus gratiae*
30 Psal[ms]. 116.7.
32 *rests. Hebr[ew].*

p. 14
14-15 Prov[erbs]. 25.11 *Heb[rew].*
15 Ps[alms]. 119.126,127.
29-35 Allusion to the Authors name *Bedle,* an officer of a Court, a Bailiffe errant κῆρυξ. *v[ide] M[i].nshewes* Dictionary. Dr. *Cowels* Interpreter.

p. 15
1-2 Mr. *Greenhams* works *folio* p. 3.

p. 15 (cont.)
17-19 B[ishop]. *Andrews* Catech[ism]. *fol[io]*. referring to Lev[iticus]. 7.15.
22 Dr. *Gouge*.
38 *Valer[ius]*. *Maxim[us]*. l[iber].2.c[aput].1.

p. 16
2 2 Tim[othy]. 3.[2].
5 Luk[e]. 6.35.
6-7 *Ingrato quod donatur deperditur. Senec[a]*.
8-12 *Ingratitudo beneficiorum perditio. Ventus ureus et siccans,* &c. *Bernard in Cantic[a]. [Canticorum] Serm[on].* 51.
19 Job 36.9.
20 Psal[ms]. 28.5.
34-38 *Ambulandum est praeceptis per viam Regiam. B[ishop]. Andrews* Catech[ism]. *fol[io]*. p. 91.

p. 17
8-9 Psal[ms]. 40.5. & 71.15. 94.
13-15 *Qui timet esse bonus non timet esse malus*.
28 Mal[achi]. 3.16.
35 Neh[emiah]. 13.2.

p. 18
18-19 *Verba vivenda, non legenda*. Aug[ustine].
18-21 *Egidius*, Abbot of *Nurimberg, Boni Catholici sunt qui et fidem integram sequntur et bonos mores*.
26-27 Dan[iel]. 8.13. *marg[in]*.

p. 21
22 Psal[ms]. 107.6,8.

p. 22
8-10 Psa[lms]. 78.40,42.
20-22 Deut[eronomy]. 4.9. & 6.12.

p. 22
33-34 Psal[ms]. 78.11,41. & 106.7,13,21.

p. 23
8-9 Mat[thew]. 16.8,9,10.
11 Luk[e]. 17.17, [18.]
18-19 Isa[iah]. 17.10,11.

p. 24
24 Exo[dus]. 16.33.
28 Josh[ua]. 4.6,9.
33-34 Numb[ers]. 15.38,39.

p. 25
5 Exod[us]. 13.3.
7 Luk[e]. 1.74.
11 1 Cor[inthians]. 11.24,26.
28 Psa[lms]. 78.5,6.
33 Exo[dus]. 17.14.

p. 28
7-8 Psa[lms]. 78.38,39.
14 Doct[rine].
28 Psa[lms]. 18. *titl[e]*.

p. 29
6 Exod[us]. 14.8.
8 Psal[ms]. 8.3.
10 Isa[iah]. 53.1.
16 Eph[esians]. 6.12.
22 2 Tim[othy]. 3.12.
34 Exo[dus]. 12.38.

p. 32
1-2 1 King[s]. 12.30.
3 2 Chr[onicles]. 31.1.
13-14 1 Sam[uel]. 16.18.

Sidenotes 175

p. 33
21 Ezr[a]. 3.3,4,10.
22 Nehem[iah]. 3.
28 Matt[hew]. 6.33.
33 Ioh[n]. 8.21.

p. 34
20 2 Chr[onicles]. 17.8.
38-39 Judg[es]. 9.4. & 3.15. & 5.31.

p. 35
8 1 Kin[gs]. 4.20.
12-13 2 Chro[nicles]. 13.17.
19-20 Act[s]. 8.1. & 9.31.

p. 37
35 Psal[ms]. 37.37.
37 Numb[ers]. 23.10

p. 38
1 Psal[ms]. 37.38.
29-30 Psal[ms]. 52.5,6,7.

p. 40
17 Prov[erbs]. 23.33.

p. 41
10 Mat[thew]. 12.34.
25 Num[bers]. 16.9.
28 1 Ki[ngs]. 11.26.
38 Lam[entations]. 5.8.

p. 42
13 Judg[es]. 9.15.

p. 43
16 Proverbs 18.19
20 Acts 15.39

p. 44
29 Jer[emiah]. 32.[39].
31 Job. 17.

p. 45
27 2 Ki[ngs]. 10.16.
29 1 Ki[ngs]. 21.13.

p. 46
5 Isa[iah]. 11.9.
8 Ezek[iel]. 47.[3-4.]
15 2 Kin[gs]. 10.8.
24 Tit[us]. 1.[16] *ult[imo]*.
34 *Aug[ustine]*. in *Psa[lms]*. 30.

p. 48
9 Jude v[erse]. 12.

p. 49
1 Heb[rews]. 10.38.

p. 52
8 1 Ki[ngs]. 20.24.
35 Jer[emiah]. 18.12.

p. 53
13-14 Exod[us]. 4.24,26.

p. 57
14 Act[s]. 22.6,7.
19 1 Tim[othy]. 1.13,14.
21 Joh[n]. 9.25.

Sidenotes

p. 58
1 Psalms 87.5, 6
2 Phil[emon]. 10.
7 Rom[ans]. 16.7.
14 Exod[us]. 13.3.
30 Gen[esis]. 21.7.

p. 59
10 1 Tim[othy]. 1.16.
36 Isa[iah]. 1.3.

p. 60
4 Isa[iah]. 40.29.
9 1 Sam[uel]. 17. [49.]
12-16 Exod[us]. 3.11,13. & 4.10.13. & 5.22. & 6.12,30.
21 2 Tim[othy]. 4.7.

p. 61
3-4 2 Tim[othy]. 4.16,17.
29-30 Gen[esis]. 39.8,9.

p. 62
6-7 2 Sam[uel]. 16.7,8,11,12.
25 2 Pet[er]. 2.9.
32 1 Sam[uel]. 17.[37.]

p. 63
13 Psal[ms]. 117.1.
15 Gen[esis]. 7.16.

p. 65
9 Joh[n]. 8.59.
15,19 Prov.[erbs] 4.3,4. & 31.1,2,3.

p. 66
26-27 2 Tim[othy]. 1.16,17.
34 Zach[ariah]. 4.10.
35 1 King[s]. 17.6,9.

p. 67
15 Deut[eronomy]. 9.18,19.
24 & 10.10
27 1 Sam[uel]. 1.27.

p. 68
2 Psal[ms]. 2.8.
7 Joh[n]. 11.42.
8 Heb[rews]. 5.7.
29 Eph[esians]. 3.20.
32 Prov[erbs]. 23.4.
36 Act[s]. 14.17.

p. 69
1 Psal[ms]. 23.5.
18 Gen[esis]. 18.33.
24-25 Gen[esis]. 21.16,17.

p.70
5 Psal[ms]. 85.8.

p. 71
11 2 Kin[gs]. 2.14.
22 Gen[esis]. 31.9.
29 & 33.10,11.

p.72
9 & 28.16

p. 73
9 Est[her]. 5.11.
14 1 Sam[uel]. 17,37.

Sidenotes

p. 74
12 2 Cor[inthians]. 1.3.
17 Psal[ms]. 84.11.
36 Psal[ms]. 18.2.

p.75
3 & 41.3.
11 Rev[elation]. 21.7.

p. 76
3 1 Sam[uel]. 30.6.
9 Hab[akkuk]. 3.17,18.
18-20 Mic[ah]. 7.1,2,3,4,5,7.
21 2 Cor[inthians]. 6.10.
24 Jer[emiah]. 9.23.
35 Ps[alms]. 144.15.

p. 77
21 Rom[ans]. 8.32.
24 1 Cor[inthians]. 3.21,22.

p. 78
5 Gen[esis]. 34.23.
26 Gen[esis]. 1.
27 Joh[n]. 1.[1]

p. 79
6 2 Sam[uel] 19,30.
22 1 Sam[uel]. 5.4.
30 Act[s]. 28.3.
34 2 Sam[uel]. 12,30.
39 Phil[ippians]. 4.15.

p.80
2 Est[her]. 6.8.
31 Josh[ua]. 23.14.

p. 80 (cont.)
36-37 2 King[s]. 9.25,36.

p.81
3 Heb[rews]. 13.4.
7 Exod[us]. 20.7.
11 Psa[lms]. 119.65.
16 2 Chr[onicles]. 6.10.
25 Jonah 1.3.

p.82
4 Luk[e]. 1.54,55,
7-8 69,70,71.
16 Psal[ms]. 84.11.
20 Prov[erbs]. 20.7.
30 1 Tim[othy]. 4.8.

p.83
4 Ioh[n]. 20.15.
8 2 Cor[inthians]. 6.17.
13 1 Cor[inthians]. 7.1.
18 Pro[verbs]. 28.13.
28 Act[s]. 9.6.
37 Col[ossians]. 3.16.

p.84
14 Josh[ua]. 1.5.
18 Heb[rews]. 13.5.
20 Psal[ms]. 84.11.
37 Psal[ms]. 18.2., 119.94
38 Psalms 119.94

p.85
5 Gen[esis]. 45.19,20.
9 Rom[ans]. 5.10.
22 Psal[ms]. 50.10.
24 & 95.4.
36 Gen[esis]. 50.20.

Sidenotes

p.86
2 1 Sam[uel]. 16,13.
11-12 1 Sam[uel]. 17,33.
16 Exod[us]. 18.[19-23.]
19 Judg[es]. 7.7.

p. 87
18 Exo[dus]. 12.35.
28 Jer[emiah]. 38.6,7.
32 Jerem[iah]. 32.3, 39.11.
38 1 Sam[uel]. 14.6.

p. 88
12 Gen[esis]. 2.5,20.
38 Gal[atians]. 4.4.

p. 89
2 Exo[dus]. 12.41.
11 Matt[hew]. 14.29.
15 Psa[lms]. 107.29.
20 Mar[k]. 5.41.
22 Luk[e]. 7.14.
23 Joh[n]. 11.39.
33 2 Sam[uel]. 16.22.
35 Prov[erbs]. 5.14.

p.90
7 Ezek[ial]. 37.2,10.
9 Psal[ms]. 123.2.
15 Act[s]. 1.7.
18 Lam[entations]. 3.26.
19 1 Kin[gs]. 10.8.
34 Prov[erbs]. 3.17.
37 Jer[emiah]. 30.18.

p. 91
7 Psal[ms]. 27.13,14.
21 Psal[ms]. 37.16.

p. 92
10 Gen[esis]. 48.18.
15 Ps[alms]. 73.3,14.
34 1 Sam[uel]. 17.39.

p. 93
24 1 Ki[ngs]. 21.13.
33 Act[s]. 3.6.
34 Matt[hew]. 4.9.

p. 94
2 Jerem[iah]. 52.[11.]
23 2 Sam[uel]. 12.7,8.
30 Gen[esis]. 23.15.

p. 95
8 Gen[esis]. 48.11.
15 Phil[ippians]. 4.12.
21 Eccl[esiastes]. 5.10.

p. 96
15 Job 42.12.

p. 97
13 Job 5.6.
15 Psal[ms]. 75.6,7.

p. 100
6 Gen[esis]. 32.10.
12 Dan[iel]. 26.5,6,7,8,9.
20 Est[her]. 6.1,2.

Sidenotes

p. 102
2 Gen[esis]. 2.17.
5 Josh[ua]. 1.1,2,7,13,15.
11 Deut[eronomy]. 3.25.
14 Mar[k]. 10.21.
24 2 Sam[uel]. 16.12.
26 Gen[esis]. 2.16.
28 Deut[eronomy]. 34.6.

p. 103
9 Est[her]. 5.11.
13 Ps[alms]. 127.4,5.
19 Deut[eronomy]. 33.24,25.
24 Gen[esis]. 49.20.

p. 104
10 Heb[rews]. 12.7.
12 1 Tim[othy]. 4.10.
26 2 Cor[inthians]. 11.22,23.

p. 105
2-4 Gen[esis]. 43.34. & 44.2.
16 1 Tim[othy]. 4.10.
24 Mar[k]. 16.15,16.
27 Rom[ans]. 8.29,30.
31 Joh[n]. 17.9.
36 Psal[ms]. 37.16.

p. 106
4 Gen[esis]. 26.12.
13 Gen[esis]. 4.12.
28 Psal[ms]. 17.14,15.
31 Matth[ew]. 5.6.
38 Psa[lms]. 106.15.

p. 107
9 Ier[emeiah]. 31.34.
13 Jam[es]. 5.11.
20 1 Joh[n]. 3.12.
21 Gal[atians]. 4.29.
21 Heb[rews]. 12.16.
22 2 Pet[er]. 2.15.
23 Jude v[erse]. 11.
26 Jer[emiah]. 50.20.

p. 108
3 1 Kin[gs]. 21.4.
4 Est[her]. 5.13.
11 Gen[esis]. 30.1.
20 & 15.2.
33 Act[s]. 25.23.
37 Est[her]. 7.10.

p. 109
31 1 Ki[ngs]. 18.38.

p. 110
22 Dan[iel]. 4.30,31,32.
32 Matt[hew]. 24.2.

p. 111
4 Eccles[iastes]. 1.2.
10 Psal[ms]. 46.1.
12 Gen[esis]. 28.15.
16 1 Cor[inthians]. 7.31.
19 Psal[ms]. 90.2.
39 1 Joh[n]. 1.5.

p. 112
11 Psa[lms]. 119.57.
18 2 Ki[ngs]. 7.6,7.

Sidenotes

p. 113
11 Eccles[iastes]. 1.2.
14 Cant[icles]. 5.10,16.
27 Jon[ah]. 4.6,7.

p. 114
17 Col[ossians]. 3.2.

p. 115
10 Isa[iah]. 2.22.
15 Psal[ms]. 39.5.
18 Phil[ippians]. 3.2.
19 Mat[thew]. 10.17.
24 Psal[ms]. 49.16.
27 [Psalms] & 62.9.
29 Isa[iah]. 40.15,17.

p. 116
1 Mica[h]. 7.4,5,6.
8 2 Ki[ngs]. 18.20.
30 Matth[ew]. 16.22.
33 Gal[atians]. 2.12,13,14.

p. 118
10 Est[her]. 6.3.
25 Act[s]. 27.23.

p.119
10 1 Sam[uel]. 25.21.
21 2 Kin[gs]. 4.13.

p. 121
17 1 Sam[uel]. 27.28.

p. 122
18 Mat[thew]. 5.47.
19 Isa[iah]. 38.3.
21 Neh[emiah]. 13.14.
31 Gal[atians]. 6.10.
32 Rom[ans]. 12.20.
36 [Romans] & 8.9.
38 1 Sam[uel]. 18.4.

p.123
4 Joh[n]. 15.13.
8 Jer[emiah]. 38.1.
26 Mat[thew]. 16.23.
28 Gen[esis]. 44.33.
38 Jon[ah]. 1.12.

p. 124
6 1 Cor[inthians]. 6.17.
22 Luk[e]. 12.33.
25 Eph[esians]. 4.28.

p. 125
16 Pro[verbs]. 28.27.
18 2 Cor[inthians]. 9.6.
25 Prov[erbs]. 9.12.

p. 126
12 Phil[ippians]. 3.13.
18 Luk[e]. 2.52.
36 Judg[es]. 8.16.
37 Psal[ms]. 94.12.
39 Mic[ah]. 6.9.

p. 127
19 1 Joh[n]. 5.13.
30 Rom[ans]. 1.8.

Sidenotes

p. 128
17 1 Thess[alonians]. 5.18.
38 2 Cor[inthians]. 5.21.

p. 129
3 Isa[iah]. 53.5.
18 Rev[elation]. 3.21.
38 Gen[esis]. 47.9.
39 1 Pet[er]. 1.6.

p. 130
11 Hos[ea]. 5.15.
32 Job 1.21.

p. 131
16 Heb[rews]. 11.25.
28 Gen[esis]. 39.9.
31 Neh[emiah]. 6.11.
36 Judg[es]. 11.34,35.

p. 132
24 1 Sam[uel]. 25.32,33,34.
34 Gen[esis]. 39.10

p. 133
2 Mat[thew]. 25.21.
29 Luk[e]. 16.24,28.

p. 134
14 Psal[ms]. 40.10.
19 Ps[alms]. 105.2.
21 & 66.16.
30 Ex[odus]. 18.8.10.
32 Mar[k]. 5.19.

p. 135
4 Psal[ms]. 148.11,12,13.

p. 137
9 Psa[lms]. 119.96.
20 Prov[erbs]. 30.8.

p. 138
18 Deut[eronomy]. 9.7.
20 Ephes[ians]. 2.11,12.
27 Eze[kial]. 20.43.
31 Act[s]. 26.9,10,11.
39 1 Cor[inthians]. 15.9.

p. 139
2 1 Tim[othy]. 1.13,
4 v[erse]. 15.
13 Gen[esis]. 42.21.
26 Phil[emon]. 15.

p. 140
2 Deut[eronomy]. 5.15.
5 & 26.5,6.
12 Gen[esis]. 32.10.
21 1 Pet[er]. 5.5.
23 Isa[iah]. 61.3.
29 Col[ossians]. 2.7.
38 Psal[ms]. 106.7.

p. 141
4 Deut[eronomy]. 29.2,3,4.
19 Matt[hew]. 16.6
36 Deut[eronomy]. 9.3,6.

p. 142
3 1 Sam[uel]. 12.24.

Sidenotes

p. 143
3 Hos[ea]. 2.15.
7 Exod[us]. 15.1.
9 Jer[emiah]. 2.2.

p. 144
4 Gen[esis]. 14.19,22.
13 Exod[us]. 3.6.
17 Exod[us]. 20.2.
22-23 Jer[emiah]. 16.14,15. & 23.7,8.
27 2 Cor[inthians]. 1.3.
28 Eph[esians]. 1.3.

p. 145
9 Psal[ms]. 31.23.
18 Deut[eronomy]. 10.12.
23 Gal[atians]. 5.6.

p. 146
4 1 Sam[uel]. 18.1.
7 & 19.2.
10 & 20.4.
17 Act[s]. 9.6.

p. 147
9 1. *Ab excellenti.*
20 Rev[elation]. 2.17.

p. 148
12 Act[s]. 27 *per tot[ii]*.
28 Joh[n]. 2.11.
32 & 4.54.

p.149
1 1 Sam[uel]. 2.27,28.
6 1 Sam[uel]. 15.17.
11 2 Sam[uel]. 12.7,8.
17-18 Amos 4.6,7,8,9,10,11,12.
21 *Ab aequo.*
27 Gen[esis]. 8.1.
29 & 19.29.
32 & 30.22-25
33 1 Sam[uel]. 1.9.
36 Gen[esis]. 8.1.

p. 150
1 Jonah 4.10,11.
6 Isa[iah]. 49.15,16.
19 Jer[emiah]. 2.2.
24 Gen[esis]. 18.12.
27 1 Pet[er]. 3.6.
31 Psal[ms]. 56.8.
35 Mal[achi]. 3.16,17.
38 Act[s]. 10.3.

p. 151
5 Gen[esis]. 40.14,23.
20 Rev[elation]. 20.12.
23 Matt[hew]. 25.35.
29 3. *A necessario.*
37 Gen[esis]. 33.1.

p. 152
1 & 25.29.
6 & 41.9.
7 Psal[ms]. 40.5.
20 Psal[me]. 9.17.
25 & 10.4.
28 & 50.16,17,22.
36 Eccles[iastes]. 9.14,15.

p. 153
13 Psal[ms]. 50.22.
37 Act[s]. 12.23.

p. 155
8 4. *Ab utili.*

p. 156
36 Ps[alms]. 107.43.

p. 157
3 1 Tim[othy]. 6.17.
7 Jam[es]. 1.17.
9 Rom[ans]. 11.29.
15 1 Joh[n]. 4.19.
18 Psal[ms]. 91.14.
24 Prov[erbs]. 8.17.
29 Joh[n]. 14.21,23.
38 2 Cor[inthians]. 1.3.

p. 158
3 Heb[rews]. 6.17,18.
6 Psal[ms]. 16.2,3.
9 1 Joh[n]. 3.14.
18 Matt[hew]. 25.34,40.
29 Ps[alms]. 8.3,4.
37 & 144.3,4.

p. 159
8 2 Sam[uel]. 9.7,8.
15 & 7.18,19.
25 1 Pet[er]. 5.5.

p. 160
2 Exo[dus]. 28.34.
6 Psa[lms]. 50.23.
9 & 67.5,6.
19-26 Exod.[us] 17.9. & 7.20. & 8.17. & 14.16.
38 Psal[ms]. 37.25.

p. 161
10 Gen[esis]. 48.15,16.
17 Rev[elation]. 21.7.
20 1 Sam[uel]. 7.12.
23 Psal[ms]. 31.19.
32 2 Cor[inthians]. 4.17.
37 Phil[ippians]. 3.20,21.

p. 162
4 Gen[esis]. 45.3.
9 Phil[ippians]. 1.23.
19 Psal[ms]. 16.*ult[imo]*.

p. 167
5 *Diarium*
9 *Itinerarium*

Corrections

p. 2
18 conld] could.

p. 5
12 inflited] inflicted.

p. 6
32 presnme] presume.

p. 18
7 arithmemetick] arithmetick.
34 then then] then.

p. 29
18 rnlers] *rulers*.

p. 45
29 *Sidenote*: I Kings 12.13] I Kings 21.13.

p. 59
12 *on*] *in*.

p. 60
21 aad] and
30 prevants] prevents

p. 61
3-4 *Sidenote*: 1 Timothy 4.16,17] 2 Timothy 4.16,17.

p. 67
4 acccount] account.

p. 78
11 he honorable] be honorable.

p. 80
14 dnties] duties.

p. 81
16 *Sidenote*: 2 Chronicles 4.10] 2 Chronicles 6.10.
30 continned] continued.

p. 83
4 *Sidenote*: John 21.15] John 20.15.

p. 86
16 *Sidenote*: Exodus 18] Exodus 18.19-23.

p. 87
18 *Sidenote*: Exodus 11.13] Exodus 12.35.
32 *Sidenote*: Jeremiah 39,11] Jeremiah 39.11.

p. 94
30 *Sidenote*: Cen. 23.15] Gen[esis]. 23.14.

p. 105
2-4 *Sidenote*: Genesis 45.2] Genesis 44.2.

p. 106
10 ye cursed at the last] yet go cursed at the last.

p. 108
3 *Sidenote*: I Kings 2.14] 1 Kings 21.4.
20 *Sidenote*: [Genesis] 15.12] [Genesis] 15.2.

Corrections to the Text

p. 121
7 unworthy thy name] unworthy of thy name.

p. 123
4 *Sidenote*: John 15.12] John 15.13.

p. 126
8 periections] projections.

p. 128
38 *Sidenote*: 1 Corinthians 5.2] 2 Corinthians 5.21.

p. 135
4 *Sidenote*: Psalms 148.1,2,3] Psalms 148. 11,12,13.

p. 138
39 *Sidenote*: 1 Corinthians 15.10] 1 Corinthians 15.9.

p. 148
11-12 how a perfect a Journall] how perfect a Journall.
17 is is] is.

p. 149
10 reat] great
32 *Sidenote*: Genesis 30.31] Genesis 30.22-25.

p. 150
9 *to us ward*] toward us.
23 *Sidenote*: Matthew 16.9,11] Matthew 16.6.
38 *Sidenote*: Acts 10.4] Acts 10.3.

p. 151
20 *Sidenote*: Revelation 20.11] Revelation 20.12.

p. 153
37 *Sidenote*: Acts 12.13] Acts 12.23.

p. 158
23 read it, over] read it over,.

p. 160
13 bnt] but.
25 *Sidenote*: Exodus 5.17] Exodus 8.17.
26 *Sidenote*: Exodus 14.15] Exodus 14.16.

p. 161
23 *Sidenote*: Psalms 31.20] Psalms 31.19.
32 *Sidenote*: 1 Corinthians 4.17] 2 Corinthians 4.17.

p. 164
25 *the the*] *the*.

p. 167
5 *colllecta*] *collecta*.

Commentary

lxxii/16-19 **Nihil tam ... ingratus homo**] Lactantius, *PL* 7: 125 (for a slightly different wording: "Nam si nihil est tam conveniens Deo, quam Beneficentia nihil autem tam alienum, quam ut sit ingratus homo.")

lxxii/20-24 **Chrysost[om]. Rom[ans]. Hom[ily]. 18]** *PG* 60: 579.

lxxiii/1-6 **Deo plane ... nostrorum engens**] Bernard of Clairvaux, *Opera Omnia*, ed. J. LeClercq, 7 vols. to date (Rome: Editiones Cistercienses, 1957-) 4: 180-181.

lxxiii/7-11 **Curatorem mei ... Foxius**] Probably John Fox; "By a covenant I have God to take care of me and my affairs. He well knows what is enough for me and when it would be good for me to have it. Thus far he has not failed me when I began to have doubts, without at the same time being actually ungrateful."

1/3-4 **Robert Earl of Warwick, Baron of Leez**] Robert Rich, born in June 1587, the second Earl of Warwick, and the eldest son of Robert Lord Rich and Penelope Devereux. He was admitted to Emmanuel College, Cambridge, on June 4, 1603. In 1625, he was appointed joint lord-lieutenant of Essex. He belonged to a Puritan family and was originally counted among the Presbyterians and the supporters of Oliver Cromwell. He died on April 19, 1658, and was buried at Felsted, Essex, on May 1 (*DNB* 16: 1014-19). Also, see Vicary Gibb, ed., *The Complete Peerage*, 13 vols. (London: The St. Catherine Press, 1959) 12.2: 407-412.

1/6 **Eleanor Countess of Warwick**] Eleanor was the daughter of Sir Edward Worthy and the Dowager Countess of Sussex. She became the third wife of Robert Rich on March 30, 1646 (*DNB* 15: 1016).

2/10-16 *Luther* . . . **as he had prayed**] Frederick Myconius (1490-1546), ordained a Franciscan in 1510, was an admirer of Augustine. He left the Franciscans in 1524 and joined Luther and Melanchthon in Wittenberg. He became pastor in Gotha and was known as the reformer of Thuringia. In 1540, when he suffered from a pulmonary infection which began to show symptoms of consumption, he believed he was near death. He received Luther's letter of January 9, 1541, where Luther prayed: "May he cause you to survive me. This I pray. This I wish. My will be done. Amen." Thereupon he recovered and, in fact, survived Luther by a few weeks. See Theodore G. Tappert, ed., *Luther: Letters of Spritual Counsel* (Philadelphia: Westminster Press, 1955), 47-48.

2/17-18 *Justus Jonas* . . . **That man could have what he would**] I have been unable to find a source for Jonas' remark.

4/22-26 **When** *Solomon* . . . **before him**] 1 Kings 3.1-13.

6/4-6 **As** *Ignatius* . . . **the least**] St. Ignatius, Bishop of Antioch, on the road to martrydom, wrote in his Letter to the Trallians, "Memores estote in omnibus orationibus vestris ecclesiae, quae est in Syria, de qua et nomen habere non sum dignus, qui sim eorum ultimus." See Franciscus X. Funk, ed., *Patres Apostolici*, 2 vols. (Tubingen: Henry Laup, 1901) *1*: 251.

6/12-13 **Christians who walk much with God**] Gen 5.22.

6/17-19 **the subject . . . gone**] Beadle was the first and only writer in the seventeenth century to write a book length study about the purpose and method of development behind puritan diary-writing.

Commentary to the Text   199

6/20 **Cloud of witnesses**] Hebrews 12.1.

6/21 **Pillar of Fire**] Exodus 13.21, 14.24, Numbers 14.14, and Nehemiah 9.12,19.

6/21 **Star to guide me**] Matthew 2.2-10.

6/25-26 and 10/1 *Qui curat oves oviumque Magistros*] Virgil, *Eclogues*, 2.33.

6/28-29 *in aurem vel in angulo*] That is, "Personally and in private." Seneca, *De Beneficiis*, 2.23.2.

7/1-6 *Considius . . . my fear*] Plutarch, *Caesar*, 14.13-17.

9/6 *Sidenote*: ἀλλά νοσῶν.] That is, "but sickly, ailing," (Walther Bauer, ed., *A Greek-English Lexicon of the New Testament and Other Early Christian Literature*, 2nd ed., Chicago and London: U. of Chicago Press, 1979), 543. 1 Timothy 6.4: "He is proud, knowing nothing, but sick about questions, strifes of words; from which arise envies, contentions, blasphemies, evil suspicions." Also, see Wisdom 17.8.

9/20-22 **with a learned . . . the Pelagians**] As the marginal note indicates, the "Ancient" is Prosper of Aquitaine, a contemporary and defender of St. Augustine writing against the Pelagian heresy. Prosper's most famous work is his dogmatic poem of over a thousand lines, *De Ingratis*, written against the semi-Pelagians (William Smith, gen. ed., *A Dictionary of Christian Biography*, 4 vols., London: John Murray, Albemarle Street, 1887) 4: 492-497. The poem is practically a verse rendition of St. Jerome's *Epistola ad Rufinum* (426-427) and *Epistola ad Augustinum* (428) and was probably written in 428. The semi-Pelagians greatly emphasized the role of man's free will in the process of salvation. They believed that the teaching of St. Augustine on grace tended towards strict predestinarianism.

9/21-26 Sidenote: *Congentiae in...Me jubet*] Prosper of Aquitaine. The passage is as follows: "Congenitae in Christo gentis mihi castus ab alto/ insinuatus amor proprias excedere vires/ me iubet atque pias accendere carmine mentes" (Charles T. Huegelmeyer, ed., *Carmen De Ingratis*, Washington, D.C.: The Catholic University Press, 1962), 42-43.

10/2-3 **Thomas Hooker**] Born at Marfield, Leicestershire, early in July of 1586, he attended and graduated from grammar school at Market Bosworth, was admitted to Queen's College as a sizar in 1604, and graduated from Emmanuel College, Cambridge, with a B.A. in 1608, and an M.A. in 1611. In 1626, he accepted a lectureship in Chelmsford, Essex. "He very quickly gained the esteem of the other Puritan ministers around Dedham and Chelmsford; there was a sort of shadow synod in that part of the county which held regular monthly meetings, and in these assemblies his voice was heard with respect" (Frank Shuffelton, *Thomas Hooker*, Princeton: Princeton U. Press, 1977), 74. On May 20, 1629, Hooker was called for the first time before Bishop Laud's High Commission to answer for his preaching and his nonconformity, after which Hooker was suspended from his lectureship and asked to leave the diocese. In November of that year, Laud received a petition in favor of Hooker, signed by forty-nine of the beneficed clergy in Essex (T. W. Davids, *Annals of Evangelical Nonconformity in the County of Essex*, London: Jackson, Walford, and Hodder, 1863), 153. John Beadle was a signer of that petition while rector of Little Leighs (*DNB 1*: 1379). In July of 1630, Hooker was ordered to reappear before Laud's High Commission. He chose not to do so and withdrew to Holland. Three years later, he sailed for New England, arrived at Boston on September 4, 1633, settled in Cambridge, Massachusetts, and became a freeman on May 14, 1634. He died July 7, 1647.

10/8-10 **I may call him as *Latimer*, Saint *Bilney*]** Hugh Latimer (1485?-1555), in his *First Sermon on the Lord's Prayer* (1552), says of his friend Thomas Bilney, "Master Bilney—or rather

St. Bilney, that suffered death for God's word sake—the same Bilney was the instrument whereby God called me to knowledge. For I may thank him, next to God, for that knowledge that I have in the word of God" (Allan G. Chester, ed., *Selected Sermons of Hugh Latimer*, Charlottsville: University Press of Virginia, 1968), 167. The two men became close friends in 1524 after Bilney, a reformer, heard Latimer, then an avid conservative, read for his B.D. thesis a violent philippic against Melanchthon. The next day Bilney visited Latimer and convinced him to abandon his ardent conservative stance. From that day a lifelong friendship began between the two men, and they were oftentimes seen in each other's company. On August 19, 1531, (for preaching without a license), Bilney was apprehended by officers of the bishop in Norwich after giving a copy of Tyndale's Testament to the anchoress of Norwich (*DNB* 2: 504-505).

10/13 **Essex Chelmford**] A town 29 miles northeast of London which lies in the Chelmer Valley.

10/19-25 **As for . . . increased**] Before becoming rector of Barnston under the patronage of Robert Rich, Earl of Warwick, in 1632, Beadle was rector of Little Leighs in Essex. The move increased Beadle's living from £50 at Little Leighs to £90 at Barnston. See Barbara Donagan, "The Clerical Patronage of Robert Rich, Second Earl of Warwick, 1619-1642," *Proceedings of the American Philosophical Society*, 120.5 (1976): 403.

10/8-13/1-2 **As *David* . . . consort of all**] Psalms 148.

11/5 **a man after Gods own heart**] 1 Samuel 13.14.

11/10 **Asher**] Asher had four sons and a daughter, Deuteronomy 33.24.

11/11-13 **many other . . . Lamps despised**] Beadle as early as 1641 was a supporter of the Commonwealth and Oliver Cromwell and by 1656, Cromwellian supporters, many of whom were Non-conformists, and their religious and political stances were becoming increasingly unpopular.

11/18-19 *Higgaion Selah*] The word "higgaion" is probably a musical term, indicating a "forte burst of joyous music" (James Hastings, ed., *A Dictionary of the Bible*, 5 vols., New York: Scribner's Sons, 1901) 2: 154. It is found in Psalms 9.16 and 92.3. It is universally agreed that Selah is also "a musical or liturgical sign of some kind. Nowhere has the word any grammatical connexion with the text. Psalm 9.16 is not an exception, for Higgaion and Selah are both used interjectionally, 'Resounding music! Up'" (James Hastings, ed. *A Dictionary of the Bible*) 4: 451.

11/20-21 **as** *Solomon . . .* **in the gates**] Proverbs 31.31.

11/23 *Sidenote*: φερώνμοι.] That is, "bearing the name of, named after" (George Liddel and Robert Scott, *A Greek-English Lexicon*, 2 vols., Oxford: The Clarendon Press, 1925) 2: 1924.

11/24-29 *Commodus, Pius,* **did**] The Commodus Fuller refers to here is most probably Ceionius Commodus (A.D. 130-169). Commodus means "agreeable, pleasant." When his father of the same name was adopted by Hadrian, the younger Commodus passed into the gens Aelia and became L. Ceionius Aelius Aurelius Commodus. Later he was again adopted by Antoninus Pius along with M. Aurelius, who after Antoninus' death transferred to Commodus the name Verus, which means "truthful" (Aelius Spartianus, in *The Scriptores Historiae Augustae*, 1.1-7). Antoninus Pius (86-?) was also adopted by Hadrian in A.D. 138, and after Hadrian died Antoninus ascended without opposition to the throne. The hallmark of his twenty two year reign was its peacefulness. It is believed that the name "Pius," which means "dutifully affectionate," was acquired upon his accession to the throne due to his deep grief upon Hadrian's death" (Julius Capitolinus, in *The Scriptores Historiae Augustae*, 1.1-13).

Commentary to the Text

11/5-6 an Ebenezer . . . a Stone of witnesse] 1 Samuel 7.12. Ebenezer was the site of the dual defeat of Israel at the hands of the Philistines near Aphlek in the north of Sharon. The name was also given to a stone which Samuel erected between Mizpah and Shen some years after this battle to commemorate his victory over the Philistines.

12/5 *Sidenote*: Os Diaboli, Irenaeus] Cf. Polycarp's (d. 155) *Epistle to the Philippians, PG 5*: 1012, where Polycarp is said to have recognized Marcion as the "firstborn of Satan." Irenaeus in *Contra haereses, PG 7*: 853 also describes this exchange as does Eusebius (*Historia Ecclesiastica PG 20*: 339-40): "And Polycarp himself, when Marcion once met him and said: 'Recognize us,' replied: `I do recognize you; I recognize the firstborn of Satan."

12/6-7 of murmuring, called it the Devils mouth] Echoes proverbial phrase, "To murmur (patter) the Devil's paternoster" (Bartlett Jere Whiting, ed., *Proverbs, Sentences and Proverbial Phrases From English Writings Mainly Before 1500*, Cambridge: The Belknap Press, 1968), D214.

12/23 it is better to give then to receive] Acts 20.35. Also, see Morris Palmer Tilley, ed., *A Dictionary of The Proverbs in England in the Sixteenth and Seventeenth Centuries* (Ann Arbor: The University of Michigan Press, 1966), G119; and Robert William Dent, ed., *Proverbial Language in English Drama Exclusive of Shakespeare, 1495-1616* (Berkeley: University of California Press, 1984), G119.

12/32 *Sidenote*: Ursin.[us] Catech.[ism]] Zacharias Ursinus (1534-1583) was a German theologian who helped author a catechism widely known as the *Heidelberg Catechism*. He was born at Breslau on July 18, 1534, and became a disciple of Melanchthon at Wittenberg. Later, he studied divinity under Calvin, and Hebrew at Paris under Jean Mercier. In 1563, at the (14/33 cont.)

request of Frederick III of Germany, Ursinus wrote the *Catechism* in cooperation with Kaspar Olevian. The *Heidelberg Catechism*, translated into English, was known as *The Catechisme or maner to teach Children and others the Christian fayth* (London, 1572?; STC 13028).

11/32-33 Some Divines . . . Thankfulnesse] In his *Catechism*, Ursinus makes thankfulness the third thing a Christian must know: 1) "QVE. How many thinges are needfull for thee to know, that thou mayst come by, and enjoy this comforte, that thou mayst both live and dye blessedly? AN. Three: first, how great my sinne and wretchednes is: The second, by what meanes I may be delivered from my sin: The thyrd is, what thanks I owe unto my Lorde God for my deliverance" (London; STC 13028), sig. Aa1.

12/39-13/1 I will praise . . . any being] Psalms 104.33 and 146.2.

13/2 Thou art my praise] Jeremiah 17.14.

13/3-4 *Paul* . . . above all] Romans 12.14, 1 Corinthians 4.12, 1 Corinthians 14.16.

13/3-4 *Job* . . . as giving] Job 1.20-21.

13/7 *Jesus Christ*. . .in his blessed lippes] Matthew 11.25 and Luke 10.21.

13/8-9 *Sidenote: Ascensus gratiarum descensus gratiae*] Bernard of Clairvaux: "Sic plane, sic gratiarum cessat decursus, ubi recursus non fuerit; nec modo nihil augetur ingrato, sed quod acceperat ei vertitur in perniciem" (*Opera Omnia*, J. LeClercq ed. *et al*) 4: 356. Also, see *PL 183*: 170. Further, see Lancelot Andrews' *A Patterne of Cathechisticall Doctrine* (London, 1630; STC 603), sig. H4v: [under the first commandment] "Thankes is never truely given to God, but there is a better thing received; as *Bernard* saith *Ascensus gratiarum est decensus gratiae*: and grace failes when our thankes faile." Also, see Andrews' *The*

Commentary to the Text   205

Pattern of Cathechistical Doctrine at Large (London, 1650; Wing STC A3145), sig. T3v: "So as Bernard saith when there is *recursus gratiarum*, a sending back of thanks, then there is a new *decursus gratiae*, a descending of benefits, and *si cessat recursus gratiarum, cessat decursus gratiae,* if thanks be not returned, there will be noe more return of grace and other benefits: that the grace we have received, if it stand still, and be not in *recursus,* in perpetual succession by returns, then like water (to which its oft compared) it stands still, and putrifies: and rots all the gifts and graces formerly bestowed."

13/16-17 **the Italian . . .** *Do good for your selves*] See Giovanni Florio's *Second Frvites* for the saying in its entirety: "Fa Bene a te, & a' tuoi, e poi a gl'altri se tu puoi" (London, 1591; STC 11097), sig. K2r, p. 103.

13/27-28 **as his Chronicles did to him in** *Esther*] See Esther 2.22. Mordecai was the deliverer of the Jews in the Book of Esther. After becoming aware of a plot against King Ahasuerus, Mordecai told Queen Esther and was rewarded by the entry of his name in the royal chronicles.

13/30 *David* **to return to rests in the plurall**] Scholars have puzzled over the unique Hebrew plural form of 'your rest' in Psalm 116.7; however, its use probably signifies "a complete, true rest" (A.A. Anderson, *The Book of Psalms,* 2 vols., Greenwood, S.C.: Attic Press, 1972) 2: 792.

13/33 *Ahasuerus* **advanced** *Mordecai*] See Esther 5.9 and Esther 6.

13/4 **Book affords . . . fire**] Genesis 22.7.

14/8-11 **Stewards . . . towards us**] See, for example, 1 Corinthians 4.1, 2; 1 Peter 4.10.

14/14 **a word . . . its wheels**] See Antonius Giggeius, *In proverbia Salomonis commentarij trium rabbinorum: Salmonis Isacidis. Abraham Aben Ezrae. Levi ben Ghersom,* Mediolani (Collegij

Abmrosiani Typographia, 1620), 407 on Proverb 25: Salomon Isacides, "*mala area* Idest tanquam poma, quae in argenti caelaturis sint efformata"; A. Aben Ezra, "*mala aurea*. Sicut forma grata est aurei pomi in claustris argenteis, quod apte, concinneque sit argento inclusum, ita est sermo, qui debita moderatione, & consentaneo modo sit pronunciatus, non autem ad alterius sceretum patefaciendum. Alia expositio. Debitus ordo est, ne alterius arcana prodas" (408); Levi Ghersom, "*mala aurea*. Postquam autem a sedo sermone dehortatus est, ad laudabilem, honorificumq; instituit, aitque sermonem pronunciatum iusta consentaneam rationem esse velut mala aurea canzellis argenteis obtecta, in quibus parua quedam foramina interniteant, e quibus facili obtutu malorum aureorum species emineat. Non ergo dissimilis ab illis est sermo rite pronunciatus; singularis n. vtilitas percipitur ob id, quod intelligitur cum primum animus sermoni intelligendo adiungitur; quodsi quis illum magis penetrare studeat, facili negotio in eo mala aurea comperiet, iuxta rationem in multis huisce libri versiculis seruatam vt explicauimus" (409).

14/21-22 **earthly Lords . . . Quit-rents**] The people most negatively affected by Cromwell's economic policies were the Catholics and the Irish. In Ireland, the expenses of maintaining Cromwell's army far exceeded the revenue raised from 'Adventurers' to pay for that army. Hence, during the early 1650's the rents of confiscated private lands, houses, bishops' lands were used to help pay for the English army (Charles Harding Firth, *The Last Years of The Protectorate*, New York: Russell & Russell, 1964), 165-167. In addition, a bill was introduced in Parliament which disposed of two-thirds of any recusant's estate that was forfeited or sequestered by any act or order of Parliament (Austin Woolrych, *Commonwealth to Protectorate*, Oxford: Clarendon Press, 1982), 304-307.

14/29-35 *Sidenote*: χῆτυε]. That is, a herald, "whose duty it is to make public proclamations" (Walter Bauer, ed., *A Greek-English Lexicon of New Testament and Other Early Christian Literature*, 2nd ed.), 431. John Minsheu (fl. 1617), a lexicographer who lived in London and made his living as a language teacher (*DNB* 13: 494), published a polyglot dictionary entitled *The guide into tongues* (London, 1617; *STC* 17944). Minsheu defines "harold," or "heraldus": "With us it signifieth an officer at armes, whose function is to denounce warre, to proclaim peace, or otherwise to be emploied by the King in martiall messages or other businesse" (sigs. T6v, T7r). Also, see a facsimile edition of *The guide into tongues* (Delmar, New York: Scholars' Facsimiles & Reprints, 1978). See further 1 Timothy 2.7, 2 Timothy 1.11, and 1 Peter 2.5.

14/34-35 Sidenote: Dr. Cowels Interpreter] John Cowell (1554-1611) was educated at Eton College and King's College, Cambridge, where he obtained his LL.D. In 1600, he became a member of the college of civilians at Doctors' Commons. In 1603 and 1604, he was vice-chancellor of Cambridge University, and in 1608 Bancroft, who was then Archbishop of Canterbury, appointed him to the post of vicar-general (*DNB* 4: 1300). Cowell's most well-known work is a legal dictionary entitled *The Interpreter, or Booke Containing the Signification of Words* where he says that "bedell (bedellus) commeth of the French (bedeau, apparitor) & it signifieth with vs, nothing else but a messenger or seruitour belonging to a Court, as a Courtbaron or Leet" (London, 1607; *STC* 5900), sig. K1v.

15/1 Mr. Greenham] Richard Greenham (1535?-1594?) was a puritan divine who attended Cambridge University. At an older age than usual, he matriculated as a sizar at Pembroke Hall in 1559. His puritanism was temperate as is evidenced by his reproval of young divines for engaging in ecclesiastical controversies (*DNB* 8: 521). In 1599, Greenham's *Workes* were collected and edited by Henry Holland (London; *STC* 12318).

14/38-15/4 Formility . . . his dayes] According to Greenham, "A Certaine man being a Papist, though not so grounded as he desired to be, tooke a view of the life of Papists, if it were as glorious in truth as they pretended; which when he found not, he turned himselfe to the Protestants, and looking into their conuersation, he found himself not contented, vntill in the end he met with Familists, in whom he so staied himselfe, that he grew in familiaritie with their doctrine. The first principle that they taught him, was that there was no God: This boyled much in him, so that he began to adde conclusions to this precept on this sort: If there be a God, he is not so iust and mercifull, as they say: if there be no God, there is neither heaven, hell; or if there be any, the ioyes are not so eternall, not the paines so continuall, as some haue taught: Why then doe I sell my certaine pleasures in this world, for vncertaine pleasures in the world to come? This diuellish illusion so farre preuailed, that he stole an horse, for which he was apprehended, imprisoned, arraigned, & condemned: but, by the prouidence of God, he conferring with a godly Minister, confessed himselfe an Atheist" (*Workes*, STC 12318), sig. B2r.

15/3 **Familisme**] The Familists, commonly called the Family of Love, were an offshoot of a Dutch sect, founded by Henrik Niclaes. Niclaes never left the Catholic Church and was not attracted to Protestantism. Instead, he was more attracted to medieval sectarianism. In his work, *Evangelium regni. A joyfull message of the kingdom* (1575?; STC 18556), he exhorts all members of all religions to forget their dogmatic differences and join together in a great fellowship of love. Also, see William Wilkinson. *A Confutation of Certaine Articles Deliuered Vnto the Familye of Love* (London, 1579; STC 25665). For modern treatments of the Familists movement in England, see the following: Alistair Hamilton, *The Family of Love* (Cambridge: James Clarke & Co., 1981); Jean Dietz Moss, *"Godded With God": Hendrick Niclaes and His Family of Love* (Philadelphia: The American Philosophical Society, 1981); Julia G. Ebel, "The Family of Love: Sources of its English History in England," *Huntington Library Quarterly* 30.4 (1967): 333-43; Lynnewood F. Martin, "The Family of Love in England: Conforming Millenarians," *Sixteenth Century Journal* 3 (1972): 99-108.

Commentary to the Text   209

15/18-21 *Sidenote*: **B.[ishop Lancelot Andrewes Catech[ism]** . . .
Lev[iticus]. 7.15] The Pattern of Catechistical Doctrine at Large
. . . [*Perfected according to the Authors own Copy, and thereby
purged from many thousands of Errours, Defects, and
Corruptions, which were in a rude imperfect Draught formerly
published,*] (London, 1650; *Wing STC* A3145). Opposite the
marginal note "Levit. 7.15." in a section on prayer and thanksgiving under the exposition of the first commandment,
Andrewes notes that the fourth sign of thankfulness is ". . .
when we defer not our thanks. A type of this was the law. The
sacrifice of thanksgiving was to be eaten the same day, not kept
longer. No procrastination of thanks. *Nihil citius senescit
gratia*, nothing grows old sooner than thanks" (sig. V1r). Fuller
mentions "fol." to distinguish the full and correct folio edition
of 1650 from the brief and sketchier duodecimo edition of
London, 1630 (*STC* 603).

15/25 *Sidenote* **Dr. Gouge**] William Gouge, D.D. (1578-1653)
who was born at Stratford-le-Bow, Middlesex. After attending
Eton for six years, he went to King's College, Cambridge in 1595,
graduated B.A. in 1598, M.A. in 1602, and proceeded D.D. in
1628. A staunch defender of Ramus, he was lecturer on logic and
philosophy at King's College, where he also taught Hebrew.
While at King's College, he earned the nick-name of "arch-
puritan" because of his strict prayer life. Throughout his life
he remained devoted to the presbyterian system, which he
believed was *jure divino* (*DNB* 8, 271-272).

15/24-25 **he commended . . . in thanksgiving**] Dr. William
Gouge's *The whole-armour of God* (London, 1637; *STC* 12110.5)
emphasizes the blindness of those "who can see no matter of
thanksgiving" (sig. Ee1v). Moreover, he asks, "Are not almost
all much more ready to crave and aske, then to give thanks? I
speake not this of the prophane men of the word, or of carnall
& carelesse professors, who regard no dutie due vnto God: but of
those who make a greater and truer profession, yea who make
conscience of their duty to God. Marke & observe if there
requests to God be not more frequent & fervent then their

thanksgiving" (sig. Ee1v). He later adds, "but to let passe those also that offend in the generall neglect of this duty: there are other who being somewhat carefull of the duty in general, faile exceedingly to the extent of it: they give not thanks for AL THINGS. Some can be thankefull for temporall blessings, as for *peace, plenty, seasonable weather, deliverance from invasions, rebellions, treasons, from fire, plagues, famine, sicknesse, etc.* But it seemeth they take no notice of spirituall blessings their mouthes are very seldome or never opened to blesse God for them. They shew themselves to be too earthly minded (sig. Ee2r).

15/31-32 **Tenants... good to them**] Cf. Matthew 21.33-40; Mark 12.1-9; Luke 20.9-16.

15/34-35 **Ingratitude ... nature**] See Seneca's *De Beneficiis* 4.18.1: "Ut scias per se expetendam esse grati animi adfectionem, per se fugienda res est ingratum esse, quoniam nihil aeque concordiam humani generis dissociat ac distrahit quam hoc vitium." Also, see *De Beneficiis* 7.27.3: "Si indignaris ingratos esse, indignare luxuriosos, indignare avaros, indignare impudicos, indignare aegros deformes, senes pallidos! Est istuc grave vitium, est intolerabile et quod dissociet homines, quod concordiam, qua imbecillitas nostra fulcitur, scindat ac dissipet, sed usque eo vulgare est, ut illud ne qui queritur quidem effugerit." Further, see Dent, I66: "And as ingratitude is the most heinous offence against God, so have I taught you that is the greatest faulte in humayne actions."

15/6 *Lycurgus*... **against it**] The reputed founder of the Spartan constitutions, who probably lived in the 9th century. Fuller most likely read this anecdote in a popular contemporary compendium of providences and historical anecdotes written by Samuel Clark entitled, *Mirrour or Looking-Glasse Both For Saints, and Sinners*, 2nd ed. (London, 1654; *Wing STC*, C4548), sig. Cc5v: "Lycurgus would make no Law against ingratitude, because he thought that no man would fall so far below Reason as not thankfully to acknowledge a benefit."

Commentary to the Text 211

15/8-18/1 **In Athens ... to bondage]** See *Valerius Maximus* 2.6. instead of 2.1 as the sidenote indicates.

16/6 **Let nothing be lost]** John 6.12 not Luke 6.35 as the sidenote indicates.

16/6-7 *Sidenote: Ingrato ... Senec*[*a*]*.*] Cf. *De Beneficiis* 4.10.3: "Quam saepe hominum donationem suam inconsultam obiurgantium hanc exaudimus vocem: Mallem perdidisse quam illi dedisse! Turpissimum genus damni est inconsulta donatio multoque gravius male dedisse beneficium quam non recepisse."

16/7 **Bernard ... God]** *Sermones super Cantica Canticorum*, Sermon 51: "Numquid non perit quod donatur ingrato? Ingratitudo inimica est animae, exinanitio meritorum, virtutum dispersio, beneficiorum perditio. Ingratitudo ventus urens, siccans sibi fontem pietatis, rorem misericordiae, fluenta gratiae" (Bernard of Clairvaux, *Sermones super Cantica Canticorum*, ed. J. LeClercq, 8 vols., Roma: Editiones Cistercienses, 1957-) 2: 87.

16/34-38 *Sidenote Ambulandum ...* **B[ishop]. Andrews, Catech[ism]. fol. p. 91]** *The Pattern of Catechistical Doctrine at Large ... [Perfected according to the Authors own Copy, And thereby purged from many thousands of Errours, Defects, and Corruptions, which were in a rude imperfect Draught formerly published,]* (London, 1650; *Wing STC* A3145): Andrewes gives the fourth fule concerning the extent of a law: "4. The fourth Rule of extension is that, which mans Law hath prescribed. *Cum quid prohibetur, prohibentur omnia per quae pervenitur ad illus, & e contra,* when anything is prohibited, all things likewise are forbidden, that are the means to it, and so on the contrary. The Jews say, *Ambulandum est in praeceptis per viam regiam,* we must walk in the commandments, not by a by-path, but in the rode, in the Kings high way. The reason is, the goodnesse of a way of motion dependeth on the end: so that if these or these means bring to an evil end, they are evil, and consequently not to be used in good things, neither are we to seek God by them. We must not so much as stand in the way of sinners. So if a thing be good, the omission as also the means be evil. *Bonae legis est, non solum tollere vitia, sed et occasiones vitiorum,* it is the property of a good law not only to take away sin it self, but the occasions also of sin" (p. 91, sig. M2r).

17/13-15 *Sidenote:* ***Qui timet esse bonus non timet esse malus*]** Cf. Bernard of Clairvaux, *Corpus Epistolarum,* Le Clerq, ed. by 8 vols. (Roma: Editiones Cistercienses, 1957-) 7: 240: "Minime pro certo est bonus, qui melior esse non vult, et ubi incipis nolle fieri melior, ibi desinis etiam esse bonus."

17/32-33 **shall we write . . . in water]** Cf. Thomas More, *The History of King Richard III,* ed. Richard S. Sylvester in *The Complete Works of St. Thomas More,* 18 vols. to date (New Haven: Yale University Press) 2, 57: "For men vse if they haue an euil turne, to write it in marble: & whoso doth vs a good tourne, we write it in duste which is not worst proued by her"; Cf. Thomas More, *Historia Richardi Tertii,* ed. Daniel Kinney in *The Complete Works of Thomas More* (New Haven: Yale University Press) 15: 430: " . . . eo diuturniore memoria quo deteriore / vt beneficia puluere / mali si quid patimur / marmori insculpimus"; Francis Beaumont and John Fletcher, *Philaster,* ed. Andrew Gurr (London: Methuen & Coltd, 1969), V.3.81-84. Also, cf. Tilley W114, Dent W114.

17/38-39 **to blesse . . . us]** Luke 6.28.

18/18-19 ***They are words . . . not read only*]** Cf. Augustine's *De Opere Monachorum, PL* 40: 565: "Qui autem se dicunt vacare lectioni, nonne illic inveniunt quod praecipit Apostolus? Quae est ista ergo perversitas, lectioni nolle obtemperare, dum vult ei vacare; et ut quod bonum est diutius legatur, ideo facere nolle quod legitur? Quis enim nesciat tanto citius quemque proficere cum bona legit, quanto citius facit quod legit?"

Commentary to the Text   213

18/18-24 Sidenote *Egidius, Abbot of Norimberg*] I have not been able to find an Abbot named Egidius in Nuremburg. There were six monasteries in Nuremberg during the Middle Ages and the Reformation: the oldest was the Benedictine house of St. Aegidius, founded in 1140, the youngest that of the Carthusians, built on the outskirts of the city in 1380. The Minorite friars had their house on the southern bank of the Pegnitz; the Dominicans, who came to the city in about 1250, built their house on donated ground north of the river; the Carmelites were located in the Lorenz parish also on donated ground; and the Augustinians established themselves in the city in 1265 (Gerald Strauss, *Nuremberg in the Sixteenth Century*, Bloomington and London: Indiana University Press, 1976), 157. According to *Die Benediktinerklöster in Bayern* in *Germania Benedictina*, 3 vols. (Ottobeuren: Bayerische Benediktiner-Akademie, 1979-), 2: 199, St. Agidienkirche Kloster, originally founded by Conrad III for a group of Scottish monks, never had an abbot named Egidius. Very possibly, the last abbot of the Kloster, Abbot Friedrich Pistorius, who was abbot from 1520 to 1525 and was "a man known to be sympathetic to Wittenberg," is the person being referred to here by Fuller (Gerald Strauss, *Nuremberg in the Sixteenth Century*, Bloomington and London: Indiana U. Press, 1976), 175.

18/20-24 Sidenote: **Boni Catholici . . . mores**] I am unable to locate the origin of this saying.

18/31-32 **who is the Way, Truth and Life**] John 14:6.

18/34-35 **lesse then . . . and mercies**] Genesis 32.10.

19/5 **John Fuller**] Nonconformist minister from Sussex who was ejected from his living at St. Martin's, Ironmonger Lane, in 1660 (T.W. David, *Annals of Evangelical Nonconformity in the County of Essex*), 541. In *An Abridgement of Mr. Baxter's History of His Life & Times*, 2 vols. (London: Printed for J. Lawrence, 1713), sig. D2v, Fuller is described as a "Most Pious

Man and Practical Preacher: He had three Sons that were Scholars and Ministers of Note. Two of them conform'd; but his Son Mr. *Francis* Fuller, dy'd a nonconformist in London." Also, see John Venn, comp., *Alumni Cantabrigienses*, 10 vols. (Cambridge: University Press, 1922) 2: 184.

21/12-13 **their adversity . . . forget him commonly**] See Ben Jonson, *Timber or Discoveries*, eds. C.H. Herford Percy and Evelyn Simpson, 11 vols. (Oxford: Clarendon Press, 1947) 8: 569: "*Affliction* teacheth a wicked person sometime to pray: *Prosperity* never." Also, Livy: "Adversae deinde res admonuerunt religionum" (Livy, V.51.9).

21/16-17 **when . . . . strength**] Ecclesiastes 10.10.

21/20 **repeats this passage**] Psalms 107.6 is repeated in Psalmes 107. 13,19,28.

21/22-23 **he doth . . . goodnesse**] Psalms 107.8 is repeated in Psalms 107.15,21,31.

23/4-5 **take heed . . . the Pharisees**] Matthew 16.6, 11-12.

23/26-31 *Summa est* **. . . contempt of God**] See Calvin's *Commentarii in Isaiam* in *Joanis Calvini Opera, in Corpus Reformatorum*, vols. 29-87 (Brunsvigae: apud C. A. Schwetschke et filium, 1863-1900) 64: 317. For the popular English translation see Calvin's *A Commentary upon the Prophecie of Isaiah* (London, 1609; STC 4396), sig. Q6v.

23/37-25/1 *Initio omnia . . . saith Vatablus*] Francois Vatable, French Hellenist and Hebraist, was born about 1493 in Gamaches in Picardy. He matriculated at the University of Paris in 1508, and his relationship to Jacques Lefévre d'Etaples and his later association with the collége Cardinal Lemoine suggest that he studied and taught there (Eugene Rice Jr., ed., *The Prefatory Epistles of Jacques Lefévre d'Etaples*, New York and London: Columbia University Press, 1972), 249. From lecture

Commentary to the Text   215

notes taken from Vatable's students, Robert Stephanus took the material for the *scholia* he added to his edition of the new Latin translation of the Bible by Leo and Juda (Paris, 1539-1545); it has been proved that these notes had been shamefully garbled by the Protestants at Zurich. The Sorbonne doctors criticized the Lutheran tendencies of the notes to Stephanus' Bible, and Vatable himself disowned them; however, the Salamanca theologians, with the authorization of the Spanish Inquisition, issued a new, thoroughly-revised edition of them in their Latin Bible of 1584 (*The Catholic Encylopedia*, 1st ed., New York: Robert Appleton Company) 15: 276. Vatable's commentary on Isaiah and the prophets, along with other popular commentators of scripture, were collected in John Pearson's *Critici sacri*, excudebat Jacobus Flesher (London 1660; *Wing STC* P994A), sig. S6v.

24/5-7 *Junius ... fructum percipias*] See Junius's Commentary in *Testamenti Veteris Biblia Sacra* (Hanoviae, Wechelianis, apud Claudium 1602), sig. Ss2r. Francois Du Jon (1545-1602), a reformed theologian and a personal pupil of Calvin, was commissioned in 1573 by Elector Frederick III to assist in a Latin translation of the Old Testament (*The New Schaff-Herzog Encyclopedia of Religious Knowledge*, 13 vols., New York and London: Funk and Wagnalls Company, 1908-1914) 6: 266.

24/11-14 **Luther had ... Gods benefits**] See Luther's *Table Talk*: "Unsere Kirch wird vonwegen der Tyrannen und ihrer Verfolgung nich so grose Noth und Gefahr leiden, al von den Unsern selbs, und von wegen unser grossen Sickerheit, Witz und Unachtasamkeit" (*D. Martin Luthers Werks: Tischreden*, 6 vols., Weimar, 1912-1921) 4: 377, no. 4557; for the sixteenth-century manuscripts and editions which contain this passage, see 1, xvii, xxii-xxiii. This passage does not appear in *Dr. Martin Luther's Divine discourses at his table ... Translated out of the high Germane into the English tongue by Capt. Menrie Bell* (London, 1652; *Wing STC* L350).

24/37 **feast of Tabernacles**] Also called the "festival of booths." See Leviticus 23.34,43; Deuteronomy 16.13.

24/38 **Pentecost**] Also called the "feast of weeks." See Exodus 23.1 34.22; Leviticus 23.16-25; Numbers 28.26; Deuteronomy 16.9,10,16.

25/35 **Book of *Jasher*]** See Joshua 10.13; 2 Samuel 1.18.

25/38-39 **Book of the Judges ... *Battails of the* Lord**] See commentary on Numbers 21.14 in *The Geneva Bible: A facsimile of the 1560 edition* (Madison: University of Wisconsin Press, 1969), sig. siiv: "Which seemeth to be the boke of the Iudges, or as some thinke, a boke which is lost."

26/2 **Book of Exodus; *Junius* and *Calvin*]** Cf. Calvin's *Commentarius in Exodi*, in *Corpus Reformatorum*, 52: 181: "Hoc preaecepto admonuit Deus, rem se gessisse quae non sermone tantum celebrari debeat, sed apud posteros quoque aeternam gloriam mereatur. Ideo enim in libro scribi iubet, ne unquam intercidat eius memoria. Quod de libro curiosius disputant interpretes, supervacuum mihi videtur: quia simpliciter vult Deus exstare omnibus saeculis huius rei monumentum: Quod hac narratione praestitit Moses, quia cum perpetua et immortali legis doctrina huius gratiae elogium scripto prodidit usque ad finem mundi. Quanquam non tantum scribi voluit memorabilem huius pugnae eventum, sed Iosuam de ea commonefieri, ne sub tot, quae enim manebant, difficultatibus fatisceret. Nihil enim melius eum potuit invicta constantia fulcire quam huius historiae recordatio: unde statuere licebat, populum sub Dei auspiciis semper fore victorem." In the *Geneva Bible* (Edinburgh: A. Hart, 1610; *STC* 2209), sig. S2v, Junius's annotation to Joshua 10.13 is as follows: "Some reade in the booke of the righteous meaning Moses, the Chaldee text readeth in the booke of the Law: but it is like that it was a booke thus named which is now lost." Likewise, in Calvin's *Commentary on Joshua* (London, 1578; *STC* 4394), sigs. Oiv Oiir:

Commentary to the Text

(26/2 cont.)
"The booke which he citeth be lost: and interpretours doe not well argue about the name Jasar. They that would have Moses noted thereby, doe fondly drawe the example, which is to be tolde, to generall predictions. But because Moses so calleth the chosen people, it will better argue, that by the booke is noted the Chronicle of the actes and deedes."

26/9-10 **sentence ... *Amalek*]** 1 Samuel 15.7-8.

26/19-21 ***Moses ... the Lord*]** Numbers 33.2.

27/31-32 **bread from heaven]** Exodus 16.4.

27/32 **water out of the rock]** Exodus 17.6.

27/31-34 **the violence of the mighty waters]** Exodus 14.26-28.

27/35-36 **cruelty of the *AEgytians*]** Exodus 14.

27/35-36 **malice of the *Amalekites*]** Exodus 17.10-16.

27/36-37 **sting of the fiery Serpents]** Exodus 7.12.

27/37-38 **Manna and Quails]** Exodus 16.13-15.

27/39**delivers them his Law]** Deuteronomy 4.5-8.

29/2-3 **vale of tears]** Cf. the hymn *Salve Regina mater misericordiae*: "Ad te suspiramus gementes et flentes / In hac lacrimarum valle." The prayer is attributed to Hermann Contractus (1013-1054). See Clemens Blume and Guido M. Dreves, eds., *Analecta Hymnica*, 52 vols. (Leipzig: O.R. Reisland, 1897-1908) 50: 318.

29/24-25 bunch... wildernesse] Numbers 13.24.

29/28-30 When *Joseph*... Sacks] Genesis 42.6-24.

29/39 Ark... Cham] Genesis 7.13.

30/2-3 seven Deacons... *Nicholas*] Acts 6.1-6. He alone among the deacons was never honored as a Saint. Moreover, the Fathers reproach him for indiscretion in words or in deeds with regard to his beautiful wife. See Irenaeus's *Contra Haereses*, *PG* 7: 687; Clement of Alexandria's *Stromatum*, *PG 8*: 1129.

30/5-6 the spirits... made perfect] Hebrews 12.23.

30/11-12 whatever was written... our learning] Romans 15.4.

31/16 Such Prince, such people] See Whiting P403, C34, J71, M408; Tilley M723; Dent M723. Also, see Hans Walther, ed., *Proverbia Sententiaeque Latinitatis Medii Aevi*, 8 vols. (Göttingen: Vandenhoeck & Ruprecht, 1966), 23250: "Qualis rex, talis populus;" See also Cicero, *De Legibus*, 3.14; Claudian, *Panegyricus de Quarto Consulatu Honorii Augusti*, 1.300; Robert Herrick, "Examples, or Like Prince, like People," in *The Poetical Works of Robert Herrick* (Oxford: Clarendon Press, 1956), 255: "Examples lead us, and wee likely see,/ Such as the Prince is, will his People be."

31/17-18 yeelding... of *Winchester*] William Paulet, the first Marquis of Winchester and Lord Treasurer during Henry VIII's reign, was perceived as an adroit political opportunist because he weathered the revolutions of four regimes (*DNB 15*: 537-539). See John S. Cerovski, ed., *Fragmenta Regalia*, by Sir Robert Naunton (Washington, D.C.: Folger Books, 1985), 48: "Paulet, Marquess of Winchester and Lord Treasurer of England, had served then four princes in as various times and changeable seasons that I may well say no time nor age hath yielded the like precedent. This man being noted to grow high in her favor as his place and experience required was questioned by an intimate friend of how he stood for thirty years together amidst the changes and ruins of so many counselors and great personalities. 'Why,' quoth the Marquess, '*ortus sum ex salice non ex quercu.* I was made of the pliable willow, not of the oak." Paulet's observation derives from Aesop's fable about the tree and the reed; see R.T. Lenaghan, ed., *Caxton's Aesop* (Cambridge: Harvard University Press, 1967), 135-136. Also, see Tilley O3 and Whiting O3.

31/24 *Constantius* the Heretick] After the death of his father, Constantine the Great, who died believing the Arian heresy, Constantius, who ruled from 337-361, became allied with the Eusebian Arian faction because of the spiritual direction of Valens, Bishop of Mursa. See Eusebius, *Ecclesiastical History*, 2.299.

31/22 *Constantine* the Reformer] That is, the emperor Constantine (288?-337), under whom the empire became Christian.

31/24 *Iulian* the Apostate] Roman emperor (331-363) was the half-brother of Constantine the Great. Constantius sent Julian to Nicodemia where he studied neo-Platonic philosophy mixed with occult superstition. He continued his studies in Athens where he became completely won over to Hellenism and was initiated into the Eleusinian mysteries. However, he continued to embrace Christianity outwardly. After becoming emperor in 355, he allowed himself to be portrayed as under the protection of Zeus. Moreover, he commanded all towns to reopen the temples for pagan worship, restored animal sacrifice, abrogated all rights, titles to lands, and immunities bestowed on Christians by Constantine, forbade the appointment of Christians as teachers of rhetoric, and demanded that monies granted to the Church by Constantine be repaid to the State. See the third book of Theodoret's *Ecclesiastical History* which records the exploits of Julian's reign and apostasy.

31/25 *Jovinianus*] Beadle is probably referring to the successor of Julian the Apostate, Jovianus (d. 364), who proclaimed his orthodox Christianity after being chosen emperor by his soldiers and supporters in A.D. 363 Jovianus also brought Athanasius out of exile and reinstated the Nicene creed as the proper symbol of the Christian Church (Theodoret, *Ecclesiastical History*, 4.1.).

32/1-2 **Regis ad exemplum**] Claudian, *Panegyricus de Quarto Consulatu Honorii Augusti*, 1. 300. Also, see Thomas Heywood, *Philocothonista* (London, 1635; STC 13356), sig. C8v: "Regis ad exemplum totus componitur orbis." See 32/16.

32/4-10 **When certain Embassadors ... another Generall**] Xenophon, *Hellenica*, 3.2.7.

32/18-19 **another Caesar ... by Arms**] Beadle is probably referring to Julius Caesar, who was a great soldier and patron of the arts.

33/6-7 **Charls the Great ... the Bible**] I cannot find the source for this anecdote.

33/7-11 **Canutus ... the best Policy**] Matthew of Westminster, (C.D. Yonge, trans., *The Flowers of History*, 2 vols., New York: AMS Press, 1968) 2: 526-527.

33/11-12 **The Lions ... pure gold**] 1 Kings 10.19 and 2 Chronicles 9:18.

33/13 **pretended**] That is, professed or claimed (*OED*).

33/33-35 **as soon as ... whither they intended**] The sidenote indicates John 8.21; however, the passage Beadle is referring to is Matthew 14.23-33.

34/3 **Bishop of *Monte Fulciano* ... of *Trent***] Not until 1561 was the city of Monte Pulciano given a bishopric (*The Catholic*

Encyclopedia, 10: 531-532). By then both Paul III and Charls V had died, in 1549 and 1558, respectively. Nevertheless, in 1543, Paul III "intended to send a special ambassador, Montepulciano, to the Emperor . . . The papal ambassador, Montepulciano, offered him [Charles V] the Pope's mediation in his troubles with France, but Charles treated the suggestion with coolness" (Karl Brandi, *The Emperor Charles V*, Atlantic Highlands, N.J.: Humanities Press, 1986), 471-474.

34/11-14 **Pope Paul . . . religion is lost**] I cannot find this instruction of Paul III.

34/15-18 **Danish King . . . the other mans**] The Dooms of Canute (1020-34): 18. "and thrice a-year let there be a 'burh-gemot,' and twice a 'shire-gemot'; unless it be oftener. And let there be present the bishop of the shire and the ealdorman, and there let both expound as well the law of God as the secular law" (William Stubbs, ed., *Select Charters and other Illustrations of English Constitutional History from the Earliest Times to the Reign of Edward the First*, Oxford: Clarendon Press, 1921), 86.

34/30-31 **Omnium rerum est vicissitudo**] Terence, *Eunuchus*, 2.2.45. Also, see Tilley C233, Dent C233.

34/36-37 **Jabin . . . yeers**] Judges 4.2,17,23,24 are more appropriate than the passages indicated in the sidenotes.

35/15 **Stephen was stoned**] Acts 7.58-59.

35/18 **Saul became Paul**] Acts 13.9.

35/30-31 **Capernaum . . . to heaven**] Matthew 11.23 and Luke 10.15.

36/7 **Marte cadunt . . . fratres**] Ovid, *Metamorphoses*. 3.123.

36/8-12 **Sylla . . . bowels**] Livy, *Summaries*, 79.

36/12-14 *Titus Vespasian* . . . **the Jews**] Josephus, *The Jewish Wars*, 5.519-520.

36/19-24 *Pliny* . . . **death**] *Natural History*, 8.11.32. and 8.12.33-34.

36/25-28 *Philip* **Duke of Burgundy** . . . **are consumed**] Philip the Good (1396-1467) is most famous for his battles with the Turks and his establishment of the Order of the Golden Fleece. For the most definitive biography of him, see Richard Vaughn, *Philip the Good: The Apogee of Burgundy* (London: Longmans, 1970). Beadle might have seen Philip the Good's favorite emblem, which is described in H. Beaune and J. d'Arbaumont, eds., *Mémoires*, by Olivier de La Marche, 4 vols. (Paris, 1883-1888) 2: 11-12: "I avoit dix huict chevaulx d'une parure, harnachez de velours noir tixuz et ouvrez á sa devise, qui furent fusilz garniz de leurs pierres, rendans feu; et, par dessus le velours, gros cloz d'or exlevez et esmaillez de fusilz, et faictz á moult grans coustz." La Marche was a ducal page in Philip the Good's court.

36/34-39 **one of their Emperors** . . . **minde.**] Suleiman I, or, as the Christian world knew him, Suleiman the Magnificant. Several contemporary historians commented on his recognition of the discord among the German Christian princes. See John Knolles, *The generall historie of the Turkes* (London, 1602; *STC* 15051), sig. Fff1r: "Whereupon *Solyman* waiting all occasions that might serue for the enlarging of his empire, and annoying of the Christians, thought it now a fit time for him to set his foot into HVNGARIE, whereinto he had alreadie laied open a way by the taking of BELGRADE. He knew right well that *Lewes* then king of *Hungarie* was but yong, altogether vnacquainted with the warres, commaunding ouer his headstrong subjects (especially his rich prelates and nobilitie) no otherwise than pleased themselues, being himselfe rather by them altogether ouerruled. Besides that, he was in good hope, that the other Christian princes neere vnto him, either carried away with regard of their owne estate, would not, or els before vnto himselfe by league fast bound, could not affoord vnto him any great aid or succour: The Germanes hee knew would make small hast vnto such warres as should yeeld them much danger, and but small pay: As for the prince of the house of AUSTRIA, *Charls* the emperour, and *Ferdinand* his brother, although they were joined vnto the young king with the neerest bonds of alliance (*Lewes* hauing married *Marie* their youngest sister, and *Ferdinand, Anne,* king *Lewes* his sister) yet was there as he thought small helpe to be expected from them; *Charls* hauing his hands full in ITALIE, and *Ferdinand* altogether carefull of himselfe: And that *Sigismund* king of POLONIA would for the young kings sake breake the antient league he had with the Turkish emperors, he could hardly be persuaded: As for other Christian princes farther off, he stood not in any great doubt;" (R. Carr, *The Mahumetane or Turkish Historie, containing three Bookes,* London, 1600; STC 17997), sig. N2v: "SOLYMAN came to his reigne the xxviij. yeere of his age, who the yeere next ensuing by the cousail of *Peribacha,* beseged *Belgrado,* & did win it from king *Lewes* of *Hungary* (the son of *Lancelot.*) who at the time was very young, hauing the Princes & Lords of his Countrie at discord among them selues, about the Regimént of their King and of his Realme: Whereby it came to passe that no maner of Order was foreseen, either for the defence or succoring of that famous Place.

The next yeere after, hee beesieged the *Rhodes,* espying alwayes after the custome of his elders, the discords & diuisions among *Christian Princes,* the which enterprice was cleerely against the minde and counsail of *Peribacha,* who accompted the Iourney very doubtfull and of no litle aduenture: Howbeit the same succeded too well with him, as he desired."

37/8-9 **Pharaoh the bloody**] Exodus 5.1-17.

37/9 **Achitophel the crafty**] 2 Samuel 15.12; 2 Samuel 16.23; 2 Samuel 17.1-23.

37/10 *Balaam* **the covetous**] Numbers 22.12-20.

37/10 *Corah* the rebell] Exodus 6.16,18,21; Numbers 16.1-50; Jude 11.

37/10 *Haman* the proud] Esther 3.1-5.

37/11 *Herod* the fox] Matthew 2.7-8,13.

37/13 *Absolom* the disobedient] 2 Samuel 3.3; 2 Samuel 13.1-18,32; 2 Samuel 15.12.

37/13-141 *Ela* the drunkard] 1 Kings 16.8-14.

37/14 *Zimri*] Numbers 25.6-15.

37/14 *Cosbi* the unclean] Numbers 25.1-18.

37/15 *Ananias* and *Saphira* those lyars] Acts 5.1-11.

37/17 Nimrods] tyrants (*OED*).

37/17 *Maxentius* the Tyrant] Roman emperor from A.D. 306 to A.D. 312. See Eusebius, *Ecclesiastical History*, 8.14.: "His son Maxentius, who secured for himself the tyranny at Rome, at the beginning counterfeited our faith in order to please and fawn upon the Roman populace; and for this reason ordered his subjects to give over the persecution against Christians; for he was feigning piety and endeavoring to appear favourable and very mild above his predecessors . . . All cowered before him, people and rulers, famous and obscure, and were worn out by his terrible tyranny; and even though they remained quiet and endured the bitter servitude, still there was no escape from the tyrant's murderous cruelty." Also, see Eutropius 10.2, Carol Santini, ed., *Breviarium ab Urbe Condita* (Leipzig: B.G. Teubner, 1979); and Book 2.9-18 of Zosimus, *Historia Nova: The Decline of Rome* (San Antonio: Trinity University Press, 1967).

37/18 *Julian* the Apostate] See 32/24 n. While fighting the Persians in June A.D. 363, he was wounded in the side by an arrow and died during the night.

37/19-20 ten . . . Histories] See Book 1 of John Foxe's *The Acts and Monuments*, 8 vols. (New York: AMS Press, 1965) 1: viii, 99-249, which describes "the three hundred years next after Christ, with the ten persecutions of the primitive church."

37/24 *wily Winchester*] Probably Stephen Gardiner (1483?-1555), whom John Foxe called "wily Winchester" in Foxe's *Acts and Monuments*, 7: 592. Gardiner was Bishop of Winchester under Henry VIII and predecessor of Edmund Bonner. On Edward's accession to the throne, Gardiner was excluded from the council of state, and also removed from the chancellorship at the university of Cambridge. However, on Mary's accession he was among the prisoners who knelt before her on her visit to the Tower and was at once set at liberty. In 1553, he was made lord high chancellor of the realm, and in this capacity placed the crown on her head at her coronation and presided at the opening of parliament. Because of his participation in the persecution of Protestants, he, in conjunction with Bonner, was held responsible for severity of the persecution. He also took a leading part in bringing back the country to its Roman allegiance against which he had written so forcibly and which he had so long repudiated (*DNB* 7: 863-864).

37/24 **bloody Bonner**] Edmund Bonner (1560?-1569), whom John Foxe calls "the bloody bishop of London," (*Acts and Monuments*) 8: 667, was committed to Marshalsea prison in 1549 and deprived of his bishopric. In 1553, at the accession of Queen Mary, he was released and took possession of his see where he restored processions, crucifixes, and images. Later, in 1555, after England had been reconciled to Rome, Bonner participated in the persecution of the Protestants at the request of Queen Mary and King Philip (*DNB* 2: 819-822).

37/12 **ruled the roste**] Cf. Dent R144, Whiting R149 and Tilley R144.

37/31-32 **God hath leaden feet... he strikes surely**] See Tilley G182; Dent G182; Euripides, *The Bacchanals*, 1.882; Juvenal, *Satires*, 2.1.23. Also, cf. "God hath Woollen feet, but Iron hands" (Thomas Beard, *Theatre of Gods Judgements*, London, 1648; *Wing STC* B1565), titlepage.

38/6-8 *Zoroastes* **the inventer... lamentable death**] Pliny, *Natural History*, 7.16.72: "Risisse eodem die quo genitus esset unum hominem accepimus Zorastren, eidem cerebrum ita palpitasse ut inpositam repelleret manum, futurae praesagio scientiae." Also, see Augustine, *De Civitate Dei*, 21.15-20 (Turnholti: Typographi Brepols Editores Pontificii, 1955), 780: "Solum, quando natus est, ferunt ririsse Zorastrem, nec ei boni aliquid monstrosus risus ille protendit. Nam magicarum artium fuisse perhibetur inventor." Clement of Alexandria, *Recognitionum, PG 1*: 1326-1327: "Ex quibus unus Cham nomine, cuidam ex filiis suis qui Mesraim appellabatur, a quo AEgyptiorum et Bablyoniorum et Persarum ducitur genus, male compertam magicae artis tradidit disciplinam; hunc gentes quae tunc erant Zorastrem appelaverunt, admirantes primum magicae artis auctorem, cujus nomine etiam libri super hoc plurimi habentur. Hic ergo astris multum ac frequenter intentus, et volens apud homines videri Deus, velut scintillas quasdam ex stellis producere et hominibus ostentare coepit, quo rudes atque ignari augere de se hujusmodi opinionem, saepius ista moliebatur usque quo ab ipso daemone, quem importunius frequentabat, igni succensus concremaretur.

Hinc enim et nomen post mortem ejus Zoroaster, hoc est vivum sidus, appellatum est ab his, qui post unam generationem Graecae linguae loquela fuerant repleti. Hoc denique exemplo etiam nunc multi eos qui fulmine obierint, sepulcris honoratos tanquam amicos Dei colunt;" Gregory of Tours tells the same story in O.M. Dalton, ed., *The History of the Franks* (Oxford: Clarendon Press, 1927), 14: "The firstborn of Ham was Chus, who by inspiration of the Devil was first inventor of the whole art of magic, and of idolatry. He first, at the prompting of the Evil One, set up a graven image to be worshipped, and by his false arts, showed mankind stars and fire falling from heaven. He passed over to the Persians, who called him Zoroaster, which is to say living star. Taught by him the custom of adoring fire, they worshipped him as a god, since he was consumed by fire" (14). Also, see Samuel Clark, *A Mirrour or Looking-Glass*, 2nd ed. (London, 1654; Wing STC C4548), sig. Gg5r: "*Zoroastres* King of Bactria, a great Astrologer and Magician was burned to death by the Divel!"; Thomas Beard, *The Theatre of Gods Judgements* (London, 1648; Wing STC B1565), sig. H3v: "*Zoroastres* King of Bactria is notisied to have bin the inventer of Astrology and Magick. But the Devill (whose ministry he used) when he was too importunate with him, burned him to death."

38/9-20 *Alphonsus Dyazius*] "On 27 March 1546, at Neuburg, on the Danube, the Spaniard Juan Díaz was murdered in Cruel fashion at the instigation of his own brother, Alfonso Díaz, a priest, because in spite of the latter's efforts and threats he stuck to his Protestant faith" (Hubert Jedin, *A History of the Council of Trent*, trans. Dom Ernest Graf., 2 vols., London: Thomas Nelson and Sons Ltd., 1957) 2: 212. Jedin also suggests that "all the indications pointed to the fact that the Neuburg murder was planned as a warning and that Díaz had only been a tool" (213). Alphonso's younger brother, Juan Díaz, studied theology in Paris for thirteen years before going to Geneva in 1545 to study reformed theology with Calvin. Beadle probably read the version of the story he relates in Thomas Beard's *The Theater of Gods Judgements* (London, 1648; Wing STC B1565), sig. Q4r, which contains all the elements to which Beadle refers. For other contemporary Protestant treatments of Juan Díaz's murder see the modern edition of Claud Senarclens, *Historia de la Muerte De Juán Díaz* (Barcelona: Librería de Diego Gómez Flores, 1983); and Philip Melancthon, "The Narratio Melanchtonis de Diasio," in G. Baum, E. Cunitz, and E. Reuss, eds., *Corpus Reformatorum* (Leipzig, 1863-1900) 123: 112-114. In addition, see the discussion of Juan Díaz's life and relationship with his brother in Edward Boehmer, *Bibliotheca Wiffeniana. Spanish Reformers of Two Centuries from 1520*, 3 vols. (New York: Burt Franklin, 1874-1904) *1*: 187-198.

38/31-36 **A Serving-man . . . 1626**] Cf. anecdote given in Samuel Clark's *A Mirrour or Looking-Glasse*, 2nd ed. (London, 1654; Wing STC C4548), sig. O7v-O8r: "A Serving-man in Lincolnshire for every trifle used to swear by Gods precious blood, and would not be warned by his friends, till at length falling into a grievous sicknesse, he was again much perswaded by his friends to repent, which counsel he rejected . . . and so he died."

39/34-39 *Scaliger* **. . . they might drink**] Julius Caesar Scaliger, *De causis linguae latinae* (Lyon: Sebastianus Gryphaeus, 1540), sig. C1: "Vasconibus quoque hoc est uitium peculiare, ut eo modo pronuncient B, quo & Graecos dicimus. Itaque lusimus in eos epigrammate, ut eorum Viuere, Bibere, sit."

40/1-3 *Seneca* **foretold . . .** *virtus esset*] I cannot locate this quotation.

40/3-5 **the Brewers horse . . . carry more liquor**] Cf. *1 Henry IV*, 3.3.9: "I am a peppercorn, a brewer's horse." Thomas Heywood's *Philocothonista* (London, 1635; STC 13356), sig. E8v: "One whom the brewer's horse hath bit." Also, see William Cecil's *Certaine Precepts, or Directions, for the well ordering and carriage of a man's life* (London, 1617; STC 4897), sig. A6r: "I neuer heard other commendation ascribed to a Drunkard, more then the well-bearing of his drink, which is a Commendation fitter for a Brewers horse, or a Dray-mans backe, then either for Gentlemen or Scruing-men."

40/7 **as drunk as a Beggar**] Tilley B225, Dent B225.

40/7 **as drunk as a Prince**] See Tilley L439.

Commentary to the Text   229

40/10-13 When *Aeschines* . . . in a Prince] Plutarch, *Demosthenes*, 16.3-4.

40/16-17 *Ebrietas* . . . *omnes*] Is probably a play on the Latin proverb: "Virtutes pietas in se complectitur omnes," Walther, 33723b. Cf. Thomas Heywood's *Philocothonista* (London, 1635; STC 13356), sig. K3v: "Nam maximum Ebrietas Malorum est omnium / Mortalibus, quod laedat hoc est maximum. The greatest evill that on earth can be, / And most hurts mankinde, is Ebrietie." Cf. "A branch of the sin of drunkenness, which is the root of alls sins" (King James I) in *The Oxford Dictionary of Quotations*, 3rd ed. (Oxford University Press, 1980), 271.

40/22-29 *Edgar* a King of England . . . much money] See William of Malmesbury, *Chronicle of the Kings of England*, ed. J.A. Giles (New York: AMS Press, 1968), 148: "Indeed, so extremely anxious was he to preserve peace ever in trivial matters, that, as his countrymen used to assemble in taverns, and when a little elevated quarrel as to the proportions of their liquor, he ordered gold or silver pegs to be fastened in the pots, that whilst every man knew his just measure, shame should compel each neither to take more himself, nor oblige others to drink beyond their proportional share." Possibly, Beadle saw this same story related in Samuel Clark's *A Mirrour or Looking-glass*, 2nd ed. (London, 1654; Wing STC C4548), sig. G6v.

41/1-2 *William Bygod* . . . *Alice* his Wife] See John Foxe, *The Acts and Monuments*, 5: 344.

41/6-7 *Omne peccatum* . . . excel other] I cannot find a source for this saying.

41/17-18 *Absalom* . . . Son] 2 Samuel 15.1-15.

41/18-19 *Hazael* . . . Subject] 2 Kings 8.7-15.

41/19-20 *Jezebel* . . . Husband] 1 Kings 21.8.

41/21-23 **lowest . . . Priests**] 2 Kings 12.31.

41/24-26 *Corah* **. . . Priesthood**] Numbers 16.7-11.

41/28-36 **How sad was . . . possessed their goods**] Junianus Justinus, *De Historiis Philippicis*, 2.5.

41/39-43/4 *Caesar* **riding . . . person in Rome**] Plutarch, *Caesar*, 11.3-6.

42/6-7 *Adam* **and** *Eve* **. . . standing**] Genesis 3.2.

42/12-13 **the bramble . . . shadow**] Cf. Avian's fable about the bush and the fir tree in Aesopus, *The Fables of Aesop* [as first printed by William Caxton in 1484 with those of Avian, Alfonso and Poggio], ed. Joseph Jacobs, 2 vols. (London: David Nutt, 1889), 1: 234: "one for his beaute ought not to despreyse some other / For sometyme suche one is fayre that soone wexeth lothely and fowle / and to hyghe falleth vnto lowe / as it apperyth by this fable / Of a fayr tree whiche mocqued and scorned a lytyl busshe and sayd / 'Seest thow not / my fayre fourme and my fayre fygure And that of me men and byldeth fayre edefyces as palays and castellis / galeyes & other shippes for to saylle on the see' / And as he auaunced & preyesed hym self thus / came there a labourer with his axe for to hewe and smyte hym to the ground / And as the labourer smote vpon the fayre tree / the busshe sayd / Certaynly my broder yf now thow were as lytel / as I am / men shold not hewe ne smyte the doune to the erthe / And therfore non oughte to reioysshe hym self of his worship / For suche is now in grete honour and worship / that herafter shalle falle in to grete vytupere shame and dishonour."

42/17-19 **simple Cobler . . . his Priest**] Pliny, *Natural History*, 35.36,85: "Ne supra crepidam sutor iudicaret, quod et ipsum in proverbium abiit." Cf. Dent C480, Tilley C480.

42/19-20 *Ye Sons of Levi . . . take too much upon you*] Numbers 16.7.

42/31 *Phaeton*] Ovid, *Metamorphoses*, 2.180-236.

42/32-36 **Scythian slaves . . . last perished**] See 42/28-36 n.

42/38 **Some wood . . . worms**] Cf. Morris Palmer Tilley, *Elizabethan Proverb Lore in Lyly's Euphues* (New York: The Macmillan Company, 1926), 351: "Every wood has its worm."

42/39 **some cloth . . . moths**] Cf. Tilley, *Elizabethan Proverb Lore*, 231-232: "The MOTH does most mischief in the finest cloth."

43/11-13 **broken bones . . . cured**] Cf. William Camden, *Remains Concerning Britain*, R.D. Dunn, ed. (Toronto: University of Toronto Press, 1984), 271: "A man is not so soone healed, as hurte."

43/17-18 *Solomon . . . strong city*] Proverbs 18.19.

43/19-20 *Paul . . . asunder*] Acts 15.39.

43/21-23 *Cosmus . . . forgive our friends*] Francis Bacon, *Apophthegms*. In *The Works of Francis Bacon*. James Spedding, ed., 15 vols. (Boston: Brown and Taggard, 1863) 13: 371, no. 206.

43/30 **bone of contention**] Tilley B518 and D237. Also, see *The Oxford Dictionary of English Proverbs*, 3rd ed., 73.

43/30 **apple of strife**] See *Oxford Dictionary of English Proverbs*, 3rd. ed., 17: "Apple of discord," meaning any subject of dissension. Also refers to apple thrown down among three goddesses who were to be judged by Paris.

43/36-37 *Iniquity shall . . . grow cold*] Matthew 24.12.

43/38-39 **Many false prophets ... seduce many**] Matthew 24.11.

44/7 **boutefewes**] An incendiary, a firebrand; one who kindles discontent and strife (*OED*).

44/13-14 **to try the spirits**] 1 John 4.1.

44/17-18 **division from the Devil**] Tilley D237.

44/21 *Machiavel's* **rule ... may rule**] Nicolo Machiavelli, *The Prince*, ed. Allan H. Gilbert, 3 vols. (New York: Henricks House, 1946) *1*: 24. Also, see Tilley D391.

44/23-26 **champion** *Milo* ... **wilde beasts**] Aulus Gellius, *Attic Nights*, 16.1-4, and Pausanias, *Description of Greece*, 2.14.8-9.

44/33-35 **unity of the spirit, with the bond of peace**] Ephesians 4.3.

44/39-45/1-7 *Melanchthon* ... **with tears**] Several eyewitnesses collaborated to publish a detailed account of Melanchthon's last days and death (*Brevis narratio exponens. quo fine vitam in terris suam clauserit reveredus vir D. Philippus Melanchthon . . . ,* Wittenberg, 1560; 2nd edition, Wittenberg, 1561). Melanchton was indeed happy to seek in heaven relief from the quarrels and attacks which oppressed him in his last years. See the modern edition of the account by Nicolaus Müller, *Philipp Melanchtons letzte Lebenstage, Heimgang und Bestattung nach den gleichzeitigen Berichten der Wittenberger Professoren* (Leipzig, 1910), 5/22-23, 18/12-15, 23/16-24, 24/42, 25/4, 27/24-32, 30/9-16, 31/1-8 and 30-38, 37/16, 39/21-25. The "contentions amongst the brethren" which helped cause Melanchthon's mortal illness was a physical quarrel about the Lord's supper between a Lutheran minister and his deacon over the communion cup at the altar of a Lutheran church in Heidelberg. As a result of their conduct and the subsequent scandal, Elector Frederick rejected the Lutheran doctrine on the eucharist and introduced the Reformed teaching (James William Richard, *Philip*

Melanchton: The Protestant Preceptor of Germany, (1898; New York: Burt Franklin, 1974), 375-377.

45/13-14 **looking . . . another**] Brian Melbancke, *Philotimus* (London, 1583; STC 17801), sig. P1v: "And so imitate the waterman, which looketh one way, and roweth another;" Thomas Overbury, *The Conceited Newes of Sir Thomas Overbury and His Friends* (Gainesville, Florida: Scholar's Facsimiles & Reprints, 1968), sig. L1r: "for like a fellow that rides to the Pillorie, he goes not that way he lookes;" Thomas Dekker, *The Wonder of a Kingdom*, Fredson Bower, ed. In *The Dramatic Works of Thomas Dekker*, 4 vols. (Cambridge: University Press, 1958) 3: V.ii.131-133: "Now in good sooth my Lord, shee has but vs'd you / As watermen use their fares, for shee look'd one way, / And row'd another, you but wore her glove;" Edmund Spenser, *Mutability Cantos* in *The Works of Edmund Spenser: Variorum Edition*, 10 vols. (Baltimore: Johns Hopkins Press, 1939) 6: 7.35.7-9: "And backward yode, as Bargemen wont to fare / Bending their force contrary to their face, / Like that vngracious crew which faines demurest grace."

45/17 **painted sepulchres**] Matthew 23.27.

45/19 **seven . . . hearts**] Proverbs 26.25.

45/27-29 *Jehu* . . . **Kingdome**] 2 Kings 10.1-11

45/29 *Sidenote*: **1 Ki[ngs]. 12.13**] The correct reference is 1 Kings 21.13.

46/2 **Isaac digged more Wells**] Genesis 26.18-22.

46/18-19 **The Toad . . . the belly**] Tilley T360. See John Lyly, *Euphues*. In *The Complete Works of John Lyly*, R. Warwick Bond, ed., 3 vols. (Oxford: Clarendon Press, 1967) 1: 202: "The foule Toade hathe a fayre stoane in his head." Also, in Shakespeare's *As You Like It*, 2.1.12-14: "Sweet are the uses of adversity,/ Which like the toad, ugly and venomous, / Wears yet a precious jewel in his head." Finally, see Edward Fenton, *Certaine Secrete wonders of Nature* (London, 1569; STC 10787), sig. L2v: "In an other cuntrie of the *Indians* is founde a stone in the heades of olde and greate toades, which they call Borax or Stelon, which Brasauolus approveth, is most commonly founde in the head of a hee toade, and yet is of opinion that it is rather a boane than a stone, which some affirme to be of power to repulse poysons."

46/20 *Cato . . . Lucullus*] Lucullus (b. 106 B.C.) was praetor under Sulla and conqueror of Mithridates. The name of Lucullus is as celebrated for his luxury as for his victories over the Mithridates which supplied him with the means of gratifying his taste for ostentatious luxury and sensual indulgence (William Smith, gen. ed., *Dictionary of Greek and Roman Biography and Mythology*, 3 vols., Boston: Little, Brown, and Company, 1867) 2: 836.

46/20-22 **Leah had bad eyes . . . she was barren**] Genesis 29.17,31.

46/27-30 *Quis non irascatur . . . factis renunciantes*] Augustine, *Ennarrationes In Psalmos, I-L* (Turnholti: Typographi Brepols Editores Pontificii, 1956) Psalm 30: 204.

47/9-14 **The *Cardinal* of *Lorreign* . . . the hypocrite**] Charles de Guise, cardinal of Lorraine (1525-1574), archbishop of Reims, founder of the University of Reims, held supreme political power in France. He endeavoured to secure a national religious settlement in France, and searched for a formula of reunion with the Calvinists and toleration of the Huguenot cults. For a definitive study of the Cardinal's political and ecclesiastical activities, see H. Outram Evennett, *The Cardinal of Lorraine and the Council of Trent* (Cambridge: University Press, 1930). In March 1564, Bernardino Ochino, an Italian reformer who had lost favor with Protestants because of publicly defending polygamy, was banished from Basel, and then travelled to Nuremburg for refuge. According to Ochino's modern biographer, Karl Benrath, Ochino met with the Cardinal in Nuremberg, and this meeting was subsequently interpreted negatively by Ochino's Protestant detractors who believed "Ochino had told the Cardinal the cause of his banishment, had given him his Dialogues, and declared himself willing to prove twenty-four errors in the Reformed Church, and that the Cardinal answered that four were already too many" (*Bernardino Ochino of Siena*, London: James Nisbet & Co., 1876), 278. For a contemporary source of this view, see Théodore Bèza, *Epistolarum Theologicarum Theodori Bezae Vezelij* (Geneva, 1573), 11: "Vix Basilea egresso (quod narro scito me non vt rumorem incertum, sed vt certam historian narrare) occurrit Lotharingus Cardinalis ex Italia rediens, cui sese operamque suam omnem obtulit, pollicitus sese centum errores istorum inter quos tandiu haesisset haereticorum demonstraturum. Spreuit hominem toties Apostatam Cardinalis. Also, see Josias Simmler, *Narratio de ortu, et obitu reverendi viri, d. Henrici Bvllingeri* (Tiguri, Froschovervus, 1575), sigs. K3v-K4r: "Itaque senex, miser magis quam miserabilis inde discessit, in Poloniam abiturus oblata itineris commoditate. Ferunt eum dum Schaphusium transiret, incidisse illic in Cardinalem Lotharingum suasque ipsi calamitates exposuisse, quod nunc exulare cogatur Dialogorum suorum gratia, quos se non alio animo scripsisse affirmabat, quam vt triginta hasce veritates, quas in sacra nostra religione obseruasset, creditu difficiles, ab aduersariorum calumnijs assereret, ac vindicaret: simul oblatis aliquot Dialogorum exemplis, rogasse Cardinalem vt eos legere digna retur: Ad quae Cardinalem respondisse ferunt, se quidem inspecturum, sed vbi non placuerint, mox combusturum: adiecisse his Ochinum, se longa ista sua peregrinatione obseruasse 24 errores in nostris ecclesijs, ac pollicitum esse de hisce facile conuicturum Euangelicas ecclesias. His siue ludens siue serio agens respondit Cardinalis, nimium esse 4. ut maxima viginti non adijciat."

47/14-18 *Trajan . . . deserved by industry*] Cassius Dio, *Roman History*, 67.6.5 and 68.6.2. Domitian, emperor before Trajan (A.D. 53-117), was compelled to make an ignominious peace with Decebalus, king of the Dacians. He agreed to pay Decebalus an annual subsidy, and to supply him with engineers and craftsmen skilled in all kinds of construction, especially fortifications and defensive apparatus. As a result, Dacia was immensely strengthened. When Trajan could no longer endure this use of Roman resources against Rome itself, he advanced against the Dacians in A.D. 99 and defeated them, in spite of the treaty by which he had incurred debts to them.

47/25-26 **the *Bonaventure*, the *Triumph*]** During the reign of Elizabeth I *Bonaventure* was a ship's name popular for merchant vessels in England, usually coupled with the Christian name of the owner. She herself owned a ship name *Elizabeth Bonaventure* (*The Oxford Ompanion to Ships & the Sea*, London: Oxford U. Press, 1976), 94. The *H.M.S. Truimph* was a 'great ship' of 1,100 tons, built in 1561, and was the first ship to take the name in the British Navy. In 1588, commanded by Sir Martin Frobisher, she fought against the Spanish Armada. The second *Triumph* was built at Deptford in 1623. This ship had a long career of sixty-five years. Ten of the seventeen battle honours which belong to the *Triumph* were added by this second holder of the name, all of them battles in the three Anglo-Dutch wars in the seventeenth century (*The Oxford Companion to Ships & the Sea*), 890. For seventeenth century descriptions of these two ships, see *Gloria Britannica; or, the Boast of the Brittish Seas. Containing A True and Full Account of the Royal Navy of England* (London, 1689; *Wing STC* B7), sigs. A1r, A2v.

47/26-27 *ventorum ludibrium*] Virgil, *Aeneid*, 6.74: "Foliis tantum, Ne carmina manda, Ne turbata volent rapidis ludibria ventis."

48/2-3 **transform ... Saints]** 2 Corinthians 11.14.

48/3-4 **the voyce of Jacob, and the hands of Esau]** Genesis 27.22.

48/21 **Iulian]** See 31/24 n.

48/24-27 **Bladwine and Bolsack ... truth**] Francis Baldwin (1520-1573), a celebrated jurist who worked for the court of Charles V, in the earlier part of his life was sympathetic toward Calvinism, and this recommended him to princes for the settlement of religious questions involving Protestants and Catholics. However, in 1560, he made a serious study of Catholic and Calvinist eccelesiastical beliefs and successfully defended Catholicism against Calvin. Baldwin did not publish a life of Calvin (*The Catholic Encyclopedia*, 1st ed.) 2: 221. Jérôme-Hermès Bolsec (d. 1584), a theologian and a Carmelite monk, left the Catholic Church in 1545 and settled in Geneva. A theological controversy soon ensued between him and Calvin over the doctrine of predestination, and Bolsec was ultimately banished from Geneva forever. He then returned to France, recanted his errors, was reconciled with the Catholic Church and published invective biographies of both Calvin and Beza (*The Catholic Encyclopedia*, 1st ed.) 2: 643. His life of Calvin was entitled *Histoire la vie, moeurs, actes, doctrine, constance et mort de Iean Calvin* (A. Lyon, par Jean Patrasson, 1577).

48/27-30 **Parsons and Harding ... Church of God**] Robert Parsons, S.J. (1546-1610), converted to Catholicism from Protestantism in 1575, and was received into the Jesuits in 1578. In 1580, he and Edmund Campion were sent as missionaries to England with strict instructions from the general of the Jesuits against involving themselves in political questions. Parsons, however, did not desist from political intrigue and conspired with Philip II of Spain in hopes of inciting a Spanish attack on England. In doing so, he hoped to reconcile the English church with the Roman (*DNB 15*: 411-418). Thomas Harding (1516-1572), chaplain to Lady Jane Grey, espoused Reformed Protestantism before his conversion to Catholicism at the accession of Queen Mary in 1552. Upon the accession of Elizabeth I, Harding was one of the first to be deprived of his appointments, so that he retired to Louvain. Harding is most famous for his disputations with John Jewel which began in 1564 (*DNB 8*: 1223).

48/30-31 **The greatest enemies ... own house**] Micah 7.6. and Matthew 10.36. Also Plautus, *Mercator*, 1.796.

48/31-32 **He ... betrayed him**] That is, Judas.

48/37-39-50/1 **Iulian the Apostate ... miserable**] Theodoret, *Ecclesiastical History*, 3.25. Sec 32.24n.

49/4-15 *Henry* **the fourth ... Apostate**] In 1594, the *parlement* of Paris expelled the Jesuits from France partly because Jean Chastel, a mentally unstable student who left a Jesuit college seven months earlier, had attempted to assassinate Henry IV on December 27, 1594 (Roland Mousnier, *The Assassination of Henry IV*, London: Faber and Faber, 1973), 217-224. But in the spring of 1603, after long and complicated negotiations, the King allowed the Jesuits to return to the towns where they used to reside and to reopen their colleges, provided they took an oath not to engage in any activity detrimental to the King, the public peace, and the welfare of the state (Mark Greengrass, *France in the Age of Henri IV: The Struggle for Stability*, New York: Longman, 1984), 160-162. Once they were reinstated, the King patronized the Jesuits by allowing them to establish a new college with a royal pension at La Flèche in the *ressort* of the *parlement* of Paris. Later, Henry's heart would be buried at La Flèche. There is no evidence that Henry IV's most trusted advisor, Maximilien De Béthune duc de Sully, a Protestant, advised against the Jesuits being readmitted into France, especially if one notes that he helped the King to put down insurrections of French nobles, whether Roman Catholic or Protestant, and that it was he who arranged the marriage between Henry IV and Marie de Médicis. Finally, on May 14, 1610, Henry was fatally stabbed in the chest by Francois Ravaillac, also mentally unstable, whose application to the Jesuits had been turned down in 1606 (Mousnier, 25).

49/32 *Circumcellians* **... Scriptures**] The Circumcellions probably first appeared before the death of Constantine. They were mostly rustic enthusiasts who joined the Donatists (who called them *agnostici*), but in fact were plunderers who roved Numidia and Mauritania. According to St. Augustine, they were notorious for their lawless violence against the Catholics as well as against property; however, there is no evidence that the Circumcellions defaced scripture. In *De Haeresibus* 69.4.32-43, Augustine describes the Circumcellions: "Ad hanc haeresim in Africa et illi pertinent qui appellantur Circumcelliones, genus hominum agreste et famosissimae audaciae, non solum in alios immania facinora perpetrando, sed nec sibi eadem insana feritate parcendo. Nam per mortes uarias, maximeque praecipitiorum et aquarum et ignium, seipsos necare consuerunt, et in istum furorem alios quos potuerint sexus utriusque seducere, aliquando ut occidantur ab aliis, mortem, nisi fecerint, comminantes. Verumtamen plerisque Donatistarum displicent tales, nec eorum communione contaminari se putant, qui christiano orbi terrarum dementer obiiciunt ignotorum crimen Afrorum" (Turnholti: Typographi Brepols Editores Pontifici, 1969), 332. Also, see Augustine's *Contra Gaudentium, PL 9*: 725; and *Epistolam Parmeniani, PL 43*: 53-54,62,96.

49/35-39 **The same grand Hereticks . . . Session]** Rev. H.J. Schroeder, ed., *Canons and Decrees of the Council of Trent* (St. Louis: B. Herder Book Co., 1941), 296: "Sacrosanctas oecumenica et generalis Tridentina synodus, in Spiritu Sancto legitime congregata, praesidentibus in ea eisdem tribus Apostolicae Sedis legatis, hos sibi perpetuo ante oculos proponens, ut sublatis erroribus puritas ipso evangelii in ecclesia conservetur, quod promissum ante per prophetas in scripturis sanctis Dominus noster Jesus Christus Dei Filius proprio ore primum promulgavit, deinde per suos apostolos tamquam fontem omnis et salutaris veritatis et morum disciplinae omni creaturae praedicari jussit; perspiciensque hanc veritatem et disciplinam contineri in libris scriptis et sine scripto traditionibus, quae ipsius Christi ore ab apostolis acceptae, aut ab ipsis apostolis Spiritu Sancto dictante quasi per manus traditae ad nos usque pervenerunt, orthodoxorum patrum exempla secuta, omnes libros tam veteris quam novi testamenti, cum utriusque unus Deus sit actor, necnon traditiones ipsas, tum ad fidem tum ad mores pertinentes, tamquam vel oretenus a Christo, vel a Spiritu Sancto dictatas et continua successione in ecclesia catholica conservatas, pari pietatis affectu ac reverentia suscipit et veneratur."

50/7-8 **Supererogation**] In Roman Catholic theology, works of supererogation are those which are not enjoined as a strict obligation, and therefore are not simply good as opposed to bad, but better as opposed to good ('opera meliora'). The term which goes back to the Latin translation of Luke 10.35—*quodcumque spererogaveris*—was probably not used in its theological sense until the Middle Ages when *opera supererogationis* was treated by Alexander of Hales and St. Thomas Aquinas—the doctrine for which the story of the rich young ruler (Matthew 19.16-22) and St. Paul's teaching on virginity (1 Corinthians 7) are usually presented as evidence (F.L. Cross, ed. *The Oxford Dictionary of the Christian Church*, London: Oxford University Press, 1974) 1324. This particular doctrine was attacked by the Protestant reformers and defended by Robert Bellarmine in his *De Monachis*. For an excellent discussion of this doctrine, see *Cyclopaedia of Biblical Theological, and Ecclesiastical Literature*, ed. John Mclintock, 12 vols. (Grand Rapids, Michigan: Baker Book House, 1970) 10: 30-32.

50/10-11 **So say the *Rhemists*...**] See the annotations in *The text of the New Test. of Iesus Christ*, tr. by the papists. With a confutation of all such annotations as conteine manifest impietie. By W. Fulke. [Rheims and Bishops Bible in parallel columns] C. Barker (London, 1589; *STC* 2888), sigs. Aaa5r-Aaa5v: "Christs paines or passions have not so satisfied for al, that Christian men be discharged of their particular suffering or satisfying fore eche mans owne part: neither be our paines nothing worth to the attainement of heauen, because Christ hath done ynough, but quite contrarie: he was by his passion exalted to the glorie of heauen: therefore we by compassion or partaking with him in the like passions, shal atteine to be fellowes with him in his kingdome" (Romans 8.17). Moreover,

Commentary to the Text   241

the annotation of Colossians 1.24, sig. Rrr3v, similarly states: "And not onely those passions which he suffered in him selfe, which were fully ended in his death, and were in them selues fully sufficient for the redemption of the world and remission of all sinnes, but all those which his body and members suffer, are his also, and of him they receiue the condition, qualitie, and force to be meritorious and satisfactorie. for though there be no insufficiencie in the actions or passions of Christ the head. Yet his wisedome, will and iustice requireth and ordaineth, that his body and members should applie to them selues and others the generall medicine of Christes merites and satisfactions, as it is effectually also applied to us by Sacraments, Sacrifice, and other wayes also."

50/23 *Gallioes*] Acts 18.12-18.

50/23 *Gadarens*] Matthew 8.28-34; Mark 5.1-20; and Luke 8.26-39.

50/34-35 **The reverend ... *many adversaries***] Beadle here refers to *A Vindication of the Presbyteriall Government and Ministry* (London, Printed for C. Meredith, 1650; *Wing STC* V523A), p. 64, sig. I4v, which defends Oliver Cromwell, his policies, and his strict implementation of presbyterial government: "We are not ignorant, that it hath many Adversaries. The obstinately ignorant hates it, because it will not suffer him to go blindfold to hell. The prophane person hates it, because it will not suffer him to eat and drink his own damnation, by unworthy coming to the Sacrament. The Heretique hates it, because after two or three adminitions, it rejects him. The Jesuite hates it because it is an invincible bulwark to keep out Popery. The Schismatique, because the main design of it, is to make all the Saints to be of one lip, one heart, and one way. And above all, the Devil hates it, because if rightly managed, it will in a short time blow up his kingdome."

51/13-14 **hedge to the Vineyard**] Isaiah 5.5-9.

51/18 *Antitrinitarians*] More often known as Unitarians, they denied the doctrine of the Trinity by opposing to it to a God without distinction of persons. In the early Church, the Antitrinitarian heresy expended itself in producing the Sabellian and Arian heresies. During the Reformation, its appearance was most widespread in Germany and Switzerland (see John Henry Blunt, ed., *The Dictionary of Sects, Heresies, Ecclesiastical Parties and Schools of Religious Thought*, London: Longmans, Green, and Co., 1903), 35-38. The most famous proponent of Antitrinitarianism was Servetus (b. 1509), a Spaniard who wrote *De Erroribus Trinitatis* (Hagenau, 1531), and *Dialogorum de Trinitate Libri Duo* (Hagenau, 1531).

51/18 *Antinomians*] Also an ancient heresy which reappeared during the Reformation. Those who espouse Antinomianism reject the authority of moral law. The opposition to the law is not the opposition of the simple transgressor of the law, but the opposition which justifies itself by alleging a supposed liberty or privilege. The most famous proponent of Antinomianism on the continent was John Agricola (fl. 1527), an Anabaptist. In England, John Eaton, minister of Wickham-Market, Suffolk, wrote *Discovery of a most dangerous Dead Faith* (London, 1641; *Wing STC* E112), and *The Honeycomb of Free Justification by Christ alone* (London, 1642; *Wing STC* E115). The object of the latter work is to show that God does not, will not, nor cannot see any sin in any of His justified children (see John Henry Blunt, ed., *Dictionary of Sects, Heresies, Ecclesiastical Parties and Schools of Religious Thought*), 33-34.

51/19 *Antiscripturists*] Or Anti-Scripturians rejected all the Scriptures of the Old and New Testament as of purely human invention, and held that the Scriptures were not the word of God because there is no Word but Christ. In addition, they maintained that the Bible was insufficient, uncertain, and not an infallible rule of faith; the writers wrote as they thought, moved only by their own spirits. The Old Testament in particular had no binding force on Christians. Only right reason

Commentary to the Text 243

could be the rule of faith; thus, they only believed the Scriptures as far as they considered them agreeable to reason (C.E. Whiting, *Studies in English Puritanism from the Restoration to the Revolution, 1660-1688,* New York: Augustus M. Kelley Publishers, 1968), 320.

51/19 *Socinians*] They derive their name from Laelius Socinus (1525-1562), a priest and intimate friend of Bullinger, Calvin and Melanchthon, and his nephew Fausto Socinus (1539-1604). In Venice, the sect began to debate the efficacy of the doctrine of the Trinity, but members were forced to flee to Poland in the 1560's, where the sect then flourished. In 1638, when the Polish Catholics insisted that Socinians leave Poland, they fled to Holland. The fundamental belief of the Socinians was that the Bible should be interpreted only in the light of reason; therefore, any mystery that could not be understood through the light of reason was rejected. Thus, only the unity, eternity, omnipotence, justice, and wisdom of God are insisted on, and His immensity, infinity, and omnipresence are considered unnecessary. As for the Christ, the Socinians maintained that since God was absolutely simple, distinction of persons is inadmissible; and thus, they denied the doctrine of the Trinity (*The Catholic Encyclopedia,* 1st ed.) 14: 113-115.

51/18-19 **Antitrinitarians . . . . Familists**] Each of the heresies Beadle lists here are specifically condemned as "carnal doctrines" and "damnable Errors Heresies and Blasphemies of these present evil times" in "A Testimony of the Ministers in the Province of Essex to the Truth of Jesus Christ . . . " found reprinted in Harold Smith, *The Ecclesiastical History of Essex* (Colchester: Benham and Company Limited, 1932), 103. The order in which Beadle lists them here is the same order in which they are listed in the "Essex Testimony." Very possibly, because Beadle was instrumental in promulgating the "Essex Testimony," he here alludes to the document and its unequivocal condemnation of the above sects.

51/19 **Quakers**] The popular name for the sect which represents the extreme form of Puritanism, and which originated about the year 1650 in Yorkshire, Durham, Lancashire, and Cumberland, under the leadership of James Naylor, Richard Farnworth, and George Fox. The idea of "quaking" and "trembling" was common among the extreme Puritans, characteristics probably borrowed from the religion of the Traskites. They believed that many texts of Scripture showed that the earth trembled and quaked, that Isaac trembled exceedingly, that Moses feared and quaked, that the Lord told his disciples to quake with fear, and therefore saints ought to be called Quakers (see John Henry Blunt, ed., *Dictionary of Sects, Heresies, Ecclesiastical Parties and Schools of Religious Thought*), 464-469.

51/30-32 **the Cartwheel . . . still**] See Tilley S768.

52/31-32 **We are become . . . them the truth**] Cf. Amos 5.10 and Romans 1.18.

52/38-39 *nititur in vetitum*] Ovid, *Amores*, 3.4.17.

53/6-10 *Franciscus Sodorinus* . . . **prepare for more**] Francisco Soderini (1453-1524), before he betrayed Adrian VI in a conspiracy with Francis I to discredit the Pope's efforts towards peace, was a trusted friend and advisor of Adrian VI. Before the betrayal, Adrian attempted to reform the practices of the Dataria and the granting of indulgences while he was also defending Catholicism against Luther's heresy in his native Germany. Adrian VI proposed a definition of indulgence which would emphasize the necessity of inner conversion; however, Cardinal Sodorini insisted that because of the Vatican's financial woes the loss of revenue from indulgences could be detrimental to the security of the Church in Italy: "Heresy has always been put down by force, not by attempts at reformation; such attempts can only be partial, and will seem to be extorted by terror; they will only confirm the heretics in the belief that they are right, and will not satisfy them. The danger of the

Holy See is not in Germany but in Italy, where the Pope needs money to defend himself. No source of revenue can be abandoned. The princes of Germany must be taught that it is their own interest to put down the Lutheran heretics" (Mandell Creighton, *The History of the Papacy*, 6 vols., London: Longman's Green and Co., 1897) 6: 244.

53/24-25 *Judas ... this waste?*] Matthew 26.8. See the annotation to this passage in *The Geneva Bible*, 1560: "This was through Iudas motion to whome they gaue credit."

53/25-26 *Jeroboam ... It is too much*] 1 Chronicles 22.14.

53/32 **Doves to the windows**] Isaiah 60.08.

53/35-36 *Depart ... wayes*] Job 21.14.

54/33-37 **Mr. *Udall* ... I have seen**] John Udall (1560?-1592), Puritan and friend to John Penry (alias Martin Mar-Prelate), secretly wrote and printed a polemic entitled, *A Demonstration of the trueth of that Discipline which Christe hath prescribed in his worde for the gouernement of his Church, in all times and places, untill the ende of the worlde* (London, 1588; STC 24499). This polemic was distributed at the same time that Penry's first Martin Mar-Prelate tract was being printed. Soon, many more Martin-MarPrelate tracts followed and Udall was suspected of complicity in their issuance. He was summoned to London on December 29, 1589, to be examined by the privy council who asked him whether he was responsible for *A Demonstration*; he refused to respond and was detained in the Gatehouse at Westminster. On July 24, 1590, Udall was placed on trial at the Croydon assizes and found guilty. Sentence was deferred, however, and he was moved to White Lion prison in Southwark where he was offered a pardon if he would recant. Again, in February 1590-91, he was brought to the bar of the Southwark assizes and was sentenced to death. A pardon was granted in 1592, but Udall died before being freed (*DNB* 20: 4-6). For the actual testimony and interrogation of Udall at the assizes, see *An Introductory Sketch to the Martin Marprelate Controversy, 1588-1590*, ed. Edward Arber (New York: Burt Franklin, repr. 1967), 88-93; and Daniel Neal, *The History of the Puritans or Protestant Nonconformists from the Reformation in 1517 to the Revolution in 1688*, 5 vols. (London: William Baynes and Son, 1822) 1: 406-415. For the story of Udall's imprisonment, examinations, and arraignments in his own words, see *A new Discouery of Old pontifcall practises for the maintenance of the prelates authority and heirarchy* (London, 1643; *Wing STC* U14).

54/39-56/2 **King of *Denmark* . . . for the Cause**] The letter Beadle refers to is not in Christian V's *Letters*, eds. Carl Frederik Bricka and Julius Albert Fridericia, 7 vols. (Copenhagen, 1878-1891). For the text of King James VI of Scotland's letter of June 12, 1591, about Udall's imprisonment, see G.P.V. Akrigg, ed., *The Letters of James VI & I* (Berkeley: U. of California Press, 1984), 110. King James VI defended the Puritan because he respected Udall's abilities as a scholar and because Udall had impressed the monarch when he preached before the King in Scotland on June 20, 1589.

56/3-8 **King *James* . . . in discipline**] When James VI had returned from Denmark in August 1589 after his marriage to Anne of Denmark, he delivered the speech to the General Assembly to which Beadle refers. The moderator and opening speaker at the Assembly, James Melvill, also delivered a similar speech on the theme of church discipline and it is from his autobiography and diary that the content of James VI's speech is described: "Also, the haill breithring war ernestlie exhorted to studie the discipline diligentlie, and practise it cearfullie, that they might be able at all occasiones to stand in defence thairof, as it hes bein of God's grait favour with the treuthe of the doctrine sett doun out of the Word of God; and the practise of the sam fund maist halsome and profitable within the Kirk of Scotland. And that at this tyme, for thrie caussas, namlie; first, because of the esteat of the godlie, guid, and zealus breithring in Eingland, our nibour Kirk, standing for the treuthe thairof, and scarlie suffering for the sam. Secondlie, because these Amaziases, belli-god Bischopes in Eingland, be all moyen, yea and money, war seikand comformitie of our realme with thairs, till invert and pervert our Kirk, as did Achaz and Urias with the King and Altar of Damascus" (Robert Pitcairn, ed., *The Autobiography and Diary of Mr. James Melvill*, Edinburgh: Printed for the Wodrow Society, 1842), 281. Also, see David Calderwood, *The History of the Kirk of Scotland*, 8 vols. (Edinburgh: Printed for the Wodrow Society, 1842-1849) 5: 105: "In end, to please the Assemblie, he fell furth in praising God, that he was borne in such a tyme as the tyme of the light of the Gospell, to suche a place as to be king in suche a kirk, the sincerest kirk in the world. `The kirk of Geneva,' said he, keepeth Pasche and yuile; what have they for them? they have no institutioun. As for our nighbour kirk in England, it is an evill said masse in English, wanting nothing but liftings.'"

55/11-12 *Not him but Barabbas*] John 18.40.

55/19 **reign over us**] Luke 1.33.

55/19 **Prince of peace**] Isaiah 9.6.

55/20 *song* **of peace**] Luke 2.14.

58/1-2 **The Lord ... born there**] Psalms 87.6.

58/6-7 *Cyprian* ... **Father**] In *De Vita et Passione Sancti Cypriani*, PL 4: 1185.

58/12-13 *Polycarpus* ... **dealt well with me**] *The Martyrdom of Polycarp*, PG 5: 1036.

58/21-22 **following** ... *David*] 1 Samuel 17.20.

58/35 **toad was of poysen**] See 48/18-19 n. Tilley T360, Dent T360.

58/36-37 **by his grace I am that I am]** 1 Corinthians 15.10.

59/2-3 **he feeds the Ravens . . . the Grasse]** Psalms 147.7-8.

59/5 *Abraham* . . . **age]** Genesis 18.10.

59/7 **mercy to** *Manasseh*] 2 Chronicles 33.12-14.

59/8 *Mary Magdalan*] Luke 8.2.

59/22-24 *Beza* . . . **of the Truth]** See Antonio La Faye, *De Vita Et Obitv Clariss Viri, D. Theodori Bezae Vezelii* (Geneva: Iacobvm Chovet, 1606), sig. K1r: "1. Gratias agit Deo immortali per D.N. Iesum Christum, quòd anno aetatis suae 16. verae Christianae Religionis cognitione ac luce donatus sit: cujus tamen fructus non ediderit tam opportunè quàm decuisset, abreptus scilicet per deuia quaedam, à quibus tandem Deus illum in rectum iter reduxit: inq; Geneuensem portum adduxit: vbi sub magno illo D. Ioanne Caluino pleniùs Christum didicit."

60/1-2 *Yet we do not consider*] Philippians 3.13.

60/32-37 **St.** *Augustine* . . . *non stas*] See Granger Ryan and Hulmut Ripperger, trans., *The Golden Legend*, by Jacobus de Voragine, 2 vols. (London: Longmans, Green and Co., 1941) 2: 488: "The Lord therefore put it into his mind to seek out Simplicianus, in whom shone the light, namely the grace of God, that he might confide his cares to him, and confer with him concerning the seemly manner of living and walking in the way of God, wherein one went one way, and the other a different way; for all that he did in the world was tedious to him, so great was his desire of the sweetness of God and the beauty of His house. Simplicianus urged him on, saying: 'How many youths and maids serve God in the Church of Christ, and art thou unable to do as they do? Or thinkest thou that they do this of themselves, and not in God? Why strivest thou to stand

Commentary to the Text 249

by thine own strength, and so standest not? Cast thyself upon Him, and He will receive thee and save thee!"

61/3-4 *Sidenote*: **1 Tim[othy]. 4.16,17**] The correct reference is 1 Tim. 4.16,17.

61/10 **Faith . . . God**] Ephesians 2.8.

61/13 **helping the heart at a sudden pinch**] Cf. the proverbial phrase found in William Bullein, *A Dialogue Against the Feuer Pestilence*, Mark Bullen and A.H. Bullen, eds., (1564; London: EETS, 1888), 10: "You are welcome, Maister doctour, with all my harte; now helpe at a pinche, or els neuer, for I doe fear my selfe verie much." Furthermore, see John Palsgrave, *Acolastus* (London, 1540; *STC* 11470), sig. Aa3r: "excepte that god him selfe, or some good saynt apperyng to me forth of a clowde, do nowe helpe me at a pynche, or forth lay to his helpyinge hande, in this great dystresse of myne."

61/15-16 **A lively faith . . . dead lift**] See Tilley F699, L271, W669, and Dent L271.

61/17-18 *Joseph . . .* **Mistris**] Genesis 39.7.

61/31-36 **David . . . an assault**] 2 Samuel 16.7-9.

62/27-29 *Jacob . . .* **remembred**] Genesis 31.12-16 and Genesis 27.40-43.

62/33-34 *Jeremiah . . .* **was saved**] Jeremiah 37.17.

62/34 **Daniel . . . escaped**] Daniel 6.23.

62/35-36 *Jonah . . .* **delivered**] Jonah 2.10.

62/37-63/2 **Mr. Beza . . . from both**] See Antonio Le Faye, *De Vita et Obitu Clariss Viri, D. Theodori Bezae Vezelii* (Genevae: Iacobvm Chovet, 1606), sig. K1r: "Quòd Lausannae peste correptus, grauissimisq; appetitus calumniis, ab vtraque lue, per Dei misericordiam liberatus sit."

63/3-5 That being ... dangers] Again, see Antonio Le Faye, *De Vita et Obitv Clariss Viri, D. Theodori Bezae Vezelii*, sig. K1r: "Quòd vocatus in Galliam, & belli primi ciuilis tempestatibus jactatus ad menses 22, à sexcentis periculis sit seruatus."

64/3-4 *Henry* the fourth ... assisted] Elizabeth I intervened in the French civil war of 1562-1563 because she believed she could aid the Huguenots and embarrass the French Catholic Guises. Besides her wish to help the French Calvinists win over their country to the Kingdom of God, Elizabeth seemed guaranteed of keeping Calais. For Elizabeth I's declaration of aid to France, see *Expositio causarum quibus Angliae regina commouebatur, vt quasdam cohortes, armis instrueret, respectu proprie defensionis, & regis Caroli* (London, 1562; STC 9187). For the text in English, see Arthur F. Kinney, ed., "A Declaration of the Quenes Maiestie, *Elizabeth*, by the Grace of God, Quene of *England, Fraunce*, and *Irelande*, Defendor of the Faiyth, &c. Conteyning the Causes which haue constrayned her to arme certeine of her Subiectes, for Defence both of her owne Estate, and of the moste Christian Kyng, *Charles the Nynth*, her good Brother, and his Subiects," in *Elizabethan Backgrounds* (Archon Books, 1975), 71-75.

65/20-22 *Lemuel* ... upon the place] John Mercer, or Jean Mercier, a loyal Huguenot and biblical commentator, was born in Uzès, France in the beginning of the 16th century. He became interested in ancient languages while studying law in Avignon and devoted much time to the study of Greek, Hebrew, and the Semitic tongues. In 1546, after having been the most noted pupil of Francois Vatable (see 24/39-25/1-3), he became his successor as professor of Hebrew in the Royal College of France. He died in 1562 (*Cyclopaedia of Biblical, Theological, and Ecclesiastical Literature*, 12 vols., New York: Arno Press, 1970) 6: 110. In his *Commentari, in Iobum, et Salomoni Proverbia,*

Ecclesiasten, Canticum Canticorum (Lugduni Batevorum, F. Hackii, 1651), 510, Mercier observes that Lemuel is the name given to Solomon: "*Verba Lamuelis* [Hebrew]. Habent quae sequuntur ad finem usque, novum titulum, nec dubium quin sint Salomonis qui se hoc loco appellavit [Hebrew] Lemuel, quasi [Hebrew] Lemoel quo modo secundo loco, v.4. in exempl. emend. scribitur, i.e. ad Deum: ut [Hebrew] Semuel, quasi [Hebrew] quòd eum mater à Deo petiisset. Scurec euponiae causa pro Holem. non est, inquam, dubium hunc Lamuelem Salomonem esse, quia non alium legimus fuisse Lamuelem regem in Israël."

65/26-30 **Dr. Andrews ... his study dore**] In "The Sermon preached at the Funeral of the Right Honourable and Reverend Father in God, Lancelot, Late Lord Bishop of Winchester," Bishop John Buckeridge (1562?-1631), a close friend of Andrews, refers to Andrews admiration for Richard Mulcaster (1530?-1611) and how "he had made Master Mulcaster his tutor or supervisor, he placed his picture over the door of his study, whereas in all the rest of the house you could scantly see a picture" (*The Works of Lancelot Andrews*, J.H. Parker, ed., 11 vols., (New York: AMS Press, 1967) 5: 289. Also, see Henry Isaacson's 1650 account of the Bishop's life in "An Exact Narration of the Life and Death of the Late reverend and Learned Prelate, and painfull Divine, Lancelot Andrewes, Late Bishop of Winchester," in *The Works of Lancelot Andrewes* (New York: AMS Press, 1967) 11: xx.

65/31-34 **Mr. Calvin ... to him**] Mathurin Cordier (1480-1564) was John Calvin's teacher when his father sent him as a young boy to study in Paris. In his Dedicatory Epistle to *Commentaries on The Epistles of Paul the Apostle to The Philippians, Colossians, and Thessalonians*, ed. John Pringle (Grand Rapids, Michigan: Wm. B. Eerdmans Publishing Company, 1948), 234, Calvin says, "It is befitting that you should come in for a share in my labours, inasmuch as, under your auspices, having entered on a course of study, I made proficiency at least so far as to be prepared to profit in some degree the Church of God ... And although I was permitted to have the use of it [Cordier's training] only for a short time, from the circumstance that we were soon afterwards advanced higher by an injudicious man, who regulated our studies according to his own pleasure, or rather his caprice, yet I derived so much assistance afterwards from your training, that it is with good reason that I acknowledge myself indebted to you for such progress as has since been made."

65/34-37 **And Persius ... high language**] Lucius Annaeus Cornutus (fl. A.D. 66), Stoic philosopher and commentator of Aristotle. He was a friend to Seneca and a teacher to Persius and Lucan. In A.D. 68, he was exiled by Nero because he openly critized the literary efforts of the emperor (Dio Cassius, *Roman History*, 62.29.

65/38-66/2 **Hinc ego ... traham pura**] Persius, *Satire* V: *To His Master Cornutus, on Stoic Freedom and on Sins and Slavery*, 26-28.

66/3-4 **Mecaenas what bountifull Benefactor**] C. Cilnius Maecenas, born April 13, between 73 and 63 B.C (see Horace, *Carminvm*, 4.9.19-20), was both friend and literary patron to Virgil, Horace, and Propertius.

66/7-10 **St. Augustine ... advanced**] Romanianus, a wealthy citizen of Tagaste and owner of property in Carthage, was the young Augustine's friend and benefactor while he studied in Carthage. Throughout his life, Augustine was grateful to Romanianus for his encouragement and kindness during times when Augustine neglected their friendship. Augustine thanks Romanianus in *Contra Academicos* (Tvrnholti: Typographi Brepols Editores Pontificii, 1970), 19: "An fortasse paululum debeo? Tu me adulescentulum pauperem ad studia pergentem et domo et sumptu et, quod plus est, animo excepisti."

66/17-21 **Plato ... of Socrates**] See Plutarch, *Caius Marius*, 46.1; Seneca, *De Beneficiis*, 5.7.5; Lactantius, *Divinarum Institutionum*, PL 6: 412-413.

Commentary to the Text   253

67/7-12 **Lord *Cromwell* . . . a meals meat**] When Thomas Cromwell was a young soldier he escaped to Florence after the Battle of Garigliano where the French were defeated in 1503. While in Florence, the impoverished Cromwell was enabled to return to England because of Francis Frescobaldi, a Florentine banker, who lent Cromwell "sixteen ducats and a good hackney" (Matteo Bandello, *The Novels of Matteo Bandello*, 6 vols., London: Printed for the Villon Society, 1890) 4: 107. Later, after Cromwell had achieved fame, he repaid Frescobaldi in full when the banker was near financial ruin (Bandello, 4: 110-114). For the dramatic accounting of the friendship between Cromwell and Frescobaldi, see W.S., *The True Chronicle Historie of the whole life and death of Thomas Lord Cromwell* (London, 1602; STC 21532), sigs. C2v, C3r, E4r, E4v.

67/15 *Selah*] See 13/19-20 n.

67/21-24 **God . . . *time also***] Numbers 3.15.

67/30-31 **hang upon a pin . . . engine**] Cf. the "Great Businesses engines turn on a little pin" (Tilley, B757).

68/2-3 ***Ask of me . . . thee***] Matthew 7.7.

68/18-21 **King *James* . . . you may receive**] According to Arthur Wilson, in *The History of Great Britain, being the Life and Reign of King James the First* (London, 1653; Wing STC W2888), 76-77, James I was "one day in the *Gallery* at *White-hall*, and none with him but Sir *Henry Rich* (who was second Son to the Earl of *Warwick*) afterwards Earl of *Holland* . . . and *James Maxwell*, one of his Bed Chamber; some *porters* past by them, with three thousand pounds, going to the *Privy Purse*: Sir *Henry Rich* whispering *Maxwel*, the King turned upon them and asked *Maxwel*, what says he? *Maxwel* told him, he wisht he had so much money; *Marry shalt thou* Harry (saith the King) and presently commanded the *Porters* to carry it to his

Lodging with this Expression, *You think now you have a great Purchase; but I am more delighted to think how much I have pleasured you in giving this money, than you can be in receiving it."*

68/21-24 *Tiberius* . . . **his bounty**] Cassius Dio , *Roman History*, 57.19.6-8.

68/29 *Give* . . . *bread*] Matthew 6.11 and Luke 11.3.

69/4-8 *Roger* **Bishop of** *Salisbury* . . . **of giving**] See William of Malmesbury, *Historia Novella* (London: Thomas Nelson and Sons Ltd., 1955), 39.

69/10-13 **Sir** *Walter Raleigh* . . . *leaves giving*] I cannot locate the source of this quotation, which is often referred to with no documentation in biographies of Elizabeth I and in Agnes Strickland's *Lives of the Queens of England*, 12 vols. (Philadelphia: Blanchard and Lea, 1854) 7: 17.

69/20 **young Ravens when they cry**] Psalms 147.9.

69/21 **Doves that mourn in the valleys**] Isaiah 59.11; Ezekial 7.16.

69/29-34 **St.** *Ambrose* . . . **should perish**] See Augustine, *Confessiones*, 3.12.21.

70/12 *Selah*] See 11/19-20 n.

71/18-19 **he that runs may read**] Tilley R211, Whiting R236.

71/25-26 *they are* . . . *given me*] Genesis 33.5.

72/3-7 *Jacob* . . . **above it**] Genesis 28.12-15.

72/29-30 **prudence of a Prince** . . . **State**] Cf. 32/16 n.

Commentary to the Text   255

72/37-73/5 **A great Cardinall . . . forgat God**] A possible reference to John Armand, Cardinal of Richlieu. According to D.P. O'Connell, *Richelieu* (New York: The World Publishing Company, 1968), 70, there is little evidence of Richelieu's personal faith and piety found in his memoirs. In *A SYNOPISIS, or Contract view, of the Life of* John Armand, *Cardinall of Richlieu* (London, 1643; *Wing STC*, S6387), sig. A3v, the author says of the worldly prelate: "And yet (which is a sad thing) he that so plainely felt God an *avenger*, would not plainely enough *acknowledge* him." Moreover, the author continues, "In that, Death approaching, rather out of a politick *Prudence*, then a Christian *Piety*, he commended his *Favorites* to the King, more then his *Soul* to God."

73/4 *Haman*] See 37/10 n.

73/5 *Zeresh*] Esther 5.14, 6.13.

73/19-20 **nor all . . . day**] The stars were thought to store light from the sun. Cf. John Donne, "A Nocturnall upon S. Lucies Day, bineg the shortest Day," in *The Elegies and Songs and Sonnets*, ed. Helen Gardner (Oxford: Clarendon Press, 1965) 84. Also, see the description of the creation of the sun and stars in John Milton, *Paradise Lost*, VII. 354-369.

73/23-28 **The *Jews* . . . the Story**] I can find no reference by contemporary commentators about "letting the book fall upon the ground." Purim is the name given to the Jewish festival celebrated for two days on the 14th and 15th of the month of Adar, the last month of the Jewish lunar calendar, in which the Book of Esther is read. The festival celebrates the miraculous deliverance of the Jews from the threat of Haman, the grand vizier of Ahasuerus, who planned a general massacre of the Jews in 473 B.C. The only religious feature of the festival, since the book does not contain the word "God," is the reading of the Book of Esther in the synagogue at the evening services. During these services the book may be read in any language and whenever the name "Haman" is mentioned the congregation stamps their feet or makes noise with rattles (Hayyim Schauss, *The Jewish Festivals*, New York: Union of American Hebrew Congregations, 1938), 234-239.

74/19-20 **the light . . . Sun**] See 73/19-20 n.

74/23-27 **shield . . . armour**] Cf. Psalm 91.4-6. Also, see Thomas More's intricate discussion about God's pavis or shield of strength in *A Dialogue of Comfort Against Tribulation* in *The Complete Works of St. Thomas More*, 18 vols. to date (New Haven: Yale University Press, 1976) *12*: 106: "as god hath faythfully promisid to protect & defend those that faythfully will dwell in the trust of his help / so will he truly perform yt/ And the that such one art, will the trouth of his promise defend, not with a litell round buckeler that scant can couer the hed, but with a long large pavice, that couereth all along the bodye, made as holy saynt Barnard sayth brode above the godhed, & narrow beneth with the manhed / so that this pavice is our saviour Christ hym selfe.

And yet is not this pauice like other pauices of this world, which are not made but in such wise, as while it defendith one part, the man may be woundid vppon the tother / but this pavise is such / that as the prophet sayth / it shall rownd about enclose & compase the / so that thyn ennymye shall hurth thy sowle on no side."

74/27-29 **speech of *Ajax . . . jacentem*]** Ovid, *Metamorphoses*, 13.75.

75/10-11 **the *Alpha* and *Omega*]** Revelation 1.8, 21.6, 23.13.

75/14-16 **All comfort . . . fountain**] Psalms 68.26.

75/17-22 **King of *Bohemia* . . . in S**] Frederick V (1596-1632), Catholic elector of the Palatinate, was crowned King of Bohemia at Prague November 4, 1619. Historians refer to him as the "Winter King" because just four days after his coronation he was forced to take refuge in the Netherlands where he lived in relative obscurity for the rest of his life. After checking several contemporary histories, I could not find the anecdote about his allies.

75/28-33 **Herod . . . or fortitude**] Josephus, *Jewish Antiquities*, 15. 138-139.

75/4-38 **Id bonum . . . be spared**] Lactantius, *Divines Institutiones*, PL 6: 123.

76/38 **cap and the knee**] Cf. Dent C63.1: "My cap (hat) to a noble (etc)."

77/27-28 **Ye are . . . is Gods**] 1 Corinthians 3.23.

77/33-34 **he . . . sweet**] Exodus 15.23-25.

78/16-17 **his name . . . every name**] Philippians 2.97.

78/38-79/5 **Germane Ladies . . . with them**] The "Emperour" Beadle refers to is Conrad III (1093-1152), king of Germany, who besieged the city of Weinsberg, Germany, in 1140. According to the seventeenth century historian Samuel Clark, "The Emperour *Conrade* besieging the City of *Winsperge* in *Germany*: and the women perceiving that the Town could not hold out long, petitioned the Emperour that they might depart onely with so much as each of them could carry upon her back, which the Emperour condescended unto, expecting that they would have loaden themselves with silver, gold, etc. but they came all forth with every one her husband on her back, whereby the men were all saved, and their wives gat immortal credit to themselves (*A Mirrour or Looking-Glasse*, 2nd ed., London, 1654; Wing STC C4548), sigs. V8r-V8v.

79/17-22 **Tiberius . . . must down**] See Tertullian, *Apologeticum*, 5.1-2; Paulis Orosius, *Seven Books of History Against the Pagans*, ed. Irving Woodworth Raymond (New York: Columbia

University Press, 1936), 325; and Eusebius, *The Ecclesiastical History*, 2.1-3.

79/39 *Sidenote*: **Phil[ippians]. 4.15**] The correct reference is Phillippians 4.13.

80/9-12 **Caesar ... consulibus**] Suetonius, *Lives of the Caesars*, 1.2.

81/14-16 **Blessed be... his mouth**] 2 Chronicles 6.4.

81/16 *Sidenote*: **2 Chr[onicles]. 4.10.**] The correct reference is 2 Chronicles 6.10.

81/39-82/1 **Careat ... putat**] Ovid, *Epistolae Heroidum*, 2.85-86.

83/4 *Sidenote*: **Ioh[n]. 21.15**] The correct reference is John 20.15.

83/24-25 **her desires ... over her**] Genesis 3.16.

83/29-32 **How few ... Originall**] The combination of the aorist subjunctive with the first οὐμή and the reduplication of the negative amount to a strong asseveration (James Moffatt, *A Critical and Exegetical Commentary on the Epistle to the Hebrews*, New York: Charles Scribner's Sons, 1924), 229.

83/34-35 **the Latines ... firmly deny**] See 127/13-15 n. See Herbert Weir Smyth, *A Greek Grammar* (Boston: American Book Company, 1920), #2754: οὐμή and the compounds of each, are used in emphatic negative predictions and prohibitions. Whereas, in Latin usage "As a rule two negatives are equivalent to an afffirmative" (Arthur Sloman, *A Grammar of Classical Latin*, Cambridge: The University Press, 1928), 208, #304.

83/39 **Vade mecum**] "A book or manual suitable for carrying about with one for ready reference" or "a thing commonly carried about by a person as being of some service to him" (*OED*).

84/2-3 *Saul*... **beds head**] 1 Samuel 26.7,12.

84/9-10 **the promise**... **go twain**] Matthew 5.41.

84/12-13 **the promise**... **old age**] Genesis 21.2.

84/24 *secundum modum recipientis*] Aristotle, *De Anima*, 424a. This scholastic commonplace is found often in St. Thomas of Aquinas. See his *Summa Contra Gentiles* (Roma: Desclée C. Herder, 1934), 316: "Superiores intellectuales substantiae perfectius divinae sapientiae influentiam in seipsis recipiunt: cum unumquodque recipiat aliquid secundum modum suum."

84/26 **Pottle-pot**] "A two-quart pot or tankard" (*OED*).

86/16 *Sidenote*: **Exod[us]. 18**] The complete reference should be Exodus 18.19-23.

86/29-37 **good Melanchthon... a god**] See *D. Martin Luthers Werke: Breifwechsel*, 16 Vols. to date (Weimar, 1930-70) 5: 415: "Tu esto fortis in Domino, Philippum meo nomine Exhortare semper, ne fiat Deus, Sed pugnet contra illam innatam & a Diabolo in paradiso implantatam nobis ambitionem diuinitatis, Ea enim non expedit nobis." Also, see *Luther's Works*, ed. Helmut T. Lehmann, 55 vols. (Philadelphia: Fortress Press, 1972) 49: 337.

86/39 **Ferdinand Alvares Duke *de Alva*]** Fernando Alavarez de Toledo, Duke of Alva (1507-1582), Spanish soldier and statesman famous for his conquest of Portugal (1580) and notorious for his tyranny as governor general of the Netherlands (1567-73), was known for his unshakable self-confidence and proud disposition (see William S. Maltby, *Alba: A Biography of Fernando Alvares de Toledo, Third Duke of Alba* (Berkeley: Univeristy of California, 1983).

260   *Beadle's* A Journall or Diary of a Thankfull Christian

87/5-10 **Cardinall *Matheo Langi* . . . be endured**] Matthew Lang (1468-1540), Cardinal, Bishop of Gurk and archbishop of Salzburg, was inclined to liberal action towards those who clamored for reform; in fact, his effort to carry out a program of reform was one of the earliest within the Church, constituting one of the first tangible signs of the Catholic reform in Germany. According to Justus Jonas, "Saltzburgensis dicitur in privato colloquio hanc vocem edidisse: 'vellem utramque speciem, coniugium libera esse, vellem Missam reformatam esse, vellem libertatem in cibis at aliis traditionibus esse, et totum ordinem sic stare; sed quod unus angulus debet nos reformare omnes hoc est turbare pacem, hoc non est ferendum'" (*D. Martin Luther's Werke: Briefwechsel*, 16 vols., (Weimar, 1930-1970) 5: 427-428. However, at the Diet of Augsburg in 1530, he openly declared himself an opponent of Luther: "Thus a great Nicholas [Roman Catholic] bishop declared in Augsburg that he could tolerate it if everyone believed as they do in Wittenberg; but what he could not tolerate was that such a doctrine should originate in and emanate from such a remote nook and corner" (See *Luthers Works*, ed. Helmutt T. Lehmann, 47, 20).

87/18 *Sidenote*: **Exo[dus]. 11.13**] The correct reference is Exodus 12.35.

87/20-21 **Ravens . . . evening**] 1 Kings 17.4.

87/22 **poor Widow . . . for him**] 1 Kings 17.9.

87/36-37 **embleme . . . heaven**] Cf. George Wither, *A Collection of Emblems: Ancient and Modern*, (1636), (Columbia, S.C.: University of South Carolina Press, 1975), sig. Q2v; Georgette de Montenay, *Monumenta emblematum Christianorum virtutum interpretatione metrica Latina* (London, 1619; STC 18046), sig. M4r.

88/25-31 ***AEgyptians* . . . to come**] In the great temple of Serapis at Alexandria, the image of the Egypto-Hellenic god was attended by a triple-headed monster resembling Cerberus, but the three heads of the beast were distinguished as wolf, lion, and dog. Macrobius's *Saturnalia*, 1.20.13 contains a detailed explanation of the image. In the Renaissance, Petrarch offers a memorable description of the Serapis in *Africa*, 3.190-200.

89/39 *Lazarus come forth*] John 11.43.

90/1 *Manasseh* the bloody] 2 Kings 21.16.

90/1 *Mary Magdalen* the filthy] Luke 8.2.

90/2 *Paul* the persecuter] Acts 8.3, Acts 9.4., Acts 22.7, Acts 26.14, and Philippians 3.6.

90/12-14 *Wilt thou ... to Israel*] Acts 1.6.

90/23-24 *Abraham* waited long for a Son] Genesis 17.16-17.

90/24 *Hanna* waited long for a childe] 1 Samuel 1.20.

90/25-26 *Zachary ... gracious issue*] Luke 1.24.

90/27-32 **When two Monkes ... the place**] King William II (d. 1100), was the third son of William the Conqueror and second Norman king of England (1087-1100). For two sources of the anecdote: "William and the honest monk," see William Thorne, *Chronicle of Saint Augustine's Abbey Canterbury*, ed. A.H. Davis (Oxford: Basil Blackwell, 1934), 62; and *Hall's Chronicles*, gen. ed. J. Johnson (London, 1809), 178.

91/1 *Charls* **King of** *Sicily*] Beadle is probably referring to Charles of Anjou, King of Naples and Sicily, brother of St. Louis (1226-1285), who, for a short time, was one of the most powerful sovereigns in Europe. Charles was known as a great soldier, possessing real political acumen; but his inordinate ambition, his oppressive methods of government, and his cruelty created enemies on all sides, and led to the swift collapse of his dominions and his rule of Sicily (See Denis Mack Smith, *A History of Sicily: Medieval Sicily, 800-1713*, 3 vols. (New York: The Viking Press, 1968) 2: 65-75. Charles eventually lost Sicily to Peter of Aragon and was forced to abandon all attempts at reconquest. However, he proposed to decide the question by single combat between himself and Peter which was to take place at Bordeaux under English protection. The Aragonese accepted, and Peter appeared on the morning of June 1 supposedly ready to do battle; however, Charles did not arrive at the battlefield until a few hours later after Peter had gone and had formally proclaimed his victory due to default.

91/1-2 *Fabius* the *Romane* **General**] Q. Maximus Verrucosus was the celebrated opponent of Hannibal. The system he adopted to check the advance of Hannibal is well known. By a succession of skillful movements, marches, and countermarches, always choosing good defensive positions, he harassed his antagonist, who could never draw him into places favorable for his attack, while Fabius watched every opportunity of availing himself of any error or neglect on the part of the Carthaginians. This mode of warfare, which was new to the Romans, acquired for Fabius the name of CUNCTATOR, or "delayer" (Livy, 22.15).

91/4-5 *cunctando restituit rem*] See the preceding note, 91/4-5 n. Also Cf. Cicero, *De Officis*, 1.24.84; Cicero, *De Senectute or Cato Major*, 4.10; Cicero, *Epistulae ad Atticum*, 2.19.2; Livy 30.26.9; Vergil, *Aeneis*, 6.846; Ovid, *Fasti*, 2.242.

91/17 **gives us our daily bread**] Matthew 6.11 and Luke 11.3.

91/31-34 **Sumpter-horses . . . gall'd backs**] Cf. Tilley H700, Dent H700, Whiting H505. Also, see Shakespeare, *Measure of Measure*, 3.1.26: "If thou art rich, thou art poor,/ For like an ass whose back with ingots bows,/ Thou bear'st thy heavy riches but a journey,/ And death unloads thee . . . "

92/24-26 **Fulnesse . . . wantonnesse**] See Tilley F787, Whiting W426.

Commentary to the Text   263

92/26-27 **surfet ... famine**] See Theognis, *Elegies*, 605: "Plenty's destroyed more men than famine's killed." Also, cf. Tilley F441, G148.

92/29-31 **Spring ... Winter**] Cf. Horace, *Odes*, 1.4.1: "Solvitvr acris hiems grata vice veris et et Favoni."

92/31-32 **meanest ... safest**] Cf. Tilley S492.

92/32 *Iob* **on the dunghill**] Job 2.8.

92/33 *Adam* **in Paradise**] Genesis 2.8.

92/36-38 **a poor man ... horseback**] See Tilley M576.

93/38-93/5 **God grant ... safe home**] Beadle is probably referring to John Welch (1570?-1622), a presbyterian divine, and son-in-law of John Knox. He was put on trial for high treason in 1603, and as a result was banished from England until 1622. The source for this particular anecdote is not found in either this short biography of Welch, called "The History of his life and sufferings . . . . " in *Forty-eight Select Sermons* (Glasgow, 1850), 11-44); or in Samuel Clark's *The lives of sundry eminent persons* (London, 1683; *Wing STC* C4538), sig. Ii2r-Kk1v.

93/11 *stellae primae magnitudinis*] Aelius Lampridius, *Alexander Severus*, 13.5.

93/15-17 *Dantur bonis ... summa bona*] I have been unable to trace this saying.

93/21-24 **Many Papists ... Hugenots**] In the Saint Bartholomew Day Massacre according to the contemporary historian Francois-Eudes de Mezeray, *A general chronological history of France* (London, 1683; *Wing STC* M1958), sig. XXXX3v, "The deluge of Blood swallow'd up many Catholicks likewise, who were dispatched by Order of the Higher-Powers, or at the Instigation of some particular Persons. It was enough to make them *Huguenots*, if they had Money, or a wished for Employment, or vindicative Enemies, or impatient heyres. Some called this Massacre *The Paris Matins*, as they formerly called that in *Sicily*, Anno 1281. *The Sicilian Vespers*." Henri Noguères, *The Massacre of Saint Bartholomew*, trans. Claire Eliane Engel (London: George Allen & Unwin Ltd., 1962), 108, lists names of devout "Catholics, who, in spite of their religion, were also thrown into the Seine: Rouillard, for instance, a church councilor who was suing a colleague for forgery, Villemor, a son of a former Keeper of the Seals and *Maître des requêtes*, who was also suing a shady colleague; even a Spaniard, the Lord of Salcede, a sworn enemy of the Huguenots but a man who was on bad terms with the Cardinal of Lorraine."

93/26-29 **Sir *Iohn Cornwall* . . . of treason]** Sir John Cornwall, Baron of Fanhope (d. 1443), married the widowed sister of Henry IV and fought in the battle of Agincourt (1415). He died at Ampthill in 1443, and was buried at Ludgate (Vicary Gibb, ed., *The Complete Peerage of England, Scotland, Ireland, Great Britain and the United Kingdom*, 3: 253-254). After returning from the military campaigns in France, Sir John invested the proceeds of his soldiering in a brand new castle at Ampthill. His acquisition of the castle caused a serious, armed disagreement between himself and Lord Grey of Ruthin, a principal and long-time resident of nearby Wrest Park. Grey perceived Cornwall's presence at Ampthill as a threat to his political prominence in Bedfordshire. In mid-January 1439, sympathizers of both men collided in a public house where negotiations were being held between their respective constituencies. At last, eighteen men were thrown down the stairs of the shire hall; some were badly hurt and others suffocated. Each side accused the other of precipitating the violence. In March 1439, the King decided to intervene in the conflict, thereby extending his grace to his kinsman-by-marriage after Cornwall had payed a punitive fine (see Ralph

A. Griffiths, *The Reign of King Henry VI: The Exercise of Royal Authority*, 1422-1461, Berkeley: University of California Press, 1981), 353, 356, 570-571. I cannot locate, in chronicles of the period, the reference to Sir John Cornwall's dying words.

93/29-32 **Solon ... your gold**] I am not able to locate this anecdote in primary classical sources which discuss the activities of Solon; for example, Ausonius, *The Masque of the Seven Sages*, 3.52-64 and 4.73-120; Herodotus, 1.28-34; Plutarch, *Solon*, 27.1-7.

93/38-39 *In sublimitate* ... **of fears**] See 92/32-34 n.

94/3-5 **Zedekiah ... into captivity**] 2 Kings 25.7.

94/5 *Mediocria firma*] See 142/6-7. The motto of Sir Nicholas Bacon (fl. 1570) (Elizabeth McCutcheon, ed., *Sir Nicholas Bacon's Great House Sententiae,* Claremont, CA: The Sir Francis Bacon Foundation, 1977), 30. Also, cf. Pindar, *Pythian Odes*, 11.1.52: "Of all the orders in the State, I find the middle rank flourishes with a more enduring properity;" Plautus, *Aulularia*, 4.10.803: "Esse in vado salutis;" Thomas More, *The Lyfe of Jhon Picus*, (1557; Scholar Press, 1978), sig. a8r: "The golden mediocrite, the meane estate is to be desired, which shall beare us as it were in handes more easily, which shal obey us and not maister us;" Philip Sidney, "Translated out of Horace, which beginnes Rectiùs viues." In *The Poems of Sir Philip Sidney*, William A. Ringler, Jr., ed. (Oxford: Clarendon Press, 1962), 143: "The golden meane who loves, lives safely free / From filth of foreworne house, and quiet lives, Releast from Court, where envie needes must be;" S.W., *The countrymans commonwealth* (London 1640?; STC 21525.1), sig. B7r: "To liue in the meane estate is the best wisdome, for high Cedars are shaken with the wind, when low shrubs are scarcely moued."

94/6-7 *food* ... **prayed for**] Proverbs 30.8.

94/8-12 Scipio Africanus ... we have] I cannot find this reference.

95/2-6 When one ... to beg] Beadle has confused Alexander the Great here with Antigonus. See Plutarch, *Moralia*, 182E: "When Thrasyllus the Cynic asked him [Antigonus] for a shilling, he said `That is not a fit gift for a king to give.' And when Thrasyllus said, `Then give me two hundred pounds,' he retorted, `But that is not a fit gift for a Cynic to receive.'" Also, see Erasmus, *Apophthegmata*. In *Opera Omnia*, 10 vols. (Hildesheim: Georg Olms Verlagsbuchhandlung, 1962) 4: 204B. It is probable that Beadle's confusion here originates from a similar story related by Samuel Clark in *A Mirrour or Looking Glasse*, 2nd ed. (London, 1654; *Wing STC* C4548), sig. I7r, which says, "One craving a small courtesie of *Alexander* the Great, he gave him an whole City, and when the poor man said that it was too much for him to receive, Yea (said *Alexander*) but not for me to give." Elsewhere in Clark's *A Mirrour*, he retells the story; "A begging *Philosopher* asking a groat of a certaine King: the King told him that it was too little for him to give; then give me a talent (quoth the other,) Nay (said the King) that's too much for a beggar to receive" (sig. K1v).

95/25-28 one told *Alexander* ... be contented] See Justin, *Philippic Histories*, 11.12.9-15, where Darius attempts to make a deal with Alexander: "Scribit itaque et tertias epistolas, et gratias agit, quod nihil in suos hostile fecerit. Offert deinde majorem partem regni usque flumen Euphraten, et alteram filiam uxorem; pro reliquis captivis triginta millia talentum. Ad haec Alexander 'gratiarum actionem ab hoste supervacaneam esse respondit; 'nec a se quicquam factum in hostis adulationem, nec quod in dubios belli exitus aut in leges pacis sibi lenocinia quaereret; sed animi magnitudine, qua didicerit adversus vires hostium, non adversus calamitates, contendere;' polliceturque, 'praestaturum se ea Dario, si secundus sibi, non par, haberi velit. Ceterum neque mundum posse duobus solibus regis; neque orbem summa duo regna salvo statu terrarum habere: proinde aut deditionem ea die, aut in posteram aciem, paret; nec polliceatur sibi aliam, quam sit expertus, victoriam.' Also, cf. *The Worlds Anotomy, Or, Reason diswading from the love of this world* (London, 1640; *STC* 25983), sig. A7r, which refers to Alexander's insatiable ambition to conquor: "Great Alexander, like the sift wing'd Sun,/ Did all the world with Conquest over-run; / Yet all the world contenting not his mind, / New [---] undertakes, new worlds to find; / But finding none, all disconted weeps, / Wishing the surging Seas, and silent deeps/ Were sollid earth, [--] with imperious hand, / All other kings as Wassals did command . . ." Also, see Samuel Clark in *The Life and Death of Alexander the Great* (London, 1665; *Wing STC* C4526), sig. F2r, who observes that "the bounded earth suffized not for his boundlesse ambition. Many Arguments he therefore used to draw on his Army farther into the East."

95/27-31 **Diogenes the Cynick . . . Craterus**] Diogenes Laertius, *Diogenes*, 6.57.

95/32-35 **It is reported . . . no need of**] Socrates is the "old Philosopher" Beadle refers to here. See Diogenes Laertius, *Socrates*, 2.25.

95/38-96/5 **with Cato . . . cannot want**] Aulius Gellius, *Attic Nights*, 13.14.1-2.

96/21-25 **Henry the fifth . . . amisse to them**] Holinshed recounts Henry V's imperviousness to the elements: "In casting of great iron barres and heauie stones he excelled commonlie all men, neuer shrinking at cold, nor slothfull for heat; and when he most laboured, his head commonlie vncouered; no more wearie of harnesse than a light cloake, verie valiantlie abiding at needs both hunger and thirst; so manfull of mind as neuer seene to quinch at a wound, or to smart at the paine; nor to turne his nose from euill sauour, nor close his eies from smoke or dust" (*Chronicles*, 6 vols., London, 1808) 3: 133. With regard to the military stamina of Gustavus Adolphus II (1594-1632), an anonymous contemporary historian of the Battle of Lutzen observes, "he never persuaded any man to an enterprise, in which he would not himself make one . . . I may add, that neither antiquity can, nor posterity ever shall produce a prince so patient of all military wants, as of meant, drink, warmth, sleep, &c. all which are necessary to the maintenance of life. In divers sufferings of his, he recalls to my mind the most accomplished of the Romans, Cato, who, leading is troops, through the contagious and poisonous desarts, was ever the last of his army that drank" (*The Great and Famous Battle of Lutzen* in *The Harleian Miscellany*, 8 vols., 1633; London, 1808-1811) 4: 184.

96/29-31 **Joseph . . . Heb.11**] Hebrews 11.21. See John Chrysostom, *Homilies on the Hebrews*, Homily 26.2: "That is, even though he was now an old man, *he bowed himself* to Joseph, shewing the obeisance of the whole people which was to be [directed] to him. And this indeed had already come to pass, when his brethren *bowed down* to him: but it was afterwards to come to pass through the ten tribes. Thou seest how he foretold the things which were to be afterwards?" (T. Kreble, trans., *The Homilies of S. John Chrysostom on the Epistle of S. Paul the Apostle to the Hebrews*, London: James Parker and Co., 1877), 298.

96/34-35 **he is sold . . . to AEgypt**] Genesis 37.28,36. and Genesis 39.1.

96/35-36 **he is advanced . . . Kingdome**] Genesis 39.4-5.

96/38-97/1 **jealous husband . . . his soul**] Genesis 39.11-21 and Psalm 105.18. Also, see Tilley I90, and Whiting I57.

97/1-2 **he is advanced . . . could permit**] Genesis 41.40.

97/12-13 **high sail of honor and greatnesse**] In the emblematic tradition, the figure of fortune is recognized by "the wind of opportunity billowing out her sial-like scarf" (Charles

Moseley, *A Century of Emblems*, Brookfield, Vermont: Scolar Press, 1989) 133.

100/31-101/1 ***Tamerlane*... had faln into]** In Jean du Bec, *The Historie of the Great Emperovr Tamerlane* (London, 1597; *STC* 7263), sig. H6r, there is a complete and detailed account of Tamerlane's habit of having Chronicles read to him before a battle.

101/10-12 ***Israel*... their journey]** Genesis 46.4.

101/12-18 ***Joseph*... in their way]** Genesis 46.28, Genesis 47.1-6, and Genesis 47.13.

101/28-29 **under a cloud]** 1 Corinthians 10.1. Also, see Tilley C441.

101/31-33 **life of the best... to the ground]** Beadle here refers to a game called "Shuttlefeather," also known as "Battledore and Shuttlecock," popular during the reign of James I of England. The battledore was a small hand bat made of a skin stretched over a wooden frame and catgut strings stretched over a frame. The shuttlecock consisted of a small cork into which feathers of equal size were fixed at even distances (G. Laurence Gomme, ed., *A Dictionary of British Folk-Lore*, 2 vols., London, 1894-1898) 2: 192-193.

101/37-102/2 **The *Germanes*... the money]** The "Palsgrave," or elector of the German king, being referred to is probably the Palsgrave of the Rhine which became the highest position among the four palsgraves. The Margrave of Brandenburg acted as chamberlain of the imperial household, and the Duke of Saxony as its marshal (see Marsilius of Padua, *De Translatione Imperii Romani* in *Monarchia Imperii*, ed. Melchior Goldast, 3 vols., Graz: Akademishce Druck-U. Verlagsanstalt, 1960) 2: 153. I am unable to locate the anecdote about the German princes.

102/2 **No man hath all**] See Tilley M315.

102/8 *Deo servire regnare est*] Walther 5401.

102/18 *one thing necessary*] Luke 10.42.

103/6-8 **poorest men . . . bill of charges**] Francis Bacon, "Of Marriage And Single Life," in *The Essayes or Counsels, Civill and Morall*, ed. Michael Kiernan (Cambridge: Harvard University Press, 1985), 25. Further, see Tilley C331, C338, and W379.

103/18 **If God send mouths, he will provide meat**] Tilley G207, G218.

103/31-35 *Galba* **. . . homely habitation**] Erasmus, *Apophthegmata*, 291E: "In Galbam Oratorem eloquentia clarum, sed gibbo deformem ita lusit M. Laelius, ut diceret, *Ingenium Balbae male habitare*. Nam animi domicilium est corpus."

103/35-36 *Aesop* **. . . very wise**] See *Aesops fables, with their moralls* (Cambridge, 1650; *Wing STC* A688), sig.P9v, which describes Aesop not only as a slave, "but amongst the men of his age most deformed, for he was of a sharp head, flat nose, crooked back, lips pendant, black, from which he had his name (*AEsopus* is the same with *AEthiops*) large belly, crooked bowlegges . . . But of all, he was most infortunate in this, his speech was slow, inarticulate and very obscure; all which, made *AEsop* fit for nothing but servitude; for a man so extra ordinarily ill-shapen could scarcely avoid that kind of life: Such was his body, howbeit Nature endowed him with a most accomplished mind, for the most sublime contemplations."

103/36-37 *Erasmus* **. . . great Scholar**] See Beatus Rhenanus, "*Compendium Vitae*," John C. Olin, ed. In *Christian Humanism and the Reformation* (New York: Fordham University Press,

1975), 29: "He was not even pleased with his own face, and it was only with effort that his friends forced him to agree to sit for a painting."

104/3 **Methuselah**] See Genesis 5.22-27.

104/3-4 **Weeping-crosse**] Used allusively, especially in the proverbial phrase *to come home by the Weeping Crosse*, to suffer grievous disappointment or failure (*OED*).

104/18-19 **eye hath ... conceive**] 1 Corinthians 2.9.

105/4 *Sidenote*: **Gen[esis]. 45.2**] The correct reference is Genesis 44.2.

105/22 **Jailor ... fellow**] The stereotype of the jailor was often written about in the seventeenth century. Sir Thomas Overbury's description of the jailor concurs with Beadle's observation that the jailor occupies the lowest estate: "His conscience and his shakles hangs up together and are made very neere of the same mettle saving that the one is harder then the other and hath one propertie above Iron for that never melts. He distills mony out of the poores tears, & grows fat by their curses, No man comming to the practicall part of hell can discharge it better, because here he does nothing but studie the theorique of it ... His eares are stopt, to the cryes of others, and Gods to his ... He must looke for no mercy ... for he shewes none, And I thinke he cares the lesse, because he knowes heaven hath no neede of Jaylours ... What estate can be worse" (Thomas Overbury, *The Overburian Characters*, W.J. Paylor, ed. Oxford: Basil Blackwell, 1936), 91-92.

106/8-9 **bit and a whip, a crust and knock**] Cf. Tilley B416: "He gives him the Bit and the buffet with it (a bit and a knock)."

106/10 **Abundance ... the last**] Cf. Luke 12.15.

106/22-23 *Jacob ... is alive*] Genesis 45.28.

106/23 **My redeemer liveth**] Job 19.25.

107/1 **fat body and a lean soul**] Cf. Thomas Overbury *The Conceited Newes of Sir Thomas Overbury And His Friends*, ed. James E. Savage (Gainesville, FL: Scholars' Facsimiles & Reprints, 1968), 247: "That a soule in a fat body lies soft, and is loath to rise."

107/16 **Faith of *Abraham***] Romans 4.9.

107/16 **Grief of *Lot* . . . wicked**] 19.7,14.

107/18-19 **Zeal of *David***] Psalms 69.9 and Psalms 119.137.

107/17 **Wisdome of *Solomon***] 1 Kings 4.30.

108/4 *Sidenote*: **1 Kin[gs]. 2.14**] The correct reference is 1 Kings 21.4.

108/16 *Sidenote*: **Gen[esis]. 15.12**] The correct reference is Genesis 15.2.

108/19-20 **Though some . . . reached higher**] Cf. commentary of Geneva Bible, 1560, sig. biiv, on this verse: "His feare was not onely lest he shulde not haue children, but lest the promes of the blessed sede shulde not be accomplished in him."

108/30-31 **the pomp . . . soon vanish**] Cf. Tilley P464: "All the pompe and Pryde, the Bodie tournes to dust."

108/39-109/5 **It hath been observed . . . to ruine**] Suetonius observes of Tiberius: "In addition to his old friends and intimates, he had asked for twenty of the leading men of the State as advisers on public affairs. Of all these he spared hardly two or three; the others he destroyed on one pretext or another, including Aelius Sejanus, whose downfall involved the death of many others. This man he had advanced to the highest power, not so much from regard for him, as that he might through his servies and wiles destroy the children of Germanicus and secure the succession for his own grandson, the child of his son Drusus" (*Tiberius*, 3.55). Mahomet II, also called Mahomet the Great (fl. 1444), killed his brother in order that he would reign more safely: "After the deathe of Ainurathes, hys sonne Mahomete, (being. xxi. yeres of age, proclaymed Prince and Emperour with the great fauour of all his souldiers) to thinkest he might more frelye and saufely reygne, comaunded eftsones his brother to be slayne" (Giovo Paolo, *A shorte treatise upon the Turkes Chronicles*, London, 1546; STC 11899), sigs. C6v-C7r. According to Kritovoulos, a chronicler of the reign of Mahomet the Great, the sultan "arrested Halil, one of his first-rank men and very powerful, and put him in prison. And after torturing him in many ways, he put him to death" (Kritovoulos, *History of Mehmed the Conqueror*, Charles T. Riggs, ed. Princeton: University of Princeton Press, 1954), 87. Also, Richard Knolles in *The generall historie of the Turkes* (London, 1603; STC 15051), sigs. Gg1r-Gg2v, describes Mahomet's early ruling years: "This young tyrant was no sooner possessed of his fathers kingdome, but that he forgetting the lawes of nature, was presently in person himselfe about to haue murthered with his owne hands, his youngest brother, then but eighteene moneths old, begotten on the daughter of *Sponderbius* . . . At the same time also he caused another of his brethren, committed by his father to the keeping of *Caly Bassa*, and now by him betrayed into his hands, to be likewise murthered . . . Thus beginning his tyrannous raigne with the bloodie execution of them that were in blood nearest vnto him, and whom of all others he ought to haue defended." Finally, Samuel Clark in *A Mirrour or Looking-Glasse*, sig. F5r, declares that "Mahomet the great, a most cruell, and mercilesse Tyrant, is said in his life-time to have been the cause of the death of eight hundred thousand men." Edward Herbert, Lord of Cherbury in *The life and raigne of King Henry the Eighth* (London, 1649; Wing STC H1504), sig. Cccc2v, describes the conditions of Henry's rule "as stiled him both at home and abroad by the name of *Cruell*; which also hardly can be avoyded; especially, if that Attribute be due, not onely to those Princes who inflict capitall punishments frequently, and for small crimes, but to those who pardon not all that are capable of mercy. And for testimonies in this kinde, some urge two Queens, one Cardinall . . . or two (for *Poole* was condemned, though absent); Dukes, Marquesses, Earls, and Earls Sons, twelve; Barons and Knights eighteen; Abbots, Priors, Monks and Priests seventy seven. Hee gave some proofs yet that he could forgive; though, as they were few and late, they served not to recover the name of a Clement Prince."

109/6-7 *Bajazet* and *Bellizarius* . . . misery] Bayazid I (d. 1403?), Ottoman sultan. His reign was characterized by military exploits, and brought to an end on July 28, 1402, when Tamerlane defeated and captured him at Ankara, after which Tamerlane subjected him to repeated humiliations: "The Emperour did not vse him at all curteouslie, but caused small account to bee made of him: and for to manifest that he knew how to punish the proud; vpon festiuall dayes, when as he mounted on horseback, they brought this proud man vnto him, and hee serued him in steed of a foot-stoole: this did hee for to manifest the follie and arrogancie of men, and how iustlie God had humbled him" (Jean Du Bec-Crespin, *The Historie of Great Emperour Tamerlan*, London, 1597; *STC* 7263), sig. I2r. Belisarius (b. 505-565 A.D.) was the greatest general the Byzantine empire ever produced. After a great career, he was accused of a conspiracy against Justinian by Theodora, his fortune was sequestered, and he was publicly humiliated: "Belisarius, although none of the charges against him were proved, was at the insistence of the Empress relieved of his command by the Emperor . . . Belisarius's lancers and shield-bearers, and such of his servants as were of military use, he [Martinus] ordered to be divided between the other generals and certain of the palace eunuchs. Drawing lots for these men and their arms, they portioned them as the chances fell. And his friends, and all who formerly had served him, were forbidden ever to visit Belisarius. It was a bitter sight, and one no one would ever have thought credible, to see Belisarius a private citizen in Constantinople, almost deserted, melancholy and miserable of countenance, and ever expectant of a further conspiracy to accomplish his death . . . Late in the evening he went home, often turning around as he withdrew and looking in every direction for those who might be advancing to put him to death. Accompanied by this dread, he entered his home and sat down alone upon his couch. His spirit broken, he failed even to remember the time when he was a man; sweating, dizzy and trembling, he counted himself lost; devoured by slavish fears and mortal worry, he was completely emasculated" (Procopius, *Secret History*, trans. Richard Atwater, Ann Arbor: University of Michigan Press, 1961), 21-22.

109/10-20 **Saladine . . . his shirt**] See Vincent of Beauvais, *Speculum Historiale*, 4 vols. (Graz-Austria: Akademische Druck - u. Verlagsanstalt, 1964) 4: 1204: "Eo autem tempore Saladinus abiit apud Damascum. Cum autem sciret sibi mortem imminere, signiferum suum vocauit dicens: Tu qui soles ferre vexilla mea per bella, fer vexillum mortis meae scilicet panniculum vilem per totam Damascum super lanceam clamitando. Ecce Rex orientis moriens non fert secum nisi hoc pallium vile, & sic mortuus est." Also, see Samuel Clark, *A Mirrour or Looking-Glasse*, Bb7r.

109/20-22 **Duke of Exeter . . . Duke of Burgundy**] Henry Holland (1430-1475), a staunch Lancastrian, and husband to Anne Plantagenet, daughter of Richard, Duke of York (see Vicary Gibb, ed., *The Complete Peerage of England Scotland Ireland Great Britain and the United Kingdom*) 5: 212-215. According to Phillipe de Comines, the Duke of Exeter and other Lancastrians "lived as banished men in the Duke of Burgundies court, who received them as his kinsmen of the house of Lancaster, before his mariage with King Edwards sister. I have seene them in so great misery before they came to the Dukes knowledge, that those that beg from dore to dore were not in poorer estate then they: for I once saw a Duke of Excester run on foote bare legged after the Duke of Burgundies traine, begging his bread for Gods sake, but uttered not his name. He was the neerest of the house of Lancaster, and had maried King Edwards sister, but when he was knowne, the Duke gave him a small pension to maintain his estate" (1596; *The History of Comines*, englished by Thomas Danett, 2 vols., New York: AMS Press, 1967) 1: 177. See also Samuel Clark, *A Mirrour or Looking-Glasse*, sig. Cc1r.

110/5 **fair weather ... under foot**] See Dent F29, Tilley F29.

110/7 **lamp of God ... of himself**] Job 29.2-3.

110/9 **I may ... for a time**] Job 30.12.

110/11-12 **God may write ... my youth**] Job 13.26.

110/12-13 **for there ... Ghost**] Matthew 12.31-32.

110/15-17 *Joseph* **... imprisonment**] Genesis 37.5-9.

110/19-22 **great city ... and none**] Seneca is referring to Lyons which was burnt in A.D. 59 and then was restored by Nero. See Seneca, *Ad Lucilium Epistulae Morales*, 91.2: "Nulla res magna non aliquod habuit ruinae suae spatium; in hac una nox interfuit inter urbem maximam et nullam. Denique diutius illam tibi perisse quam perît narro."

110/37-39 *O quantum* **...** *Perseus* **long agoe**] Persius, *Satires*, 1.1.

111/5 *Vanitas* **...** *vacuitas*] I cannot locate this saying which sounds very much like a scholastic definition of vanity.

111/14 **our pleasures end in pain**] See Tilley P408, P412, P420; Dent P408, P420.

111/15 **our plenty in penury**] See Tilley P427 and Dent P427.

111/23 *Nihil est ab omni parte beatum*] Horace, *Odes*, 2.16.27.

Commentary to the Text   277

111/29-30 *Augendi ... metus*] Cf. Tilley C86, B723, B724, P23, R108; Whiting B595.

111/33-34 *Quae ... displicent*] Cf. Tilley T199. Also echoes Seneca, *To Polybius on Consolation*, 9.5: "Omnia ista bona, quae nos speciosa sed fallaci voluptate delectant, pecunia, dignitas, potentia aliaque complura, ad quae generis humani caeca cupiditas obstupescit, cum labore possidentur, cum invidia conspiciuntur, eos denique ipsos, quos exortant, et premunt; plus minantur quam prosunt."

111/36-38 **Like *Calipolis* ... expectation**] The modern Gallipoli meaning "Fair City." Agathias Scholasticus, a Byzantine historian, refers to the physical character of the city: "Not far from Sestos is another small town which despite its extreme smallness, its lack of beauty and generally unprepossesssing appearance is called Callipolis. The surrounding country is graced with fields and roadsteads, dotted with a great variety of trees and blessed with streams of good drinking water and with a rich, fertile soil that produces a plentiful store of all the neccessaries of life" (*The Histories*, ed. Joseph D. Frendo, 2 vols., Berlin: Walter De Gruyter, 1975) 2A: 147.

112/12 *I will be thy God*] Genesis 17.8.

112/18-19 **as the Syrians ... treasure**] 2 Samuel 10.14,18 and 1 Chronicles 19.15.

112/29-30 *omnium rerum ... fulsomnesse*] Cicero, *De Senectute*, 20.76.

113/23-24 ***Quantum canis Appula tantum***] Persius, *Satires*, 1.60: "nec linguae quantum sitiat canis Apula tantum!"

113/24-27 **Like the dog ... by them**] See Macrobius, *Saturnalia*, 2.2.7; Phaedrus, *The Aesopic Fables*, 1.25; Pliny, *Natural History*, 8.61.148. Aelian, *Various History* (London, 1665; Wing STC 679), sig. B2r: "This also is wise in the *Aegyptian* Dogs;

they drink of the River not greedily or freely, stooping and lapping till they have at the same time satisfied their thirst, for they are afraid of the Creatures in it; but run along the bank, and catch up drink by stealth at times, till at last they have allayed their thirst by snatches without receiving harm." Also, see Tilley D604, Dent D604.

113/38 ***Magistratus virum indicat***] See Aristotle, *Nichomachean Ethics*, 5.1.16; Diogenes Laertius, *Pittacus*, 1.77; Plutarch, *Moralia*, 811B; Sophocles, *Antigone*, 1.175; Erasmus, *Adagia*. In *Opera Omnia*, 10 vols. (Hildesheim: Georg Olms Verlagsbuchhandlung, 1961) 2: 389F; Daniel Rogers, *Matrimonial honour* (London, 1642; *Wing STC* R1797), sig. G3r: "The old speech is, Magistracy makes not the man, but discovers what mettell is in him." Walther, 14196a.

114/4-9 **reported of Pope *Sixtus quintus* . . . crown**] A probable source of the legend about Cardinal Montalto's (1520-1590) supposed physical change from a poor, old, bent Franciscan friar to a spirited, younger looking Pope is Gregorio Leti (1630-1701), a seventeenth century Italian biographer of Sixtus V: "It was observed, that after it [the election] had begun; Montalto walked backwards and forwards, and seemed to be in great agitation of spirit; but when he perceived there was a sufficient number of votes to secure his election, he threw the staff, with which he used to support himself, into the middle of the Chapel, stretched himself up, and appeared taller, by almost a foot, than he had done for several years, hawking and spitting with as much strengh as a man of 30 years old" (*The Life of Pope Sixtus the Fifth*, Dublin: W. Colles, Dame Street, 1779), 203-204.

114/10-13 ***Judas* . . . his Master**] Allusion to John 12.6 and John 13.29. In John 12.6 in *The Geneva Bible*, 1560, sig. NNi, refers to the "money-box" as a "bagge": "Now he said this, not that he cared for the poore, but because he was a thefe, and had the bagge, and bare that which was giuen."

Commentary to the Text   279

114/23 **set your hearts on them**] Psalms 4.4.

114/24-25 **you shall lye down in sorrow**] Isaiah 50.11.

114/25 **good servants but bad Masters**] Cf. Tilley F253, M1055, Whiting S158. Also, cf. Francis Bacon, *De Augmentis Scientiarum*, ed. James Spedding, 15 vols. (Cambridge: Riverside Press 1863) 2: 468: "Divitiae bona ancilla, pessima domina."

114/28-29 **If riches ... thy slave**] See Tilley M1055. Also echoes Seneca, *Ad Lucilium Epistolae Morales*, 104.34: "Spernendae opes: auctoramenta sunt servitutum."

114/30-32 **Serve it as** *Diagorus* **... with it**] See Clement of Alexandria, *Cohortatio Ad Gentes*, PG 8: 94.

114/33 *All these things will I give thee*] Matthew 4.9.

115/5-6 **like ... excepted**] This familiar phrase is not scriptural although Hebrews 4.15 does serve as its source: "For the high priest we have is not incapable of feeling our weaknesses with us, but has been put to the test in exactly the same way as ourselves, apart from sin." Later, in 451, the Council of Chalcedon formulates this Christian dogma in its Symbol: "Sequentes igitur sanctos Patres, unum eundemque confiteri Filium Dominum nostrum Iesum Christum consonanter omnes docemus, eundem perfectum in deitate, eundem perfectum in humanitate, Deum vere et hominem vere, eundem ex anima rationali et corpore, consubstantialem Patri secundum deitatem et consubstantialem nobis eundem secundum humanitatem, 'per omnia nobis similem absque peccato' (Henry Denzinger, ed. *Enchiridion Symbolorum*, 32nd ed., Rome: Herder, 1963, p. 108).

115/12-13 *Put not ... of man*] Psalms 146.3.

115/29 *Canaan ... Anak*] Numbers 14.1-35.

116/15 **Bashan for their Og**] Numbers 21.33-35, and Deuteronomy 3.1-3.

116/15-16 **Philistines for their Goliah**] 1 Samuel 17.4.

116/17-18 **where goes . . . the bucket**] Cf. Miguel De Cervantes, *The History of Don Quixote*, trans. Thomas Shelton, 4 vols. (1612; New York: AMS Press, 1967) 3: 71: "Speake mannerly, Sr., (quoth Don Quixote) of my Mistrisses things, and let's be merry and wise, and cast not the rope after the bucket." Also, see Tilley B694 and R173.

116/23-25 **I will . . . carry it**] See Ro: Ba:, *The Life of Syr Thomas more, Somtymes Lord Chancellour of England*, eds. Elsie Vaughan Hitchcock and P.E. Hallett (1950; London: EETS, 1957) 222: 205. Also, see Tilley F32 and S533.

116/28 **old man . . . best man**] Allusion to Colossians 3.9-10.

117/3-6 **Have . . . none**] I have been unable to locate these sayings.

117/9 **Alexander and Ephestion**] Hephaestion, a Macedonian, celebrated as Alexander's companion (Plutarch, *Alexander*, 39; Plutarch, *Moralia*, 180D, 340A).

117/9-10 **David . . . Jonathan**] 1 Samuel 18.1-4.

117/10-11 **Court . . . Kings friend**] 2 Samuel 15.37 and 2 Samuel 16.16.

117/11-14 **Christ . . . the rest**] John 19.26, 20.2, 21.7, and 21.20.

117/14-16 **wise man . . . *Pater-noster***] Tilley P96.

117/17-19 ***Give unto . . . are Gods***] Mark 12.17 and Luke 20.25.

Commentary to the Text   281

119/26-27 the alpha ... thankfulnesse] Cf. Revelation 1.8, 21.6, and 22.13.

119/29-30 There ... him] Esther 6.3.

120/30-38 brave speech ... given him] Louis XIII (1601-1643), who was staunchly Catholic, reached the gates of Pau (of which a majority of the population were Huguenots) on October 15, 1620, and declared that he would not enter a city which contained no consecrated Catholic church where he could worship God according to the rites of his religion: "Ce pays étant de ma souveraineté, j'y devrais recevoir les honneurs qui appartiennent aux souverains; et s'il y avait une église, j'irais y descendre comme j'ai fait en toutes les autres villes où j'ai passé. Mais puisqu'il n'y en a point, je ne veux point d'entrée, ni qu'on me présente li poële; car il serait malséant de recevoir des honneurs en un lieu où il n'y a nulle église pour en rendre grâces à Dieu" (*Declaration des Béarnais au roi sur ce qui s'était passé en leur pays depuis le partement de Sa Majesté de la ville de Bordeaux, avec la réponse du roi à ladite déclaration* ... Paris, 1620), 12.

121/3-8 *Boleslaus* ... thy name] Probably a reference to Boleslaus I, called "The Great," (992-1025), first Christian prince of Poland. He succeeded in converting the court from paganism to Christianity. At his death in 1025, Poland had become one of the mightiest states of Europe. As for the anecdote concerning the respect he had for his ancestors, it is similar to one related in George Pettie, trans., *The Civile Conversation of M. Steeven Guazzo*, 2 vols. (1581; London: Constable and Co., Ltd., 1925) 1: 183: "Yea and gentry is to be honored for this respect, that for the most part better lineage we come of, the better behaviour wee are of. And therefore Q. Max. Scipio, and others said, that beholding the pictures and ymages of their auncestours, they felt themselves marvaylously stirred up to vertue ... And truely it happeneth seldom that he doeth ill, who seeth thereby the honour of his auncestours together with his owne brought in danger."

121/26-31 **Cardinall Wolsey . . . hath done**] See George Cavendish, *The negotiations of Thomas Woolsey* (London, 1641; *Wing* STC C1619), sig. P1r: "And master *Kingston*, had I but served God as diligently as I have served the King, he would not have given me over in my gray haires." Also, see *The Life and Death of Thomas Wolsey*, ed. Richard S. Sylvester (Oxford: EETS, 1959), 178-179.

122/1-3 **Seneca . . . no good**] Seneca, *Ad Lucilium Epistulae Morales*, 82.1

122/6-8 **Moses . . . Midian**] Exodus 2.15.

122/24-29 **Our charity . . . ditch**] Cf. Proverbs 5.15-18.

123/4 *Sidenote*: **Joh[n]. 15.12**] The correct reference is John 15.13.

123/14-16 **Trajan . . . Souldier**] Cassius Dio, *Roman History*, 68.8.2.

123/17-23 **Pompey . . . I live**] Plutarch, *Pompey*, 50.2; see also Erasmus, *Apophthegmata*, 217F.

123/36-38 **Charls the fifth . . . saved**] On October 24, 1541, Charles V landed 20,000 troops 8 miles east of Algiers. On October 25, an attack on the city was to take place; however, during the night a severe storm struck the Spanish army causing severe losses of ships, military supplies, and food. The eyewitness account of N. Durand, the Chevalier de Villegagnon, describes Charles' decision to throw horses overboard in order that troops could be saved: "Thre Dayes after, the See somewhat assuaged, but yet not so, that it was possible to haue entreprised the goynge for enye Vytayles; and The emperour, in this Necessite, coulde none otherwyse prouyde for his Armye, but commaunded that the Horses whych he had caused to be brought with hym in the Barques, to be kylled for the Sustentacion of the poore Souldyers, the which by the

Space of. iii. Dayes dyd eate none other Meat; for the Tempest, in brusynge and noyenge of the Shyppes, had loste and drouned a great Quantyte of Meale, Corn, and Bysket, and other Vytayles, as Peason, Beanes, Wyne, Oyle, and poudred Fleshe, with the whiche they were wel laden at their Commyng foorth. And so, by this meanes, there was loste many Horses, and a great Nombre of Artillarye, aswell of that which serued for the Safegarde and Defence of Shippes" (*A lamentable and piteous Treatise, verye necessarye for euerie Christen Manne to reade, wherin is contayned, not onely the high Entreprise and Valeauntnes of The emperour Charles the v. and his Army (in his Voyage made to the Towne of Argier in Affrique against the Turckes. . .* in *Harleian Miscellany,* 8 vols., London, 1744-1746) 4: 512. Also, see *Collection des Voyages Des Souverians des Pays-Bas,* ed. L.P. Gachard, 4 vols., (Bruxelles: F. Hayez, Imprimeur de La Commission Royale D'Histoire, 1876-1881) 3: 443, for an anonymous sixteenth century French account of the Algiers disaster.

124/11-16 **Mr. Fox . . . the poor**] See Samuel Fox, "The Life of John Fox" in John Fox, *Acts and Monuments* (London, 1684; *Wing STC* F2036), sig. C4r: "The money, which sometime rich men offered him, he accepted, returning it back to the Poor." Also, Thomas Fuller, *The History of The Worthies of England,* 2 vols. (London: F.C. & J. Rivington, 1811) 2: 22: "He was one of prodigious charity to the poor seeing nothing could bound his bounty but want of money to give away."

124/16-19 **A Student . . . gave it him**] On February 27, 1532, Martin Luther wrote his wife concerning his *famulus,* John Rischmann, who was about to leave Luther's household. Luther urges his wife to find the means necessary for an appropriate farewell gift for Rischmann and suggests that if there is no money available one of their silver goblets, given to them on their wedding day, should be given to him: "Remember how often we have given something to bad boys and ungrateful students, in which cases all that we did was lost. Now therefore reach into your wallet and let nothing be lacking of this fine fellow, since you know that it is well used and God-pleasing. I certainly know that little is available; yet if I had them I wouldn't mind giving him ten gulden. But you shouldn't give him less than five gulden, since we didn't give him a new suit of clothes. Whatever you might be able to do beyond this, do it, I beg you for it . . . Yet under no circumstances should you let anything be lacking as long as there is still a fine goblet [in the house]" (Helmut T. Lehmann, ed., *Luther's Works*, 55 Vols., Philadelphia: Fortress Press, 1975) *50*: 47-50. See also *D. Martin Luther's Werke: Briefwechsel*, 16 vols. (Weimar, 1930-1970) 6: 270-271.

124/21-22 **Cyprian . . . charity**] Cyprian, *De Opere et Eleemosynis*, ed. M. Simonetti. In *Opera* (Tvrnholt: Typographi Brepols Editores Pontificii, 1976), 3A: 66: "Vt in hac uita saeculari alendis sustinendisque pignoribus quo maior est numerus hoc maior et sumptus est, ita et in uita spiritali adque caelesti quo amplior fuerit pignorum copia esse et operum debet maior inpensa."

124/35-125/4 **Mauritius . . . judicia tua**] See Theophylactus Simocattae, *Historiarum*, 8.10-11 and Zonaras, *Epitomae Historiarum*, 14.13.7-45 to 14.14.1-15. Mauricius (582-620) was one of the greatest emperors of Constantinople. When he fought the Avars in 602, twelve thousand of his men were taken prisoner by the chagan (not Saladin) who demanded 6000 pieces of gold for their ransom. Mauricius refused to pay it, and the prisoners were then slaughtered. After which the army despised him and elected as emperor Phocas, a simple centurion, to march against Constantinople. Mauricius was then forced to flee with his wife and five sons, and was captured and executed on November 27, 602.

124/2-3 *Justus . . . tua*] Psalms 118.137.

124/4-13 **Pyrhias . . . the pitch**] Plutarch, *Moralia*, 298E.

Commentary to the Text   285

126/5-6 **All grace in truth hath growth**] Cf. John Ayre, ed., *The Governance of Virtue*, by Thomas Becon, in *The Early Works of Thomas Becon* (Cambridge: The University Press, 1843), 395: "Grace groweth after governance."

126/6-7 *Ulterius* . . . **Motto**] See *Mottoes and Badges of Families, Regiments, Schools, colleges, States, Towns, Livery Companies, Societies, etc: British and Foreign*, ed. W.S.W. Anson (London: George Routledge Sons, Ltd., 1975), 114: "Plus ultra: Thus far and further."

126/8 **periections**] Since this word does not appear in the *OED*, it is quite likely that Beadle wrote "projections" (projects). The abbreviated prefixes "per-" and "pro" were frequently confused. Neither is "perjectio" a Latin word.

126/22-25 *Mundus* . . . **full beauty**] Genesis 1.11-12. See Benedictus Pererius, *Commentariorum et disputatione in Genesim* (Cologne, 1601), sig. D1r: "Verum mundi primorida fuisse in autumno . . . " Also, Andrew Willet, in *Hexapala in Genesim* (London, 1608; *STC* 25683), sig. A5r, observes that some prove by these verses "that the world was made in the Autumne, because the trees were created with ripe fruite." Willet also says "Others doe thinke, that the world was made in the Autumne, in the moneth *Tisri*. 1. because that moneth was the beginning of the yeare, as Iosephus thinketh, before Moses by a new institution appointed Nisan (which answereth to the moneth of March and April) to be the first moneth: and therefore it is called the end of the yeare, Exod. 34.22. from whence they beganne the account of the Iubile . . . Concerning the other obiection of ripe fruit, we shall not neede to answere as some doe, that the fruit did hang still vpon the trees till the autumne, or that some trees in paradise bare fruit in the spring, some in the autumne: or that they might beare fruit twice in the yeare, as Plinie reporteth of India" (sig. A5r).

127/10-11 **house of *David* . . . weaker**] 2 Samuel 3.1.

127/14-15 **higher the Sun ... shadows**] See Tilley S989, Dent S989.

127/18-19 **the elder ... should be**] Luke 5.39.

127/32-38 *Grave William ... a tree*] Maurice of Nassau, Prince of Orange, second son of William the Silent (1567-1625), was made stadtholder of Holland and Zeeland and president of the council of the state despite his youth. In 1586, the States of Holland conferred upon him the title of prince; in 1588, he was appointed by the States-General captain and admiral-general of the Union; and in 1590, he was elected stadtholder of Utrecht and Overysel. Maurice was especially famous for his superior military knowledge of the science of seiges. The letter to which Beadle refers is not found in *Archives où Correspondance Inédite de la maison D'Orange-Nassau*, 15 vols. (Utrecht: Kemink et Fils, 1835-1896). Moreover, in Aubrey du Maurier's *The Lives Of all the Princes of Orange* (London, 1693; *Wing STC* A4184), sig. L8r, there is no mention of a letter by Prince Maurice containing his motto; however, Du Maurier does mention that Prince Maurice "took for the body of his Device the Trunk of a Tree, cut off so as to seem about two foot high, from whence there grew a vigorous Sprout, which apparently would renew the noble Tree which had produced it, with these words, *Tandem fit circulus arbor, At last the Sprout becomes a Tree*: To show that he would revive the glories of his Father." For the sources of this proverb, see Matthew 13.32, Walther 31034, Tilley S211, and Aeschylus, *Libation-Bearers*, 1.204: "From a little seed may spring a mighty stock."

128/5-7 *Si vis ... periisti*] St. Augustine, *De Verbis Apostili Sermonis, PL 38*: 926: "Semper tibi displiceat quod es, si vis pervenire ad id quod nondum es. Nam ubi tibi placuisti, ibi remansisti. Si autem dixeris, Sufficit; et periisti."

128/20-28 **say a benediction ... befalls them**] Benedictions, in this context, are Jewish blessings or prayers of thanksgiving and praise recited either during divine services or on special

Commentary to the Text 287

occasions. According to rabbinical tradition, they were instituted and formulated by the founder of the synagogue, the "Men of the Great Synagogue, the hundred and twenty elders" at the head of the commonwealth in the time of Ezra. There are benedictions said at reading of Scripture, before and after meals, for personal benefits and enjoyments, upon seeing natural phenomena, and upon seeing remarkable persons. By the second century, it was the duty of every Jew to say one hundred benedictions daily beginning with the formula: "Blessed art Thou, O Lord, our God, King of the Universe!" (*The Jewish Encyclopdia*, ed. Isidore Singer *et al*, 12 vols. New York: Ktav Publishing House, 1964) 3: 8-12.

128/31 **He loves a cheerful giver**] 2 Corinthians 9.7.

128/38 *Sidenote*: **1 Cor[inthians]. 5.2**] The correct reference is 2 Corinthians 5.21.

129/11-17 *Cyrus* . . . **go unrewarded**] Cyrus the Elder (d. 529 B.C), founder of the Persian empire agreed to increase the rank of his soldiers if they defeated the Armenians in battle. See Xenophon, *Cyropaedia*, 2.1.24-25.

130/3-4 **like a top** . . . **whipt**] Cf. Tilley T439.

130/6-10 **King of** *Scotland* . . . **palace**] I cannot find the anecdote.

130/13-14 *Out of* . . . *O Lord*] Psalms 130.1.

130/16-17 **Afflictions** . . . **humble**] Cf. Tilley A53: "Afflictions are sent by God for our good. Also, see Walther 33277a: "Vexatio dat intellectum."

130/17-18 **lowest humility** . . . **highest majesty**] Reference to Matthew 23.12. Also, see George Pettie, trans., *The Civil Conversation of M. Steeven Guazzo*, 2 vols. (1581; London: Constable and Co. Ltd, 1925) *1*: 192: "According to that philosophical and Christian saying, That the more loftie we are placed, the more lowly wee ought to humble our selves: which is in deed, the way to ryse higher;" and also "because least greedie desire of domination and enlarging my royall estate, pricke mee no further to use tyrannie over my subjects, so to purchase a perpetuall blot of infamie, I will goe into some quiet solitude, fortifying my designed purpose with this saying: 'Whosoever humbleth himselfe in earth shalbe exalted in heaven'" (124).

130/19-23 *Aristippus . . . his feet*] Aristippus (fl. 366 B.C.), founder of Cyriac school of philosophy and disciple of Socrates. For this anecdote, see Diogenes Laertius, *Aristippus*, 2.79.

130/34-38 **one came to Mr. Bradford . . . thank her**] John Bradford (1510?-1555), a Protestant divine, was brought up for examination in 1554-55 before Bishops Gardiner and Bonner. He was burned at the stake June 30, 1555 (*DNB* 2: 1065-1067). The testimony of Bradford before the royal commissioners was first published in 1561 as *All the examinations of Iohn Bradforde* (London; *STC* 3477); the testimony Beadle quotes is found on sigs. Ciiv-Ciiir. The "one" who came to Bradford was Percival Cressewell, a friend of Bradford's, who did not ask Bradford to recant, but asked, "Tell me what suet I should make" (sig. Ciiv).

131/3-7 **Ecclesiastical Histories . . . *thanked*]** See St. Gregory the Great, *Dialogues, PL* 77: 341-344 and *Homiliarum in Evangelia, PL 76*: 1133-1134, which tell of Servulus' thanksgiving and which contain all that is known of the saint. Servulus (c. A.D. 590) was a beggar, afflicted with palsy from infancy. Every day his mother and brother carried him to the porch of St. Clement's church in Rome, where he lived on the alms of those that passed by, and whatever was left over he gave to others in need.

131/21-24 *Socrates . . .* **delighted in**] See Plato, *Phaedo*, 31E: "And it is likely that those are not souls of the good, but those of the base, which are compelled to flit about such places as a

Commentary to the Text 289

punishment of their former evil mode of life. And they flit about until through the desire of the corporeal which clings to them they are again imprisoned in a body. And they are likely to be imprisoned in natyures which correspond to the pracies of their former life . . . I mean for example, that those who have indulged in gluttony and violence and drunkenness, and have taken no pains to avoid them are likely to pass into the bodies of asses and other beasts of that sort . . . And those who have chosen injustice and tyranny and robbery pass into the bodies of wolves and hawks and kites . . . Then is it clear where all the others go, each in accordance with its own habits?"

131/24-27 **Major sum . . . my body**] Seneca, *Ad Lucilium Epistolae Morales*, 65.21.

131/33 **sons of Zerviah . . . us**] 2 Samuel 3.39.

131/39 **We all . . . the way**] Cf. 1 Corinthians 9.24, 2 Timothy 4.7.

132/5-6 **little flock . . . mischief**] Cf. 1 Samuel 36-37, Matthew 10.16, Luke 10.3 and Acts 20.29.

132/17-18 **heels have not been tript up**] Proverbial phrase found in Shakespeare, *As You Like It*, 3.2.210: "It is young Orlando, that tripped up the/ wrestler's heels, and your heart, both in an instant;" John Taylor, "The Kings Most Excellent Majesties" in *The Works of John Taylor*, 4 vols. (New York: Burt Franklin, 1967) 1: 5: "Thy Constancie hath trip'd up *Fortunes* heele."

133/2 **the best is yet to come**] Cf. Seneca, *Ad Lucilium Epistolae Morales*, 12.5.

133/7 **a throne without a thorn**] Cf. Tilley C839.

133/8-9 **treasure without moths**] Matthew 6.19.

133/21-22 **our mansions . . . ever**] John 14.2.

290   Beadle's A Journall or Diary of a Thankfull Christian

134/8-9 *non amotis* . . . **of others**] See Sallust, *Bellum Catilinae*, 20.1; Seneca *De Beneficiis* 2.23.2. Also, see Tilley F683: "Admonish your Friend in secret, commend him in public."

135/4 *Sidenote*: **Psal[ms]. 148.1,2,3**] The correct reference is Psalms 148.11,12,13.

135/7-8 **Comemmoration . . . excellent**] Before the official university wide celebration of Commemoration was started at Oxford in 1669, commemoration sermons or orations were delivered to honor founders and benefactors of the University and its colleges. An example of a commemmoration oration is *Camdeni insignia* [In honour of W. Camden.] (Parentatio historica: sive commemoratio G. Camdeni per D. Whear.) (Oxford, 1624; STC 19028).

137/11-12 **When things . . . quickly fade**] See Tilley B165, Dent F386.

137/12-13 **Lute string . . . breaks**] Cf. Tilley L201: "At Length the string cracks by being overstrained;" also, see *The Oxford Dictionary of English Proverbs*, 3rd ed., 781.

137/20 *Agur*] The author of a small collection of proverbs incorporated into the Book of Proverbs (30.1-14).

138/39 *Sidenote*: **1 Cor[inthians]. 15.10**] The correct reference is 1 Corinthinas 15.9.

139/9-10 *Omne peccatum* . . . **eminency**] Cf. 42/6-7 n.

139/20-24 *Themistocles* . . . **distressed**] Leader of Athenians in the second Persian war, 480 B.C. See Plutarch, *Moralia*, 328F: "For, when Themistocles in exile had obtained great gifts from Artaxerxes, and had received three cities to pay him tribute, one to supply his bread, another his wine, and a third his mean, he exclaimed, `My children, we should be ruined not, had we not been ruined before.'" Also, see Erasmus, *Apophthegmata*, 243F; Plutarch, *Themistocles*, 19.7.

140/8-11 *Agathocles* . . . at first] King of Sicily, tyrant of Syracuse flourished in the latter part of the third century B.C. See Plutarch, *Moralia*, 176E, 544B, 544C.

141/19 *Sidenote*: Matt[hew]. 16.9,10] The correct reference is Matthew 16.6.

142/11-12 *Omnis festinatio* . . . observers] See Lucius Apuleius, *The Golden Ass*, 8.6; Walther 37371l.

142/27-28 *Omne novum* . . . *Scaliger*] Since there are no modern editions of Scaliger's work and because the early editions cannot be loaned, I do not have access to this reference.

142/30 *Omnia subita* . . . *Cicero*] Cicero, *Tusculan Disputations*, 3.22.52.

142/17 strike . . . hot] See Plautus, *Poenulus*, 1.914; Seneca, *Hercules Octaeus*, 1.435. Also, see Whiting I60, Tilley I94, Dent I94.

142/35-36 *Qui tardè*. . . *Seneca*] *De Beneficiis*, 1.1.8.

143/21-25 *November* 1605 . . . true Religion] The Gunpowder Plot is the name given to a "Romanist" conspiracy intended to blow up King James I and the Parliament on November 5, 1605. The plot was a reaction against severe anti-Catholic legislation reinvigorated by James I in February 1604. The "Act concerning Jesuits and Seminary Priests, 1604," banished priests and contained statutes against Jesuits, seminarians, seminary priests, and recusants. In November of 1604, recusancy fines were demanded of 13 wealthy Catholic families. After the Gunpowder Plot an even more intense enforcement of the penal laws, the extreme limit of anti-Catholic legislation, was codified in "An Act for the better discovering and repressing of

Popish Recusants, 1606." Finally, in 1610, "The Oaths Act" contained clauses imposing penalties on married Catholic women. The texts of these legislative documents can be found in *Constitutional Documents of the Reign of James I*, ed. Joseph Robson Tanner (Cambridge: University Press, 1960), 83-109. For a contemporary Protestant account of the Gunpowder Plot, see *A True And Perfect Relation of the proceedings at the seuerall Arraignments of The Late Most barbarous Traitors* (London, 1606; STC 11618). For the Catholic view of the plot, see John Gerard, S.J., *A Narrative of the Gunpowder Plot*, ed. John Morris (London: Roehampton, 1871). Finally, see Hugh Ross Williamson's exhaustive modern study, *The Gunpowder Plot* (New York: The Macmillan Company, 1952).

143/26-30 **City of *Berne* . . . of gold**] In 1528, the Disputation of Berne was held to the establish the Reformation in that city. Among the results of this disputation were the abrogation of the Mass, and the removal of images from the churches. John Foxe in *The Acts and Monuments*, 4: 338, reports: "The day and years when this reformation from popery to true Christianity began with them [Bernese], they caused on a pillar to be engraven with golden letters, for a perpetual memory to all posterity to come. This was A.D. 1528." Also, see Samuel Clark, *A Mirrour or Looking-Glasse*, sig. Cc2v, which relates the same incident.

143/39-144/2 *Melchisedech* . . . *earth*] Genesis 14.18.

145/2 *Oh!* . . . **Saints**] Psalms 31.23.

145/11 **bucket goes . . . come up**] See Whiting B575, Tilley B695, Dent B695.

145/12 *Pharaoh* . . . **saved**] Exodus 14.28.

145/12-13 *Haman* . . . **advanced**] Esther 7.9-10.

Commentary to the Text 293

145/20-21 **love is ... Law**] Cf. Romans 13.10. Cf. Pseudo Origen, "Tractatus origenis de libris ss. Scriptarum tractatur," *Neue Kirchliche Zeitschrift* 13 (1902), 134: "Unde iam planum vobis esse debet, dilectissimi fratres, sicut istam imaginem legis habuisse, sicut et botrum constat Christi esse figuram, quia nec Christus sine lege nec lex sine Christo esse potest. Testimonium enim evangelii lex est et evangelium complementum est legis."

145/31-32 *ubi amor* ... **minde is**] Cf. Walther 32035a: "Ubi amor, ibi fides." Also, see Whiting S634: "One's spirit is where his affection is;" and Whiting T240: "Where one's Thought is there is he."

145/32-33 **Where our treasure ... heart be**] Matthew 6.21. Also, see Whiting T451; Tilley T485; Henry Hawkins, *The Devout Hart, or Royal Throne* (London, 1634; STC 17001), sig. A8v: "Where our treasure is, there is our hart. Iesvs is a treasure, wherin our hopes, our riches, and al we haue, are lodged & laid vp in store;" and John Payne, *Royall Exchange* (London, 1597; STC 19489), sig. F2v: "Where a mans threasure ys there is his hart/ that is yf God be our heavenly threasure."

145/34-35 **eye sees ... desires not**] See Whiting E216; Tilley E247, E251; *Oxford Book of Proverbs*, 236.

145/35 **love came in by the eye**] See Tilley L501, Dent L501, Whiting L496.

146/3 *Amore unionis*] See St. Thomas Aquinas's discussion concerning the Trinity and the "love of union in *Summa Contra Gentiles*, 4.8.11: "Per hoc autem quod Dominus ad Patrem dicit de discipulis, *ut sint unum sicut et nos unum sumus*, ostenditur quidem quod Pater et Filius sunt unum eo modo quo discipulos unum esse oportet, scilect per amorem: hic tamen unionis modus non excludit essentiae unitatem, sed magis eam demonstrat."

146/6 *amore complacentiae*] See St. Thomas Aquinas, *Summa Theologiae*, 1a.2ae.25,2: "Ipsa autem aptitudo sive proportio appetitus ad bonum est amor, qui nihil est aliud quam complacentia boni."

146/9 *amore benevolentiae*] See Cicero, *Epistulae ad Familiares*, 3.9.1: "Nihil est enim, quod studio et benevolentia, vel amore potius, effici non possit."

147/11-17 **It hath ... white stone**] See Ovid, *Metamorphoses*, 15.41-47: "mos erat antiquus niveis atrisque lapillis,/ his damnare reos, illis absolvere culpa;/ tunc quoque sic lata est sententia tristis, et omnis/ calculus inmitem demittitur ater in urnam:/ quae simul effudit numerandos versa lapillos,/ omnibus e nigro color est mutatus in album."

147/24-27 ***Persius*** **... better stone**] Persius, *Satires*, 2.1.

148/1 ***Theophilus's***] Luke 1.1-4.

148/6 ***Bonaventure***] See 48/25-26 n.

148/18 **seige of *Ostende***] Ostend was beseiged for three years and was finally surrendered to the Archduke Albert of the Netherlands' general, Ambrose Spinola, on September 20, 1604. The contemporary account of the seige Beadle refers to is probably an anonymous French history called *A true historie of the memorable siege of Ostend* (London, 1604; STC 18895), which contains meticulous descriptions of "the assaults, alarums, Defences Inuentions of warre, Mines, Counter-mines and Retrenchments, Combats of Galleys, and Sea-fights, with the portrait of the Towne" (title-page).

149/32 *Sidenote*: **[Genesis] 30.31**] The correct reference is Genesis 30.22-25.

150/5 ***No* ... *cannot***] Isaiah 1.13.

150/11-12 ***I have* ... *hands***] Isaiah 49.16.

Commentary to the Text   295

150/38 *Sidenote*: **Act[s]. 10.4**] The correct reference is Acts 10.3.

151/20 *Sidenote*: **Rev[elation]. 20.11**] Correct reference is Revelation 20.12.

151/32 **Memoria primùm senescit**] See Elder Seneca, *The Controversiae*, 1.2.

152/32-33 **an ungrateful . . . wicked man**] See Walther 6157: "Dixeris male dicta cuncta, cum ingratum hominem dixeris."

152/33-35 **Dixeris ingratum . . . any thing**] See Walther 6156; Tilley M435; *Oxford Dictionary of Proverbs*, 98.

153/2-8 **Tamerlane . . . wicked man**] This anecdote is found in a popular seventeenth century biography of Tamerlane by Samuel Clark called *The life of Tamerlane the Great* (London, 1653; *Wing STC* C4535), sig. E4v: "Then did *Tamerlane* aske him [Bajazet] if he had ever given thanks to God for making so great an Emperor? *No*, (said he) *I never so much as thought upon any such thing.* Then said *Tamerlane*, its no wonder that so ungrateful a man should be made a spectacle of misery." Also, Clark includes the same story in *A Mirrour-or Looking Glasse*, sigs. Cc5r-Cc5v.

153/15-16 **Eli forgat God**] 1 Samuel 2.28-29.

153/16 **so did Saul and Jeroboam**] 1 Samuel 13.10-14 and 1 Kings 12.28-32.

153/21 **David forgat God, and so did Solomon**] 2 Samuel 11.17,26-27, 12.9-11 and 1 Kings 11.1-10.

153/26-29 **A Souldier . . . shame**] I am unable to find this anecdote.

153/29-33 **Caesar . . . unthankful man**] I am unable to find this anecdote.

153/33-36 *Because... to stink*] Beadle seems to be referring to Ezekiel 29.3-4, which in the *Geneva Bible*, 1560 read, "Behold, I come against thee, Pharaoh King of Egypt, the great dragon, that lieth in the middes of his riuers, which hathe said, The riuer is mine, & I haue made it for my self. But will put hokes in thy chawes, & I wil cause the fish of thy riuers to sticke vnto they scales, & I wil drawe thee out of the middes of thy riuers, & all the fish of thy riuers shall sticke vnto they scales." See Ezekiel 30.12: "And I wil make the riuers drye..."

153/37 *Sidenote*: Act[s]. 12.13] The correct reference is Acts 12.23.

154/2 **gave up the Ghost**] See Job 14.10, Matthew 22.50, John 29.30, Acts 5.3-5; Whiting G55.

154/6-11 *Timotheus* ... **had gotten**] See Plutarch, *Sulla*, 6.4.; and Plutarch, *Moralia*, 856.

155/31 **people believe ... ears**] Walther 11088a, 19711a1, 21660; Herodotus, 1.8; Seneca, *Ad Lucilium Epistolae Morales*, 6.5; Petronius, *Poems*, frag. 30; Horace, *Ars Poetica*, 1.180; Erasmus, *Adagia*, 67E.

155/33-36 *Mahomet ... imitate*] According to Richard Knolles, *The generall historie of the Turkes* (London, 1603; STC 15051), sig. Pp1r: "He [Mahomet] delighted much in reading of histories, and the liues of worthie men, especially the liues of *Alexander* the Great, and *Iulius Caesar*, whom he proposed to himselfe as examples to follow."

155/37-39 *Themistocles ... imitated him*] See Plutarch, *Themistocles*, 3.3; Plutarch, *Moralia*, 84C, 92C, 184F, 800B; Valerius Maximus, 14.1; Cicero, *Disputations*, 4.19.44.

156/1 **cloud of witnesses**] Hebrews 12.1. See 9/19-20 n.

156/2-5 **pillar ... Canaan**] See Exodus 13.21-22, 14.19, 33.9-10; Numbers 12.5, 14.14; Deuteronomy 31.15, Nehemiah 9.12,19, Psalms 99.7.

156/14 *stir ... them*] 2 Timothy 1.6.

156/14 **stir the coals**] Cf. Job 41.12.

156/17-24 **The *Lacedemonians* ... honour**] Possible reference to Plutarch, *Lycurgus*, 27.1-2, which describes how Lycurgus allowed the Lacedemonians to "bury their dead within the city, and have memorials of them near the sacred places, thus making the youth familiar with such sights . . To inscribe the name of the dead upon the tomb was not allowed, unless it were that of a man who had fallen in war."

157/7-8 **with ... turning**] James 1.17.

157/21-23 *Even Publicans ... are rewarded*] See Matthew 5.46-47.

160/24 **he brought frogs**] Exodus 8.2-3.

160/24 *Sidenote*: **[Exodus] 5.17**] The correct reference is Exodus 8.17.

160/26 *Sidenote*: **[Exodus] 14.15**] The correct reference is Exodus 14.16.

160/38 **He ... done**] Psalms 115.3.

160/38-39 *I am* **is his name**] See Exodus 3.13-14.

161/7 *I cannot ... done*] Cf. Romans 7.15.

161/23 *Sidenote*: **Psal[ms]. 31.20**] The correct reference is Psalms 31.19.

298   Beadle's A Journall or Diary of a Thankfull Christian

161/32 *Sidenote*: 1 Cor[inthians]. 4.17] The correct reference is 2 Corinthians 4.17.

161/7 **vale of tears**] See 30/4-5 n.

161/7 **Fear not, it is I**] Matthew 14.27 and Mark 6.50.

167/1-18 *In Reverendi . . . facit*] trans. On the pious and learned treatise by the reverend gentleman John Beadle, namely by a mind thankful to God. [referring to the phrase "of a thankfull Christian" in Beadle's title].

Astronomers publish daily almanacs among the people. This diary by a theologian surpasses all others. One person in exile commits to paper what he has seen simply because he wants to. Another does so in order to be certain of retracing his steps on the way back. May the pious mind learn to follow the blessed route from here to the heavenly regions on high—for this is the milky way. Alas. there is too much writing, pure paper is smeared over, the presses groan under the weight of foolish trifles put out by the mad sects of the Anabaptists or the Quakers. Books are full of obstinate quarrels. But piety and kindness shine forth in this book; every page reveals the heart of its author. Whoever you may be who look at it, learn of the parent by the child; it has the looks of its father. He practises what he preaches.

167/18 *Quod docit, ipse facit*] See Tilley P537a. Also, Columbanus, *Carmen Monostichon*, 1.23; Plautus, *Asinaria*, 1.644; Chaucer, *The Prologue to Canturbury Tales*, 1.498: "This noble ensample to his sheep he yaf,/ That first he wroghte, and afterward he taughte."

169/6 **Dr. Richard Sibbs . . . Corinthians**] Puritan divine (1577-1635) whose *A learned commentary . . . upon the first chapter . . . S. Paul to the Corinthians* was sold by Thomas Parkhurst in London, 1655; see *Wing STC* S3738.

Commentary to the Text   299

169/9 **Mr. *John Cotton* . . . Uses**] Puritan clergyman (1584-1652) who left England for Boston Massachusetts in 1633 and became a leading figure in the colony's public and religious life (*DAB* 4: 461). Cotton's *A practical commentary, or an exposition on the First Epistles of John*, by R.I. and E.C for Tho. Parkhurst, was published in London, 1656; see *Wing STC* C6451.

169/13-16 **Cathechizing . . . the word**] Mr. Zachary Crofton (d. 1672) was a Nonconformist clergyman who moved to England from Ireland in 1644. In 1651, he obtained the vicarage of St. Botolph, Aldgate, which he held until the Restoration. He published many controversial tracts and a few sermons (*DNB* 5: 114-115). One of his chief works, *Catechizing Gods ordinance*, by E. Cotes for Tho. Parkhurst, appeared in London in 1656; see *Wing STC* C6990.

166/20 *some new Pieces of Mr.* **William Fenners**] Puritan divine (1600-1640). *Four profitable Treatises very useful for Christian practises*, by H. Maxey for J. Rothwel, and Tho. Parkhurst, appeared in London in 1657; see *Wing STC* F690.

Bibliography

The following bibliography includes titles which are frequently referred to in the introduction and notes. Full references to works cited only once are given as they occur. When I cite in the explanatory notes scriptural references Beadle neither documents in the marginalia nor in the text, I have used *The Geneva Bible: A facsimile of the 1560 edition.* Madison: U. of Wisconsin Press, 1969.

I have used the following abbreviations:

Dent = *Proverbial Language in English Drama Exclusive of Shakespeare, 1495-1616.*
DNB = *Dictionary of National Biography.*
OED = *Oxford English Dictionary,* 2nd edition.
PG = Migne, Jacque Paul, ed. *Patrologiae Cursus Completus.* Series Graeca. 161 vols. Paris, 1857-1866.
PL = Migne, Jacque Paul, ed. *Patrologiae Cursus Completus.* Series Latina. 221 vols. Paris, 1844-1864.
STC = Pollard and Redgrave's *Short Title Catalogue.*
Tilley = *A Dictionary of The Proverbs in England in the Sixteenth and Seventeenth Centuries.*
Walther = *Proverbia Sententiaeque Latinitatis Medii Aevi.*
Whiting = *Proverbs, Sentences and Proverbial Phrases From English Writings Mainly Before 1500.*
Wing STC = Wing's *Short Title Catalogue.*

Bauer, Walter, ed. *A Greek-English Lexicon of the New Testament and Other Early Christian Literature.* Chicago and London: U. of Chicago Press, 1979.
Bernard of Clairvaux. *Opera Omnia.* ed., J. LeClercq, 7 vols. to date. Rome: Editiones Cistercienses, 1957-.

Blunt, J. Henry, ed. *The Dictionary of Sects, Heresies, Ecclesiastical Parties and Schools of Religious Thought*. London: Longmans, Green, and Co., 1903.

Calamy, Edmund. *The NonConformist's Memorial*. 3 vols. London: Printed by J. Cundee, 1802, Vol. 2.

Calendar of State Papers, Domestic Series, Charles I, 1628-1629. John Bruce, ed. London: Longman, Green, Longman, & Roberts, 1859.

Calendar of State Papers, Domestic Series, Charles I, 1629-1631. John Bruce, ed. London: Longman, Green, Longman, & Roberts, 1860.

Calendar of State Papers, Domestic Series, Charles I, 1631-1633. John Bruce, ed. London: Longman, Green, Longman, & Roberts, 1862.

The Catholic Encyclopedia. 1st ed. 15 vols. New York: Robert Appelton, 1912.

Clark, Andrew. "Barnston Notes, 1641-1659." *Essex Review* 25 (1916): 55-69.

Clark, Samuel. *Mirrour or Looking-Glasse Both For Saints, and Sinners*. 2nd ed. London, 1654; Wing STC, C4548.

D. Martin Luthers Werke: Breifwechsel. 16 vols. to date. Weimar, 1930-70.

D. Martin Luthers Werks: Tischreden. 6 vols. Weimar, 1912-1921.

Davids, T. W. *Annals of Evangelical Nonconformity in the County of Essex*. London, 1856.

Dent, Robert William, ed. *Proverbial Language in English Drama Exclusive of Shakespeare, 1495-1616*. Berkeley: University of California Press, 1984.

Dictionary of National Biography. 30 vols. London: Oxford University Press, 1921-1986.

Donagan, Barbara. "The Clerical Patronage of Robert Rich, Second Earl of Warwick, 1619-1642." *Proceedings of the American Philosophical Society* 120 (1976): 388-417.

Essex Record Office. *Wills at Chelmsford*. London: British Record Society, 1958.

Foxe, John. *The Acts and Monuments*. 8 vols. New York: AMS Press, 1965.
The Geneva Bible: A facsimile of the 1560 edition. Madison: U. of Wisconsin Press, 1969.
Gibb, Vicary, ed. *The Complete Peerage*, 13 vols. London: The St. Catherine Press, 1959.
Hastings, James, ed. *A Dictionary of the Bible.* 5 vols. New York: Scribner's Sons, 1901.
Laud, William. *The Works of the Most Reverand William Laud, D.D.* 7 vols. Oxford: John Henry Parker, 1853, Vol. 5, part II.
Liddel, George and Robert Scott. *A Greek-English Lexicon*, 2 vols. Oxford: The Clarendon Press, 1925.
Luther's Works. ed., Helmut T. Lehmann, 55 vols. Philadelphia: Fortress Press, 1972.
Matthews, A.G. *Calamy Revised: Being a Revision of Edmund Calamy's Account of the Ministers and Others Ejected and Silenced, 1660-2.* Oxford: Clarendon Press, 1934.
The New Schaff-Herzog Encyclopedia of Religious Knowledge. 13 vols. New York and London: Funk and Wagnalls Company, 1908-1914.
Newcourt, Richard. *Repertorium Ecclesiasticum Parochiale Londinense.* London: Printed by Benj. Motte, 1710.
The Oxford Companion to Ships & the Sea. London: Oxford U. Press, 1976.
The Oxford Dictionary of English Proverbs. 3rd ed. Oxford: Clarendon Press, 1970.
The Oxford Dictionary of Quotations. 3rd ed. Oxford: University Press, 1980.
Oxford English Dictionary. 2nd ed. 20 vols. Oxford: Clarendon Press, 1989.
Migne, Jacque Paul, ed. *Patrologiae Cursus Completus.* Series Graeca. 161 vols. Paris, 1857-1866.
Migne, Jacque Paul, ed. *Patrologiae Cursus Completus.* Series Latina. 221 vols. Paris, 1844-1864.
Peck, Francis. *Desiderata Curiosa: or, A Collection of Diverse Scarce and Curious Pieces Relating*

Chiefly to Matter of English History. 2 vols.
London: Printed for Thomas Evans, 1729, Vol. 2.

Pollard and Redgrave. *A Short Title Catalogue of Printed Books in England, Scotland, & Ireland, 1475-1640.* 2nd ed. 2 vols. London: Bibliographical Society, 1976-1986.

Smith, Harold. *The Ecclesiastical History of Essex: Under the Long Parliament and Commonwealth.* Colchester: Benham and Company Limited, 1932.

Smith, William, gen ed. *A Dictionary of Christian Biography.* 4 vols. London: John Murray, Albemarle Street, 1887.

Strother, James B. "Families of Catelyn and Beadle." *Miscellanea Genealogica et Heraldica* n.s. 4 (1884): 418-419.

Tilley, Palmer ed. *A Dictionary of The Proverbs in England in the Sixteenth and Seventeenth Centuries.* Ann Arbor: The University of Michigan Press, 1966.

Tilley, Morris Palmer. *Elizabethan Proverb Lore in Lyly's Euphues.* New York: The Macmillan Company, 1926.

Walther, Hans, ed. *Proverbia Sententiaeque Latinitatis Medii Aevi.* 8 vols. Göttingen: Vandenhoeck & Ruprecht, 1966.

Whiting, Bartlett Jere, ed. *Proverbs, Sentences and Proverbial Phrases From English Writings Mainly Before 1500.* Cambridge: The Belknap Press, 1968.

Wing, Donald. *A Short-title Catalogue and of Books Printed in England, Scotland, Ireland, Wales, and British America and of English Books printed in other Countries 1641-1700.* 3 vols. New York: Clarendon University Press, 1945-1951.

Glossary

This glossary of *A Journall or Diary of a Thankfull Christian* is based on the *Oxford English Dictionary* and includes words which have forms or meanings which are obsolete, rare, or archaic according to the *OED*.

admiration the action of wondering or marveling 59/18
affections passions for 113/33
aggravated increased, magnified 36/16
an hungry (indefinite article retained before *h* down through the 17th c.) 151/23
Antipodes those in direct opposition 14/15
apostatize to abandon or renounce one's religious faith 48/36
arm-holes arm pits 63/33
aspersed calumniated, slandered, defamed 62/39
bags moneybags 145/8
Barbarian foreigner 83/2
battle-dores a small racket used in a game called shuttlefeather 101/33. See 101/33 n.
begat begot 35/38, 58/5
bestrides straddles over 64/18
bewitched influenced by withcraft 16/34
bill of charges a load of trouble, expense, and responsibility 103/8. See 103/8 n.
boutefewes firebrand (fig.), incendiary 45/7
boysterous violent 105/22
brake broke 63/37
brake out broke out 35/26
broachers those who introduce 52/16
brake up broke up 63/37
brave famous 133/13
break out burst forth 131/10-11
brokennesse contrition 139/18
burthen burden 54/10, 60/26
by in the presence of 65/29
Carman a man who drives a cart 93/4
carriage conduct 62/9
cast up to add up 18/8, 101/8, etc.

chalk up to reckon 150/17
charge to impute to one as a fault 61/5
Check reproach 72/1, 86/24
Chirurgeon surgeon 66/38, 94/14
chirurgery surgery 64/22
civill well-bred, refined 48/11,
clouts rags, or cloth put to mean use 123/9
Colliar one who carries coal 93/4
comfort aid, succour 3/3
comfortable affording spiritual delight 81/9
comfortably encouragingly, reassuringly 96/28
company accompany 34/23
compassed encompassed, encircled 13/13, 112/38
complement a formality 135/13
compounded made up, or composed 71/4
conceit idea, thought 112/14
Consort a company or set of musicians making music together 13/2
contended argued (with a person) 74/28
contents pleasures 113/7
convenient appropriate, suitable 68/31, 94/6, 120/21
Conventicles a place where dissenters or nonconformists meet 54/20
conversation behavior 107/17, 158/6
Court-Rolles the record kept containing entries as to rents, holding, deaths, etc. 15/24
cruse drinking vessel 84/2
curious exquisite, choice 45/20
cypher the number zero which increases or decreases value based on its position 67/1
Dagons idols 79/23
dainties choice viands 103/26
dark Lanthorn a lantern with a slide by which the light can be concealed 81/35
day hole the surface of the ground over a mine 6/19
decline to avoid 99/39
delicates luxuries 132/17

Glossary

descanting singing a melodic embellishment above a basic tune 13/27
dexterity suitableness 61/12
digged dug 47/2
Directory a book containing directions for public and private worship 16/39
discomfited defeated completely 34/38
discommended expressed disapprobation of 15/25
discovering revealing, making known 100/27
discovers betrays 96/20
dispose disposal 88/34
dispositions normal or natural conditions of mind 113/35
distemper disorder 39/14, 39/25
Diurnal a diary, journal, or day-book 10/9, 13/38, 58/27
divers diverse 54/32, 63/26
domesticall domestic 36/29
dresser one who prepares food for cooking 9/12
durst dared to 93/27
earnest a sum of money an installment paid to secure a contract or bargain 2/1
easinesse indifference 44/9
edged provoked 61/34
edition the action of putting forth or making public 143/34
effectual calling the embracing of Jesus Christ 57/10
eminent conspicuously displayed 50/21
engaging obliging, securing 85/12
engine device 67/31
enjoyned commanded 54/1
enlargednesse the state or condition of being free in heart and spirit 9/33
entrance the opening words of first part of a book 21/8
Ephemerides diary 15/22
Epidemicall prevalent 39/11
estate status, standing or position in the world 94/6, condition of existence 95/4
estates exalted ranks 91/39
evidences proofs of personal salvation 67/33
evill (adv.) wickedly, wrongfully 101/16

exceeded gone to far, transgressed 16/18, 16/19
exceedings a surplus of food or goods 68/36
excepted left out 79/2
experiment example 5/2
experiments proofs 5/28, 70/10, 125/31
Factors bailiffs 14/8
faln fallen 52/28, 111/1
Familisme Familism 15/3. See 15/3 n.
Firebrands pieces of wood kindled at the fire 44/2
first-fruits the earliest products of the soil with special reference to the custom of making offerings of these to God 100/10, 140/4
forgat forgot 23/32, 73/4
forward eager, zealous 32/3, 48/21
froward naughty, perverse 14/16, 52/34
frustrate ineffectual, fruitless 54/29
gathergood unifier 4/19
glister glitter, sparkle 42/23
godly (adv.) in a godly fashion 29/22
Gown-men civilians 156/20
Grave Count 127/32
graven engraved 150/11
of great parts of high intellectual ability, highly clever 45/37
hang upon the pin that on which something depends 67/30. See 67/30 n.
heads headings 13/36
heart-breakings intense sorrows, crushing griefs 44/32-33
heart-burnings intense feelings of jealousy 44/32
higher more arrogant 53/5
holpen helped 82/4, 119/16, 161/20
humor, humour temporary state of mind or feeling 6/1, 42/5, 42/9, temperment 86/38
Husband farmer, husbandman 72/22
imbruing staining 132/22
imputation the attributing to Christ of human sin, by substitution 129/3
incomes divine influences brought into the soul 129/27
ingenuity generosity 17/21

Glossary

ingenuous one of favorable stature 64/7, noble 99/9
issue luck in an undertaking 81/37
Journall book diary 148/6
lash not out do not lavish, squander 113/17-18
latitude a wide compass or extent 137/7
Landskip landscape; a description or depiction of something in words 99/20
lift up lifted up 144/4-5
like (adv.) likely, probably 22/23
listed desired 108/5
lively (adv.) vividly 36/28
lyen lain 89/23
make it good cause it to be 4/31-32
making even with adjusting 95/28
mean of low or humble degree 32/32, 84/28, 93/38
meanest humblest 92/31, 104/23
meat food 28/34
memorandums reminders 24/39
mend our pace travel faster 130/4
Merchant adventurer a merchant engaged in trading expeditions overseas 3/32
messe a serving of food 105/7
minding reminding 11/29
mischief misfortune, trouble 36/30, 38/28, etc.
moveables property capable of being moved 133/21
murther murder 38/11
name reputation 47/4
Nimrods tyrants 37/17
notional speculative 18/12
noysome harmful 110/2
open it unfold the sense of 83/14
originall origin 31/30
overplus surplus 2/7, 104/23
Paganish pagan 102/39
painfulnesse careful industry 10/19
Paltsgrave palsgrave, count palatine 101/38
parts abilities, talents 120/20
passages events, 27/24, etc.

peers nobles 96/36
peradventure by chance 45/10,
Pottle-pot A two-quart pot or tankard 84/26
Practicall a practicalist; one who advocates what is practical 10/32
pranks wicked tricks 89/33
precise puritanical 16/32
preferment promotion 31/25
prejudice hurt, loss 79/27
presidents precedents 14/2, 15/3, etc.
pretended held forth, proposed 33/14, 52/2
prevalent powerful 32/27
prevarication violation of trust 47/17
prevented anticipated 24/23, 68/23
probatum demonstration 125/30
promotions progress made 97/14
proper their own 33/1
proper good character 86/5
prosecution carrying out 31/3
provoked urged, spurred on 6/14, 134/13, etc.
punctuall exact or precise 35/1
punctually accurately 57/25-26
quicken to revive 9/9
Quit-rents rents paid by a freeholder in lieu of services which might be required of him 16/22, 16/30
Rabbins Rabbis 128/18, 127/27
rank excessive 94/14
reckon to count 102/21, 103/10, etc.
refreshed renewed 66/27
remisly moderately 113/21
reserved set apart for some fate 62/23, 62/25, etc.
ribband ribbon 24/34
Rood a crucifix 33/8
roste roost 37/25
royalties the privileges of a king 107/39
salvable capable of being saved 105/19
savourest care for 123/27
savoury of saintly repute 143/1

Glossary

scope goal, end, purpose 5/33
scumme refuse which rises to the surface in the purifying of metal 37/27
security freedom from fear 24/13
are as far to seek have to go as far 42/26
seethe to boil or stew 114/32
severall various and different 37/1
shewed showed 22/33, 25/20, etc.
shipping voyage 148/11
make shipwrack bring to destruction 47/30
shoe-latchet a shoe-lace 144/7
shrimpled withered 45/36
snuffes partly consumed wicks 11/14
spake spoke 76/4, 80/32
sped speed, prospered 42/30
speed prosper 80/8
spire blade 71/17
spirits vital powers 84/25
springheads sources or foundations 31/29
sprung exploded 148/15
stoutest most arrogant, haughtiest 114/8
straight hardship 55/29
straight strict 4/16
straightned restricted 4/10
sullens a state of gloomy ill-humor 108/13
summa totalis sum total 78/30, 151/10
surfet surfeit 92/26
sware swore 39/3
Swordman a military man 156/20
tale number 89/4
tallies records of amounts due 18/3
tell told 150/38
tender solicitations for 64/37
then than 6/4, 54/25, 104/38
tilt run on in opposition 111/3
to too 12/3
totall sum sum-total 78/33
travell travail, suffering, labor 134/26

try to separate a good thing from the rest 44/13
twitched to jerk a person by some part of the body 14/33
typicall symbolical 24/38, 28/34
tyre of Ordnance simultaneous discharge of a battery of artillery 148/16
unspeakable ineffable 12/20
varlets rogues 69/24
venture a commerical speculation 4/5, 4/11, etc.
vicinity near neighborhood 9/26
vie match one thing with another by way of comparison 104/24
virtue power 1/20, 88/6, 88/7
want lack 94/2, 96/5
want to go or do without 96/5
wanted lacked 35/23
wants hardships, sufferings 101/16, 101/24
ware wore 114/9
waxed grew gradually in strength of body 106/6
waxen grown 150/24
Weeping-crosse to suffer grievous disappointment or failure (used proverbially) 104/3-4

Index

Achilles, 74
Adolphus, Gustavus, King of Sweden, 96
Act of Uniformity, xxviii
Adrian VI, Pope, 53
Aeschines, 40
Agathocles, 140
Ajax, 74
Alexander the Great, 95, 117, 153, 155
Alvares, Ferdinand, Duke of Alva, 86
Ambrose, Isaac, xxxi-xxxii
Amphtel, 93
Andrewes, Launcelot, 65, 205
Antinomians, 51
Antiscripturists, 51
Antitrinitarians, 51
Arians, 31
Aristippus the Cynick, 130
Athens 17
Augustine of Hippo, 46, 60, 66, 69, 128
Ausburg Confession, 86, 87

Bajazet, 100, 109, 152
Baldwine, Francis, 48
Baxter, Richard, xxx, xli
Belizarius, 109
Beadle, John
    Barnston, Essex, xvii, xix, xx, xxiii
    birth xi
    brothers and sisters, xii
    Braintree, xiii
    Cambridge, xiii
    children, xiii, xiv, xviii
    classis, xxii
    death, xxviii
    defense of Hooker, xiv-xvii
    dissent, xvii-xxi
    The Essex Testimony,.xxii
    illness, xxvii-xxviii
    Journal or Diary, xxiv-xxvi
        account book, xlv
        antecdents, xxx-xxxv
        providences, lv-lxv
        confessional, xxxviii-xlv
        vehicle,
        influences, xxxxvi-xlv
    Little Leighs, xiii, xiv, xviii, xxiii
    parents, xi-xii
    Protestation of 1641, xx
    publication of *A Journal, xxvi*
    schooling, xiii
    sermonizing, xxiv
    Solemn League and Covenant, xxi, xxii, xxiii
    wife, xxviii
    will, xxviii
Beadle, Joseph, xxix
    children, xxix
Beadle, Rose, xiii
    will, xxix
Beadle, Samuel, xi, xii
Beard, Thomas, lx
Berne, 143
Beza, Theodore, 62-63
Bibulus, 80
Bilney, Thomas, 10
Boleslaus I, 121
Bolsack, Jerome, 48
Bonaventure, 47
Bonner, Edmund, 37
Boyle, Mary (Countess of Warwick), lxiii
Bradford, John, 130
Bruno, Vincenzo, xllv
Burgundy, Duke of, Philip the Good, 52, 109
Bygod, William, 40

Caecellius, 58
Caesar, Julius 7, 41-42, 80, 153
Calvin, John 23, 26 48, 65
Cato, 95, 129
Canutus, 33
Carpenter, John, l
Cervantes, Miguel, 116
Charlemagne, 33
Charles I, England, xx
Charles V (Emperor), 34, 123, 126
Charles, King of Sicily, 91

313

Index

Chelmsford, Essex, xiv, 11
Christian IV, King of Denmark, 54
Cicero, 142
Circumcellions, 49
Clark, Samuel, lx
Clerk, Henry, 41
Collins, Abigail, xi-xii
Collins, Samuel, xvii
Commodus (Emperor), 11
Conon, 154
Considius, 7
Constantine the Great, 31
Constantius the Heretick, 31
Corderius, Maturinus, 65
Cornutus, 65
Cornwall, Sir John, 93
Cotton, John, 169
Craterus, 95
Croesus, 93
Crofton, Zachary, 169
Cromwell, Oliver, xix
Cromwell, Thomas, 67
Council of Trent, 38, 49
Cyprian, 58, 124
Cyrus the Great, 129

Demosthenes, 40
Diagorus, 114
Diaz, Alphonsus, 38
Diaz, John, 38
Diocletian, 31
Diogenes the Cynic, 95
Dionysius, 130

Edgar, King of England, 40
Edward IV, King of
Egyptians, 88
Electors of Germany, 101-102
Elizabeth I, Queen
of England, 55, 64, 69, 199
Eliot, John, xvi
England, 35, 55
Erasmus, Desiderius, 103
Essex, 38
Exeter, Duke of, 109

Fabius, 91
Familists, 51
Fenners, William, 169
Fox, John, 40, 124
Fortunate Island, 35

France, 63
Frederick V, King of Bohemia, 75
Friscobald, 67
Fuller, John, 19, "To the Reader," xiv-xv, xxxiii

Galba, 103
Gellius, Aulus, 95
Geneva, 47
Germans, 39, 78-79, 101-102
Grecians, liii
Greenham, 15
Gunpowder Plot, 143

Harding, Thomas, 48
Henry IV, King of France, 49, 64
Henry V, King of England, 96
Henry VIII, King of England, 101, 189, 121
Hephestion, 117
Hercules, 114
Herod the Great, 75
Hooker, Thomas, xv-xix, 10
Huguenots, 93
Hull, John, lxii

Inatius of Antioch, 6
Ithaca, 125

James I of England, see James VI
James VI of Scotland, 55, 78,
Jews, 36, 73
Jonas, Justus, 2
Josselin, Ralph, xlv
Jovinianus, 31
Julian the Apostate, 31, 37, 48
Junius 24
Justin, 41

Lacedemonians, 32, 156
Lange, Matthew, 87
Latimer, Hugh, 10
Laud, William, xv-xvi, xvii, xix-xx, xxiv
Louis XIII, King of France, 120
London, 32
Lorraign, Cardinal of, 47
Lucullus, 46
Luther, Martin, 2, 24, 86, 124
Lycurgus, 23

Machiavelli, Nicolo, 44

Index

Macrinus, 149
Mahomet the Great, 109, 237
Malynes, Gerard, li
Marius, 36
Maurice of Orange, 127
Mary, Queen of England, 27, 130
Mauritius (Emperor), 124
Maxentius the Tyrant, 37
Maximus, Valerius, 23
Mecaenas, 66
Melanchthon, Philip, 44, 86
Mercer, John, 65
Mildmay, Carew Hervey, xxvii
Milo, 44
Miltiades, 155
Ministers of London, 50
Mohamet the Great
 St. Monica, 69
Monte Pulciano, Bishop, 34
More, St. Thomas, 116
Mulcaster, Richard, 65
Myconius, Frederick, 2-3

Newcome, Henry, lxii

Ochino, Bernard, 47
Ostende, the siege of, 143

Pacioli, Luca, xlviii-l-liii
Parkhurst, Thomas, 256
Parsons, Robert, S.J., 48
Paul III, Pope, 34
Paulet, William, 31
Peele, James, l
Pelagians, 10
Pepys, Samuel, xlvi
Persius, 65, 110
Phaeton, 42
Philip, King of Macedon, 40, 153
Phocas, 124
Pius (Emperor), 11
Plato, 66
Pliny, 36
Polycarp, 58
Pompey the Great, 123
Prosper of Aquitaine, 12
Purgatory, 50
Pym, John, xx
Pyrhias, 125

Quakers, 51

Raleigh, Walter, 69

Cardinal Richleiu, 72-73
Rhemists, 50
Romanianus, 66
Rudierd, Edmund, lix
Rufus, King William, 90

St. Bartho-lomew's Day
 Massacre, 90
Saladin, 109, 124
Salisbury, Roger of, 69
Scaliger, Julius Caesar, 39, 142
Scipio, Africanus, 94
Scythians, 41, 42
Sejanus, 68
Seneca, 40, 111, 122, 142, 110, 131
Servulus, 199
Sixtus V, Pope, 114
Socrates, 66, 131
Socinians, 51
Sodorini, Francis, 53
Solon, 93
Spalatine, George, 86
Staunton, Edmund, xxxi
Stephen, King of England, 69
Suffolk, 38
Sylla, 26

Tamerlane, 100, 153
Tartars, 100
Terra Florida, 35
Themistocles, 139, 155
Tiberius (Emperor), 68, 179, 166
Timotheus, 154
Trajan, 47, 123
Trent, Council of, 34, 39, 49
Triumph, 47
Tudor, Mary, Queen of England, 54
Turks, 36, 100, 109
Udall, John, 54
Ulysses, 74

Vatable, Franáois, 24
Vespasian, Titus (Emperor), 36
Vindication of Presbyterial Government, 50

Warford, William, xliv
Warwick, Eleanor Countess of, 1,
Warwick, Robert Earl of, xiii, xxiii, xxiv, 8-10

Welsh, John, 92-93
William, Prince of Orange, 127
Wilson, Arthur, xxiv-xxv, xxvii
Wincesther, see Stephen
    Gardiner, 31
Winchester, Marquesse of see
    Paulet, William
Wolsey, Cardinal, 121

Zoroaster, 38

For Product Safety Concerns and Information please contact our EU
representative GPSR@taylorandfrancis.com
Taylor & Francis Verlag GmbH, Kaufingerstraße 24, 80331 München, Germany

www.ingramcontent.com/pod-product-compliance
Lightning Source LLC
Chambersburg PA
CBHW050834230426
43667CB00012B/1991